Secret Empire

The KGB in Russia Today

J. Michael Waller

Westview Press
BOULDER • SAN FRANCISCO • OXFORD

Published in 1994 in the United States of America by Westview Press, Inc., 5500 Central Avenue, Boulder, Colorado 80301-2877, and in the United Kingdom by Westview Press, 36 Lonsdale Road, Summertown, Oxford OX2 7EW

Library of Congress Cataloging-in-Publication Data
Waller, J. Michael.
Secret empire : the KGB in Russia today / J. Michael Waller.
p. cm.
Includes bibliographical references and index.
ISBN 0-8133-2322-3 (hard). — ISBN 0-8133-2323-1 (pbk.)
1. Soviet Union. Komitet gosudarstvennoĭ bezopasnosti—History.
2. Soviet Union—Politics and government—1985-1991. 3. Secret service—Soviet Union—History. 4. Russia (Federation). Ministerstvo bezopasnosti—History. 5. Sluzhba vneshneĭ razvedki Rossiĭskoĭ Federatsii—History. 6. Secret service—Russia (Federation)—History. 7. Russia (Federation)—Politics and government—1991 . I. Title.
HV8224.W35 1994
363.2'83'0947—dc20 94-19531
CIP

Printed and bound in the United States of America

The paper used in this publication meets the requirements of the American National Standard for Permanence of Paper for Printed Library Materials Z39.48-1984.

10 9 8 7 6 5 4 3 2 1

To my great teacher, Monica E. Cuddy,

and to Maria, Jocelyn, Jack, Patrick, and Mary

Contents

Acknowledgments

Many people helped make this book possible, either as part of the research and writing process or unknowingly beforehand as inspirations and mentors. I would like to give particular thanks to Professor Uri Ra'anan, Director of the Institute for the Study of Conflict, Ideology, and Policy of Boston University, under whom I studied for my doctorate as an institute fellow. It was as a member of his research team to develop an electronic database on changes in the Soviet and post-Soviet governments that I assembled the core material for this book.

I also thank three other professors at Boston University: Dr. William C. Green, for his strong interest in my studies and his encouragement to choose the topic as a doctoral dissertation; Dr. Elie D. Krakowski, for his enthusiastic participation on my dissertation committee; and Dr. Lawrence Martin-Bittman for his two years of guidance on Soviet disinformation and active measures, which drew my attention to the KGB's image-making campaigns. Gratitude is also due to Dr. John J. Dziak, my undergraduate professor at the George Washington University whose course more than a decade ago, "The History of Soviet Intelligence Services," and subsequent interest converted my curiosity about the subject into an academic and professional pursuit.

For their diverse and individual assistance with information, contacts, and analysis, I thank Fredo Arias-King, founding editor of *Demokratizatsiya: The Journal of Post-Soviet Democratization* at the American University and Moscow State University; the indomitable Sergey and Tamara Grigoryants of the Glasnost Foundation in Moscow, for their selfless and historic work as Soviet dissidents and now as documenters of the KGB's secrets of yesterday, today, and tomorrow; James L. Holmes III of the Institute of World Politics, for his diligent referral of articles of interest as well as editorial criticisms and logical challenges; Paul M. Joyal, President of Integer/Intercon; and Sven Kraemer, for his great friendship and support.

I also thank Dr. John Lenczowski, Director of the Institute of World Politics, for his unique insights into judging the progress of reform including his critique on the "unintended consequences" of glasnost and perestroika; Stanislav Levchenko, one of the brave few who came over from the wrong side at the right time for the cause of freedom and who shared with me his insider's insights and encouragement; Dr. H. Joachim Maitre, who initially brought me to graduate school at Boston University; Herman Pirchner, President of the American Foreign Policy Council, who so generously helped my work in its final stages; Herb and Pat Romerstein, whose advice, admonitions, and perspectives have been so beneficial for so many years; Duncan W. Sellars, Chairman of the International Freedom Foundation, whose generosity with foundation time, resources, and institutional support was critical to my research and to the completion of this book; and the ever-informative Victor Yasmann of Radio Liberty. I also wish to thank my friends at *Izvestiya, Moscow News, Nezavisimaya gazeta, Segodnya,* and elsewhere in Russia for their time and contacts. Given the sensitive nature of the subject matter and the uncertain state of affairs, there are several people in Russia, including current and former state security officers, who helped me with information, contacts, and insights whom I cannot thank by name or organization under present circumstances but to whom I am most appreciative.

The people at Westview Press, including Peter Kracht, who welcomed my initial manuscript, project editors Deborah J. Lynes and Darice Whetstone, and my extremely diligent copy editor Katherine H. Streckfus, were truly a great team to work with. Eric Lebson also helped in the final stages. Any errors are my own.

My gratitude is also due to the John M. Olin Foundation and the Earhart Foundation, whose fellowships respectively with the Center for Defense Journalism and the Institute for the Study of Conflict, Ideology, and Policy at Boston University permitted me to undertake graduate studies to research this book while raising a family.

Most of all, my deepest thanks go to my wife, Maria, whose dedication, initiative, enthusiasm, patience, sacrifice, and love encouraged me to see this project to its completion. Lastly, I thank the four little people who have made my life so full: our children Jocelyn, Jack, Patrick, and Mary. This book is for them. May it contribute in some small way to help make the world a better place.

J. Michael Waller

Introduction

As the world sifts through the ruins of the former Soviet Union to work with new generations of leaders in constructing and establishing democratic institutions and the rule of law, a persistent question arises: What has happened to the former Committee for State Security or Komitet Gosudarstvennoy Bezopasnosti, which the world knew as the KGB? Was it indeed abolished after the attempted coup of August 1991, which spelled the end of the Soviet Union? Were its institutions of abuse, repression, and aggression—especially in Russia—dissolved and dispersed? Are they still a major problem? What is their political and economic power? Were new organizations more sensitive to pluralism and human rights created in their place? What happened to KGB leaders, officers, staff, agents, and informers? What is the role of Russian security forces today? How have they changed? What is their actual or potential effect on other countries? Perhaps most important, how are these secret services controlled and by whom?

This book attempts to address these questions and in so doing, to contribute to the debate over the future of democracy and rule of law in Russia and the rest of the former Soviet Union. To find out what happened to the KGB after the Soviet collapse, it is necessary first to discuss what the KGB was before the fall of communism and how it affected the country's political culture. Scores of personal and literary accounts, a number of journalistic works, and several academic studies have provided broad and rather deep knowledge of the KGB, its structure, and its actions during the heyday of communism. The academic studies, however, are few. Only a handful of observers have discussed the KGB's role during the perestroika years of Mikhail Gorbachev.

Many scholars are only now beginning to discuss this and other serious gaps in the study of the Soviet system. Writes historian John Lewis Gaddis in *Foreign Affairs*,

> The evidence now becoming available suggests strongly that conditions inside the U.S.S.R., not just under Stalin but also under Lenin and several of Stalin's successors, were worse than most outside experts had ever

> suspected. . . . What is emerging from the archives are stories more horrifying than most of the images put forward, without the benefit of archives, by the Soviet Union's most strident critics while the Cold War was still going on.[1]

Should such scholars be so surprised? While the Soviet Union existed, serious academic study of the KGB was rare, and virtually unwelcome, in much of the field called sovietology. Gaddis, in retrospect, addresses this problem, acknowledging that American scholars resisted such inquiry because of the "lingering effects of McCarthyism" that "so traumatized American academics that for decades afterward many of them avoided looking seriously at the possibility that communism might indeed have influenced the behavior of communist states." That response prompted many scholars to embrace "a kind of moral equivalency doctrine in which the behavior of autocracies was thought to be little different from that of democracies."[2]

As a consequence, many Westerners may be surprised to learn that the KGB was virtually the only major Soviet institution unscathed by perestroika. The decision to preserve the KGB was made not only by the KGB itself but also by the entire Soviet leadership, which depended on the protection of the sword and shield of state security. On this issue there was no battle between the enlightened Gorbachev and nonreformist hard-liners. Gorbachev enjoyed the strong support of the KGB leadership and vice-versa. His was a conscious policy to strengthen the KGB while attempting to create the conditions for Soviet society to become more creative and dynamic under the continued guidance and regulation of the Communist Party of the Soviet Union (CPSU). Rejecting the appeals of reform Communists and democrats, Gorbachev showed full confidence in and dependence on the KGB until the coup attempt of 1991.

The decision to maintain the instruments of state control even as repression eased was masked by an image-making campaign intended to convince Soviet citizens and the world that the KGB had been reformed and that it had become similar in nature and function to security services in democratic countries. Glasnost and perestroika were supported by the KGB institutionally because they were seen as means of rejuvenating a dying political and economic system with doses of human innovation and creativity, greater access to foreign markets and technology, and large infusions of foreign aid. Such themes helped make the West less resistant to an immense Soviet peacetime military buildup, more open to including the USSR and its ruling Communist Party in international political and financial affairs, and even eager to keep the Soviet system afloat with grants, credits, and loans. Perestroikist rejuvenation had unintended consequences* that gave reforms a life of their own, well beyond the dramatic but limited scope envisioned by the Politburo. These unintended consequences threatened Party supremacy. Yet whereas the Party collapsed, the KGB did not.

Disintegration of the Communist Party and the Union of Soviet Socialist Republics was not on the Party leaders' agenda. Glasnost (the word is more equivalent to "publicity" than "openness") and perestroika or restructuring, had as end goals the reinforcement of the nomenklatura ruling class, renewal of the economic system under its control, and cohesion of the Soviet empire. Preservation of all three formed the raison d'être of the KGB, which rolled into one all-powerful organization foreign intelligence; counterintelligence; military and police counterintelligence; information collection and analysis; secure communications; codes and ciphers; signals intelligence; border guards and customs; coastal defense and river and lake patrols; ideological enforcement and repression; religious persecution; political surveillance; prison camps; torture; special investigations; terrorism and counterterrorism; leadership protection; domestic and foreign assassinations; covert operations abroad; nuclear bunker maintenance; internal troops; ecological and "social" matters; facilitation of corruption within the Party leadership; and a range of other functions.

This massive apparatus, in conjunction with other institutions that held vested interests in keeping the reform process as controlled as possible, initially supported glasnost and perestroika but attempted to retard and reverse the processes when they loomed out of the Party's control in a series of events that led to the coup attempt of August 1991. The putsch, which unwittingly dealt the blow that smashed the largest institutions that the KGB had sworn to protect, was the supreme illustration that perestroika had failed to touch the security system, a machine that operated outside the control of the civilian Party leadership.

The aftermath of the putsch provided reformers the best opportunity to do away with the smothering security apparat. Highly

---

*I am indebted to John Lenczowski, director of the Institute of World Politics, for prompting me in 1989 and 1990 to examine Gorbachev's most progressive reforms not as part of a strategic plan but as responses to "unintended consequences" of his "openness" and restructuring efforts, which were largely restricted to the party. Dr. Lenczowski, along with my dissertation chairman Uri Ra'anan, director of the Institute for the Study of Conflict, Ideology and Policy at Boston University, were among the very few sovietologists to study Gorbachev's reforms so skeptically at the time.

charged public opinion ran strongly in favor of destroying the KGB once and for all. The opportunity was squandered, however, by indecision, by division, and ultimately by lack of will on the part of the Soviet and Russian political leadership, which appeared more concerned with preserving the powers of the KGB, albeit in new packaging, for their own personal use than with creating new democratic institutions. Substantial steps were taken to reduce the KGB's singular powers by splintering the organization into different services and decentralizing its bureaucracy, dividing it among the republics that chose commonwealth ties to Moscow, but other even more fundamental steps were not taken.

Aside from a largely cosmetic removal of the few most visible putschists, no attempt was made to dismantle and disperse the apparatus beyond its largest components. No attempt was made to bring to justice perpetrators of the most heinous crimes, such as organized criminal activity, physical and psychological torture, mass repression, and murder. Nor were serious attempts made to assure that what remained was accountable to the public. On the part of various KGB organs there was virtually no acknowledgment or assumption of responsibility for having initiated or carried out crimes at the Party's behest.

The relatively few admissions that did emerge either came under great pressure, such as when the Party attempted to cleanse itself of Stalinism, or seemed designed to suit the KGB's own purposes. Some were useful in controlling damage caused by leaks and independent revelations; others discredited certain historical and living personalities. The security apparat placed itself at the service of (and went into private business with) new elites from the same nomenklatura ruling class and played political games with the electoral system and the gargantuan and unreformable bureaucracy to perpetuate itself into the post-Communist age. Yet it did not place itself at the mercy of either. There was no break with the past. Indeed, in all these respects, the past was restored by the new Russian Federation.

Few of the handful of reformers installed in positions of responsibility after the putsch held their posts for more than a few months. Even they wanted to salvage the system, not scrap it and start afresh. The machinery's worn-out or obsolete parts were removed, others repaired or rearranged, and still others carefully cleaned of superfluous elements that prevented the rest from functioning with greater efficiency. Much work went into polishing outside appearances to conceal the fact that little was new within. The image-making campaigns were merely repeats of earlier efforts going as far back as Lenin to save the security organs amid outrage at their excesses.

The reformists preserved not just the structures and personnel but also the essence of Moscow's state security organs. That essence, a human factor beyond visible physical components, presents one of the greatest impediments to Russian civil society's achievement of the Western status to which the country's most reformist political leaders profess to aspire. The essence is summed up in the Law on Security that the Supreme Soviet passed and President Boris Yeltsin signed in 1992, which stated that the security organs would define and defend national "morality" and "spirituality." In other words, the new KGB would still be responsible for everything, everywhere.

In post-Soviet Russia, the secret system would be more of the same. Today's Russian security and intelligence officers preserve a set of deeply inculcated professional traditions comprehensively developed with great deliberation and continuously refined since the Bolsheviks founded the All-Russian Extraordinary Commission for Combating Counterrevolution and Sabotage, better known as the Cheka, in 1917. Indeed, they continue to refer to themselves as *chekisti,* or what I will call "chekists." In so doing they consciously carry forward the legacy of a security organ designed specifically to deprive citizens of their civil, political, economic, and human rights.

Chekism was not a mere perversion of Leninism that emerged under Stalin. It was the most fundamental offensive and defensive mechanism for Lenin's consolidation of power. In the name of the revolution and with Lenin's express orders, the Cheka carried out a systematic campaign of murder perpetrated against hundreds of thousands of civilians and armed resisters in the span of a few years. Cheka chief Feliks Dzerzhinskiy, architect of what he himself called the "Red Terror," marked not only individual opponents but entire classes of people for physical liquidation because of their social origin. Meanwhile, the chekists were free to loot and pillage for themselves.

When Dzerzhinskiy died in 1926, Stalin inculcated a cult following of the chekist founder among securitiy personnel. The Dzerzhinskiy craze diminished as Stalin's own cult of personality grew, but it was renewed under Khrushchev and even more so under Brezhnev and Andropov as a means of idealizing the successor KGB. Gorbachev inherited the chekist system in toto, and instead of marking it for reform, he insulated it from the publicity of glasnost and the structural changes of perestroika. Under Boris Yeltsin the Russian Federation maintained the cultural continuum. There was no break; chekism changed but remained the same.

Although the security services of the post-Stalin era had become progressively less lethal and more sophisticated, the changes were due not as much to the nature of the organs themselves as to the political leaders who directed them. They never lost their potential for committing human rights abuses on a massive scale.

It was not long ago that the government of Yugoslavia was considered the most benign Communist regime in Europe. The collapse of Communist ideology in Yugoslavia was not enough to bestow liberal democratic tendencies upon the leaders or even the citizens of any of the post-Yugoslav republics. This is especially true in Serbia, where the institutions remain intact. Horrors such as systematic mass rape, large-scale summary executions, and ethnic cleansing committed chiefly by the forces of the rump Yugoslav state are testimony to the dangers inherent in the survival of totalitarian instruments of control as well as to the continued presence of the Party officials and uniformed professionals who led these forces and carried out abuses at every tier of society. The case of Yugoslavia shows all too well that the surviving instruments of totalitarian repression could act in a similar manner in Russia at some point in the future.

The coup attempt of 1991 presented an opportunity for Soviet and Russian leaders to attack the chekist machine at its base, to erect transitional structures in its place, to ensure that those who had abused their power in the past would never be positioned to do so again, to bring to light the terrible truths of the past, to uproot all agent and informant networks and allow citizens access to their files, and to lay the groundwork for a completely new system consistent with the stated democratic and, in the case of Russia, free-market national goals. In Moscow's post-putsch exhilaration, a crippled Gorbachev, an almost token Soviet legislature, and a powerful Yeltsin endowed by the Russian Supreme Soviet with near absolute emergency authority vowed to dismantle the KGB so that such power grabs would never again occur. For some reason they chose not to strike at the heart of chekism itself. Perhaps, as products of the Party apparatus, the concept did not occur to them. More likely, they thought better of it so they could use the organs to fit their own ends. The gradualist approach, though hailed as an historic breakthrough, overestimated the comprehensiveness of the reforms and underestimated the powers of the entrenched security apparat.

With little frame of reference beyond the Soviet dark ages from which Russia had emerged, the leaders perceived any advance—such as splitting up the KGB, theretofore an impossible dream—as a revolutionary break with the past. Yet careful observers with a pluralistic frame of reference could see at the time that the apparat, broken down into components, remained intact. By 1994 those components consisted of five main bureaucracies: the Federal Counterintelligence Service, which inherited most of the KGB's internal security functions; the border troops; the Federal Agency for Government Communications and Information, responsible for electronic intelligence and secure communications; the Main Guard Directorate, a 25,000-man Kremlin guard; and the External Intelligence Service, formerly known as the KGB First Chief Directorate. Around them were created about eight other agencies, staffed almost completely by KGB officers answerable directly to the president, whomever that may be. This arrangement ensures that power will be concentrated in the hands of one man or a small group as before.

Russia is trapped in a twilight zone of neither dictatorship nor freedom, where "democracy," "law," "security," and "human rights" can mean anything, and as such mean nothing. In this situation everyone is a democrat. Everyone supports the rule of law and human rights. But fundamental interpretations of these concepts can be vastly different. Post-Communist societies in the former Soviet Union have yet to recover from the corruption of their languages: words can be so grotesquely twisted by the ruling apparat that they come to mean the opposite of their true definition. The cynicism in posttotalitarian culture is as extreme as the rhetoric.

Thus today's Russian laws generally are designed less to protect citizens from bad government than to protect bad government from citizens. The Supreme Soviet, or "parliament," which President Yeltsin abolished in 1993, was incapable of writing just laws, as appears the new institution he created in its place. Civil oversight of the security apparatus remains a poorly understood concept. Competition between the executive and legislative branches of government did not stay within the parameters of the balance of power but turned into a zero-sum game ending in bloodshed. The parliament building was physically destroyed. Constitutional, cultural, and sociological questions beyond the scope of this study make the problem profound. There is little practice and no tradition of an independent and impartial judiciary. The courts are caught in an uneasy balance of ruling on the base of old Communist tradition and a very different, new constitution worded in such a way that past abuses could return with a simple legislative majority or a presidential decree.

This book is an attempt to explore the Soviet KGB under Gorbachev and its successors under Yeltsin and beyond, while paying careful attention to structures and practices of civil oversight and controls to limit the services' powers. I discuss four major areas: the KGB under the Soviet Union, the KGB's successors in the post-Soviet period, civil controls over Moscow's security and intelligence services, and the image-making campaigns waged by the services to help legitimize and perpetuate themselves.

Chapter 1 provides an historical background of the KGB and focuses on the "cult" of a secret state within a state designed mainly to crush or otherwise neutralize opponents of the ruling class, as well as opponents of the organs themselves. Comparisons of the KGB and its successors with Western security and intelligence services are completely inadequate given the KGB's carefully preserved traditions drawn from its early Bolshevik period of mass murder and repression. In Chapter 2 I look at how the KGB under Yuriy Andropov set out to rejuvenate the moribund Party by recruiting the new generation of elites who developed and implemented perestroika. I examine the post-perestroika dismemberment of the KGB following the coup attempt of August 1991—and the end of the Soviet Union—in Chapter 3.

What happened to the KGB once it was dismantled and largely absorbed by the Russian Federation is explained in Chapter 4. Chapters 5 and 6 discuss the question of civil controls over the KGB and its successors during the perestroika and early post-Soviet periods, paying close attention to the comprehensive attempts of the security apparat and its allies to maximize the imagery of reform while minimizing the actual substance of civilian control and oversight. The image-making campaigns themselves are described in Chapters 7 and 8.

1

The Cult of Chekism

We represent in ourselves organized terror—this must be said very clearly.
—Feliks Dzerzhinskiy, Chairman, Cheka, 1918[1]

The words of Feliks Edmundovich Dzerzhinskiy, that a security officer must have a 'cool head, a warm heart, and clean hands,' are not an empty slogan as far as our personnel are concerned.
—Vladimir Kryuchkov, Chairman, KGB, 1989[2]

Dzerzhinskiy was a great man. You should think of the positive things he did.
—Lt. Gen. Vadim Kirpichenko, Chief of Council of Advisers, Russian External Intelligence Service, 1993[3]

No Western Counterpart

Abuse of intelligence and counterintelligence to preserve the power of political elites is not unique to the Soviet Union or to communism, but its far reach into almost every aspect of private life is a unique element of Lenin's legacy. Repressive regimes around the world, and even the most established democracies, have abused secret services for political purposes, but those abuses cannot be compared with the systematic, comprehensive, permanent scope of the system devised by Lenin to control not just outward expression or behavior, but innermost thought and even spirit.[4]

Helping to create the false impression that the KGB was somehow analogous to the FBI and CIA, critics in the 1960s and 1970s cited numerous U.S. security agencies to support their claims that the United States was a "police state,"[5] and that the U.S. intelligence community was a "cult" obsessed with subverting democracy and national independence around the world, that the agencies constituted an "invisible government."[6] There is a definite national security mindset distinct from the general population among Western security and intelligence officers, but this is due to the nature of the profession—keeping secrets in the interests of a democratic society. The mindset among today's Russian security officers, nearly all veterans of the KGB, links secrecy with conspiracy to repress democratic values—a constant search for enemies among their own people.

A Seldom Studied Area

The mirror imaging that erroneously compared the Western and Soviet services, combined with more scholarly attempts to view the Soviet system through new models related to the industrialized democracies, led many observers and students of the USSR to underestimate the KGB as a component of the power structure and its role in the decisionmaking and policy execution process. On the first page of his 1988 history of the KGB, John J. Dziak notes, "There is an excessive amount of generalization and mirroring based on Western intelligence and security systems, with the result that the unique historical, ideological, and political ethos of a non-Western system becomes force-fit to the Western paradigm."[7] Amy W. Knight, in the introduction to her study of the KGB's internal role published the same year, makes a similar observation. The KGB, she writes,

> looms as an uncertain variable for scholars examining these issues, mainly because we have no commonly accepted conceptual framework to explain its role in the system. The KGB has never received much scholarly attention in the West. Unlike the Soviet military, which has been the subject of numerous institutional studies and analyses, the KGB has been virtually ignored by Western experts. The dearth of serious scholarly research on the KGB has left a deep gap in our knowledge of how the Soviet system works and what factors influence Soviet decision making.[8]

Knight also attributes a propensity to develop explanations through mirror imaging with Western society to the lack of scholarly study of the modern Soviet security and intelligence services. She adds, "It is ironic that at the very time [during the Brezhnev period] Western analysts were looking for new models to replace totalitarian theories of Soviet politics, the security police were gaining political prominence in the Soviet Union."[9]

Most of the scholarly work that did emerge was of a historical nature. Popular studies of the Soviet political and decisionmaking systems tended to minimize and, for all practical purposes, ignore the role of the security services. Jerry F. Hough's revision and expansion of Merle Fainsod's *How Russia Is Ruled*, published by Harvard in 1979 as *How the Soviet Union Is Governed* and widely regarded then as an exemplary study of the system under Brezhnev, completely deleted Fainsod's chapter on the state security apparatus and made no serious attempt to discuss the KGB as it had been rehabilitated in the late 1960s and 1970s or its role in the Soviet power structure.[10]

Seweryn Bialer's celebrated work on Soviet foreign and domestic policy during the transition into the Gorbachev era, with the exception of references to Yuriy Andropov's career as KGB Chairman, devoted only two paragraphs to discussion of the KGB as an institution.[11] Likewise, Raymond L. Garthoff's extremely important survey of U.S. and Soviet foreign policy from 1969 to 1984 made only two passing references in its 1,126 pages to the role of the KGB as a formulator and executor of Soviet foreign policy.[12]

Even major studies of Soviet national security policy, such as *Perestroika and Soviet National Security* by Michael MccGwire, and *Hostage to Revolution: Gorbachev and Soviet Security Policy, 1985-1991* by Coit D. Blacker gave virtually no attention to the KGB. In MccGwire's case, the KGB is mentioned—but not discussed—only on seven of the book's 466 pages of text.[13] Blacker names the KGB twice, in passing.[14] These examples are the rule, not the exception, to the major studies of Soviet government, foreign policy and strategy. As a result, the KGB's role in the Soviet power structures was widely misunderstood and underestimated.

What was it that made the KGB so different from Western security and intelligence services, and how does that difference affect Russia's post-Soviet society and its relations with the West? The problem is not the existence of security organs as such, since they are a requirement for any society. The problem in Russia is their essence, which is rooted in the creation and sustenance of a totalitarian form of government that viewed all opponents as enemies. Western secret services are products of democratic society. Russia's secret services are products of Communism.

One is tempted, after Communism's collapse, to assume that Russia's security and intelligence services have likewise broken with their Leninist legacy. Several factors may give casual onlookers the impression that a new world order has begun: the officially stated potential for mutual cooperation in areas of common concern, meetings between two successive CIA directors and their Russian counterpart in

Moscow, and new business relations begun by former KGB officers. Leninism, long dead, was buried with the collapse of the USSR.

Such a conclusion is based on false premises and disregards widely available facts on which most of this study is based. Although Leninist ideology is effectively dead as an official guiding force for society, the psychological and cultural damage it inflicted on society is very much alive. Statist and collectivist psychology, lack of individual initiative, and ultra-bureaucratization are pervasive throughout Russian society. Though its intellectual theories and political practices are no longer widely revered or observed, Leninist iconography, even if neglected, dominates the former USSR. It has not been replaced by new symbols to which people can adhere or aspire.

Lenin's personal legacy is still something held dear among ordinary citizens, much more so than, say, George Washington's legacy among Americans (who no longer celebrate his birthday, it seems, except to sell automobiles). People still pay homage to Lenin without quite knowing why. His printed image on small, drab red banners still adorns the humble walls of high-rise flats that also host icons of Christ, the Virgin Mary, and the saints. Yellowed portraits still hang in public buildings and individual offices. Young married couples, hopeful for a future in a market economy, still ritualistically lay flowers by his statues which remain by the thousands in cities and towns across Russia. No historical figure or present leader, symbol, or idea has even begun to take Lenin's place.

Even more profound has been the legacy within the relatively closed world of the Russian security services. Here, although Leninism has been abandoned as an official political and economic theory, the system's central psychological and cultural components—the core values and practices that shape the worldview upon which policies and actions are based—have been adapted to post-Soviet realities. Instead they have been nurtured carefully through peer pressure, discipline, increasingly frequent personnel purges at all levels, and careful selection and training of new recruits. Notably, the purges have not been of hard-liners but of officers espousing more reformist tendencies. All senior KGB officers who had been outspokenly reformist prior to the 1991 putsch were removed from the Russian security services by 1992, and by 1993 and 1994 a number of officers known for their active involvement in political and ethnic repression had been promoted.

From the beginning, the Soviet security services and the Communist Party quickly evolved into what Dziak calls a "permanent counter-intelligence enterprise to which all other major political, social, and economic questions are subordinated." He observed that even into the Gorbachev era, "the commonweal is not the principal objective of such an amalgam of esconced power and security screen; self-perpetuation is." Such a system he termed a "counterintelligence state."[15]

The Counterintelligence State

The counterintelligence state is characterized by the presence of a large, elite force acting as the watchdog of a security defined so broadly and arbitrarily that the state must maintain an enormous vigilance and enforcement apparatus far out of proportion to the needs of a real democracy, even one as unstable as that of Russia. This apparatus is not accountable to the public and enjoys immense police powers with few checks against it. The powers are not designed to protect the rights of the individual, despite rhetoric to the contrary, but to protect the privileges of the ruling class and the chekist organs themselves. Whether the civilian government is able to control the security bodies is an open question; indeed, the civilian government is so penetrated by the apparatus that there is no clear distinction between the two. In the Soviet era, massive security organs were required to destroy and prevent opposition to the Communist Party, and since the Party was the guiding force for every aspect of society, every facet of daily life fell into the KGB's domain.

Despite the changes of glasnost and perestroika, a large portion of the Soviet public still felt the KGB's invasion into their lives. In a poll commissioned by the state security service, 30 percent of Soviet citizens responded that they or their relatives had suffered at the hands of the KGB or its predecessors, and 25 percent felt that the KGB continued to monitor them. Almost as high a percentage of young people reported the same, indicating that even with Gorbachev's other reforms, citizens sensed that the KGB under glasnost was as active and pervasive as before. Among the most educated and politically active population, the number was even greater. Thirty-five percent of those with a higher education, and more than half of those with advanced degrees, felt that they had been monitored by the KGB. Similar levels of surveillance were reported by Soviet citizens in the academic, cultural and artistic professions.[16]

The collapse of Communism reduced but did not eliminate this pervasive political spying. With the breakup of the Communist Party as a control structure, the chekists developed more than ever into an organized criminal enterprise, networking into business, banking, the news media, the political process and government, often in partnership with violent mafia elements. The blurry distinction between civilian society and the chekists grew even murkier in Russia's new "democracy."

What the KGB Was

The KGB's coat of arms was a sword and shield bearing a hammer and sickle. This symbol proclaimed the Soviet security force to be the offensive and defensive weapon of the Soviet Communist Party, even though its name, Committee for State Security (Komitet gostudarstvennoy bezopasnosti) identified it as an instrument of the state. Party and state were one and the same. Founded shortly after Lenin and his Bolsheviks seized power in 1917, the security agency was originally known as the All-Russian Extraordinary Commission for Combating Counterrevolution and Sabotage, known as the Vserossiyskaya chrezvychaynaya komissiya po borbe kontrrevolyutsiyey i sabotazhem (VChK) or more familiarly as Cheka. Its main task was to liquidate all opposition to the newly installed Communist Party. It went through a succession of name changes and reorganizations, serving as Stalin's personal terror apparatus, until 1954 when Nikita Khrushchev gave the agency its current name and attempted to bring it under control so that it would never again threaten the Party leadership.

What became the modern KGB was a result of additional reorganizations in 1959, and refinements, improvements, and massive expansion under the leadership of Yuriy Andropov, whom Leonid Brezhnev named KGB chairman in 1967. Andropov served in that capacity for fifteen years and poised himself to succeed Brezhnev as general secretary of the Soviet Communist Party.[17] The KGB inherited by Mikhail Gorbachev, who became Party chief in 1985, bore the hallmarks of Andropov's long term at the helm and was essentially the same as the KGB of Brezhnev. It received different orders from the Party, but its structure, duties, capabilities, and essence were preserved. The KGB's main functions follow.

Foreign Intelligence

The First Chief Directorate was the espionage branch of the KGB. It collected and analyzed nearly all foreign intelligence of a non-military nature for the Soviet Union, as well as significant military foreign intelligence, especially in the high-technology area. The First Chief Directorate was also responsible for foreign counterintelligence, recruitment of foreigners within the Soviet Union, and a range of covert operations, including provision of funds and technical support to foreign Communist parties and other organizations and movements, dissemination of covert propaganda and disinformation in the foreign press and among foreign leaders, support for terrorist and guerrilla organizations, and assassinations abroad. Soviet diplomats, journalists, athletes, academicians, and cultural and religious figures who traveled abroad ordinarily collaborated with this directorate as a quid pro quo for their privileges.

Counterintelligence

Counterintelligence and other internal security functions were carried out by the KGB Second Chief Directorate. In addition to full-time officers, the Second maintained armies of full- and part-time agents and informers in universities, factories, research and scientific institutes, farms and agricultural collectives, editorial offices of publications, and other locations. The Second was also responsible for the KGB's meager activities to counter organized crime and narcotics trafficking. Unofficially it helped procure illicit goods and services for Party leaders.

Military Counterintelligence

A lineal descendant of the World War II-era Armed Forces Counterintelligence Directorate known as SMERSH, a contraction of Smert Shpionam ("death to spies"), the Third Chief Directorate was responsible for military counterintelligence, including counterintelligence within the military's own intelligence organ, the Main Intelligence Directorate of the General Staff (Glavnoye razvedyvatelnoye upravleniye, GRU); security of ships and aircraft abroad, including all Aeroflot jets; physical security of nuclear warheads; and maintenance of secret assassination units within the Soviet armed forces assigned to kill military officers who refused to follow orders in time of war.

Political Police

To ensure political conformity with the Communist Party and to monitor, harass, and repress dissidents in government, politics, culture, science, religion, education, industry, and all other walks of life, the KGB maintained a Fifth Directorate. Under glasnost and perestroika the Fifth was elevated to chief directorate status. Soon after it was renamed the Department to Defend the Constitution and subsequently Directorate Z in an attempt to convince the public that the KGB was out of the political police business. The Fifth eavesdropped, ran millions of secret political informants, maintained files on individuals, and arranged for the arrest, conviction, and imprisonment of dissidents.

Signals Intelligence and Cryptography

The Eighth Chief Directorate was a massive signals intelligence and cryptography apparatus within the KGB consuming up to one-quarter of its budget. This high-tech unit was responsible for intercepting and analyzing international telecommunications, decrypting coded information, and designing and administering codes for secret communications of the Soviet government and state-run companies.

Border Guards

The Border Guards Chief Directorate, which was unnumbered, was responsible for the physical security of the land borders of the USSR and maintained a standing army of more than 240,000 troops for this purpose. The Border Guards also maintained the KGB's own navy for coastal defense and interceptions and patrols of inland rivers, canals, and lakes.

Economic Security

Although the Soviet system destroyed its own economy, the KGB maintained the Sixth Directorate for what it called "economic security." The Sixth watched against free market activity or "speculation" (as did the Cheka), theft of goods from state enterprises, and financial transactions that were not authorized by the Party as well as attempts by foreign interests to collect information on the Soviet economy.

Other Functions

Other major KGB functions included training and education of its recruits and personnel, protecting the physical security of Soviet leaders and key government buildings, installations, and transportation systems; maintaining archives, housing internal institutes or funding outside academic centers for specialized research, conducting information analysis, overseeing certain types of military construction, and developing and maintaining nuclear bunkers for the party leadership. The KGB reigned supreme over the ministries of defense and internal affairs by running counterintelligence and other operations within those two huge bureaucracies as well within all other government entities.

It maintained its own armed forces—a 240,000-man standing army and a well equipped navy—and its own prisons. The judicial system, rigged to ensure Party power, was doubly compromised by the KGB, which penetrated and exerted deference from the State Procuracy and courts; an Inter-Regional Bar Association allowed KGB lawyers to practice anywhere in the country. The KGB screened Communist Party personnel before they could be admitted or promoted, and provided one Party faction with incriminating evidence about another for use during power struggles. Rather than serve the state or country, the KGB served the military-industrial complex and the nomenklatura ruling class.

In so doing, the chekists served themselves as well, enjoying more freedom of action than the Party itself, and wielding immense influence in the processes of making and executing policy. Even under Gorbachev, the KGB not only monopolized the collection and analysis of information vital to running affairs of state but also was a main source of information for the Soviet leadership. Therefore it could shape the political leaders' actions by regulating what they saw and knew, by reinforcing or challenging perceptions and policies as the chekists saw fit. The KGB also proposed plans of action then carried out the orders. It controlled all communications of Soviet leaders, and monitored their every move by providing physical security.

In short, Communist Party officials at every level, and especially in the Politburo, depended completely on the KGB for the most critical information and resources required to govern the country, conduct foreign policy, and maintain power. As if to underscore an unwillingness or inability to challenge the KGB, Gorbachev never seriously attempted to break the KGB's monopoly on information and leadership security or to construct checks and balances against the KGB's central position in Soviet government and civil life.[18] The KGB was the foil against the Party leadership's internal adversaries and outside critics, though it also acted on its own against ruling Party officials when it saw fit.

Fraternal Conformity

Although the collapse of the USSR in late 1991 saw the Communist Party thoroughly discredited, stripped of its powers, property, and records, and briefly banned, its members and former members continue to occupy the leading positions in every sector of Russian government. All mid- and upper-level officers in the Russian security and intelligence services by 1994 were former Communist Party members, with the exception of one who reportedly had been a KGB academic reserve officer within the democratic opposition.[19] All mid-level officers and all but the newest recruits at the lower level were either full Party members or belonged to the Party youth organ, the Komsomol, which was the KGB's main recruiting ground for officers. Although it would not be accurate to assume that by virtue of his past membership a government official cannot be reformist, the facts remain that the security organs have had no infusion of new personnel free of the social, political, and professional baggage of the Communist Party or chekism and that, indeed, conformity has been enforced since early 1992 by purges of officers at the upper levels who espouse the faintest liberal inclinations.[20] The safety of Russia's emerging democracy is in the hands of the structure that created totalitarianism and the individuals who enforced it. A similar situation exists throughout the Commonwealth of Independent States.[21]

If political conformity with the Party line is no longer an issue, then what conformity is being enforced? The question is more social than political. The Russian security and intelligence services conscientiously have preserved the icons and mythology of the Soviet security organs, particularly the Cheka of Bolshevik Russia, in their training academies and headquarters.[22] They have made no break with the past but continue to hold it dear. Thus to understand the mindset of the security services of the Russian Federation it is important to review the conduct of the first Soviet security service and the ideals of Cheka leader Feliks Dzerzhinskiy, whose portraits and sculptures still adorn the halls and offices of the security bureaucracy, and whose professional descendants in 1994—with great deliberateness and sense of purpose—continued to call themselves chekists.[23]

The Essence of Chekism

Chekist ideology and attitudes have insulated the security and intelligence services from the society they are supposed to serve. Assaulted, buffetted, and not unscathed, the state security culture has survived the Soviet collapse. As the Russian government continues gradually if slowly to de-Leninize, it has been unable—perhaps unwilling—to challenge the culture of the phalanx of enforcers the

Soviet Communist Party created to maintain its rule: an insular culture of elites endowed with far-reaching and unchecked powers to guard "state security."

Lenin chose Feliks Dzerzhinskiy, the Polish commandant of the Bolsheviks' Smolny headquarters in Petrograd, to build the main instrument of the counterintelligence state. Whereas Lenin's image has become tarnished even in official government propaganda, Dzerzhinskiy's has not. Therefore it is important to approach the post-Soviet security services by looking at their founder and ancestor—Dzerzhinskiy and the Cheka. The Cheka was founded by order of Lenin on 20 December 1917 in a decree that endowed it with the following responsibilities:

> 1. To persecute and liquidate all attempts and acts of counter-revolution and sabotage all over Russia, no matter what their origin.
> 2. To hand over to the Revolutionary Tribunal all counterrevolutionaries and saboteurs and work out measures of struggle against them.
> 3. The Commission is to make preliminary investigations only in so far as that may be necessary for suppression.
>
> . . . The Commission is to watch the press, sabotage, etc. of the Right Socialist-Revolutionaries, saboteurs, and strikers. Sanctions [to be enforced]—confiscation, confinement, deprivation of food cards, publications of lists of enemies of the people, etc.[24]

Initial summary executions carried out by the Cheka were of bandits and criminals outside their own control, but they expanded quickly to include political and military opponents of Lenin's regime, and anyone who engaged in market activity. By February 1918, the Cheka had publicly instructed local revolutionary councils to:

> seek out, arrest, and shoot immediately all members . . . connected in one form or another with counterrevolutionary organizations . . . (1) enemy agents and spies, (2) counterrevolutionary agitators, (3) speculators, (4) organizers of revolt . . . against the Soviet government, (5) those going to the Don to join the . . . Kaledin-Kornilov band and the Polish counterrevolutionary legions, (6) buyers and sellers of arms to equip the counterrevolutionary bourgeoisie . . . all these are to be shot on the spot . . . when caught red-handed in the act.[25]

Definitions of "enemy agents," "spies," and "counterrevolutionary agitators" were often left up to the imagination of the individual chekist. More often than not they were individuals engaged in legitimate political or business activity. Lenin's Council of People's Commissaries issued a published decree whereby "counterrevolutionaries were to be shot on the spot," as one observer reported. Counterrevolutionary crimes punishable by death were "speculation," i.e., any form of buying and selling; disrespect toward the Soviet government; unauthorized public assembly; and violation of an 8:00 p.m. curfew.[26] Yet, along with rival revolutionaries or armed resisters, they were to be murdered on the spot. Declared the head of the Cheka in Kangur to the Urals Communist Party Central Committee, "We do not need to have proof, examination, suspicions, in order to shoot anybody. We find it necessary to our purpose to execute the person in question, and we shoot him. That is all!"[27]

Months after taking power, Lenin instructed the Cheka in a telegraph message to "put into effect a merciless mass terror against the kulaks [wealthier peasants], priests and White Guards" and to incarcerate suspects in concentration camps.[28] By this time, widespread and organized armed resistance was mounting. Mass executions were carried out as reprisals for assassinations of Bolshevik officials, especially for the 30 August 1918 attempt against Lenin in Petrograd, which killed city Cheka chief Moysey Uritskiy. More than 152 White Russians were executed to avenge the shooting of one Communist in Penza, and 500 Petrograders were murdered by the Cheka in retaliation for Uritskiy's death.[29] Within days, the Bolshevik commissar of internal affairs called for taking hostages and for imposing "mass terror," and the Commissar of Justice released a decree, "On the Red Terror," which instructed the Cheka to round up "class enemies" in concentration camps and to kill all suspected of involvement with the White Russian side of the Civil War.[30] The Bolshevik party newspaper *Pravda* approvingly declared on 18 October 1918: "Henceforward let the watchword 'All Power to the Soviets' be replaced by the cry, 'All Power to the Cheka!'"[31]

As the civil war escalated, the Cheka expanded its list of targets of liquidation by hunting down people of a given social origin or class. A top Cheka official characterized the mission:

> We are no longer waging war against separate individuals, we are exterminating the bourgeoisie as a class. Do not seek the dossier of the accused for proofs as to whether or not he opposed the Soviet government by word or deed. The first question that should be put is to what class he belongs, of what extraction, what education and profession. These questions should decide the fate of the accused. Herein lie the meaning and the essence of the Red Terror.[32]

The Red Terror campaign lasted three years. To the consternation of some Bolshevik leaders, the Cheka was accountable only to Lenin and

Dzerzhinskiy, who did little or nothing to restrain its activities as long as they were directed at opponents of Bolshevism. The Cheka chief in Orel boasted, "I am responsible to no one; my powers are such that I can shoot anybody."[33] A chekist named Peters plainly noted, "In its activity the Cheka is completely independent, carrying out searches, arrests, shootings, afterwards making a report to the Council of People's Commissars and the Soviet Central Executive Committee."[34]

Legality in the western sense was never a concern. Bolshevik laws and decrees were strictly observed but had been written so that the political ends justified the means, which were virtually limitless.[35] John J. Dziak quotes a "candid interview" with Dzerzhinskiy, who scoffed at the notions of courts and laws and made macabre reference to the use of forced confessions to administer revolutionary justice to the condemned:

> [The society and the press] think of the struggle with counter-revolution and speculation on the level of normal state existence and for that reason they scream of courts, of guarantees, of inquiry, of investigation, etc. . . . We represent in ourselves organized terror—this must be said very clearly. . . .
>
> Of course, we may make mistakes, but up till now there have been no mistakes. This is proved by the minutes of our meetings. In almost all cases the criminals, when pressed against the wall by evidence, admit their crimes. And what argument would have more weight than the confession of the accused himself.[36]

Dzerzhinskiy saw the Cheka not only as a tool to consolidate the revolution but also as "an organ for the revolutionary settlement of accounts with counterrevolutionaries"—a vehicle for revenge.[37] Staggering numbers died by outright execution, incarceration, and starvation. Merle Fainsod of Harvard University called the figure of 50,000 Red Terror victims during the Civil War a conservative estimate, and said that the total number of victims could be in "the tens of thousands and perhaps hundreds of thousands."[38] George Leggett, in his exhaustive study, estimates 250,000 to 300,000.[39] Robert Conquest surmises from the evidence that official executions by the Cheka may have numbered 200,000, with an additional 300,000 in the aftermath of the Bolshevik Revolution.[40] Some estimates are even higher.[41] Whatever the actual total—neither the KGB nor its present-day Russian successors have released the figures—the Cheka carried out a horrific campaign of mass murder with Lenin's express authority.

The early chekist killing method was designed so as not to create martyrs around whom opponents could rally. The doomed, naked prisoner would be brought to a normally drunken executioner armed with a tsarist-era Colt pistol. The Colt was favored for its large caliber; when fired into the back of the head, the bullet would mutilate the face upon exiting the skull, making the body unrecognizable. This method saved chekists the problem of dealing with relatives searching for the bodies, and made recovery of a potential martyr impossible.[42] Mass deportations and death camps were a later development to make liquidation more efficient and cost-effective.

This campaign could not have been waged without substantial participation of a large sector of society. Faced with the prospect of instant execution, people easily allowed themselves to become collaborators. As the Party and Cheka consolidated control over every aspect of daily life, collaboration was induced by the provision and denial of privileges. Commenting in 1993 on the formation of the Soviet security organs, Russian human rights figure Sergei Kovalev observed that society "accepted deliberately unlawful doctrine based on the notion of 'social justice.'" Revolutionary demands embraced not only the inevitability but also the moral justification of mass violence to achieve political and economic ends. Thus a systematic machine of state terror was required. Kovalev added that the system "wasn't brought from the outside or imposed by occupation, but it was a natural combination of those deliberately distorted doctrines which were formed within society itself. So we entered the vicious circle which is awfully hard to break, which we are unable to break still."[43]

In the process of imposing socialism by extermination, the Cheka did not necessarily uphold Marxist economic ideals. Chekists were particularly materialistic, using their power for personal material enrichment, either by exacting bribes or looting their victims outright. Many early chekists were recruited from prisons where they had first met Bolshevik leaders, including Dzerzhinskiy, who had been jailed under the tsars. In its own newspaper, *Yezhenedelnik*, the Cheka openly admitted that it attracted criminal and sadistic elements.[44] A few top Cheka leaders, Dzerzhinskiy a notable exception, were troubled by this and said so to the Party leadership. One of them, Martin Latsis, who himself was "notorious for his bloody pronouncements on class war," complained:

> Work in the Cheka, conducted in an atmosphere of physical coercion, attracts corrupt and outright criminal elements which, profiting from their position as Cheka agents, blackmail and extort, filling their own pockets. . . . However honest a man is, however crystal clear his heart, work in the Cheka, which is carried on with almost unlimited rights and under

> conditions greatly affecting the nervous system, begins to tell. Few escape the effect of the conditions under which they work.[45]

Lenin also acknowledged the problem because fellow Bolsheviks criticized the Cheka for the same reason. However he urged his comrades not to let it bother them, arguing that the ends justified the means. At a Cheka conference in November 1918 he made reference to "strange elements" in the security force's ranks but said that they were indispensable to the process of "putting into practice the dictatorship of the proletariat."[46] Thus the criminal beginnings of the KGB were mandated by Bolshevism's founder, expressly to impose the power and protect the privileges of the new ruling class of which the chekists were part.

The Permanence of Chekism

Constructing Lenin's Union of Soviet Socialist Republics required much more than the liquidation of class enemies and political opponents. Old institutions—political, economic, commercial, educational, legal, cultural, spiritual, and social—had to be destroyed or subverted to serve the regime.

With its chekist enforcement arm, the vanguard Party created new institutions in place of the old. Everything had to be under the party's political control. Entrepreneurship and barter were criminalized as "speculation." Political control of schools was implemented to turn out obedient citizens and to shape a New Soviet Man. A new legal system was built that functioned as a political tool of ruling elites against the public. The Party forged a Soviet culture to extinguish free human creativity, co-opting most artists and driving a determined few to write their literary works or paint their pictures underground or in exile. It mutated a deeply devout church, inducing many of its priests and bishops to serve chekism before God in order to escape the imprisonment or execution that befell those who resisted, or merely to preserve their ministries. And it reinforced social movements to channel the cowed population's energies and talents for the Party and its grandiose schemes for world revolution.

The Party was designed and maintained as an exclusive club. Ninety percent of the population was barred, and the most elite members occupied positions of privilege on the ruling class nomenklatura list. The people were required to serve the interests dictated and implemented by the nomenklatura, which dispensed favors and meted out punishment by virtue of the fact that it controlled every aspect of a citizen's life, from education and employment to food distribution, housing, and health care.

So paranoid was the security system that it compelled every citizen to fill out forms in longhand instead of typed, so their handwriting could be registered and used to trace subversive correspondence—a system that survived at least through 1993.[47]

To survive, individuals became loyal only to themselves, informing on their neighbors, friends, and family members, often bearing false witness to spare themselves. The chekists promoted the destruction of personal relationships to eliminate "conspiracies" and ensure obedience to the ruling class; betrayal of loved ones to the Party was officially touted as a virtue. Generations of Soviet schoolchildren were taught to be like Pavlik Morozov, the child-hero who turned in his parents to the secret police for execution. The Party line was dictated daily by a newspaper called *Truth* (*Pravda*). People sold themselves to an ideology in which they did not believe or bought their job, diploma, or judicial verdict by bribing those who governed them, and in so doing made themselves permanent captives of the party.[48] Those who resisted were turned over to the chekists for punishment or disposal. Most members of society became witting, unwitting, or meekly compliant collaborators.

Pervasive secrecy was the glue holding the power structure together, as former KGB Col. Peter S. Nikulin explains:

> Secrecy was a tool of violence and means of struggle for power. State secrets helped form the image of an enemy. Secrecy was needed to impart Messiah-like character to the KGB and to such figures as Dzerzhinskiy. . . . Had it not been for the all-embracing secrecy, terror and totalitarianism would not have been possible on such a scale. And all those legends and myths of the revolution and our lives would not have been possible either.[49]

So systematic and comprehensive was the apparatus that even former dissidents felt that they too had been co-opted. The situation was the same wherever a Soviet-style system was implanted. Czech President Václav Havel called the system a "contaminated moral environment" that corrupted the entire population. Havel, who as a dissident playwright resisted the Soviet-imposed regime in his country, considers himself as culpable as anyone else. In his January 1990 New Year's Address as president of what was then Czechoslovakia, Havel blamed all citizens, including himself, for having succumbed to the corruption of the system. He said,

> We fell morally ill because we became used to saying something different from what we thought. We learned not to believe in anything, to ignore each other, to care only about ourselves. Concepts such as love, friendship, compassion, humility, or forgiveness lost their depth and dimensions. . . .
>
> I am talking about all of us. We had all become used to the totalitarian system and accepted it as an unchangeable fact and thus helped to perpetuate it. In other words, we are all—though naturally to differing extents—responsible for the operation of the totalitarian machinery; none of us is just its victim: we are also its co-creators.
>
> . . . We have to accept this legacy as a sin we committed against ourselves. If we accept it as such, we will understand that it is up to us all, and up to us only, to do something about it. We cannot blame the previous rulers for everything, not only because it would be untrue but also because it could blunt the duty that each of us faces today, namely, the obligation to act independently, freely, reasonably, and quickly.[50]

Where chekism ceased to be a mere tool and became an engine of communist power is difficult to determine. It was first a producer and then a product of the society it created by force and fear. It reached into the entire population, compelling the people to serve from below and directing the course of their lives from above and even directing the Party itself. It built a society of collaborators.

The man who began to dismantle the KGB after the 1991 coup attempt acknowledged, "All of us were bad. The good ones have long ago perished in prisons. Very few have stayed."[51] Thus in Russia, as in most of the rest of the Soviet Union, chekism remains the main core remnant of the old regime. Not only does it have a culture of its own as an institution of the counterintelligence state that was nurtured in isolation from society for more than seven decades, but it has enculturated the society that it insulated from the world and continues to shape the way people think and act.

Chekist Cadres

The contamination of which Havel spoke was spread early. So notorious was the Cheka that in early 1922 when Lenin imposed a New Economic Policy to restructure the dying economy and attract foreign capital, the Soviet leadership saw fit to change the security organ's name. The fear-inducing Cheka became the bland and colorless State Political Directorate (Gosudarstvennoye politicheskoye upravleniye, GPU). Its structures, resources, personnel, and missions remained the same. Nevertheless, the fledgling Soviet government staged an extensive public relations campaign to make it appear as though the Cheka had been abolished. Russian-American journalist George Popoff, who was based in Moscow at the time and who saw the GPU from the inside during his detention and interrogation there, wrote of the name change in this 1925 account:

> This procedure was simply a deliberate piece of play-acting, calculated to influence the public opinion of the world. It happened that I arrived in Moscow a few days before the "dissolution" of the Tcheka, and so had an excellent opportunity of personally witnessing this historical event.
>
> . . . The theoretical dissolution of the Tcheka . . . took place under the influence of the so-called New Economic Policy, when for some months Moscow seemed seriously to intend to change its course. The Bolsheviks wished to trade with foreign countries, to get credits, etc., and recognized quite reasonably that this aim could never be attained unless the chief obstacle, the Tcheka, were removed. The first measures were taken as follows: Dsershinsky left the Lubjanka and became Minister of Communications. He was replaced by Unschlicht, the Commissar for Refugees, a man generally known throughout Moscow as "humane" and "good-natured." At the same time a decree was issued abolishing the death penalty (once more!). . . . The words "Extraordinary Commission" were abolished and the "new" institution received the harmless-sounding name "State Political Direction." . . . That was what was done in theory.[52]

Popoff added,

> How completely convinced the Tcheka was that, in order to influence foreign countries, it was quite enough formally to declare the Tcheka dissolved and announce the fact in the Press . . . is proved by the fact that it was not even considered necessary to change either the abode or the personnel of the Tcheka. Here, too, everything remained as it had been; not a single Tchekist stirred from the Lubjanka. The only changes that I could discover were new notices on the outer doors and in the inner rooms of the Tcheka. But even this was mere cynicism and comedy. In the interior of the Tcheka administration placards were to be seen over every door bearing the name of the section to which the room belonged in finely printed letters. . . . The only change . . . which was made after the publication of the famous dissolution decree was the following. Small white labels were everywhere pasted over the letters "Tche-Ka" and "G.P.U." written on them in ink. The other designations remained untouched.[53]

Although the name change did satisfy many witting and unwitting observers abroad, it failed to impress others. In Prussia a decade later, local Nazi Hermann Goering created a political terror force for Hitler's National Socialist Party and debated what to call it. He first proposed Geheime Polizei Amt (Secret Police Agency), but reconsidered because its initials were too similar to the disreputable GPU. His unit's eventual name, Geheime Staats Polizei or Secret State Police, became known by a contraction invented by a Berlin postal clerk who needed a convenient acronym: Gestapo.[54]

The Gestapo survived for only thirteen years, too short a period to inculcate itself in the national psyche as a legitimate tool of government. As Nazi Germany was crushed by the Allies, the Gestapo was dissolved, its networks uprooted, its leading officers banished from public life, and its chiefs either imprisoned or dead by execution or suicide. Its headquarters in Berlin was razed and its archives—at least those captured by the Americans, British and French—carefully catalogued and made public. American occupiers and other authorities in western Germany created not only a new democratic constitution and legal structures but also police and counterintelligence services consistent with the liberal democratic ideals of the new Federal Republic. In the Soviet-occupied eastern portion of the country, a new state security organ was created along chekist lines. This organ became known as the Ministry of State Security, or Stasi.

Everywhere, Nazi ideology was thoroughly discredited, its crimes exposed for all the world to see. Thus all instruments of Nazi ideology, command, control were completely obliterated by the end of 1945. The same cannot be said about their chekist counterparts. Although the Soviet secret services underwent bureaucratic and name changes no fewer than thirteen times between the early 1920s and 1994,[55] the staff and officers continued throughout that span of history to preserve their identification in the cult of chekism.

In contrast to the well-trained staff of the KGB from the 1970s through 1991 and of its successor services today, the early chekists were not particularly well educated. Just over 1 percent of Cheka cadres in 1921 had a higher education, and slightly more were completely illiterate.[56] Their methods were crude and violent. As the level of education and training increased, especially after the 1950s, so did the security services' sophistication of methods. Outright brutality was, with many exceptions, abandoned in favor of less messy but equally cruel means. Simple harassment or persecution could usually be resolved if the victim agreed to collaborate. The few who kept their principles were punished with denial of professional or cultural advancement, defamation, internal exile, and under the "enlightened" KGB chairmanship of Yuriy Andropov, were administered forced injections of drugs and institutionalized in psychiatric hospitals.

Beneath its image as an invisible army of men of sterling character, the KGB maintained the Cheka's corruption, which despite the morale problems it caused among dedicated professional personnel has prevailed from 1917 to the present post-Soviet era. Security officials enjoy almost total impunity, with the power to compel false confessions or frame individuals when evidence is lacking, and whereby few officers are held accountable for their mistakes and crimes; its sense of superiority over elected government officials; and its view of almost everyone as potential criminals, enemies, and traitors.

Indeed, the search for enemies remains constant. Without the specter of internal and external enemies the services would not have needed to become so large and powerful. Moreover, the existence of enemies could be "proven" before the fact because the security organs penetrated the state prosecutorial and judicial systems. Under the Soviet-era legal and criminal codes which, though amended, were still in force in 1994, state security agents could obtain the desired verdict without regard for actual guilt or innocence.

There was no true deference to civilian authority because the security services were free to recruit, blackmail, frame, or manipulate bureaucrats and other officials in order to provide the regime with the network of informants it desired and required to stay in power. Not even the military or uniformed police could be trusted; the chekists formally penetrated those institutions as well to root out suspected spies and wreckers. These networks remain in post-Soviet society as potential mechanisms to permit the security organs to maintain their near impunity.

Yet no one monitored the chekists. Commitment to law was and remains a bureaucratic procedural matter rather than one of due process. As cynical as the laws were in the USSR, the chekists went even further by applying a double standard for those who were members of the Party or nomenklatura and those who were not. Such a legal and political culture survives among revanchists and many "democrats" alike. Furthermore, although technically illegal, it was not uncommon for chekists to be instructed to conduct surveillance of high Party leaders so that they could be blackmailed or discredited in political faction struggles, especially during the implementation of perestroika. At times the chekists waited for no instruction but apparently took it upon themselves to initiate such actions.

The Cult of Dzerzhinskiy

Over the decades, especially as part of Khrushchev's de-Stalinization campaign and during the years when Andropov was chairman, the state security services developed their own mythology of the chekist: an idealized, heroic figure within a specially ordained corps of fellow chekist elites charged with defending both Party and state. The Cheka and the KGB were in many ways secretive brotherhoods, privileged cults that kept their cadres pure amid the treasonous population. In all official de-Stalinization efforts, the state security organs were carefully spared of any taint of complicity with Stalin's crimes, even though they were absolutely the core of his nearly three decades of rule. Chekists emerged unsoiled, selfless, even superhuman yet at the same time were painted as victims of past abuses like everybody else.

The cult of chekism survived both the Communist Party and the Soviet Union, a fact noted not only by Russian human rights figures but by Party careerists such as Vadim Bakatin, the Gorbachev insider who became the last chairman of the KGB after the 1991 putsch. A year later, he said,

> The specific ideology of "chekism," idealized and licked clean by the subsequent generation of idealists of the CPSU and by the publicists living parasitically on the "criminal patriotic" romantic, takes its beginning from that time of revolutionary tyranny. This ideology proved to be more tenacious of life than . . . its begetter.[57]

Chekism centers around the personality of its founder, Feliks Dzerzhinskiy. This aspect of state security ideology began under Stalin's sponsorship after the Cheka chief died in 1926. An effigy made up of death masks of Dzerzhinskiy's face and hands and clothed in his uniform was displayed in a glass coffin in the GPU officers' club "as an object of veneration similar to Lenin's embalmed remains in the Red Square mausoleum."[58]

Dzerzhinskiy's image faded as Stalin's own cult of personality grew, but it was restored under Khrushchev in the midst of the de-Stalinization campaign of the late 1950s, when the Politburo sought to distance the KGB from the concentration camps, mass terror, executions, and purges. The KGB Border Guards school in Alma-Ata, Kazakhstan, was named after him,[59] as was a special motorized division of Internal Troops under the Ministry of Internal Affairs.[60] Streets and squares were renamed to honor him in cities and towns across the USSR. A 14-ton statue of the Cheka leader was installed in front of KGB headquarters at Lubyanka Square, which itself was renamed Dzerzhinskiy Square. Similar statues were erected in cities across the Soviet Union. Miniature versions of Dzerzhinskiy in various poses were cast in aluminum, iron, white metal, and bronze for adornment of the sparse Party and KGB offices and even offered for sale to ordinary citizens and tourists in the GUM department store across Red Square from Lenin's tomb. Dzerzhinskiy even adorned postage stamps and the ubiquitous aluminum badges and pins for tourists. The government officially celebrated his birthday every September 11.

Glorification of Dzerzhinskiy continued within the security and intelligence services under Mikhail Gorbachev and Boris Yeltsin, even as Lenin's image was allowed to tarnish and ultimately blacken. During the peak of glasnost, the cult of Dzerzhinskiy was second only to that of Lenin, and both figures still evoke strong feelings among members of the general public. A 1990 poll of Soviet citizens listed ten personalities from the Bolshevik revolutionary era and asked which stirred the greatest sympathy and antipathy. Respondents could list more than one personality. Lenin was by far the most popular, with 64 percent, followed by Dzerzhinskiy, with 41 percent. The poll showed that although the USSR had effectively de-Stalinized (Stalin was viewed sympathetically by only 7 percent of respondents, with 50 percent expressing antipathy), it had not "de-chekized." Indeed, 51 percent of the respondents said that "there was a need" in 1917 to create the Cheka and grant it "the broadest rights." Only 23 percent disagreed. Dzerzhinskiy even evoked less antipathy than did Lenin, at 7 versus 8 percent.[61]

Glasnost-era and post-Soviet security and intelligence leaders went to absurd lengths to portray the Cheka founder as a symbol of purity and justice. Viktor Chebrikov, who chaired the KGB from 1982 to 1988, proclaimed,

> Feliks Edmundovich [Dzerzhinskiy] whole-heartedly sought to eliminate injustice and crimes from the world and dreamed of the times when wars and national enmity would vanish forever from our life. His whole life was in keeping with the motto which he expressed in these words: "I would like to embrace all mankind with my love, to warm it and to cleanse it of the dirt of modern life."[62]

Gorbachev's second KGB chairman, Vladimir Kryuchkov, similarly extolled the Cheka's founder: "The words of Feliks Edmundovich Dzerzhinskiy, that a security officer must have a 'cool head, a warm heart, and clean hands,' are not an empty slogan as far as our personnel are concerned."[63] One may suspect that such slogans are still regarded seriously given the fact that Dzerzhinskiy's legend has not been repudiated but reaffirmed.

Christopher Andrew and Oleg Gordievsky observed in 1990, "Feliks Dzerzhinskiy is nowadays the object of a KGB-inspired personality cult, which showers on him greater adulation than the combined total of that bestowed on all his successors."[64] A large bust of Dzerzhinskiy on a marble pedestal at foreign intelligence headquarters is almost an object of veneration; it is always surrounded by fresh flowers. All young Soviet intelligence officers had to lay wreaths or flowers by the bust and meditate with their heads bowed in solemn contemplation.[65] Reportedly the custom has not changed since the Soviet collapse.[66]

More progressive officers have intellectually dispensed with chekism and realize that the real-life Dzerzhinskiy was markedly different from the virtually deified figure that he became. But to many if not most officers, chekist culture is deeply ingrained. Following the failure of the August 1991 coup attempt, revelations streamed out of Lubyanka headquarters portraying the depth of the cult-like mentality inculcated among KGB personnel. After interviewing a number of KGB officers, a Russian parliamentary investigator observed:

> Meetings and conversations with KGB leaders of various ranks clearly highlight one detail. They have no understanding in their minds that they are serving the constitution or the law, they have no reverence for the rule of law and citizens' rights. They unquestioningly and consistently fulfilled only the orders of their superiors, this for them was the main value, even though there may have been declarations of the "We serve the people and the motherland" type.[67]

Vadim Bakatin, the reform Communist member of Gorbachev's security council and for two years USSR interior minister, encountered the same problem after becoming KGB chairman in the wake of the 1991 putsch. He complained that among KGB officers, "The law service, the juridical service—they have simply not yet come to light, or I have not yet acquainted myself properly with all of them. So far I am dissatisfied. I thought that the level was considerably higher here."[68]

In trying to carry out reforms in the KGB during his 107-day tenure, Bakatin said that doing away with the chekist mentality was as important as the physical dismemberment of the KGB along functional lines and to its decentralization from Moscow. To him, what he called "de-ideologization" transcended mere depoliticization. It was not enough merely to resign from the Communist Party. Bakatin called for "the repudiation of the ideology of 'Chekism,' the repudiation of the constant search for an enemy because, without a clearly defined enemy, whom previously the Politburo used to indicate, the KGB in the old sense simply could not exist. . . . Those are all the things that had to be repudiated, and it is hard to picture the KGB as the KGB without those things."[69]

The rapidity of the Soviet collapse made it impossible for de-ideologization to be carried out or even begun during Bakatin's brief leadership, but a revolutionary break affording such an opportunity occurred in December 1991 when the Russian government took control of the entire KGB apparatus on its territory.

That opportunity was not taken. Although Lenin is starting to fade away as the Russian government officially if slowly eliminates images and names of Bolshevik leaders from its currency, documents, place names, and public areas, Dzerzhinskiy is not, at least as far as the chekists are concerned. Following the putsch, the imposing statue of Dzerzhinskiy at the traffic circle outside headquarters was removed not by the KGB but by mobs of ordinary citizens who took advantage of the chekists' momentary paralysis to topple the hated symbol. Fearing that people would get hurt as they struggled to knock the massive icon from its pedestal, someone from the Moscow city government ordered a crane to pull it down.[70] Riding the crest of popular opinion, the progressive Moscow City Council restored Dzerzhinsky Square to its original name, Lubyanka.

On state security property, however, Dzerzhinskiy's memory is carefully preserved. Bronze sword-and-shield KGB crests still adorn the perimeter of the state security Lubyanka headquarters. Busts and statues of the Cheka founder are found throughout the Lubyanka complex in corridors, foyers, and offices. Portraits of the secret police chief are hung in nearly every room. Polished brass memorials to chekists killed in action remain embedded in red marble, illuminated from the floor by an eternal flame.[71] A small museum maintains Dzerzhinskiy iconography like a religious shrine. Those who have not had the chance to visit Lubyanka can still notice the continued attempts to keep the names of Dzerzhinskiy and the Cheka untarnished. Although the KGB reluctantly released information documenting the crimes of Stalin carried out by the organs when they were called United State Political Directorate (Obyedinennoye gosudarstvennoye politicheskoye upravleniye, OGPU) and People's Commissariat for Internal Affairs (Narodniy komissariat vnutrennikh del, NKVD),[72] neither it nor its Russian successors have made public the crimes of Lenin carried out by the Cheka.

Indeed, the new Russian security services have gone out of their way internally to maintain continuity with the Cheka in their own esoteric manner while giving the opposite impression in their public relations campaigns. Inside the apparat, many officers found it impossible to adapt to a democratic system. Reform-minded officers often had their motives questioned and many who tried to change the system from within found that they had to quit instead. One such officer, Col. Peter S. Nikulin, argued strongly during a 1993 working group meeting that the chekists submit draft legislation to parliament liberalizing secrecy laws. He got into an argument with the head of the internal security ministry's legal department, who banged his fist on the table and shouted, "Comrade Nikulin! Who pays you money? KGB or CIA?"[73]

Talk was different on the outside. During a visit to the United States in January 1993, Lt. Gen. Vadim Kirpichenko, chief of the council of advisers to Yevgeniy Primakov, director of the External Intelligence Service (Sluzhba vneshney razvedki, SVR), told Americans over and over how much the Russian service had changed from the KGB.[74] Kirpichenko was politely received wherever he went, and few difficult questions were posed to him. At one small gathering of lawyers, intelligence practitioners, and scholars that I attended, most of the discussion focused on legal and bureaucratic issues, and Kirpichenko stressed his service's adherence to law.

Then, in asking a cultural question at the table, I noted that just weeks before, on 20 December 1992, the SVR had celebrated not its first anniversary but its seventy-second, marking the founding of the Cheka's foreign intelligence arm on the same date in 1920. I asked, "This being the case, what is the SVR doing to do away with the culture of Chekism?" Kirpichenko termed it an "interesting question" but failed to give a satisfactory answer, asking sarcastically if I had a better date in mind. "Celebrate December 20th if you must," I responded, "but why not celebrate it as the first anniversary of something new, created by a democratically elected president, instead of the seventy-second anniversary of a discredited old service that was founded by a mass murderer?"

At this, Kirpichenko became slightly agitated. He leaned forward, and with tension in his voice, launched into a defense of the Cheka chief and his legacy. "Dzerzhinskiy was a great man. You should think of the positive things he did," the general began, whereupon he rattled off purported accomplishments in transportation and communications. He added, "December 20 is very important to us," and noted that security and intelligence personnel have been paid on the twentieth of the month ever since 1917 and that the practice would continue.[75] The holiday was celebrated again in 1993.

Conclusion

Chekism is a phenomenon without parallel and completely alien to liberal democracy. Thus comparison of the chekists with American, Australian, Canadian or West European security services is a completely misleading premise. The phenomenon is not limited to the security structures themselves but is ingrained in the societies that survived under totalitarianism. The system transformed nearly every citizen into a potential informer. It was characterized by a siege mentality; everyone was a suspected criminal or traitor. It was involved in a never-ending search for enemies, and when it could find none it created them by compelling the innocent to write false confessions by which they would be condemned. It routinely acted above even Soviet law. It was fixated with conspiracy and counterconspiracy. It exacted constant deference from the individual; it was not loved but hated, not respected but feared. It claimed to fight corruption while actually engaging in it on a grand scale as the greatest organized criminal syndicate in history. It reached into every aspect of civilization and human relations—political and economic, legal and cultural, personal and spiritual—and attacked body, mind, and soul. It forced people to live a lie that destroyed normal human relations, friendships, and families. For the chekist, the ends justified the means. They still do. Beyond the dead ideology that it officially shed in 1991, those ends seem to be power for power's sake.

Political control over that force was a constant concern of those in the Kremlin. In July 1918, a Bolshevik commissar of justice pointed to the lack of controls and warned that unless the party limited the Cheka's powers, "We shall have a state within a state."[76] Those were precisely the words the KGB's last chairman used to describe the chekist machine three-quarters of a century later.[77]

2

Stormtroopers of Perestroika

Perestroika will not work without the party and its fundamental influence on all aspects of social life. . . . There are attempts to create the impression that perestroika is founded upon deviation from the bases of Marxist-Leninist thought and is therefore plunging the country into chaos. This is all slander against the Party. . . . We say perestroika is the renewal of socialism, not its dismantling. . . . We say perestroika is the revival of creative Marxism, a new awareness of Leninist ideas.

—Mikhail Gorbachev,
Communist Party General Secretary, 1989[1]

We in the KGB contributed quite a bit to the process of perestroika because . . . without it the Soviet Union could not move ahead.

—Filipp Bobkov, Deputy Chairman, KGB, 1990[2]

The Party: Reform or Perish

Mikhail Gorbachev and the men with whom he surrounded himself owed much of their political careers to a common sponsor: Yuriy Andropov, who took control of the Soviet Communist Party after fifteen years as chief of the KGB. Andropov recruited the men who fathered perestroika and glasnost and promoted them through the ranks from the 1950s until his death in 1982. All were among the Party elite, though they constituted a different breed from the Brezhnevites who drove the country further and further toward inevitable collapse. Generally far more educated than the average apparatchik, they were part of a Party intelligentsia that recognized that the Soviet system as it was could not work and needed to be changed.

Their ideas for reform, however, never strayed outside the blinders of their Marxist-Leninist frame of reference, even if they did not necessarily believe in Marxism-Leninism itself; Party ideology and political reality had inculcated within them a dictatorial worldview from which few could escape. Never did they set out to destroy the USSR, or even the Communist Party, and as such they could never permit true democratization, free markets, or national self-determination. John Lenczowski terms these three fruits of Gorbachev's reforms the "unintended consequences" of glasnost and perestroika. One of the first Western policymakers or scholars to criticize the Soviet leader openly, Lenczowski wrote in 1989, "It is essential to make the distinction between intentions and unintended consequences. . . . From all indications, the Communist Party's intentions spring from a desire to preserve and renew the socialist system, and not from some sudden change of political philosophy."[3] This was highly unorthodox and controversial thinking at the time, but it was based on study of official Soviet actions and statements that were not designed for foreign consumption.

In an important speech that received little attention in the West, Gorbachev assured the Party faithful that glasnost and perestroika would not threaten socialism or CPSU supremacy and that, to the contrary, the twin slogans were quite Bolshevik in themselves. The speech was given in 1989, when Gorbachev's program was well underway. He assured the cadres, "the Party has been, and remains, the main organizing and coordinating force capable of leading the people along the path of profound socialist renewal, playing an integrating and consolidating role in society and, *let us be blunt, preventing an undesirable and dramatic development of events. Perestroika will not work without the Party and its fundamental influence on all aspects of social life.*" (emphasis added).[4]

For Gorbachev, his program was consistent with Leninism: "There are attempts to create the impression that perestroika is founded upon deviation from the bases of Marxist-Leninist thought and is therefore plunging the country into chaos. This is all slander against the Party." Socialism, he claimed, was still the wave of the future:[5]

> Socialism is one of the most powerful ideas which ever gripped the minds of people. Paradoxically, just here, at home, you can hear voices saying that supposedly the socialist idea is some kind of fruit of intellectual fantasy, a certain anomaly not corresponding to human nature, that is deprived of substance and future. Those are not the voices which reflect the opinion of communists and workers and the profound trends of the historical process. The CPSU firmly stands on principled positions. It remains devoted to the socialist ideals, socialist principles.

What different rhetoric from his public statements to the West! Gorbachev's speech cannot simply be brushed off as an attempt to appeal to Party hard-liners. Unlike Boris Yeltsin and so many others, Gorbachev never renounced Marxism-Leninism. The Soviet leader wanted to revive Bolshevism by reasserting political influence on "all aspects of social life," not weaken it with uncontrolled pluralism. He sought to energize idealism within the Party and renew the Soviet system. In his words,

> Our people made a choice in October of 1917, and despite the deformations of socialism and its Leninist concept which have taken place in the past, we will firmly go along this path. We say *perestroika* is the renewal of socialism, but not its dismantling. We say *perestroika* is revolutionary transformation, the elimination of the deformations of socialism, not the restoration of capitalism. We say *perestroika* is the revival of creative Marxism, a new awareness of Leninist ideas.[6]

These were no mere quaint paeans to the old guard; by 1989 Gorbachev had the Party firmly under his control. He hardly could have been more adamant. His words clashed with his public persona in the West, especially since he had just built a new system of government whereby a multiparty Congress of People's Deputies with a revamped Supreme Soviet and a new state presidency replaced many of the duties of the Central Committee and, just a month before the speech, its Politburo.

In assessing Gorbachev's intentions, one must ask the following questions. Did these steps do anything at the time to drive the CPSU and its leaders from power, or did they keep them in their positions of control during a turbulent period when the Party was discredited and in dire need of international financial assistance? Was the nature of the changes to bring non-Party members to positions of state power? Were the personnel changes genuine, or did they merely preserve the same Party clique under new state titles? Were Gorbachev's heavily ideological reassurances to the Party merely platitudes of political protocol devoid of real meaning? Most important for the purposes of this discussion, did perestroika do anything to challenge and reform the most Leninist of institutions—the chekist KGB?

In order to answer these questions, it is first necessary to examine the KGB as the key organism that drove the perestroika process. That institution had the historical responsibility to protect the Party from threats to its supremacy, guarding against not only counterrevolution but also "sabotage" and "speculation" (or free markets) as the expansion of the Cheka acronym suggested. By the time of Brezhnev, the Age of Stagnation, the real saboteurs of the Soviet economy—and thus the system and state—were those who controlled the Party itself.

The KGB Under Andropov: Engine of Party Renewal

Two sharply divergent views have emerged concerning the role of the KGB as an engine of political reform in the Soviet Union. One holds that under Andropov's leadership, the KGB helped drive the Party ultimately to open itself to criticism and competition so as to make it stronger.[7] The opposite view, held by such pivotal reform figures as former Soviet Interior Minister and KGB Chairman Vadim Bakatin, claims that the KGB was incapable of thinking or acting progressively, and that reforms were driven by Party activists close to Mikhail Gorbachev, such as Aleksandr Yakovlev and Eduard Shevardnadze.[8] Yet Bakatin himself acknowledges that he was a newcomer to the Gorbachev inner circle, a Siberian construction foreman and rather latecoming Party official who did not enter Moscow politics until 1985, more than two decades after Andropov began to recruit the glasnost generation of Party leaders. Nevertheless, both views may be correct without being contradictory. It was Andropov the man, who became KGB chairman, who foresaw the need for the Party to reform itself or face self-destruction.

Bakatin's hard-line predecessor KGB chairman, the stalwart Vladimir Kryuchkov, credits Andropov personally, instead of the secret police as a whole, with the impetus for reform. Asked in a 1989 interview if he thought Andropov would have initiated perestroika had he lived longer, Kryuchkov replied:

> Yes, I think so. He would have taken this path. He was perfectly well aware of the country's situation, he had been a party official, then he had been a diplomat, and, finally, he was head of the KGB for 15 years. He knew the party well and his position as head of the KGB gave him access to a vast amount of information. All that helped him to form a realistic idea of what was happening in the country. His first acts as general secretary were aimed at restoring order, at increasing the activities of state institutions, the soviets, the party. . . . Andropov understood very well that we would not make any progress unless we changed something in our economic and political mechanisms. I think that Andropov and Gorbachev had the same approach, the same ideology, perhaps even the same methodology for resolving the problems.[9]

Long before he became USSR KGB chairman, Andropov had a deep involvement with the men who would form Gorbachev's inner circle. He cultivated them for future leadership. *Pravda* editor Ivan Frolov noted in a 1989 interview that in the late 1950s and early 1960s under Andropov's direction, the Central Committee Secretariat division responsible for relations with other socialist regimes was a "training school for future Gorbachevites, and it was Andropov himself, many years later, who introduced Gorbachev—newly arrived in Moscow from Stavropol—to some of those later to become his close aides, including [Georgiy] Shakhnazarov, [Aleksandr] Bovin, and [Georgiy] Arbatov."[10]

Fyodor Burlatsky, who became editor of *Literaturnaya gazeta* when it served as a major propaganda arm of the perestroika campaign, elaborated further. He recalled that in 1960 Andropov asked him to work for his department as a consultant. Then:

> He asked me to create a group of consultants under him, so I brought in a number of people who are now very prominent—Georgii Shakhnazarov, who's a personal aide to Gorbachev; Gennadii Gerasimov, who's the spokesman of the Foreign Ministry; Oleg Bogomolov, who is Director of the Institute on the Economics of the World Socialist System; [Institute of the USA and Canada Director] Georgii Arbatov and [*Izvestia* political writer] Aleksandr Bovin . . . and others. It was a very unusual group of young party intellectuals, perhaps the first ever in the Central Committee.[11]

Andropov also attracted young Party officials who would follow him to the KGB. According to Burlatsky, Andropov "was absolutely a reform-minded person," within the narrow context of the Communist Party at least, in the early and mid-1960s. At that time, Andropov "expressed in his speeches and articles reformist ideas about modernizing the economy and changing the way the Party and state functioned. He understood the need for major reforms as well as his group of young advisers, which I headed."[12] Upon becoming CPSU General Secretary in 1982, Andropov installed Burlatsky as a political commentator at *Literaturnaya gazeta*. Gorbachev ultimately named him editor-in-chief. (In this position, Burlatsky not only spread messages helpful to glasnost but he surfaced disinformation themes against the United States, such as the false story that the AIDS virus was invented by the U.S. military as a biological weapon).[13]

Perhaps the Andropovites who tried to cobble a strategy of reforms to breathe new life into the Soviet system were encouraged by the Soviet experiment in Hungary. As Soviet Ambassador to Budapest, Andropov personally played a major role in the 1956 removal of nationalist reform leader Imre Nagy, the Soviet invasion, and the installation of the reluctant but pliable Janos Kadar. (One of Andropov's aides at the embassy was Vladimir Kryuchkov, who would become Gorbachev's KGB chairman thirty-two years later.) Kadar then embarked on a socialist economic strategy that, though far behind democratic Europe, was the most successful in the entire bloc. By the 1970s, it was clear that a Communist regime could survive and rather flourish with a significant degree of economic and political liberalization and that such reforms would not threaten the power of the ruling class. Glasnost and perestroika, then, could be used to implement needed reforms within a Marxist-Leninist institutional framework and under strict Party control. Human rights would still be lacking and securitiy forces would remain strong, but economic liberalization would endear the reforming government to the West and thereby attract Western loans, credits and other financial assistance as well as investments and high technology.

With the Andropov ascendancy, the KGB's foreign intelligence capabilities became world-class despite the Soviet Union's dramatic overall technological backwardness. A source who knew Andropov socially and professionally in the late 1960s said that the KGB chief recruited young officers with "unexpected personal concern" for their talent instead of their political connections, though all were Komsomol and Party members in good standing. By the early 1980s the officers had become majors, lieutenant colonels, and colonels in a reinvigorated service.[14]

As CPSU general secretary, Andropov embarked on a far-reaching purge of Party officials at all levels of government, utilizing an anti-corruption theme as a political rationale for discrediting and removing Brezhnevites. In the process, he promoted younger and more reformist apparatchiks to positions of responsibility. The Party housecleaning was sharply but temporarily slowed after Andropov's death in February 1984, when successor Konstantin Chernenko relaxed the anticorruption drive. However, by summer of that year, the campaign resumed, inspired by the strong shadow cast by Gorbachev, whose broad portfolio included Party cadres, and by Central Committee Secretary Yegor Ligachev, who headed the Party-Organizational Work Department.

The KGB assisted the effort by collecting, maintaining, and supplying the information needed for controlled publications such as *Literaturnaya gazeta* to make public several scandals of official corruption that reflected negatively on Chernenko and his allies. Upon succeeding Chernenko in March 1985, Gorbachev continued the massive Party purges that Andropov had begun. Without a political base or patronage network of his own, he nevertheless had the power to remove not only the Brezhnevites from the Central Committee but potential rivals like Grigoriy Romanov as well. The officials he dismissed occupied higher positions of authority than those whom Andropov had removed in the first spate of anticorruption actions. They included republic ministers as well as the MVD and Procuracy leaders.[15]

Amy W. Knight of the Library of Congress explains Gorbachev's unusual political clout:

> While the regular law enforcement agencies were subjected to sharp attacks for their failure to combat crime, the KGB remained unscathed. Despite the fact that it is actually empowered by law to conduct investigations into certain types of economic crime, in particular misappropriation of state property, the KGB was not held responsible for having allowed white-collar crime to become so pervasive.[16]

Not only was the KGB unscathed under Gorbachev. Its status in Soviet society grew. The 1986 CPSU program, the first since 1961, contained a new reference to state security organs that reflected both the KGB's new status within the Party and its status in relation to the long-glorified armed forces: "The CPSU regards the defense of the socialist homeland, the strengthening of the country's defense, *and the safeguarding of state security* as one of the most important functions of the Soviet state and the whole people" (emphasis added).[17]

This new mention was important as a definitive Party statement and a guide for Party cadres under glasnost and perestroika; for the first time since the early Khrushchev period, the Party had acknowledged state security as an integral part of national defense. Concurrent with this new stature, the KGB enjoyed increased power especially in decisionmaking, visibility, and prestige. Gorbachev constructed palatial office buildings for the KGB across the USSR, including a beautiful large annex at Dzerzhinskiy Square in the capital. Reasons for the KGB's enhanced position during perestroika are grounded in its role in the rise of Mikhail Gorbachev the politician.

The KGB and the Rise of Mikhail Gorbachev

Like other Party leaders who emerged to sire perestroika, Mikhail Gorbachev had a career of privileged interaction with the KGB, and with Andropov in particular, during his political ascent. From humble peasant beginnings in rural Stavropol where hard work for the Party won him a medal before his entry to Moscow State University,[18] Gorbachev against great handicaps earned the respect of those around him for diligence, temperance, and patience. He grew to trust the KGB completely. Although few Western observers seemed to notice, a number of seasoned Soviet émigré political scientists, citing his special relationships with KGB personnel, suggested that he was a kept man of the chekists.[19]

He seems to have owed his career to the service, with which he was probably involved since his early twenties while studying law at Moscow State University. At the time, the study of law in Stalin's Soviet Union was merely a study of a means of political control and had nothing to do with jurisprudence in the Western sense of the term, even though many Western commentators attributed his liberalism to his legal training.

A number of his mates from the Stromynka dormitory, the best-known being Zdenek Mlynar of Czechoslovakia, have commented for the record about of the bright and ambitious student who would become leader of the USSR. While Gorbachev's exposure to Mlynar is credited by some biographers as having helped to shape his reformist views, it also indicated something less praiseworthy. Biographer Zhores Medvedev observed that in the 1950s, "Only 'trustworthy' Soviet students are distributed amongst the better rooms allocated to foreigners." He added that it was "not unlikely that Gorbachev would have been asked to give periodic reports on his roommate" to the secret police.[20]

Medvedev's assertion is bolstered by accounts of former classmates and roommates of Gorbachev from 1950 to 1955. Many found him likable and, in private, humble, if not as sophisticated as his urban colleagues. Others recall that he was unpopular with many and was suspected of being an informant. Their suspicions gained credence when the law students took internships in various police and judicial agencies such as the Ministry of Justice, the Ministry of Internal Affairs, and the Procuracy. Gorbachev's internship, former classmates said, was at NKVD headquarters in Lubyanka, run at the time by one of the most notorious of chekists, Lavrenti Beria.[21]

Although there is no verifiable record that Gorbachev conclusively did serve in the state security organs, he did choose to make his mark in the Komsomol, which the law faculty recommended for students who sought a career in the chekist apparatus.[22] Building a career in the Komsomol would have been unusual because he was already a full member of the Communist Party when he was in the university, itself an almost unheard-of position for a man as young as he was. His place of internship in college is not even known to well-connected biographer Medvedev.[23] Still, no conclusions can be drawn from the evidence. Victor Yasmann of Radio Liberty speculated, "It is quite possible that [Gorbachev] would have liked to have been a KGB officer but was rejected for being too bright and too cultivated during that anti-intellectual Stalin period."[24]

Another former classmate, Lev Yudovich, said that when Gorbachev joined the Party in 1952, the university climate was "strictly Stalinist," that some students disliked Gorbachev "because he had actively supported Stalin's 'anti-cosmopolitan' [anti-Jewish] policies, and because he took a hard line during discussions of people's personal affairs."[25] Gorbachev's arch-defender Mlynar, asked about the allegation, did not deny it,[26] and major biographers agree that Gorbachev must have been an ardent supporter of Stalin.[27] To be fair, nobody with any sense of survival during the Stalin period did not support the *vozhd*. Yet unlike most, Gorbachev chose to be an active organizer as a Komsomol propagandist.

Yudovich recalled that Gorbachev pursued the Stalin line as the law school Komsomol secretary.[28] This may be another symptom of opportunism and lack of conviction, however. On one emotional occasion following the Doctors' Plot of 1952 when Stalin began blaming Jews for conspiring against him, Gorbachev defended the only Jew at one of his Komsomol meetings.[29] Yet this act of bravery also signaled possible protection from state security. Open defense of a Jew at such a delicate time would not have been without penalty unless the defender had protectors of his own in the Party or state security, and Gorbachev had no known powerful political sponsors. Furthermore, one is challenged to find deep-seated principles against anti-Semitism, as Gorbachev also exposed non-Jews as "enemies of the people," according to Vladimir Solovyov and Elena Klepikova.[30]

Biographer Gail Sheehy concluded, "No one was ever quite sure what he stood for."[31] Fellow biographer Dmitry Mikheyev, speculating on how a poor peasant from the Caucasus could advance as far and as quickly Gorbachev he did politically at Moscow State in the Stalin era, concluded that Gorbachev may have been an agent provocateur to help root out the potential traitors that the chekist organs were convinced lurked among the student body.[32]

On-the-record defenses of Gorbachev by men who remained in the Communist system must be treated with some skepticism. In fact, some of Gorbachev's main defenders rely heavily on Mlynar's accounts to portray him as enlightened even as a Stalinist.[33] Mlynar's published defenses of Gorbachev appear to have been officially sanctioned by the

Kremlin; they were first published by *L'Unita*,[34] the newspaper published by the Italian Communist Party and therefore funded and directed by the CPSU International Department. The KGB itself used *L'Unita* to surface new public relations themes in Europe.[35]

Gorbachev's critics, by contrast, were either émigrés beyond the reach of retribution or Soviet citizens who spoke only on the condition of anonymity for fear of reprisal.[36] Another classmate related, "He was really like the plague of the law school. We feared Misha like the devil himself. When he walked by, everybody stopped talking."[37] Yudovich and ex-classmate Fridrikh Nezansky remember him as a "hard-liner" who denounced the shortcomings of his fellow Komsomol members. Nezansky recalled "the steely voice of the Komsomol secretary of the law faculty, Gorbachev, demanding expulsion from the Komsomol for the slightest offense, from telling inappropriate political jokes to trying to avoid being sent to a collective farm."[38]

An account of how Gorbachev became Komsomol cell leader, if true, demonstrates the raw ambition and opportunism that propelled him. According to Nezansky, during his second year of school, in 1951, Gorbachev got his local cell leader, identified only as Nikitin, excessively drunk, denounced him for drunkenness the following day, and took his place as cell chief.[39] Regardless of how it was accomplished, the fact that a rural farmboy could become Komsomol chief in his second year of college was highly unusual.

Gorbachev's enthusiasm for Stalin and his probable collaboration with state security earned him nothing in Moscow by the time he graduated from law school in 1955, two years after the dictator's death. Speculation as to the causes of this interruption in his rise to power centers on Party politics as they related to the NKVD. The late Petr Deriabin who served in the NKVD at the time, wrote that after Stalin's death in March 1953 and Beria's execution in July, "The command apparatus inside the Central Committee was paralyzed by mistrust and factional disputes," and was accompanied by internal turmoil among the chekists.[40]

Suspicion and maneuvering was at extreme levels. Robert Conquest noted, "three successive heads of the KGB Section for Investigating Specially Important Cases were executed" between December 1953 and December 1954.[41] According to Yasmann, "The Party didn't want Beria-linked functionaries. That's why Gorbachev lost his position as Komsomol leader and why he was sent back to Stavropol. . . . Suddenly, he wasn't so attractive to the Party any more."[42]

Without a sponsor in the Soviet capital, Gorbachev returned to Stavropol, where he and his new wife, Raisa, would spend the next twenty-three years. Despite three years of Party membership, elite education, and Moscow experience, he was able to gain only a humbling entry-level position as assistant chief of the regional or *kray* Komsomol propaganda section, which required none of the skills he had learned in school.[43]

Gorbachev earned a reputation as a diligent, obliging, honest, and straightforward subordinate in the Stavropol Party apparat, but not as a leader. His skills were recognized by kray Party First Secretary Fyodor Kulakov, who in 1962 named Gorbachev to lead the department in charge of cadres. The position meant a working relationship with the local KGB, which screened potential Party members.[44] Gorbachev skipped over the third secretaryship and was elevated to kray second secretary in 1968. This position would have made him curator of the local branches of the Procuracy, the Ministry of Internal Affairs, and the KGB, like most other local second secreatries; therefore his career in the Party depended on KGB reporting and protection.[45] This quick move suggests the blessing of state security. Gorbachev reportedly had strong social relationships with two top kray KGB officers, according to a former apartment building neighbor,[46] which would not have been extraordinary for a Party official of his position.

Gorbachev gained an advocate in the Kremlin in 1964 when his local sponsor, Kulakov, was named Central Committee secretary for agriculture and transferred to Moscow. With Politburo member Mikhail Suslov, also a former Stavropol Party chief, Kulakov was part of the successful KGB-backed plot hatched in Stavropol to oust Nikita Khrushchev.[47] Through Kulakov, Gorbachev gained the attention and support of Suslov. By the time Gorbachev became kray first secretary in 1970, he had met a much more powerful sponsor, USSR KGB Chairman Yuriy Andropov, another Stavropol native. His relationship with Andropov could have begun in the early 1960s, when he was first promoted under Kulakov, as he once said that he had had a "twenty-year friendship" with Andropov by the time the KGB chief had become CPSU general secretary in 1982.[48]

Ill with diabetes and kidney disease, Andropov and his wife vacationed at the Krasniye Kamni spa in the resort town of Kislovodsk, where protocol dictated that Gorbachev play host by meeting Andropov and Politburo guests at the airport or train station, escorting them to and from the sanitoria, and visiting them to inquire about their needs during their stay. Raisa Gorbachev became friends with Andropov's wife, also a diabetic, and the two would go on walks together. According to Solovyov and Klepikova, who interviewed witnesses in Stavropol, "Andropov's autumnal visits to Kislovodsk provided a rare, almost unique opportunity. Urged on by his wife, Gorbachev took advantage of the situation for career purposes." Andropov had few friends in whom he could confide, they reported, but apparently felt a special bond with his younger host:

> Gorbachev was perhaps the only person outside Andropov's family circle who quite often socialized with him. He was able to observe him not in official or on-the-job circumstances but when he was on vacation, in the atmosphere of leisure and relaxation, when the KGB chief was in his pajamas and bedroom slippers instead of his usual dark suit and dark tie, chatting with his wife. When Gorbachev scheduled his own vacations in Kislovodsk to coincide with the Andropovs' visits there, whether by chance or deliberately, he established with the inscrutable top cop relations that were even more trusting and friendly, almost familial. For Andropov, his landsman and younger comrade Gorbachev was the only man of his kind with whom he felt completely at ease and could be frank—within certain limits, naturally. And Gorbachev knew how to please a superior, especially such a high-ranking one from the Kremlin.[49]

Biographer Christian Schmidt-Häuer's research similarly finds that the KGB chairman was crucial to Gorbachev's ascendancy:

> There can be no doubt that even before his brief time as General Secretary, Andropov was one of Gorbachev's patrons. For a number of years the two had shared the same ideas about the urgent need for modernization. This feeling had been strengthened by meetings in the Caucasian mineral spas, where Andropov, suffering from kidney disease, frequently took the waters and where Gorbachev as the Regional Party chief had to welcome distinguished visitors from Moscow. . . . What is certain is that Andropov, always a single-minded worker, suffered a collapse at the spa of Kislovodsk long before the West knew anything about his illness. It seems likely, therefore, that in the prolonged and thorough preparations for his own accession, Andropov included Gorbachev in his plans as his principal organizer and as his "crown prince."[50]

Despite Andropov's notoriously paranoid character, he felt complete confidence in Gorbachev. The late KGB chief's son Igor confirms the relationship, saying, "They were two intelligent, honest, uncorrupted persons with a lot in common, but they were completely different in their personalities." Never "buddies"—Andropov was too stiff and formal—they shared interests and talked incessantly about politics. According to Igor Andropov, the Gorbachevs were often invited to his father's dacha at Kislovodsk. He admits to having felt some jealousy at the attention his father gave Gorbachev, in whom the elder Andropov saw "great political potential."[51]

The young Stavropol Party chief, who had demonstrated a commitment to improving efficiency and to cracking down on corruption, assisted Andropov in his anticorruption campaign of 1977. The effort was designed to undermine Brezhnev's regional support bases within the Party. Gorbachev gladly assembled a dossier on Brezhnevite rival Sergey Medunov in neighboring Krasnodar kray and provided it to the KGB chief.[52]

Andropov prepared for Gorbachev's appointment to the Politburo when Kulakov died in 1978. Andropov, Mikhail Suslov and Aleksey Kosygin all had similar kidney and diabetic problems, and all had been prescribed the hot mineral water spas at Kislovodsk, where they could have talked politics and discussed the possibility of bringing Gorbachev to Moscow. In September, Andropov arranged for a Baku-bound special train carrying General Secretary Brezhnev and fellow Politburo member Chernenko to make a special stop at a resort town near Kislovodsk where he was convalescing. Andropov greeted Brezhnev and Chernenko at the station, and introduced them to his young protégé, who was able to impress Brezhnev by reporting a local grain harvest that was well over the official state quota. The brief visit, by virtue of the fact that it was mentioned in the then-controlled central Soviet press in far-off Moscow, was viewed as a significant milestone in Kremlin politics.[53] As it turned out, it was the first meeting between the sitting general secretary and his three successors.

Within three months, and with Suslov's strong support, Gorbachev was installed on the Politburo as a candidate member. He became a full member in 1980. During his candidate membership, Gorbachev was the Party secretary who shared supervision of the Administrative Organs (AO) Department with Chernenko, an unusual arrangement between a man so senior and one so junior. Gorbachev became the senior Party secretary with AO management in 1980, a position he held until 1984. In that five-year period, Amy Knight observes, he appeared at AO functions, signed key obituaries, and chaired the USSR Supreme Soviet Legislative Proposals Commission, which, officially at least, had parliamentary supervision of the administrative organs.[54] At the levers of party controls, Gorbachev was well positioned for advancement.

Consistent with Andropov's desires, the KGB treated Gorbachev well and even helped the junior Politburo member to shine among his much elder colleagues. According to Oleg Gordievsky, "The KGB put great care into briefing Gorbachev in a way that would allow him to impress the rest of the Politburo with his grasp of both Soviet and world affairs. And the reports that it provided the Politburo as a whole were deliberately designed to support Gorbachev's arguments."[55] In Brezhnev's final days, Gorbachev used files provided by the KGB on Andropov's behalf to attack members of the Soviet leader's family, including his daughter and her boyfriend. (Gorbachev would later use the same tactics to discredit his own political opponents once he became General Secretary.)

The ailing Andropov, after succeeding Brezhnev, appointed Gorbachev his spokesman in early 1983. He soon positioned Gorbachev to lead a handpicked group of young Politburo members described as a "dynamic operational team for internal and economic changes."[56] The team included Politburo members Vitaliy Vorotnikov, who would become premier of the Russian Soviet Federated Socialist Republic and in charge of choosing new members of the Soviet government; Yegor Ligachev, who would become Gorbachev's second-in-command on the Politburo; Nikolay Ryzhkov, who would become chief of the Soviet Council of Ministers; and KGB Chairman Viktor Chebrikov.[57] This was the team that rode out the brief Chernenko interregnum.

Gorbachev was a product of KGB input. In Gordievsky's words, "Gorbachev's new thinking was . . . powerfully influenced by his many briefings by the KGB."[58] (Revelations after the 1991 putsch proved this to be the case throughout Gorbachev's tenure as CPSU general secretary.) Alex Alexiev of the Rand Corporation argues that during the March 1985 Politburo meeting that made Gorbachev the successor to Chernenko, KGB Chairman Viktor Chebrikov's vote "was almost certainly the decisive one."[59] Chebrikov used a KGB dossier publicly to discredit another potential candidate, Viktor Grishin, in favor of the reformer from Stavropol.[60]

Apparently in exchange for the support, General Secretary Gorbachev promoted Chebrikov from candidate to full membership in the Politburo within a month. In Medvedev's estimation, the promotion made the KGB chairman an "independent figure" in the Party leadership, giving him the "same kind of independence that Andropov had achieved in 1973." Medvedev states that when the KGB chief was outside the Politburo or was a nonvoting candidate member, he tended to defer directly to the general secretary; as a full member he was "answerable to the Politburo or Central Committee, not to the General secretary."[61] Full membership made the KGB leader a peer and not a subordinate of the general secretary, a leader instead of a servant of the Central Committee. Gorbachev not only needed Chebrikov's help before assuming the reins of the CPSU, but he depended on the KGB more than ever because he had enabled its chief to become a more independent actor. Thus Gorbachev became Party leader without the full control of the KGB that Andropov had enjoyed.

Thanks in great part to Chebrikov's support, Gorbachev consolidated his position quickly, launching the most comprehensive personnel turnover since the Great Purge. The KGB immediately revived the anticorruption campaign begun by Andropov against the Brezhnevites. It also helped to discredit Gorbachev's main rival, Grigoriy Romanov, by spreading rumors about alleged personal indiscretions involving alcohol and women.[62]

Soon Gorbachev replaced one-third of the Politburo and regional Party officers with younger people. The reasons were varied: old age and poor health, and reasons Andropov had used, including drunkenness, bribery, corruption, and incompetence. Yet the four vices were found at all levels of government and even within the Gorbachev camp. The real reasons for the removals were political. Gorbachev broke with the Party elites of Kiev, Leningrad, and Moscow and took in new cadres from the periphery, especially from Siberia, while forging an alliance with the Party intelligentsia, whom he partially unshackled to attack the moribund aspects of the apparatus. Notably, he had no use for non-Party intellectuals or dissidents, many of whom he allowed to languish in prisons and concentration camps for another two years.

Even though Gorbachev quickly brought about massive personnel changes at all levels of the Communist Party and was unanimously elected president of the USSR Supreme Soviet in 1988, the KGB remained off-limits to the new campaigns of glasnost and perestroika Despite his powerful political base, he never used his immense political capital to touch the chekists. Knight observed halfway through the Gorbachev era,

> The KGB has not been subjected to the sweeping personnel changes that have been imposed on other institutions, such as the armed forces and the Party. It might have been expected that Gorbachev, like his predecessors, would attempt to assert control over the KGB by bringing in some of his own men, or at least neutral outsiders, to fill top KGB posts. Instead, longtime KGB professionals remain at the helm.[63]

Noted Mikheyev in retrospect,

> If Gorbachev had no burden of allegiance to the KGB and was determined to reform the system, the KGB would have been a logical place to start democratization and liberalization. Gorbachev was well aware of the terrible reputation of the KGB, particularly among the intelligentsia whose

> help he had begun to solicit in 1982. Therefore, he could have won a great amount of trust among the intelligentsia and the *narod* by lowering the KGB's status, narrowing its responsibilities, cutting its budget, putting it under some sort of public control, and punishing those responsible for the most serious crimes. But he didn't. He did not even bother to rename this institution.[64]

As in his college days and during his political years in Stavropol, as CPSU general secretary and unelected Soviet president, Gorbachev was a driven, energetic operative but not a leader of men. He protected the KGB, and the KGB protected him until the unintended consequences of the reforms and his own indecisiveness prompted chekist leaders to attempt to impose emergency powers to preserve the CPSU and the USSR. Instead of challenging the KGB's increasing illegal power, Gorbachev sought to fortify the state security organ by allowing it to portray itself as an essential element of perestroika. He utilized it as an engine of his own political agenda—both to discredit political opponents and to muzzle the newly freed dissidents who wanted to push reforms far outside the Party's narrow parameters. He willingly increased the KGB's power and prestige. If he issued no directives for the KGB to conduct itself as a professional service, he bears ultimate responsibility for abuses. If he did issue directives that were ignored, then he was never really in control. He was in no position to challenge the KGB and thus, at the very least, acquiesced. Evidence now shows that he went further and in many cases signed the orders for human rights abuses.[65]

Political Intrigue in the KGB and Politburo

Gorbachev's strategy to court Western public opinion and convince the West to finance perestroika with hard currency and favorable trade terms forced the Soviet leader to walk a fine line between assuaging the concerns of Party skeptics and introducing broad enough reforms to show that he merited large-scale infusions of aid. In this sense his foreign policy was intertwined with his domestic agenda.[66]

However, two years into his Party revivication program, it became apparent that changes were spinning out of the Party's control. On the heels of a series of calls for protection of individual rights and far-reaching legal reform came exposés of past crimes perpetrated by the Party via the KGB. Initial reports were relatively minor in retrospect, but at the time they were unprecedented; not even during the de-Stalinization campaign of the Khrushchev period had the state security organs been questioned or criticized. To add insult to the chekists' injury, political prisoners were finally released after years of international pressure. Even some KGB officials on the periphery began to admit mistakes, though it cannot be discounted that the KGB allowed limited criticism of the obvious in response to public opinion.[67]

While Gorbachev, Foreign Minister Shevardnadze, and others continued to woo the West, Chebrikov chafed at the forces he had helped to unleash. On 11 September 1987, in celebration of Dzerzhinskiy's 110th birthday, Chebrikov gave a powerful speech in which he said the KGB was restructuring along with the rest of society but warned the intelligentsia against adventurism and accused them of being aligned with collaborators of Western intelligence services—an official theme to discredit critics that would continue the next seven years or more.[68]

In so doing, Chebrikov affirmed the strength of the political and social blinders that channeled KGB perceptions of the world and revealed anew the chekist propensity to view domestic political opposition as some sort of foreign subversive conspiracy. In response, Gorbachev had his chief of staff, Anatoliy Lukyanov, give an interview to Novosti in which he minimized the KGB's role in Soviet decisionmaking, falsely saying that its main function was limited to protecting the state from espionage from abroad. Lukyanov added that the government had placed strict controls on the state security apparatus.[69] Yet the obvious understatement, combined with Gorbachev's failure to rebuke Chebrikov, made it apparent that the KGB chairman was untouchable and that, indeed, he wielded substantial influence in the political and decisionmaking process. By the end of the year, Gorbachev removed not the hard-liner Chebrikov or even Ligachev from the Politburo, but the most reformist member of all: Boris Yeltsin.

The KGB chief was still not satisfied. Celebrating the fiftieth anniversary of the founding of the Cheka, Chebrikov again raised the specter of foreign subversion:

> Imperialism's special services are trying to find new loopholes through which to penetrate our society and are exerting targeted, differentiated influence on various population groups in the USSR with the aim of instilling in Soviet people a bourgeois understanding of democracy, removing the processes of increasing the working people's socio-political activeness from the party's influence, splitting the monolithic unity of party and people, and installing political and ideological pluralism.[70]

Such speeches did little to reinforce the international image that Gorbachev and Shevardnadze were crafting, but few in the West seemed to notice. In an April 1988 speech the KGB chairman complained that there was too much criticism of the past and again accused foreign intelligence services of being behind nationalist and political ferment, warning, "The danger of this method of subversive activity against our country must not be underestimated."[71] Concurrently, Gorbachev began to back away from continued reforms. Though by this time the Party was collapsing on itself, the Soviet leader could not put reforms on hold, let alone reverse them, lest he lose the loans, credits, and other forms of aid streaming in from the West.

Throughout the summer, he devised a new system of government that would shift decisionmaking from the Party apparatus to the government bureaucracy. This change helped to streamline the process without sacrificing Party hegemony because every government official who mattered was a member of the Party and would continue for the time being to adhere to the stated line. It also projected the image that perestroika was moving the government away from the Communist Party toward a more pluralist regime without actually doing so.

The change yielded another important by-product for Gorbachev's image-making needs. It removed Chebrikov from the post of KGB chairman without alienating either Chebrikov or the KGB. The chekist's departure from state security caused him no loss of face. Upon leaving the KGB, he was made a powerful Party secretary and remained a full member of the Politburo—despite the lack of support for him on the Central Committee—and became chief of a new CPSU Commission on Legal Affairs, which officially supervised the KGB and other security organs.[72]

Vladimir Kryuchkov, who for so long had walked in the shadow of the late Andropov, was appointed to become full KGB chairman. Many observers in the West interpreted these changes as "kicking Chebrikov upstairs," as he no longer had day-to-day control over the chekist apparat, and speculated that Kryuchkov, who was not yet made a candidate Politburo member, served at the pleasure of Gorbachev and thus was less well positioned to assert himself against the Soviet leader.

However, the dynamics remain unclear. Chebrikov's powers actually may have expanded. The switch did not occur in isolation but was part of a major restructuring of the Kremlin decisionmaking system. Until that point, the CPSU Politburo decided policy, whereas the Secretariat ran day-to-day operations and prepared matters for the Politburo to discuss and approve. The system could be confusing:

Politburo members were often secretaries with sometimes poorly defined or overlapping jurisdictions. Under the new system, each Politburo member became analogous to a "cabinet" minister and had a clearly and publicly defined portfolio. Gorbachev remained Party general secretary; the premier, the Moscow Party chief, the Ukrainian Party chief, and the foreign minister retained their titles; and each of the six remaining Politburo members became head of a new CPSU commission.[73]

Chebrikov's Commission on Legal Affairs gave him a well-defined rank and a set of responsibilities far more broad than those he had as KGB chief. He now supervised the Administrative Organs Department of the CPSU Central Committee as well as the Ministry of Internal Affairs, the Procuracy, the courts, and the KGB—all without having a political base of his own within the Party. His official strength suggested that he continued to wield considerable influence over the security apparatus, and therefore over the Party. Gorbachev's initial decision not to name Kryuchkov to the Politburo suggests that Chebrikov remained the main KGB advocate in the CPSU leadership.[74] The new arrangement may even have placed the KGB in de facto control of the Ministry of Internal Affairs, the procuracy, the courts and the Party Administrative Organs Department.

Following the practices of the late Andropov, Gorbachev made no attempt to ensure political control over state security by naming a Party official to the KGB chairmanship. From the removal of Beria in 1954 until 1982 when Andropov appointed professional chekist Chebrikov,[75] Party leaders had named fellow civilian Party functionaries to run the KGB. Now, Gorbachev consolidated chekist supremacy in Lubyanka by permitting Chebrikov to designate his own successor from inside the organs, namely, fellow Andropov protégé Kryuchkov, whose fourteen years as head of the First Chief Directorate gave him vast knowledge of international affairs. This background would be a key advantage when it came to selling glasnost and perestroika abroad. The Kryuchkov appointment marked a break with Gorbachev's usual management style, which rather liberal by Soviet standards. He tended to surround himself with Communist Party intellectuals and create his own teams to reform various sectors of Soviet society. By keeping new-thinking intellectuals from having anything to do with the security apparatus, Gorbachev further insulated the organs from perestroika.

From his Politburo perch, Chebrikov continued to act as an author of abuse inside the USSR, alienating Party stalwarts by supporting Gorbachev while remaining a nemesis of reformers because of the force for which he stood. His power was on the ascent as the limited freedoms allowed by glasnost cleaved the first major fissures in the Soviet system. One observer said, "Throughout the fall and winter of 1988-89 and spring and summer of 1989, Chebrikov presided at numerous important public meetings and functions involving: the law-and-order sector, or 'Organs,' related to the Central Committee's erstwhile Administrative Organs Department, the KGB, the MVD, the army, and international ('imperial,' or nationalities affairs) as well as presiding at sessions of the Party's Legal Affairs Commission."[76]

Chebrikov authored repressive decrees that Gorbachev unquestioningly signed, such as the 8 April 1989 edict criminalizing criticism of the government and the Communist Party. The order was immediately used as a pretext to use violence to crush mass demonstrations in Tblisi, Georgia, where security forces murdered twenty-one civilians.[77] Chebrikov then authored propaganda statements to justify repressive measures with the Soviet public. Moscow intellectuals claimed that two major articles explaining the need for the decree, published in the 11 April and 11 May 1989 issues of *Pravda,* actually had been written by the Central Committee Commission on Legal Affairs, which Chebrikov chaired. Chebrikov also penned an article for the Party's theoretical journal *Kommunist* stating that the decree was needed to preserve law and order.[78]

The Party finally started to move against Chebrikov in May 1989, but it was not alone. KGB Chairman Kryuchkov began to assert himself and pushed at Chebrikov from below. Two authoritative publications of the reform Communist movement with close ties to the KGB, *Argumenty i fakty* and *Moscow News,* began publishing articles by jurists critical of the Commission on Legal Affairs.[79] Then came the USSR Supreme Soviet, which under the personal administration of Gorbachev and Anatoliy Lukyanov was becoming more of an open forum for critics and taking its first baby steps toward exercising legislative powers. Bowing to calls from democratic reformers, the legislature established the politically significant but impotent Committee on Defense and Security, a well-publicized emerging challenge to Chebrikov's commission.

The security services, and especially the KGB, came under unprecedented intense public criticism by reformist Supreme Soviet members who denounced abuses passionately during the nationally televised parliamentary sessions. Their speeches after long silence reflected a strain of public mood, especially in light of the Tblisi outrages, which were widely reported in the Soviet press. Demands for radical reform of the security services began to mount. KGB Chairman

Kryuchkov responded, making an effort to take the moral high ground and pledging that his service would be under parliamentary, and not Party, control.

A visible shift of authority was now occurring whereby the state Supreme Soviet began to overshadow the Party Central Committee, although real power remained with the executive central Party apparat. Likewise, Kryuchkov's shadow began to eclipse Chebrikov. The KGB chairman starred in a dramatic "confirmation" appearance before the Supreme Soviet in July 1989 and in a very high-profile electronic and print media public relations follow-up. However, he never publicly dishonored his predecessor. By September, Chebrikov was on the way out. A Politburo meeting followed Gorbachev's return from vacation in the first week of September, and Kryuchkov began to replace Chebrikov at state security-oriented events.[80]

Later that month, with support from the Central Committee, Gorbachev unceremoniously removed Chebrikov from the Politburo. Even then, this ouster seems to have been instigated more by Foreign Minister and Georgia native Eduard Shevardnadze and by Kryuchkov than by Gorbachev personally.[81] Nevertheless, the change did not lessen Gorbachev's dependence on the state security apparatus and may have even deepened it. In apparent exchange, or as a reward for KGB support in removing Chebrikov, Gorbachev made the unusual leap of appointing Kryuchkov to full Politburo membership without making him a nonvoting candidate member first as was the custom. The Soviet leader also made former Latvian KGB Chairman Boriss Pugo a Politburo candidate member.[82]

Even then, Gorbachev was powerless or unwilling to banish Chebrikov to political oblivion. More than a year after Chebrikov was officially removed, he continued to play a major behind-the-scenes role in security policy. He was part of the glasnost charade to "legalize" the KGB's powers. During the spring 1991 parliamentary debate on a new KGB-authored Law on State Security Organs, he was observed accompanying Kryuchkov to and from the USSR Supreme Soviet where Kryuchkov was a member, and advising him during the debate.[83] Chebrikov may have lost his post, but his influence, though diminished, apparently remained.

As Chebrikov's stock dwindled, so did that of Gorbachev. The Soviet leader was, by mid-1989, overtaken by events. Pulled by Party hard-liners on one side and reformers on the other, and with no political legitimacy of his own, Gorbachev had nowhere to turn but to the comforting bosom of the KGB.

The KGB in the Decisionmaking Process

Although the KGB, like the Party, permitted the public exercise of certain civil liberties such as freedom of the press, the censorship bureaucracy still existed and most outspoken reformers exercised a degree of self-censorship. Meanwhile, state security carefully monitored Gorbachev's political opponents—and attempted to discredit them on an as-needed basis by means of whispering campaigns, stories planted in the press, and public accusations. In private, the KGB discredited the opposition to Gorbachev personally.

According to former Interior Minister Vadim Bakatin, KGB Chairman Kryuchkov told Gorbachev the worst about the democratic opposition, convincing the Soviet leader at one point that demonstrators in Red Square had fashioned iron hooks and lengths of rope with which to scale the Kremlin walls and storm government offices. Bakatin says that he constantly had arguments with Kryuchkov in Gorbachev's presence but usually lost out to the KGB chief. Gorbachev, recalls Bakatin, "displayed unconditional trust in Kryuchkov. He did everything Kryuchkov suggested."[84]

Externally, the KGB collected intelligence and conducted covert operations vital to Gorbachev's success in making the USSR an acceptable part of the world community, especially in attracting large infusions of foreign aid. Noted Gordievsky, "Gorbachev . . . was convinced that a dynamic foreign policy required a dynamic intelligence service. The unprecedented range of initiatives on which he embarked abroad made it vital to have the fullest possible political intelligence on Western responses to them."[85]

A Leader Who Could Not Bring Himself to Lead

Mikhail Gorbachev was always the youngest among his peers: in law school, in the Stavropol apparatus, and on the Politburo. His youth among elders might be seen as a positive trait in Western societies, but in Communist Party politics it meant he was riding on an elder's coattails—being led instead of leading. The initiative and drive that propel younger politicians in the West were not characteristics traditionally rewarded by the CPSU. Imagery aside, Gorbachev was a follower, not a leader, even as general secretary and President of the Soviet Union. Solovyov and Klepikova insightfully observed in 1986,

> Persons like Gorbachev never belong to their own generation; they're already old when they're still young. Being not very independent and usually rather weak-willed, such a person does not make a political career himself: it is made for him by a series of patrons. They pass him on from hand to hand, like a baton in a relay race, and he ultimately becomes a puppet manipulated by others. But sooner or later the time comes when the mentors and sponsors have all died and their protégé is left to his own devices, personally responsible for everything. For persons who have always yielded to others, that is the most difficult time.[86]

Solovyov and Klepikova foresaw, as few others did at the time, that Gorbachev would follow those who would lead him, first Yakovlev and Shevardnadze, then Kryuchkov and Pugo. A year after the putsch, when asked whether Gorbachev was a leader or a follower, Vadim Bakatin weighed the question for a while before concluding,

> He was General Secretary, which made him a leader. . . . He was the first to do and say what he did. Yet he was not a leader. He did not want to break the socialist structure. He did not want to ruin the Communist Party. He stayed devoted to socialism until the end. He started without aiming at what he ultimately achieved. What Mikhail Gorbachev did happened by accident. . . . In the end, the system collapsed because it could only survive through control.[87]

KGB Chairman Kryuchkov led Mikhail Gorbachev down a tortuous path of repressive half-measures that ultimately destroyed everything they had tried to preserve. Glasnost and perestroika—a state of limbo that was neither totalitarianism nor freedom—would not survive without the support of the KGB.

Conclusion

The data show that the KGB had a vital and vanguard role in creating and steering glasnost and perestroika. Most of the main figures in the Party reform movement were recruited and cultivated by Yuriy Andropov, who saw like few others that the Party had to undergo radical changes if it was to survive. Gorbachev himself had strong, if perhaps not always comfortable, relations with the KGB that probably started when he was a university student and that continued in his early Party career in Stavropol, during his phenomenal rise on the Politburo, and through his tenure as CPSU general secretary. Indeed, the special relationship helped make the man into one of the twentieth century's greatest figures as much as it destroyed him in the end. Had he been true to his slogans and used his immense political capital to subdue the KGB, he might have done away with chekism forever.

3

Yeltsin Takes Over the KGB

The traditions of chekism must be eradicated, must cease to exist as an ideology.

—Vadim Bakatin, Chairman, KGB, November 1991[1]

Two political battles drove the historic changes that occurred in the KGB in 1991. The first involved the mailed fist of Boris Yeltsin, who hammered away at the Soviet Communist Party and its leaders—especially Mikhail Gorbachev—for restraining and even reversing the country's moves toward reform. Yeltsin's war was not only with Gorbachev but with Soviet central power as a whole. He led a Russian nationalist charge against the Russian Communist empire and, in so doing demanded a state security apparatus for his own government. In the USSR Supreme Soviet, he was one of the first people's deputies to demand civil accountability and dismemberment of the KGB.[2] The Russian Federation was the only one of the fifteen union republics that did not have its own KGB and Yeltsin, at the mercy of the Soviet structures which abused him as much as they had protected him, was determined to have one.

A KGB for the Russian Soviet Federated Socialist Republic (RSFSR) was finally created in May, but it had no apparatus and served no useful purpose until the culmination of the second political battle: that of Communist hard-liners whose co-optation of Gorbachev was readily apparent by late 1990. Always reluctant to commit himself, Gorbachev was not quite in lockstep with them. Although he was silent about Lithuania and did nothing public to oppose, reverse, or even criticize the actions or their perpetrators, he insisted on going ahead with the Union Treaty to cede more power to the republics. It is unclear whether he opposed hard-line plans to impose a state of emergency or went along with them. In any case, after unsuccessfully attempting to impose emergency rule legally through the USSR Supreme Soviet, KGB Chairman Vladimir Kryuchkov and his coconspirators imposed it by force in August 1991, succeeding not in reasserting Party control but in speeding the collapse of the union. A chastened Gorbachev, owing his political life to Yeltsin, went along with demands that the KGB be dismantled. By the end of the year the KGB as the world knew it was gone, divided up along functional and geographical lines, with the Russian Federation receiving the vast bulk of operations. An image-making campaign made it seem as if the chekist apparatus had been dissolved. But the apparatus and the culture that permeated it remained.

Pre-Putsch Russia and the New RSFSR KGB

The fact that Russia did not have its own republican KGB was moot until Yeltsin broke the Federation away from the Soviet center. The USSR Committee for State Security was dominated by ethnic Russians and functioned as an instrument of Russian Communist hegemony over the Union's scores of nationalities. As such, Russia needed no KGB of its own. Curiously, the first public demand for a separate Russian KGB was made not by a reformer calling for greater autonomy from the center but by a ranking hard-line KGB official during the February 1990 CPSU Central Committee plenum. Aleksandr Ovidev, head of a department in the Second Chief Directorate for counterintelligence, called for creation of a Russian KGB while attacking the process of democratization and calling on officers to protect Lenin's legacy.[3] Ovidev's intention was not clear, though he may have proposed a KGB for the RSFSR as a means of shoring up the hard line because he was alarmed at the unintended consequences of perestroika and the drift of the Party and the Union away from hard-line ideals.

Russian President Yeltsin sought a KGB for the Federation for a different reason. In the process of asserting his government against that of Gorbachev and the USSR, he apparently broached the idea with USSR KGB Chairman Vladimir Kryuchkov. He told the RSFSR Supreme Soviet in September 1990 that Kryuchkov had consented in principle, although it is clear that the KGB chief did not intend to give such an organ real powers. Yeltsin envisioned a Russian security service subordinate to him and his government and said that legislation could be drawn up within two months. To distance itself politically from the

KGB, the RF service was to have been renamed the State Committee for Public Security.[4]

Kryuchkov appeased Yeltsin by going along with the idea but played a double game. The two signed a protocol establishing a Russian KGB on 6 May 1991. As Yeltsin had long insisted, the RSFSR KGB was to have been subordinate to the Russian Supreme Soviet Presidium and the Council of Ministers, both of which he controlled, but Kryuchkov, in a surprise 40-minute negotiation with Yeltsin on the day of the signing, maneuvered Yeltsin to accept an amendment to the protocol making the Russian KGB a union-republic organ subject to dual jurisdiction between the governments of the RSFSR and the USSR.

Cosmetically, the protocol paid attention to the Russian Federation's sensitivities. The preamble, according to one account, "enshrines respect for the declaration on the republic's sovereignty." Kryuchkov, it was reported, "sugared the pill somewhat by saying that the status of the Russian committee [would] be special from all points of view (staff, budget, rights and so forth)." He explained to Yeltsin that the amendment for "dual" control was necessary "at the present stage" because of the expected signing of Gorbachev's Union Treaty, which would have relinquished much of the center's authority to the individual union republics.[5] He portrayed dual control as a mere legal technicality. Unknown to Yeltsin at the time, Kryuchkov was plotting to thwart signing of the Union Treaty by preparing for a state of emergency and the eventual putsch of August.

Yeltsin apparently was caught off guard and acceded to Kryuchkov's sugar-coated poison pill. Russia would have its own state security service, but as far as Kryuchkov was concerned, it would be an impotent one. A Russian Supreme Soviet member who was also a KGB officer noted that the "demarcation of functions and powers between the center and the republic" was not determined in the protocol and that vague reference was made in the document to basic principles of intelligence and counterintelligence activity being determined by the USSR KGB. Regional or *oblast* administrations in Russia, except for Moscow, would be transferred to the RSFSR KGB, with the fate of the Moscow KGB undetermined at the point of the signing.[6]

Nor did Yeltsin get his way in determining who would chair the new service. The circumstances surrounding this issue are less than clear. Kryuchkov named Major General Viktor Ivanenko, while Yeltsin's government reportedly sparred with the Soviet leadership to name a more reformist officer, Major General Nikolay Sham, who was deputy chief of the USSR KGB Sixth Directorate for economic counterintelligence. The Russian president approved Ivanenko's appointment as an apparent compromise. Under Ivanenko the RSFSR KGB never had more than twenty-three employees until after the August putsch, even though the protocol stated that it would begin with a staff of 300 to 350.[7]

With such a small staff, its dependence on the USSR KGB for all communications and security, and its physical location in the Lubyanka complex at Dzerzhinskiy Square, the Russian KGB was powerless to protect the Yeltsin government from Kryuchkov prior to the putsch. Yet Ivanenko did nothing to threaten Yeltsin and broke with the KGB leadership by standing with the Russian president during the August coup attempt. However, he did nothing against the CPSU either. After the putsch, when Party-bashing became politically acceptable and virtually universal, Ivanenko stated that, consistent with Yeltsin's objectives and contrary to those of the center, he had tried to ban Communist Party controls within the RSFSR KGB. He told a BBC correspondent that when the first all-Russian conference of senior KGB officers was held on 18 and 19 July 1991, it was resolved that "we should completely abolish the principle of Communist Party control and that, instead, we should base ourselves on the law and the legal authority."[8]

Yet this after-the-fact explanation of affairs seems disingenuous. With fewer than two dozen people in the RSFSR KGB including himself, Ivanenko could have depoliticized his unit instantly. However, he made no such moves until after Yeltsin issued a decree to that effect following the putsch and after interim USSR KGB Chairman Leonid Shebarshin, an unrepentant hard-liner by any standard, banned Party cells from all KGB structures.[9]

Yeltsin had no personal security, intelligence, counterintelligence, analysis, information, or communications services under his authority prior to the putsch. Nevertheless, Ivanenko may have been able to warn the Russian leadership of the impending coup attempt. Evidence indicates that Yeltsin had advance knowledge that something was going to happen. Certainly there were many who sympathized with Yeltsin within the USSR KGB.[10] Channels may have been opened with Ivanenko, who received some support from elements in the center, as evidenced by his ability to work in Lubyanka and broadcast support for Yeltsin during the putsch.[11] Yeltsin entrusted Ivanenko afterward to supervise physical absorption of USSR KGB structures. However, within five months of the putsch he was fired.

The Collapse of the Soviet Union, 22 August-19 December 1991

The crisis precipitated by the coup attempt seemed to demonstrate to all but the most die-hard totalitarians that the KGB had to be stripped of its overwhelming grip on power. The earliest changes in the KGB were dictated by Yeltsin while Gorbachev was still under apparent house arrest. Upon returning to Moscow, Gorbachev signed a number of decrees—some of the most important engineered by Yeltsin's people—to discharge key KGB officers and name replacements.

The initial quick actions by both leaders were encouraging. The KGB's top layer of leadership was removed. Reformist former USSR Interior Minister Vadim Bakatin was named as the new KGB chairman and given authority to prepare to dismantle the organization. A Soviet State Commission to Investigate the Security Organs led by Russian Supreme Soviet Committee on Defense and Security Chairman Sergey Stepashin, a career MVD officer with rank of lieutenant colonel, was created to assist Bakatin with recommendations for reform.[12] To complement Stepashin's Union level work, a Russian parliamentary commission led by progressive People's Deputy Lev Ponomarev was formed to "Investigate the Causes and Circumstances of the August Putsch."

Both the Stepashin and Ponomarev commissions would, with Bakatin's support, issue recommendations for sweeping reform of the KGB. Party archives were immediately impounded and a special Russian state commission was created to preserve, inventory, and classify or release the documents. These developments marked what appeared at the time to be a decisive beginning of civil control over the Russian security and intelligence services by democratically elected leaders.

Action was needed immediately. Public opinion was highly charged, demanding swift and sweeping action—even the executions of those responsible for the coup attempt. Changes were immediately made by the KGB itself, not out of self-discipline but "to soothe popular unrest and prevent the lynching of KGB people, vandalizing of buildings and plundering of archives," as a security spokesman later acknowledged.[13] Members of the Soviet state and Russian parliamentary commissions demanded that the KGB be dismantled. Disgraced, without direction, stricken with malaise, and uncertain of the future, the KGB lay, like the dragon on the city of Moscow's ancient coat of arms, with its back to the ground, on the verge of being impaled by the gallant knight on horseback. But Gorbachev squandered the opportunity, and surprisingly, Yeltsin did as well. After a few short bursts of decisive decrees, the Russian government's following steps were tentative, and before long the security services managed to assert themselves and limit the damage to their positions of power and privilege.

Bakatin Is Appointed the KGB's Final Chairman

Immediately following his return to Moscow on 22 August, Gorbachev signed a decree, officially subject to approval by the USSR Supreme Soviet, relieving KGB Chairman Kryuchkov of his duties.[14] He named Lt. Gen. Leonid Shebarshin, a longtime Kryuchkov protégé who had served as foreign intelligence chief since February 1990, as acting chairman.[15] However, Shebarshin lasted only a day. In the first of a series of encouraging moves, Bakatin, the reform Communist and former interior minister whom Gorbachev had fired eight months earlier for opposing Kryuchkov, was appointed to head the KGB.

The appointment was a collective decision made by Gorbachev, Yeltsin, and the presidents of the seven other republics that had not yet announced their secession from the Soviet Union. Bakatin was caught completely unprepared. On 22 August Gorbachev had directed him to write a plan to remove the KGB Alfa commando unit from state security and to place it under direct presidential control. On the afternoon of 23 August, Bakatin received a call from the Soviet leader, who summoned him immediately to the Walnut Room in the Kremlin. "I thought I was to present him with the Alfa plan," Bakatin recalled:

> I entered the room and Gorbachev was seated at the end of a table, with Yeltsin to his right. To Gorbachev's left was an empty chair. The other seats were occupied by the presidents of the other republics. Gorbachev motioned to me to sit next to him in the empty chair and as I did so, he said, "We want you to be Chairman of the KGB." I said that I should not, and that [Yuriy] Ryzhov should be. Some of the presidents said they didn't trust Ryzhov. I said that I had always said the KGB should be liquidated. Yeltsin then stood up and said, "That is what you will do when you become Chairman." Yeltsin then told Gorbachev, "Write that on the decree." I looked around the room, and all the other presidents nodded in agreement. That was that.[16]

Bakatin received instant authority to prepare to dismantle the KGB. He recalled, "Gorbachev had the decree in front of him naming me as KGB chairman. He took out his pen and wrote on the decree, 'Assign Comrade Bakatin to prepare a proposal for the reform of the state security organization.'" To the left he printed "NDP" in block letters, indicating that the addendum was not for publication.

Gorbachev's barely legible scrawl reflected the pressure he was under amid the amazing turn of events, as well as his own indecision.[17]

Bakatin said that the entire episode, including his appointment, was a series of "impulsive" acts amid the Soviet and republic leaders' euphoria at having defeated the coup attempt and their confusion about what to do next. The implication, though he did not state it, was that these swift actions would not have occurred had there been no emotional tide. There was no contingency blueprint to dismantle the KGB. Thus, without a plan, there was no way the moment could be seized to dissolve chekism in a systematic and comprehensive way. When Russian and Soviet leaders—all products of the system—settled back to earth, they opted not to make such far-reaching reforms after all.

Gorbachev was the first to announce Bakatin's appointment, in a live televised address to the Russian Supreme Soviet that afternoon. It appeared from his remarks that his nominations of Bakatin and new USSR Defense Minister Yevgeniy Shaposhnikov were really a ratification of decisions made by Yeltsin, though this is speculation. Throughout his speech to the deputies, Gorbachev was repeatedly interrupted and humiliated by his gleeful rival, who pressured him to read documents aloud and meekly sign decrees, including one to abolish the CPSU. Part way through Gorbachev's 90-minute address, Yeltsin went outside the Russian Supreme Soviet building to address a crowd, where he, too, announced Bakatin's appointment. Neither leader stated in public who had chosen the new KGB chairman; Gorbachev said that he and Yeltsin had "endorsed" Bakatin, while Yeltsin said that the two had "agreed" on the choice.[18]

Personnel Changes

Bakatin was empowered immediately to purge the KGB while plans were being drawn up for the service's dismemberment. He deliberately did not set out physically to abolish the KGB as Václav Havel had done with its Czechoslovak counterpart, but merely to break its monopoly of power by dividing it into smaller components and decentralizing it among the republics while reforming and de-politicizing its cadres from within and making them answerable to new laws. Hoping to demilitarize the service and remove military ranks by way of example he declined Gorbachev's proposal that he hold the rank of colonel general, a promotion from the lieutenant general rank he held as Soviet interior minister.[19]

Unprepared for the job—he had no background in intelligence or security, no warning of his imminent appointment, and no time to prepare for his new role—Bakatin hastily assembled a reform team to carry out his mandate. In the first few days after the defeat of the coup plotters, Bakatin fired a key Kryuchkov deputy but refrained from carrying out further personnel changes for a week until he could weigh the situation, single out officers to be removed and choose reliable replacements. Advice, solicited and unsolicited, was coming seemingly from everywhere. Personnel decisions were left to Bakatin alone, who wrote the decrees for Gorbachev's signature and with Yeltsin's support.[20] A week after taking office, on 28 and 29 August, Bakatin carried out his first set of personnel changes, including many members of the KGB Collegium, though he would not comment publicly on them.[21] In the second week of September he conducted a more comprehensive shake-up at the uppermost level.

Mass firings and forced retirements seemed imminent. Bakatin anticipated that "hundreds" would go. Russian KGB Chairman Viktor Ivanenko predicted in a television interview that "the changes in the leadership of the KGB will come very quickly and will go very deep. I cannot tell you the exact percentage, but I think that most of the leadership of the KGB will be changed within the next few months."[22] The KGB, as well as the entire Soviet government, was in a state of turmoil and shock. Top officers involved in the putsch busily tried to cover themselves while rank-and-file personnel suffered from low morale, wondering what would happen to them.[23] Following the arrest of Kryuchkov and the quick removal of his interim replacement, Shebarshin, the two first deputy chairmen of the USSR KGB and other key security leaders were next.

Yet Bakatin quickly retreated from a comprehensive purge. Speaking to an assembly of KGB officers shortly after settling into Lubyanka, he tried to win over personnel by pledging that there would be no "witch hunt" and promising that the majority of chekists had no reason to fear for their jobs.[24] In retrospect, he said his attempt to be popular was a "naive address and vain hopes."[25] Once settled and able to grasp the dynamics of the KGB bureaucracy, Bakatin staged a second round of forced retirements in September, removing a few ranking officials who had been promoted just days before. In choosing a new KGB leadership, he looked not outside for skilled administrators without a chekist taint but into the third and fourth echelons of the apparatus itself. Nearly all his choices were disappointing. None was from outside the security apparat, save perhaps his incompetent director of personnel, an air force officer whom Bakatin himself had hired, who curiously kept more reformist indivuals from being appointed. Key personnel changes, listed below, followed the recommendations of a departmental commission that Bakatin organized.

First Deputy Chairmen. The USSR KGB had two first deputy chairmen in 1991. Prior to and during the putsch they were Viktor Grushko and Geniy Ageyev. Both were removed in the aftermath. Grushko was "detained on suspicion of involvement" and formally arrested 48 hours after Bakatin took over; Gorbachev signed a decree relieving Grushko of his duties a few days later.[26] Grushko, whose portfolio included foreign intelligence, was replaced by longtime protégé Lt. Gen. Gennadiy Titov. They had served together for years in the Anglo-Scandinavian department of the KGB First Chief Directorate. In 1989 Grushko was transferred from foreign intelligence to become head of the Second Chief Directorate. When Grushko was promoted to KGB first deputy chairman in February 1991, Titov took his place at the helm of internal security.[27] Titov's replacement of Grushko as first deputy chairman following the putsch was not well received by reformers or by professional officers. One former officer who had served with Titov described him as "deeply unpopular among his KGB colleagues," "feared by his subordinates," and especially "unpleasant and unprincipled."[28] Bakatin apparently discovered shortcomings on his own. He removed Titov as first deputy chairman on 29 August but allowed him temporarily to retain leadership of the Second Chief Directorate.[29]

Titov's replacement was fifty-one-year-old Col. Anatoliy Avvakumovich Oleynikov, one of the new leaders from the third and fourth echelons who joined the KGB in 1968 as one of the wily, bright young Andropovite recruits. He had risen rapidly from posts in the Moscow KGB to head of state security in the closed industrial city of Perm, and later to deputy chief of the new Directorate for Combating Organized Crime, where he had come to the attention of Russian President Yeltsin. Bakatin says that Yeltsin intervened personally after the putsch to urge him to give Oleynikov a leading role in reorganizing the KGB. Accordingly, Oleynikov was promoted to major general and on 29 August replaced Titov as a first deputy chairman of the USSR KGB. Bakatin placed his complete confidence in Oleynikov and a year later reflected, "He faithfully carried out my instructions."[30] Oleynikov headed the departmental commission that Bakatin created to recommend further leadership changes effective 25 September.

The other of Kryuchkov's first deputy chairmen, Col. Gen. Geniy Ageyev, was dismissed by presidential decree on 28 August.[31] Ageyev held the portfolio for supervision of the dissident-hunting Directorate for the Protection of the Constitutional System (the former Fifth or Ideological Directorate), the archives, the public relations center, and the Seventh (Surveillance) Directorate, which included the Alfa unit. It was later found that he organized Gorbachev's isolation in time for the putsch and orchestrated the attempted seizure of the Russian parliament building and the attempted overthrow of Yeltsin and his government. He was also accused of having ordered the arrest of large numbers of Soviet and Russian officials.[32] Ageyev's post as first deputy chairman was filled temporarily by Valeriy Lebedev, a professional analyst from the Information Analysis Directorate, who lasted only fourteen days. Ageyev's deputy, Aleksandr Fokin, chief of the Tenth Department (Archives), was also dismissed.[33] However, despite reports that he ordered the closure of all newspapers during the putsch, Lebedev himself was not forced out of the KGB; Bakatin named him deputy chief of the Information Analysis Directorate.[34]

Ageyev's ultimate replacement became Maj. Gen. Nikolay Sham, the first deputy chief of the Directorate for the Protection of the Soviet Economy (Sixth Directorate), who was popular with many Russian reformists prior to the putsch.[35] Kryuchkov earlier had opposed attempts by Yeltsin's government to have Sham appointed RSFSR KGB chairman when Viktor Ivanenko became the compromise choice.[36]

First Chief Directorate (Foreign Intelligence). Lt. Gen. Leonid Shebarshin had been head of the First Chief Directorate with the parallel position of KGB deputy chairman since March 1989.[37] Slighted at being unceremoniously removed after only a day as acting USSR KGB chairman following the putsch and alarmed at the reformist trend, Shebarshin presented Bakatin with his retirement from the KGB. Bakatin rejected the resignation and instructed Shebarshin to develop proposals to cut the bloated foreign intelligence personnel rolls by one-third.[38]

The intelligence officer apparently continued to chafe at his treatment. He sent Bakatin a report on 18 September protesting "favoritism" for top posts and complaining that a "non-professional" was named as his deputy. With that report, he is said to have tendered a second resignation.[39] At the recommendation of Bakatin, Gorbachev formally approved Shebarshin's departure in a subsequent decree declaring his "dismissal."[40] Shebarshin publicly complained, "I was treated intolerably crudely, even insultingly," and said that Bakatin "did not have time to phone and announce his decision." Instead, Shebarshin said, he was informed of the decree by a member of the presidential Secretariat.[41] He was replaced temporarily by an anonymous acting chief whose name was not published in the Soviet press. The acting chief was identified as Vyacheslav I. Gurgenev.[42]

Bakatin wanted a prominent civilian to head foreign intelligence. He picked his colleague on the presidential Security Council, academician Yevgeniy Primakov, for the job. Gorbachev and Yeltsin agreed with his decision.[43] Although the appointment irritated some intelligence professionals who preferred one of their own to head the service, Bakatin felt strongly that Primakov, with his academic and political status, would bring to the service "a clear-cut selection of political priorities, moral directions, and understanding of for whom and in the name of what it works."[44]

Primakov, who speaks excellent English and Arabic and who can be charming and sophisticated, represented anything but a break with the past. A career journalist and "academician," he was one of the CPSU's architects of support for radical anti-Western regimes in the Middle East that sponsored terrorism against the United States and its allies and for the extreme factions of the Palestine Liberation Organization (PLO) that utilized terror as a political tool and trained other violent revolutionary groups worldwide.

During the Brezhnev regime's "Zionism is racism" campaign of the 1970s, Primakov was a Middle East correspondent for *Pravda,* dutifully supporting the PLO even in the midst of its most notorious bombing and murder campaigns against civilians. He authored the Party's most authoritative ideological justification for the 1979 invasion of Afghanistan and subsequently issued strong statements in support of the invasion and occupation.[45] He later deplored the Iran-Iraq war, saying, "It diverts the forces of Iraq and Iran from the struggle against imperialism. It promotes the strengthening of certain trends which are needed by the United States in the region as a whole."[46] In 1985, lamenting deep splits in the PLO, Primakov urged that the organization remain hostile to the West because it was the PLO's "anti-imperialist nature which guaranteed the vital interests of the Palestinian people."[47]

His rhetoric became more conciliatory after Mikhail Gorbachev settled into position. On Christmas Day 1986, he said that the Kremlin wanted to cooperate with Washington in counterterrorism, but stopped short of supporting sanctions against terrorist sponsoring governments such as that of Libya. Referring to Soviet arms shipments to the Qaddafi regime, Primakov said, "We don't make any conditions for the use of these arms and we're not going to trade off some conditions with Libya."[48] He affirmed the Brezhnev policy toward the PLO in 1987, telling reporters that the USSR sought to keep the PLO as a "mighty, unified, anti-imperialist force."[49] In 1990 and early 1991, he worked tirelessly on behalf of Gorbachev to prevent the U.S.-led coalition from driving the Iraqi military out of Kuwait.[50]

Primakov had long-standing ties to the state security services. He had served as a KGB informant as early as 1957, with the cryptonym "Maxim," according to a former KGB officer who worked with him at the time.[51] As a journalist in the early 1970s, Primakov was identified by scholars as being close to the security and intelligence apparatus.[52]

In 1989 and 1990, as chairman of the Council of the Union chamber of the USSR Supreme Soviet, Primakov worked to ensure that the new parliamentary oversight committee would remain loyal to the security and military organs. During a June 1989 plenary meeting, Primakov announced the membership of the various new joint committees. When challenged as to how these memberships were determined (rank-and-file deputies were unable to participate in selection) and why the Committee on Defense and Security was dominated by representatives of the military-industrial complex and the KGB, Primakov, along with Supreme Soviet Chairman Anatoliy Lukyanov, hedged and failed to give satisfactory answers. As Lukyanov did when faced with calls to eliminate conflicts of interests on the committee, Primakov intervened when debate began to challenge the methods of committee membership selection. When a voice from the floor called for creation of a committee of people's deputies instead of unelected and anonymous "technical personnel" to choose memberships, Primakov called a recess. Debate was thus squelched.[53] He was, in retrospect, a perfect "outsider" to head KGB foreign intelligence and protect its interests.

Second Chief Directorate (Counterintelligence). Although he lasted only a week as a USSR KGB first deputy chairman, Lt. Gen. Gennadiy Titov initially kept his post as head of the Second Chief Directorate, to which he had been named seven months before the putsch. However, Bakatin sought a much more reformist individual, preferably a civilian, to lead counterintelligence. His first nominee was jurist Konstantin Lubenchenko, who served as deputy chairman of the USSR Supreme Soviet Committee for Legislation. Lubenchenko declined the appointment, saying that he did not want to wear KGB shoulderboards and be subject to military discipline.[54] Maj. Gen. Fedor Myasnikov was appointed head of the Second Chief Directorate and deputy chairman of the USSR KGB by a Gorbachev decree on 13 September.[55] Myasnikov was previously deputy chief of the KGB Inspection Directorate.[56]

Third Chief Directorate (Military Counterintelligence). The chief of military counterintelligence was replaced by Yuriy Bulygin;[57] deputy chief Nikolay Ryzhak was removed on 25 September.[58]

Fifth Chief Directorate (Ideological/Political Police). No public announcements were recorded indicating a change of personnel in the Fifth Directorate, then called Directorate Z, perhaps to avoid drawing attention to the continued existence of the unit. Bakatin later said that Directorate Z chief Valeriy Vorotnikov and his deputies Dobrovolskiy and Perfilyev were fired on 25 September.[59] (Directorate Z was briefly known as the Directorate for the Protection of the Constitutional System.)

Border Guards. Because he was not actively involved in the putsch, Border Guards chief Ilya Kalinichenko was retained. However, Nikolay Britvin, chief of the Border Guards Military Political Directorate, and his first deputy Boris Golyshev, were fired 25 September.[60]

Eighth Chief Directorate (Signals Intelligence and Cryptography). This unit, responsible for signals intelligence and cryptography and comprising one-quarter of the KGB's entire budget, was transferred from the Soviet government to the control of the Russian government by a 24 August decree of President Yeltsin.[61] The Eighth's leader, Gen. Andrey Grigoryevich Beda, was dismissed on or before 29 August and replaced by his deputy, Lt. Gen. Aleksandr Starovoytov.[62]

Fourth Directorate (Transportation). KGB Transportation Directorate chief Yuriy Storozhev was retained.[63]

Sixth Directorate (Economic Counterintelligence and Industrial Security). With the promotion of Sixth Directorate leader Sham to KGB first deputy chairman, the unit's new leader was brought up from below, though his identity could not be ascertained. Bakatin dismissed his own son Aleksei, who served in an ecological subunit of the Sixth, and was quoted as saying that he "found it impossible" to have relatives serve as subordinates.[64]

Seventh Directorate (Surveillance). Research found no reports of personnel changes.

Protection Service (Ninth Directorate, Presidential Security/ Guards). Protection Service (formerly Ninth Directorate) chief Plekhanov and his deputy, Generalov, were arrested and charged with "betraying the homeland" for their involvement in the putsch.[65] The new chief was Vladimir Redkoborodiy.[66]

Tenth Directorate (Archives). Directorate Chief Aleksandr Fokin, a subordinate of Deputy Chairman Valeriy Lebedev, was dismissed by Bakatin in early September, possibly 11 September; the dismissal was confirmed by a decree of the Soviet president.[67] Lebedev was replaced by Anatoliy Krayushkin.[68] The Tenth was immediately removed from the KGB and placed under official presidential control, though it does not appear that that control was operational.

Twelfth Directorate (Electronic Surveillance). Gen. Yevgeniy Ivanovich Kalgin, chief of the Twelfth, was fired for involvement in the putsch.[69]

Fifteenth Directorate (Government Installation Security/Bunkers). Also known as the Bunker Directorate, the Fifteenth provided security for government installations and administered the USSR's system of blast-proof underground shelters for nuclear weapons and government officials. Some Party officials fled the CPSU Central Committee headquarters to seek shelter during the putsch. One report said that leaders of the Fifteenth supported the putsch (and that following General Vladimir Gorshkov's orders, they went on "combat readiness" alert on the morning of 18 August.[70] However, Bakatin writes that Gorshkov did not follow orders to form a "reserve group" of 200 to storm the Russian parliament building.[71] Research could not ascertain the new leaders of this unit.

Information Analysis Directorate. Lt. Gen. Nikolay Leonov, chief of the directorate, was retired on pension. He had an accomplished career in foreign intelligence and supposedly was credited by Khrushchev with having recruited Raúl Castro into the Soviet camp prior to the Cuban revolution of 1959.[72] Leonov openly supported the hard-line Communist "Soyuz" faction of the USSR Supreme Soviet and declared that all chekists stood with Soyuz.[73] In leaving the KGB, Leonov is said to have removed all documents from his offices—a serious breach, as one observer reported, "it was said of this directorate that it keeps its finger on the pulse of everything that happens in the KGB."[74]

Leonov was replaced by KGB Col. Vladimir Rubanov, who as a true professional was a longtime critic of the apparatus under Kryuchkov. He was fired from the KGB in 1988 after writing an article accusing the body of being obsessed with a "cult of secrecy" and of inventing foreign threats. Bakatin, then USSR interior minister, retained him as a personal aide until Gorbachev fired them both in December 1990. As a Russian people's deputy, Rubanov was also briefly a deputy chairman of the RSFSR Supreme Soviet Committee on Defense and Security.[75]

In early September when Bakatin had demoted USSR KGB first deputy chairman Valeriy Lebedev, he had instructed the KGB Personnel Department to find him a new position. Gen. Lebedev accordingly was appointed Col. Rubanov's deputy in the Information Analysis Directorate.[76] This was one of many poorly considered appointments that served only to cause frictions and undermine reformist state security officers such as Rubanov.

Moscow and Moscow Oblast KGB. Lt. Gen. Vitaliy Prilukov, chairman of the KGB for Moscow and Moscow oblast, was relieved of this position and his KGB deputy chairmanship in a decree issued by Gorbachev on 28 August.[77] Control of the Moscow KGB was transferred from the center's Second Chief Directorate to the new RSFSR KGB. Yeltsin, with the approval of RSFSR KGB Chairman Viktor Ivanenko, placed the city and oblast KGB under the supervision of the Moscow mayor. Then-mayor Gavriil Popov, a radical democrat, named thirty-nine year-old Deputy Mayor Yevgeniy Savostyanov to the post. Savostyanov, a geophysicist, had cofounded the Democratic Russia movement and served as parliamentary campaign manager for Popov and Andrey Sakharov. A vocal anti-Communist who was never a member of the Party, he refused the military rank of colonel. It is known that he was a reserve junior officer, though his service was not known and it is suspected that as a scientist he served in the KGB "academic reserve."[78] He was a close associate of the new Moscow police chief, thirty-four-year-old Arkadiy Murashev, another anti-Communist founder of the Democratic Russia movement who had been appointed by Popov.[79] Bakatin fired Moscow KGB deputy chiefs Korsak and Karabanov,[80] but Savostyanov was not able to bring in his own team, and his office was completely staffed by chekists.[81]

Other Regions. Bakatin initiated an investigation into the conduct of KGB leaders on the USSR periphery. The probe resulted in the removal of KGB chiefs in Amur, Bryansk, Vologod, Irkutsk, Minsk, Novosibirsk, Pskov, Samar, and Saratov oblasts, as well as Primorsk kray.[82]

Personnel Directorate. Cadres determine policy among chekists as anywhere else. The leader of the KGB Personnel Directorate, Lt. Gen. Vitaliy Ponomarev, was removed on 28 August. He was replaced by an outsider handpicked by Bakatin: Aviation Maj. Gen. Nikolay Stolyarov,[83] an Air Force Academy teacher. Naming Stolyarov turned out to be another terrible mistake. Bakatin said he thought that Stolyarov would be a good candidate because he had a paper trail of relatively reformist (though still Communist) writings and published statements. Furthermore, with Russian Vice President Aleksandr Rutskoy, a fellow Air Force officer then allied with Yeltsin, Stolyarov played an important role in defending the Russian Supreme Soviet building during the putsch. Stolyarov's weakness was that he was a poor manager; in Bakatin's words, "My reforms were stalled by his inability to administer."[84]

The early failure to install committed reformers in key positions was a fatal move in the attempt to uproot chekism. One of Bakatin's key outside advisers gave the new KGB chairman a list of individuals from inside the service who sympathized with radical anti-chekist views. Although Bakatin tried to minimize resistance to the appointment of such officers few were placed in critical positions.[85] Many resigned or were forced out. The reforms that began so hopefully stalled upon takeoff.

Personnel Problems

Bakatin did not have a physical blueprint to deprogram the security organs of the cult of chekism. He did, however, arrive with a plan to move in three directions: It entailed the "disintegration" or dismemberment of the KGB into functional components; "decentralization" among republics and other political units; and "de-ideologization," or what he termed "the repudiation of the ideology of Chekism."[86] He entered the KGB without bringing along a large team of loyalists, choosing instead to recruit aides from within. This was a mistake he would later regret. In retrospect, he noted, "one of my main errors included that I came into the KGB without my own staff and without a large group of like-minded people devoted to the matter. I overestimated my own powers. Without my own staff to turn over this bulky and cumbersome thing called the KGB, it proved to be almost impossible."[87] A handful of academics he brought on as personal staff found themselves isolated.[88]

He said after his initial leadership changes in September 1991, "I count on being able to create a team with its own identity, and I am already doing that. . . . A healthy nucleus can be found here." He counted on these officers to carry out a large-scale personnel change at all levels, especially near the top: "There is a very great stagnation of the cadres here, and they have already become well in with the powers that be, and have already been too long in their generals' posts; and it is necessary to have a very robust shakeup and rejuvenation of these cadres."[89]

Bakatin reported that eight generals (out of several hundred) had been fired within two weeks of the coup attempt and promised that there would be "quite a few more dismissals. We may be talking about hundreds or thousands across the country."[90] In the end, a purge never took place. An internal KGB report completed less than three weeks after the putsch sought to sacrifice a few top officers identified with Kryuchkov in order to preserve the overall apparat. The report, never published, called for the dismissal of thirteen KGB generals for "dishonorable behavior," the dismissal of thirteen generals and colonels as "unfit to serve"; the retirement of six generals who had reached pensionable age; the demotion of two generals; a warning of unsatisfactory performance for four generals; and strict reprimands for another four generals.[91] A Russian parliamentary commission later found that of thirty-two pro-putsch KGB leaders due to have been dismissed, only one—Kryuchkov—was forced out in public disgrace or charged with crimes. Six were retired, and the other twenty-five were allowed to remain in state security; none was publicly identified. The situation was similar in the Ministry of Internal Affairs and the armed forces, according to the commission.[92]

Bakatin's rapid firings and demotions along the uppermost echelons, and his continued insistence that the KGB would be broken up, caused a combination of uncertainty, discontent, malaise, intrigue, and conflict. He tried to assure cadres that "professionally trained KGB personnel will further continue their work" and added, "Only an insignificant part of KGB personnel that would not be able to reorganize their work will resign."[93] Intra-service grudges were settled in the putsch aftermath as KGB personnel accused one another of having supported the action. Bakatin commented on the problem:

> That is what I fear more than anything else. There have already been some people laying information against each other, intrigues, investigations, telephone calls, there are even some memoranda. You see, this might go down as far as the smallest units, and inside these small units arguments will break out. . . . Yesterday I even risked making an appeal to the personnel on this. . . . Defamation is still going on.[94]

The center was willingly ceding control to the periphery, which caused further concern among core personnel (although it was apparently supported by chekists in the other republics, where the transition from central control went smoothly).[95] The greatest source of alarm, however, was Moscow Mayor Popov's appointment of Savostyanov, an anti-Communist, as chief of the Moscow KGB.[96]

To make matters worse for the KGB, stories poured out of Lubyanka, foreign intelligence headquarters at Yasenevo and offices across Russia and the USSR about the poor quality of security and intelligence officers at all levels of the apparatus. A deputy mayor of Moscow publicly complained that he received "so-called analytical memos from the Moscow Directorate [of the KGB] . . . of an appallingly low standard."[97] Russia's most progressive newspapers such as *Komsomolskaya pravda*, *Moscow News*, and *Nezavisimaya gazeta*, received so many reports (as well as documents) from disaffected KGB officers that their correspondents were saturated with high-grade material that could not be published for lack of space.

Most of the sources tended to be reformist officers who sought to discredit the cult of chekism and the KGB as Kryuchkov and his predecessors had built it and who wanted to see the government develop entirely new security and intelligence services comprised of high-quality personnel. Some had been openly or anonymously vocal prior to the putsch. They blamed poor leadership for a series of crippling defections to the West. Many of these critics were intelligence officers from the First Chief Directorate who had been exposed to the industrialized democracies and believed that if the country was to develop, Russia and the Union would have to pursue freer markets and more democratic government. Others were counterintelligence officers who finally realized that they had been rooting out not spies and traitors but hard-working citizens who were trying to survive in a system without opportunities. Yet they did not talk of "abolishing" the KGB.

Post-putsch reform attempts were stunted by the poor quality of top-echelon officers, even those sympathetic to the new policies. Chairman Bakatin, who had come to the Politburo's attention in 1985 as an unusually adept administrator within the Party bureaucracy in Siberia, commented that he found among his own retinue a disturbing number of officers who "have simply not been accustomed to fast work. They do not know the sense of the tasks it is their duty to explain; they go away only to come back with documents that are not always literate. . . . There are times when information through our mass media is more precise and credible than the information that lands on my desk, which at times is very impoverished."[98]

High-level ineptitude, cronyism and corruption, which for so long had trickled down through the ranks, stuck to the security superstructure and hastened the decay. One disgusted officer told *Moscow News* that young officers who saw abuses committed with impunity risked being co-opted by those abuses. He accused the recently removed director of KGB training, an officer identified only as Orlov, as one of the culprits. The officer cautioned, "Decent people will simply not be able to work in the KGB if we don't get rid of our legacy and the fear that everything will continue as before."[99]

There was also deep-seated resentment and resistance to Bakatin's reforms within the KGB bureaucracy. Lower-level officers who sympathized with what he was trying to accomplish were purged by their corrupt or ideological superiors. Oleg Zadkirov, a former major in the Smolensk KGB, reported such activity in his city unit, and in so doing felt pressure to leave.[100]

The emergence of a market economy made the personnel problem worse. Now, talented officers had an alternative. Rather than tolerate toadies and criminals in the security bureaucracy, they could leave. As the KGB was broken up, many of the best and brightest began to abandon the service, demoralized because their careers no longer held status or promise, and lured by better working conditions and stunningly higher salaries, in hard currency no less, with foreign joint ventures.

This personnel exodus, though perhaps somewhat disruptive at first, was not necessarily a net loss for the chekist organs. In many ways it was a gain. Many officers left the KGB officially to go into business, but remained in the service of the security and intelligence organs to penetrate Western institutions and obtain funds and technology as continued collaborators or as members of the "active reserve." Some took care of their friends still inside. The least inventive, energetic, and outgoing officers were the least likely to quit a secure job to become entrepreneurs or work for private business. So they remained in the apparat and filled the spaces of those who left.

Businesses, both Russian and foreign, thought they could benefit by hiring KGB personnel, while Russian banks and other companies offered golden parachutes for chekists of all ranks. KGB toughs found lucrative careers as private security guards, while the more urbane set up consulting firms to perform due-diligence investigations for domestic and foreign companies. Former KGB First Deputy Chairman Filipp Bobkov, who was the right-hand man to KGB Chairman Kryuchkov, reportedly is an adviser with a large banking firm.[101] Large companies extracting and selling petroleum, natural gas, and diamonds also retained ranking former KGB officials for important corporate posts.[102]

In addition to challenging laziness and incompetence, Bakatin faced another hurdle: the deeply ingrained mentality of the chekist. Russian reformers point to this problem again and again. In the midst of Bakatin's reforms, a top RSFSR Supreme Soviet investigator observed,

> Meetings and conversations with KGB leaders of various ranks clearly highlight one detail. They have no understanding in their minds that they are serving the constitution or the law, they have no reverence for the rule of law and citizens' rights. They unquestioningly and consistently fulfilled only the orders of their superiors, this for them was the main value, even though there may have been declarations of the "We serve the people and the motherland" type.[103]

The followers were more likely to remain in the service than the entrepreneurial self-starters. Some of the latter were concerned that Bakatin might not succeed against the cutthroat machinations. An anonymous reform officer sent a warning through *Moscow News*: "Intriguers eager to square accounts are already flocking to see him. . . . I have no doubts about his good intentions, but I am afraid that the absence of professionalism and detailed knowledge of professional work, personnel, the atmosphere and situation in intelligence will be a hindrance for him. It has also occurred to me that an attempt may be made to manipulate him."[104]

As a product of the Party himself, Bakatin grappled with the problem of doing an effective housecleaning of personnel. Rather than conduct wholesale firings—which he initially advocated—the new KGB chairman felt he could reform most chekists as individuals. He admitted in an interview that one of the services' "most difficult tasks" would be to change the ideology of the personnel, saying, "It cannot be solved merely by a substitution of people. Furthermore, we have no other people. All that will help now is sustained work to persuade each person individually." The "ideological dogmatists" who refused to reform, he said, would be compelled to retire. "The traditions of chekism must be eradicated, must cease to exist as an ideology."[105]

In the closing days of his three-month tenure as the USSR's last security chief, Bakatin was asked again about the nature of the personnel who still served in the special service. A journalist from *Literaturnaya gazeta* inquired, "You are today having to work with the same people who persecuted dissidents, hounded Sakharov and all that. . . . Is that not embarrassing?" Bakatin's response was frank. The problem, he said, was not limited to state security officers but reflected of the sickness of Soviet society as a whole:

> Yes, they are the same people. But we are, after all, from the same world, from the same society, from the same system. All. And the editorial office [of *Literaturnaya gazeta*] also, most likely. So what should we do, then? Remove all those people and bring in some new ones? Where would we find them? Who would undertake to be the judges?[106]

To Bakatin, it was not enough to change the KGB; for reform to take root, all of Soviet society would have to change. This presented a huge dilemma affecting much more than the narrow sliver of society called chekists. He continued his line of reasoning:

> All people, each of us, change, I believe. Should change, at least. Not only our skin, our suit, but in essence also. And the question is not whether people

have remained the same but whether they are capable of changing or not. The majority are, but for some: Can a leopard change its spots, as they say? There is a problem here.[107]

Bakatin's perspective holds that society had emerged from communism so damaged and disfigured that simply reforming the KGB would do little until the entire public underwent a long-term cultural healing process. Although this excuse might seem like a cop-out, since it provided a rationale to preserve the chekist apparat—which was inherently unreformable and therefore would fester any long-term societal healing process—his view that "all of us were bad" was shared by such heroic resistance figures as Václav Havel, who wrote of the "contaminated moral environment." Bakatin voiced the daunting dilemma confronting post-Soviet Russia, namely, that there was no one who could build a new security apparatus who was not tainted.

The society of the New Soviet Man, of *homo sovieticus*, was thoroughly poisoned by the living lie by which individuals informed and denounced to the secret police in order to survive. At the same time it was up to individuals like Bakatin to lead society in redeeming itself by making that total break with the past. For some reason they could not bring themselves to go that far.

Dismemberment of the KGB

Bakatin, Gorbachev, and Yeltsin made the decision not to "destroy" the KGB on the Czech and German models of dissolving State Security (Statni tajna Bezpecnost, StB) or the Stasi, respectively. Bakatin believed that chekism should not be uprooted immediately from without, but cleansed away over the long term from within.[108] Soviet and Russian political leaders agreed to this approach, though probably not without cynicism that they would need KGB resources for their own purposes besides legitimate intelligence and counterintelligence needs. Thus, while the KGB was to be dismembered, it was also to be saved.

A joint commission, dominated by the RSFSR but accountable to both governments, was formed to guide Bakatin and serve as a check in the course of dismembering the KGB. The most significant aspect of this body was that it marked the first step toward civil oversight of the security and intelligence services in Moscow; it was created by a democratically elected president and comprised mostly of nominally elected officials. Although subject to conflicts of interests and shortcoming similar to those that marked the farcical USSR Supreme

Soviet Committee on Defense and Security which was dominated by loyalists of the KGB and military-industrial complex, it nevertheless served as an instrument intended to bring the organs under some semblance of civil control. However, limited and co-opted, the commission failed, perhaps willingly, to confront the essence of chekism.

The State Commission to Investigate the Activity of the Security Organs, known as the Stepashin Commission after its chairman, was created six days after the putsch failed. Its formation left little doubt that Russian President Yeltsin was taking the initiative to determine the fate of the Union structures and to keep as much of the KGB as possible for himself. Yeltsin signed the 28 August 1991 decree forming the Commission for the USSR and appointed as its chief Sergey Stepashin, the MVD officer who chaired the RSFSR Supreme Soviet Committee on Defense and Security. Significantly, the commission's first news conference was held not in the Kremlin but in the Russian Supreme Soviet building.

The commission had three main functions: to determine the role of the USSR KGB in the putsch; to develop proposals to reform and restructure the KGB; and to draft a new state security law, new state regulations for the Russian Federation and the Union, and amendments to the Russian and Union constitutions. Investigation of specific individuals was left to the Russian procurator.[109] The majority of the commission's members were Supreme Soviet members but not completely free from the influence of the KGB. Most of them were reformers of the status quo but not real agents of change.

Stepashin's own presence, while positive, was nevertheless self-constraining and indicated a continuation of the conflicts of interests that had erased the distinction between the police or security services and representative government. A lieutenant colonel in the MVD and firmly in the Yeltsin camp, he was slated to become a KGB deputy chairman with the rank of major general. The first members of the Stepashin Commission were RSFSR Supreme Soviet members Nikolay Konstantinovich Ryabov, named deputy chairman of the commission; Aleksandr Alexeyevich Kotenkov, Igor Aleksandrovich Bezrukov, and Nikolay Kuznetsov (a tough career KGB officer who served with Stepashin as a member of the RSFSR Supreme Soviet Committee on Defense and Security); reformist USSR Supreme Soviet members Yuriy Ryzhov, Sergey Stankevich, and Konstantin Lubenchenko; RSFSR KGB Chairman Ivanenko; and USSR KGB First Deputy Chairman Titov.[110] When Titov was fired from the KGB in September, he was replaced on the commission by KGB First Deputy Chairman Anatoliy Oleynikov.[111] The commission also included nongovernmental experts. The few genuinely anti-chekist reformers on the commission, such as *Moscow News* investigative reporter Yevgeniya Albats, were quickly isolated and ultimately expelled from the commission at the instigation of fellow members who were KGB officers.[112]

Maj. Gen. Oleynikov was the nexus between the commission as a whole and KGB Chairman Bakatin.[113] Actual destruction or dissolution of the KGB was never on the commission's agenda; indeed, the group—after the purge of real reformers like Albats—was committed to preserving the KGB's basic structures and functions. In this sense, there would be no fundamental change. There was no challenge from above. What made the commission important were the mechanisms it would recommend to attempt to ensure that the preserved basic structures would not return to their political police functions and, more important, would never again be able to threaten the political power of the government.

This objective was just what Yeltsin had demanded to Kryuchkov in the USSR Supreme Soviet two years before. Said commission member Ryzhov, "We should not allow the concentration of functions within one department that exists in the present KGB. It must be broken down, and as a matter of priority its shameful components such as the services dealing with political investigations and the comprehensive surveillance of dissidents must be dismembered and abolished."[114] Control over these mechanisms was to be changed radically, with actual central power of the internal security services to be transferred to each union republic, but there was no challenge to chekism itself. This fundamental failure ensured that the back of the chekist system would not be broken.

Recognizing the trend of most republics toward greater independence from Moscow, commission members indicated that they sought to make the decentralization process as orderly as possible while maintaining the integrity of the Union. A preliminary document stated,

> during the process of forming new forms of statehood now underway in the country, it would be impermissible for the state security organs to be disorganized and lose their effectiveness on account of the growing tension. . . . Therefore the abolition of the USSR KGB organs is not on the agenda; on the contrary, the issue is that of their gradual reorganization with the aim of creating a rational system of state security organs that respond to the interests of the republics and the Union as a whole.[115]

This first step, at least as far as responsiveness to the interests of the USSR was concerned, was seen as contingent on successful negotiation of the Union treaty that the coup plotters had attempted to thwart. TASS paraphrased Ryzhov as saying,

> "A doctrine for the existence of a future community of sovereign states must be formulated, and from this should stem an understanding of the questions of this community's security." He said that until this doctrine was developed, it would be "difficult to determine the size, functions, and even the orientation of the special services, which . . . should be formed on the basis of existing KGB services."[116]

The preliminary commission document proposed that the USSR State Council execute a "radical reorganization" of the KGB, "proceeding from the view that the Union Republics are the legal successors to the KGB structures in the relevant territories." To carry out this reorganization, the commission proposed creating "inter-republican commissions" comprised of "authorized representatives of the republics" to "work out, during talks, proposals for the reorganization of KGB structures, determining the volume of the powers and functions delegated to the bodies being reorganized." Questions concerning the social protection of KGB staff members, financing of operations, and resolution of property ownership of KGB facilities would be resolved by the interrepublican commissions. The Stepashin Commission also proposed creation of an interrepublican body that would function "within the joint security system of a future union of sovereign states" as a coordinating mechanism.[117]

Bakatin technically was supposed to have implemented structural reforms once the commission officially recommended them. The decree creating the body gave it five months to issue recommendations. However, Bakatin criticized the group for wanting to wait the full five months before issuing final proposals. In the course of developing a final set of recommendations, the commission, through KGB First Deputy Chairman Oleynikov, provided Bakatin with ideas upon which he acted, but Bakatin later complained, "They kept having meetings, and kept writing, but would not present their ideas to Gorbachev or Yeltsin. . . . I implemented their ideas on my own while they talked." For their parts, commission members complained directly to Gorbachev that Bakatin was moving too quickly. However, only the speed of reforms, and not the reforms themselves, was the point of contention between Bakatin and the commission.[118]

Insulation from Reform

In all there were five separate investigations of the KGB's role in the putsch: They were conducted by the USSR State Commission to Investigate the Activity of the Security Organs, led by Stepashin; the USSR Supreme Soviet Commission for Investigation into Reasons and Circumstances of the Putsch, headed by lawmaker Obolensky; the Russian Supreme Soviet Commission to Investigate the Causes and Circumstances of the August Putsch, led by democratic member of parliament Lev Ponomarev; the Special Interdepartmental Commission to Investigate the Activities of State Security Officers During the Putsch, formed by Bakatin and headed by KGB First Deputy Director Anatoliy Oleynikov; and an investigative unit of the Russian State Procuracy.

According to a reformist former KGB officer who helped the Ponomarev group, however, the KGB had agents on each commission who "frustrated their work at every turn, [and denied] them access to archives and personnel." The inexperienced commission members "reached no conclusions, published no final report, and submitted no recommendations to the legislature." None of the probes was conclusive: The Obolensky and Stepashin commissions lasted only three months; the Ponomarev commission was abolished by the Russian Supreme Soviet leadership shortly afterward; the Procuracy investigation focused only on the top coup leaders who were on the State of Emergency committee; and the internal Oleynikov commission claimed, without much credibility, to have finished its inquest in only ten days, and few officers were fired as a result.[119]

Post-KGB Structures

Under Bakatin's direction, the USSR KGB was dismembered along functional and regional lines. From the center, it was split into five major separate bodies: foreign intelligence, counterintelligence, secure communications and electronic intelligence, presidential security, and border guards. Bakatin told *Izvestiya* his reasons for dismembering the KGB in this fashion:

> The most dangerous thing is that the KGB has had an absolute monopoly on government communications, total surveillance, secrecy, encryption and decryption of documents, protection of USSR borders and of the president.

> This may have had a decisive part to play in the coup. That is, the danger to the Soviet Union lay in the very structure of the state security organs. It is my job to make the KGB an organization that really does guarantee the country's security. We must deal only with intelligence, counterintelligence, and crimes by top Soviet state officials. Anything else is none of our business.[120]

On the periphery, republican governments were given control over the KGB structures, including facilities and personnel, that were situated on their territories. This transfer included structures responsible for secure communications and ciphers, which benefitted the center by permitting permanent surveillance of the coded government messages of all other republics. Most of the KGB's internal structures on Russian territory were transferred to the Russian Federation. Foreign intelligence and border guards were intended to remain under Union control, as at that point Soviet leaders had not yet envisioned the total breakup of the USSR. Bakatin drew from his ideas in reforming the USSR MVD in 1989, when he planned a three-tier apparatus at the federal, regional, and local levels, reasoning that central police authority could be maintained only by delegating as much responsibility as possible to Internal Affairs bodies at the republican level.[121]

A "soviet union" could no longer exist as before. The upsurge in nationalism and greater assertions of national independence made it impossible for a central state security apparatus to serve the "national" interests of each Soviet republic objectively and effectively. Enlightened officers serving with Bakatin noticed this dilemma, which was articulated by Vladimir Rubanov, head of the USSR KGB Analytical Directorate. National "vital interests" could no longer be determined by the center, he said:

> There is no common denominator for disparate national interests, nor can they be supplanted by some kind of unionwide interest formulated by the center. Pressure 'from the top' is impermissible here. At union level it is merely possible to coordinate vital national interests and try to balance them to the advantage of all the republics. In seeking to achieve this balance, the preponderance of any one of the vital interests must not be tolerated, and the domination of any of the structures of state management, especially of a strong-arm or repressive character, in the security system as a whole must be avoided. It must be admitted that we have a long way to go to achieve harmony.[122]

In the process of restructuring, Bakatin took measures to establish legal civil controls over the organization and its successor services. Although dismantlement of the KGB and formal creation of new services were accomplished by decree, Bakatin did not neglect the need to back the decrees with the force of law, illegitimacy of the union or republican constitutions and legislatures notwithstanding. In a meeting with U.S. Secretary of State James A. Baker, he requested that American experts help Soviet lawmakers draft legislation to bring the new services under civil control. Prominent Russian Supreme Soviet members also sought U.S. help; during an October 1991 visit to Washington, Stepashin reportedly asked for CIA assistance.[123]

Bakatin's was a sincere approach, though made from the worldview of a lifelong Party official who had no firsthand appreciation of the fundamental differences between Soviet and U.S. political and legal culture. Nevertheless it was an extremely important gesture. In late November, after the USSR Supreme Soviet was reorganized to grant more powers to reformist members, Bakatin addressed its Council of the Republics chamber to urge adoption of a draft law to reorganize the state security services as proposed by the Stepashin Commission.[124]

Partition of the KGB was not entirely a move toward curbing abuses. It was a move supported by many chekists toward greater efficiency. The essence of the change was to maintain an extremely strong apparatus, but one that ceded internal security powers to the republics. Bakatin had to back away from the prospect of large-scale firings. RSFSR KGB Chairman Ivanenko wanted to absorb a large apparatus, not a truncated one, arguing that Russia needed such a security service to protect President Yeltsin from a future coup attempt.[125]

Even hard-line chekists such as espionage chief Leonid Shebarshin, despite his bitter differences with Bakatin, said it would be wise to separate foreign intelligence from the security apparatus,[126] but for a reason far removed from democratic reform. Shebarshin believed that intelligence should be completely severed so as to distance it completely from "the objectionable KGB 'tail' which dragged behind it."[127] So partitioning the KGB, while revolutionary in a bureaucratic if not practical sense, was not necessarily a threat to the cult of chekism Nevertheless Bakatin's moderate approach failed to endear him to many, who resented him as an unwelcome intrusion into their domain, and there remained strong resistance to his methods within the apparatus.

Sketches of the initial post-putsch Soviet intelligence and security services that were carved from the KGB follow.

Central Intelligence Service

The First Chief Directorate (foreign intelligence), became the USSR Central Intelligence Service (Tsentralnaya sluzhba razvedki, TsSR). This first break from the KGB was largely dictated by fears that non-Russian republics would try to peel away parts of the KGB foreign intelligence apparatus for themselves.[128] Primakov remained in charge and was formally appointed director general on 6 November.[129] The Soviet leadership was decidedly against parceling out the intelligence bureaucracy among the republics, as the service, in Bakatin's words, would cease to function.[130]

The main structures, including the directorates and services, were essentially unchanged, although there bureaucratic modification to remove unnecessary offices and positions that once served the CPSU and to rearrange the department level to divide geographical responsibilities more efficiently. The TsSR continued the KGB's economic intelligence work, and Primakov planned for it to engage in economic counterintelligence abroad to make sure that foreign business partners "do not rob us"[131] or, just as likely, to continue to purloin proprietary information from Western firms, industries, and financial institutions for Soviet enterprises run by the chekists and their friends.

Personnel cuts were planned for 50 percent of manpower abroad and 30 percent of manpower overall.[132] These reductions were dictated by the presence of officers assigned to service the newly defunct CPSU International Department, by general bureaucratic overstaffing, by hard currency shortages, and by a reassessment of strategic priorities.

Independent Counterintelligence/Internal Security Services

The Second Chief Directorate, responsible for counterintelligence and internal security, became decentralized. Control within each of the 11 remaining Soviet republics was transferred to each of the union republics, with the exception of the three Baltic states. The Russian Federation rapidly took the lion's share. Most of these transfers took place officially on 23 and 24 September. The newly independent republican KGBs, some of which immediately changed their names to give the appearance of a break with the past, maintained links with the center and with one another at the Union level by means of a new Inter-republic Security Service (Mezhrespublikanskaya sluzhba bezopasnosti), described below. The state security bodies responsible for Moscow were placed under control of the city government, then led by Mayor Popov, per an agreement with Yeltsin and Russian KGB Chairman Ivanenko.[133]

Government Communications Committee

The USSR Government Communications Committee (Komitet pravitelstvennoy sviazi, KPS) was formed to absorb the KGB Eighth Chief Directorate (signals intelligence and cryptography, though it is unclear to the author whether the Eighth had been reorganized as the Radioelectronic Intelligence Chief Directorate, the Government Communications Chief Directorate, and the Communications Security Chief Directorate, which were listed as part of the KPS); the Sixteenth Directorate (technical penetration of foreign missions); the KGB Government Communications Troops; the Information-Analysis Directorate; the RSFSR Government Communications Directorate; the Military Construction Directorate; the Commercial Department and the Scientific Center; the Mobilization and Personnel directorates; the Press and Internal Security Services; the Academy of Cryptography; the Orlov Higher Command School of Communications; and other units. Thus it absorbed approximately one-fourth of all USSR KGB resources.[134] Bakatin named Lt. Gen. Aleksandr V. Starovoytov to be KPS chief.[135]

Committee for the Protection of State Borders

The Border Troops Chief Directorate was split from the KGB and became an autonomous USSR Committee for the Protection of State Borders (Komitet po okhrana gosudarstvennoy granitsy, KOGG) when the USSR KGB was dismembered on 6 November 1991. Ilya Kalinichenko, the sitting chief, was formally appointed KOGG chairman and commander-in-chief of the Border Troops in a decree signed by Gorbachev on that date.[136] Total troop strength was estimated by Western sources at between 175,000 and 220,000,[137] though Bakatin says it numbered 240,000.[138]

The KOGG was described by its deputy chief of staff as "an interrepublic organ of state management defending the interests of the Union and the sovereign republics within it on the border and in the economic zone. All its activity will be carried out within the limits of the powers delegated by the sovereign republics." A key role of the KOGG was to "help Union and republic customs and law-enforcement organs, and also environmental and public organizations to protect citizens and the natural environment in border areas, in territorial and inland waters, and in the economic zone."[139] The KOGG's central purpose was to coordinate among republics and to defend USSR borders. Direct border guard functions between republics were to be carried out by the individual republics themselves.[140]

The "supreme leadership" of the Border Troops, a "unified troop command" comprised of representatives of each of the republics and the Union government, was supposed to have organized and supervised implementation of relevant legislation, regulations, and treaties by the periphery and the center and to have ensured readiness.[141] A Kremlin decree issued 3 December confirmed temporary regulations governing the KOGG.[142] Apparently the Commonwealth of Independent States (CIS) Border Troops, which briefly succeeded the KOGG, continued to abide by the Soviet regulations after the USSR collapsed. There was no time for any effective changes to take place.

The unified border guard concept failed from the perspective of the republican governments and the rank-and-file conscripts. Balts left their posts in droves and were provided sanctuary in their newly independent, non-Soviet republics. Moldova and Ukraine quickly announced the formation of their own border guards, and Belarus considered creating its own unit in February 1992. Desertions across the Union were high—troops of one nationality felt no fealty to guard the borders of another republic—and uncertainty and aggravated morale plagued border forces throughout the CIS, especially in the volatile Caucasus, where troops and their families were kidnapped or attacked by nationalist forces.[143] However, by mid-1994 not all republics had developed their own border guards, and Russian Border Troops predominated around much of the CIS, especially in Tajikistan where they became embroiled in combat with Tajik and Afghan Islamic guerrilla forces. Russian Border Troops were also sighted along the Georgian-Turkish border, though at the time Tblisi was hostile to Moscow and had refused to join the CIS.[144]

Main Guards Directorate

Presidential security, the former Ninth Directorate or Government Guards Directorate, was split from the KGB and named the USSR Main Guards Directorate.[145] Answerable to the Soviet president, the unit was also responsible for protection of the Russian president, at Yeltsin's suggestion. A special commission was set up in early September 1991 to prepare proposals on upgrading the guard system and to clarify its legal status. Most of the unit was loyal to the Soviet presidency during the putsch.[146] The unit's new chief was Col. Vladimir Redkoborodiy. A separate armed force that was merged into the guards, the Alfa group of the former KGB Seventh Directorate (surveillance), also provided security to the Russian and Soviet presidents, even though Alfa was an offensive shock commando and antiterrorist unit, and not a guard force. The USSR Main Guards Directorate and the Alfa group became the Russian Federation Main Guards Directorate.

Inter-Republic Security Service

Anticipating that the KGB in each republic would become autonomous within the context of a preserved Soviet Union, Bakatin conceived of the Inter-republic Security Service (Mezhrespublikanskaya sluzhba bezopasnosti, MSB) to help coordinate the security services and provide them with necessary technical and personnel assistance from the center. The Stepashin Commission agreed with his proposal.[146] With the formation of the MSB on 6 November 1991, the USSR KGB ceased formally to exist. Bakatin continued as MSB chairman.[147] A coordinating body was comprised of the MSB chief, the foreign intelligence (TsSR) chief, and the chiefs of state security for the remaining Soviet republics. Some structures and personnel from the USSR KGB, including the Information Analysis Directorate, the Public Relations Center, and an unnumbered directorate for producing special equipment and forged documents, were transferred to the MSB. The KGB Third Chief Directorate for military counterintelligence and the former Fifth Chief Directorate for political repression were separate units within the MSB.

One of Bakatin's first acts as USSR KGB chairman had been to instruct the entire Third Chief Directorate, which had responsibility for physical control of nuclear warheads, to suspend all activities and concentrate on ensuring the security of nuclear weapons. The nuclear problem plagued Bakatin and USSR Defense Minister Yevgeniy Shaposhnikov as a daily concern throughout the last four months of 1991.[148]

Bakatin intended to transfer military counterintelligence and related units to the Soviet Armed Forces General Staff.[149] Reports to the contrary and an official announcement notwithstanding, this transfer never took place,[150] even though Shaposhnikov wanted the armed forces to take on this role.[151] The unit's new chief, Army Maj. Gen. Yuriy Bulygin, was originally very keen about making the transfer to the military, but Bakatin recalls, "Later, with the greatest enthusiasm, Bulygin began to demonstrate the necessity for the Third Chief Directorate to remain in the KGB, alluding to the unpreparedness for the transfer organizationally and psychologically."[153] Bakatin himself became convinced of the KGB argument that by keeping the Third as part of state security, it would act as a check and balance against army "monopolism." The Soviet leadership would not approve transfer to the military, and Bakatin withdrew his suggestion.[154]

Outward signs at the time also indicated that the Third would remain in the hands of the chekists. Bulygin addressed the purpose of military counterintelligence in an interview with *Izvestiya* published on 6 December. He said that the Soviet military's main threat was an internal enemy and that his service would protect the armed forces not only from espionage and terrorism from abroad but also from internal threats such as organized crime, narcotics trafficking, and other forms of corruption. In the same interview, he called for a new military police service and proposed renaming military counterintelligence the Main Military Administration of the Inter-republic Security Service.[155] This new name indicated that military counterintelligence would remain affiliated with the old KGB structures. Within two weeks, the organization was absorbed by the Russian Federation and the matter was closed.

The notorious Fifth Chief Directorate, established by KGB Chairman Andropov in the 1960s for more sophisticated surveillance and persecution of dissent, supposedly had been abolished under Gorbachev prior to the putsch and replaced by the Directorate for the Defense of the Constitutional System. This was only a name change. Sometime in 1991 the unit was renamed Directorate Z, the "z" standing for *zashchita* or "defense." Again, this was done only to convey the false impression of change. Plans to dissolve the directorate were announced in September. The official reason was that "ideological counterintelligence [was] not yet provided for in the structure of the [reformed] organs."[156] Its abolition was announced in mid-October by USSR KGB First Deputy Chairman Oleynikov in an interview with *Izvestiya*.[157] However, a ranking state security official admitted that the unit was still in existence by December; indeed, it survived the Soviet collapse and many of its personnel were transferred to counterintelligence, counter-crime, a new tax police, and other state security subunits.[158]

The MSB bureaucratic structure included four main directorates: Counterintelligence, Information Analysis, Operational-Technical, and Inspectorate-Administration. The Counterintelligence Directorate was designed to coordinate and facilitate counterintelligence functions in and among the republics as well as to combat narcotics trafficking, organized crime, and terrorism. It may have absorbed KGB analytical and operational units that were not specifically designated to the other new services. The unit's director, F. A. Mestnikov, was a reformist KGB officer who had been in counterintelligence in Leningrad. Oleynikov, who had been drawn from the USSR KGB directorate for combating organized crime after the putsch, may have supervised the crimefighting element of the MSB Counterintelligence Directorate.[159]

The Information-Analysis Directorate was headed by Vladimir Rubanov, a reform professional KGB officer who as a colonel was fired by Kryuchkov in 1988 for publicly denouncing the service's "cult of secrecy." He later became an aide to then-USSR Interior Minister Vadim Bakatin until the latter was dismissed by Gorbachev in December 1990.[160] Rubanov described his directorate, which was lifted from the Analytical Directorate of the KGB Second Chief Directorate, as the central unit responsible for systematizing information and analysis. It also prepared assessments on a daily basis. Another MSB unit, composed of regional experts, refined these basic assessments and prepared them for designated policymakers or other users among the republics. In Rubanov's words, his directorate would "objectify" assessments, and the other unit would "individualize" them. He said that the directorate did not serve as a central analysis center.[161]

The Operational-Technical Directorate, responsible for "special equipment production," was an unnumbered KGB directorate that produced custom equipment and forged documents for use in operations. The Inspectorate-Administration Directorate handled personnel, training, material and technical support, and logistics.[162]

A Coordination Council was designed to serve as the actual mechanism within the MSB through which individual republican services would channel information and coordinate activities with one another. Foreign intelligence gathered by the Union TsSR and information from other Union services was to have been provided to the republics through this same mechanism. The MSB would then, in theory, analyze the information and provide assessments to a USSR National Security Council, which would have coordinated among the Union services and the republics had the Union not collapsed.[163]

Cooperation between the MSB and the republican KGB services was not automatic. Separate agreements were negotiated between the center and each republican capital. Belarus, Kazakhstan, Kyrgyzstan, Moldova, Tajikistan and Ukraine were the first to sign the accord.[164] The other republics, aside from the three Baltic states and Georgia, later signed. All signatories, including the KGB chiefs of warring Armenia and Azerbaijan, subsequently signed a protocol on mutual cooperation.[165] Because of the suddenness of the changes, the MSB financed the republican KGBs for the remainder of 1991.[166]

The highest body of the MSB was a council. All republican KGB chiefs, along with USSR Central Intelligence Service Director General Primakov, State Communications Committee Chairman Staravoytov, Committee for the Protection of State Borders Chairman Kalinichenko, and MSB Chairman Bakatin, were members. The atmosphere, Bakatin recalled, was collegial, a change from the hierarchical arrangement of the old KGB collegium: "Nobody on the council was the subordinate of anyone else."[167]

Conflicting interests among the republics, and political differences between the more progressive center and the reactionary periphery doomed the MSB to failure. When Bakatin, in a good-faith gesture to Washington, provided U.S. Ambassador Robert Strauss with samples of KGB electronic eavesdropping equipment planted in the American Embassy, as well as charts showing the location of all KGB devices inside the complex and the tunnels beneath it, he caused an uproar not only within the MSB, but among chekists outside Russia. Some demanded that he be tried under the notorious Article 64 of the RSFSR Criminal Code for "high treason."[168] The Belarus KGB went so far as to warn that it might stop collaborating with the MSB, accusing Bakatin of "flagrant" violation of the MSB-BKGB agreement on ensuring state security.[169]

The organization of the Inter-republic Security Service occurred in the context of the collapse of the Soviet Union, the bureaucratic atomization of the KGB, crippling uncertainty and demoralization among the cadres, and the Russian Federation's rapid and often uncoordinated absorption of Union security structures. Civil authorities were overwhelmed by the changes. Rubanov observed complete disarray in the intelligence analysis and dissemination process. Despite formal structures on paper, no central mechanism existed to integrate reports from the other Union services, the MVD, or the military. Most telling, perhaps, was the spare time officials such as Rubanov had that enabled them to travel outside Russia during such an intense period. The MSB information-analysis chief visited Germany to attend a four-day conference on intelligence in November and the United States for a week to speak with sovietologists in December. Perhaps he saw that his efforts to preserve a Union structure were futile.[170]

RSFSR KGB

As Bakatin mapped out his reforms from the center, he ceded large sections of the USSR KGB to the RSFSR KGB (RKGB), which quickly took the spoils and indeed successfully resisted Bakatin's attempt to fire hundreds or even thousands of officers. Gorbachev made these transfers of bureaucracies official by issuing presidential decrees for each. In a 13 September announcement Bakatin authorized the Russian KGB, headed by Viktor Ivanenko, to assume command over the state security organs of all autonomous republics, krays, and oblasts, with a simultaneous transfer of all structures, personnel, property, vehicles, computer and communications equipment, and other resources in their possession within the boundaries of the Russian Federation.[171]

The Moscow city and oblast KGB was placed under the control of the city council, then led by reformist Mayor Gavriil Popov, on 26 September.[172] Although the central KGB could do nothing legally to prevent the appointment of Deputy Mayor Yevgeniy Savostyanov, an anti-Communist political activist, as Moscow KGB chief, the security apparat surrounded him with chekist officers to serve as advisers, subordinates, and minders. Even though he was reputed to be a lieutenant in the KGB "academic reserve," Savostyanov's presence drew concern even from reform professionals like Information Analysis Director Rubanov, who called the decision of the Moscow city leadership "dangerous games." He added, "This could, to say the least, split the [KGB] collective and create confusion. And it is hardly sensible to underrate the strength of the KGB."[173]

On 27 September the chairman and deputy chairmen of the USSR KGB directorate for the city and oblast of St. Petersburg resigned. Unlike the special status of the Moscow KGB, the St. Petersburg KGB was not made subordinate to the city council. City and oblast KGB Chairman Anatoliy Kurkov stepped down effective one month from giving notice. His unnamed deputies were to have left their posts in a shorter period.[174] Kurkov was replaced by Sergey Stepashin, one of the prime organizers of state security restructuring and chairman of both the RSFSR Supreme Soviet Committee on Defense and Security and the USSR State Commission to Investigate the Activity of the Security Organs. A career MVD officer with the rank of lieutenant colonel, Stepashin became a KGB major general upon his appointment.

Bakatin directed an orderly transition of state security power and personnel to the Russian Federation beginning with the periphery of the republic. By late September, the RKGB had grown a thousandfold, from 23 men to more than 20,000.[175] Most of these individuals were dispersed throughout the Federation; in October, 22,000 RKGB officers were in regional offices, and only 189 were based at Lubyanka.[176] The RKGB was made the "legal succesor" to the USSR KGB on Russian territory in a decree issued by President Yeltsin on 5 October. The decree also proposed holding talks with the union republics about establishing a state security coordinating body, which became the USSR Inter-republic Security Service (MSB) headed by Bakatin.[177]

Russia's absorption of the USSR KGB structures on its territory was carried out by RKGB Chairman Viktor Ivanenko and overseen in the presidential apparatus by State Secretary Gennadiy Burbulis, although Burbulis's influence is not known to have been particularly strong. Because he felt that the USSR could survive as a loose federation of autonomous states, Bakatin tried to ensure that his organization was not swallowed whole by the RKGB. This attempt caused a disagreement with Burbulis, who wanted the RKGB to absorb the Union services completely, changing little more than the names to reflect Russian ownership. Such a comprehensive transfer would have precluded the possibility of an Inter-republic Security Service. Stepashin sided with Bakatin on this point, although the commission as a whole did not, and Burbulis was momentarily thwarted.[178]

Russian President Yeltsin had two strong allies in the top echelon of the USSR security and police apparats who helped ensure the Russian Federation's interests against those of the center, and both agreed with Bakatin on most issues. Those allies were USSR KGB First Deputy Chairman Anatoliy Oleynikov, the organized crime fighter who had been appointed Bakatin's deputy at the Russian president's insistence, and Viktor Barannikov, who had been Russian MVD chief until he was named to replace USSR MVD Minister Boriss Pugo, who shot himself when the putsch failed.

Oleynikov and Yeltsin were not personal friends and their relationship is not well understood. Barannikov, by contrast, earned Yeltsin's confidence well before the putsch when he headed Russian Internal Affairs, and he was at the Russian president's side with a weapon in hand almost constantly during the three-day ordeal in the Russian White House. In the first year of the Russian Federation's independence, Barannikov reportedly enjoyed access to Yeltsin unparalleled by anyone except his personal secretary.[179] Barannikov was widely known as a close personal friend of the president; one former senior KGB officer described him as Yeltsin's "right-hand glass."[180] Others, noting Barannikov's constant access to the president, referred to him with a note of sarcasm as Yeltsin's bodyguard. While neither Oleynikov nor Barannikov were of the Kryuchkov mold and both advocated some significant changes, neither could be termed a real reformer, and neither had any demonstrated democratic leanings. In retrospect, many Russian democrats view Oleynikov as one of the most progressive chekists of the time.

Bakatin maintained a friendly and cooperative professional relationship with Barannikov and had a "good relationship" with RKGB Chairman Ivanenko, although Ivanenko's deputies were resentful of the Soviet KGB chief.[181] These personal relations helped to smooth and coordinate the transition from the center to the republics, although the atmosphere of change and uncertainty was highly charged and frequently chaotic within the bureaucracies themselves. The lack of resistance to the republics' absorption of the KGB on their territories suggests that the regional chekists supported the changes as power slipped from Moscow's grasp to the peripheral capitals. At the same time, Ivanenko saved many KGB officers from Bakatin's dismissals, countermanding his orders to cashier chekists in the Far Eastern Border Guards District and in a signals intelligence facility at Khabarovsk. Indeed, Ivanenko insulated the KGB on Russian territory from Bakatin's most sweeping reforms.[182]

The USSR KGB was officially abolished on 26 November 1991 by decree of Soviet President Gorbachev. In its place stood the shaky Inter-republic Security Service (MSB) headed by Bakatin, the stable Central Intelligence Service (TsSR) led by Primakov, the Government Communications Committee (KPS) led by Starovoytov, and the Committee for the Protection of State Borders (KOGG) chaired by Kalinichenko. On the same day, Russian President Yeltsin issued Decree No. 233, which renamed the RKGB the RSFSR Federal Security Agency (Agentsvo federalnoy bezopasnosti, AFB) and provided provisional statutes for the service.

Russian Federal Security Agency

The Federal Security Agency assumed the USSR KGB Second Chief Directorate staff of 20,000 in Moscow and 22,000 throughout the Federation.[183] RSFSR KGB Chairman Ivanenko automatically became AFB director general and had responsibility for overseeing the transition process. The transition was not led entirely by reformers. Ivanenko was the compromise figure; prior to the putsch he had kept the RSFSR KGB a rump organization of only twenty-three staffers. No fewer than six leading AFB officers had been involved in the August putsch, according to a parliamentary finding.[184]

Three days after its formation, on 29 November, the AFB was formally "presented" to the public at a Lubyanka news conference. Ivanenko set the theme, which differed not at all from the one devised by Kryuchkov two years before, or even that set by Chebrikov before him. The AFB, he said, would focus on "the struggle to combat organized crime, terrorism, the narcotics business, contraband and corruption." The AFB would seek "fruitful relations" with Western services. Most important, Ivanenko claimed, creation of the AFB marked a permanent break with state security's "sad past," as if the present corps of chekists was brand new and free of abusive figures. The new leadership of the AFB was presented. Ivanenko's deputies were Vladimir Podelyakin, first deputy director general; Stanislav Orlov, deputy for organized crime matters; Stanislav Pyatakov, deputy for counterintelligence; Vladimir Fisenko, deputy for intelligence; Valeriy Yampolskiy, deputy director general for personnel; Yevgeniy Savostyanov, deputy director general for Moscow and Moscow oblast; Sergey Stepashin, deputy director general for St. Petersburg and St. Petersburg oblast; Andrey Oligov, head of the Public Relations Center.[185]

None of these was completely from outside the organs, although in comparison to most chekists, Ivanenko, Podelyakin, and Yampolskiy were rather reformist, as was the MVD veteran Stepashin. This is not to say that they advocated the undoing of chekism itself—they only wanted to adapt it. Savostyanov, as the only one with a track record of fighting communist abuse of power and as the only ranking official of the AFB who had never been a member of the Communist Party, was still an outsider. He had no team of his own and depended completely on career KGB officers.[186] Notably, he was the only top official not appointed by Ivanenko or Yeltsin, but by the Moscow city government.

The AFB did not exist long enough for it to distinguish itself in any way. Nor did Ivanenko. Three weeks after the AFB was formed, it was taken over in an inter-service putsch of sorts, with Yeltsin's approval. Ivanenko, Podelyakin, and Yampolskiy were prematurely retired shortly afterward. The probable reason why Savostyanov kept his position, and Stepashin was promoted, was because they soon embraced chekism and became part of the problem.

Conclusion

In the course of dividing itself up, the KGB, with the support of the Soviet and Russian leadership, went to great lengths to preserve itself institutionally. Ranking officers who displayed tendencies toward even modest reform were either removed or conformed to the status quo. Despite a few important revelations, there were no large-scale exposures of wrongdoing. Nor was there any systematic or meaningful attempt to come to terms with the past. Five post-putsch investigations notwithstanding, there were no conclusive probes or public reports. Like stones tossed into a pond, "dissolution" of the KGB was characterized by some brief splashes, momentary ripples, then calm as if nothing had occurred.

4

Post-Soviet Security and Intelligence Services

You cannot make a white dog by washing a black one.

—Russian proverb

The Survival of the KGB

The Soviet Union ceased to exist well before it was signed into history on 25 December 1991. The Communist Party was already destroyed and the Soviet Army languished as a discredited, demoralized, and almost dysfunctional force. The Party's KGB enforcement arm, dismembered and assumed by the Russian Federation and the control of the newly independent republics, stripped the USSR of the last mechanism by which it could exercise hegemony.

Russian President Yeltsin had three basic options: He could attempt to abolish the services outright and start afresh; he could try to reform the apparatus that already existed by removing the top layers and promoting younger, more reform-minded officers;[1] or he could simply assume the old-style system and attempt to use it for his own purposes. USSR People's Deputy and prominent journalist Yuriy Shchekochikhin wryly noted the problems that lay ahead for the president:

> As far as the KGB is concerned, there has always been discussion about whether creating new structures of any kind on the basis of this organization is permissible. The danger was that employees from the KGB—or even worse, whole, unchanged subunits of the Committee for State Security—would be automatically transferred to the new organization and

that this would mean that they would retain all of their pleasant characteristics, as well.[2]

He added, "The post-putsch reform of the KGB, despite the promises of a drastic reduction in the number of the KGB departments, has been subjected to acute criticism, precisely because in the organizational sphere the skeleton of the old secret services has remained inviolable." He called for the total dissolution of the old services and a case-by-case selection of personnel for new security organs.[3]

This did not happen. Yeltsin chose option number three. Despite three reshufflings in late 1991 and the first month of 1992, what was once known as the KGB was re-formed by the Russian Federation without being reformed. Rather than naming civilians with known democratic tendencies to lead the internal security and foreign intelligence services of the new Russian state from the top, and promoting younger and less tainted officers into the middle ranks, President Yeltsin appointed remnants of the old regime. Their underlings, with the sole exception of the Moscow security chief, were career servants of the CPSU. Some had reformist tendencies but fundamentally did not want to break the back of chekism.

Sergey Stepashin, as chairman of the Russian Supreme Soviet Committee on Defense and Security, chief of the USSR State Commission to Investigate the Activity of the Security Organs, and chief of state security for St. Petersburg, all pivotal positions, recognized the superficiality of the reforms. He termed the "abolition" of the KGB mere "facelift."[4] Vadim Bakatin, who oversaw the partitioning of the KGB, agreed. Speaking in the third person, he underscored that his reforms as KGB chief in reality had accomplished very little:

> Everyone keeps saying that Bakatin has torn down the KGB structure. For goodness' sake, this is not so. If you come to Kazakhstan, not a single hair has fallen from the head of any official in Kazakhstan. Or to Kyrgyzstan—I just got back from there, everything is still as it was there. The situation is the same in the Moscow department, and in the Keremovo one. That is, all the capillaries at the bottom and the structures have remained the same. . . .[5]

He assessed the Russian secret services in a separate interview:

> It must be said plainly here that success was not achieved. I do not believe that it was possible anyway to significantly reform anything in such a short time in the conditions that actually exist. . . . Nor do I think that the incipient Russian service, like the others, achieved great success in ideological restructuring equal to the building of a democratic state. This still has to be

> achieved. Thus I do not think that our special services have already become safe for our citizens. There are no laws, no control, no professional security services.[6]

President Yeltsin's first acts with the newly acquired services ensured that few reforms among the chekists would be forthcoming. Now that he had the KGB at his disposal, he would try to make it work for him.

Ministry of Security and Internal Affairs (MBVD)

As he stood on the tarmac at a Moscow airport on 19 December 1992 before flying to Rome for a summit with Western leaders, President Yeltsin was hurriedly handed some papers by a member of his farewell party, interim Soviet Interior Minister Viktor Barannikov, his close friend. The sheaf contained several decrees requiring a presidential signature. One, which bolstered Yeltsin's image prior the trip, abolished the USSR Foreign Ministry and transferred all its facilities and responsibilities to the Russian Federation. A second decree, however, would shock both the public and officialdom at home. It abolished the USSR MVD and Inter-republic Security Service (MSB) and ordered the immediate merger of those bodies with the Russian MVD and Federal Security Agency, creating a giant and unchallenged police and security force. The new bureaucracy, with cabinet status, would be the Ministry of Security and Internal Affairs (Ministerstvo bezopasnosti i vnutrennykh del, MBVD).[7] Without a hard surface to write on, Yeltsin raised one foot on a step leading up to the aircraft and signed the decrees on his knee. He handed them back to Barannikov and boarded the plane.[8]

News of the merger detonated intense controversy throughout official Moscow. The decree had come without warning. Liberal critics likened it to Stalin's merger of state security (United State Political Directorate, OGPU) with the *militsiya* in 1932, which led to the creation of an even more powerful All-Union People's Commissariat for Internal Affairs (NKVD) two years later. Although the MBVD differed substantially from the NKVD, it bore enough common basic features to allow reasonable people to draw parallels to Stalin's service. The last-minute delivery of the decree to Yeltsin and the hasty manner in which he signed it indicated the haphazard nature of the Russian president's governing style and the deliberate way in which the organs took advantage of the situation. Barannikov had to obtain Yeltsin's signature on 19 December because of the powerful symbolism for the cadres. There would be no break with the past. The new MBVD would be born on 20 December, the seventy-fourth anniversary of the creation of the Cheka.

The Ouster of Bakatin

Many saw the MBVD as a power grab by Barannikov, who had named himself minister of the huge armed bureaucracy. The original concept, however, had been developed by Bakatin, who conceived of the idea when he was Soviet interior minister between early 1988 and December 1990. At that time Bakatin made overtures to the United States for joint cooperation to combat organized crime, but conditions in the Soviet Union precluded meaningful U.S. participation. He was equally unsuccessful working with Soviet KGB Chairman Kryuchkov, who rejected a structural merger of state security elements with the police to maximize the government's ability to fight criminal syndicates.

Bakatin, a construction engineer by profession with no background in law enforcement or security and thus unburdened by chekist culture, yet with no extensive knowledge or experience of Western democracies, envisioned a merger of police and counterintelligence into a service he mistakenly anticipated would be similar to the Federal Bureau of Investigation (FBI) in the United States. In the autumn of 1990 he found himself increasingly at loggerheads with Kryuchkov and concluded that it was senseless to await reforms from state security. Bakatin began demanding that the KGB, especially its internal repressive apparatus, be abolished. What he did not know at the time was that Kryuchkov was planning to provoke a state of emergency to reassert Party supremacy and to crush nationalist movements that threatened the USSR.[9] In December 1990, Bakatin was replaced as MVD chief by KGB General Boriss Pugo, but this event proved only an interim break from his attempts at reform.

Following the putsch, with Pugo dead, Bakatin became USSR KGB chairman and found new USSR interior minister Barannikov (who had been Russian interior minister prior to the coup attempt) to be supportive of his idea, although no steps were taken in Lubyanka to develop the concept. For Bakatin, only the MVD, though weaker and less prestigious than the KGB, could hope to bring the chekists to heel. By late 1991, however, Barannikov had no use for him.[10] Barannikov never arranged to show Bakatin advance drafts of his December MBVD decrees. Yeltsin's signing of the surprise edicts was a major coup for the militsiya and a blow to the chekists, who had just seen their apparatus truncated and dismembered.

The decrees placed the merged Soviet and Russian interior ministries under the directorship of Barannikov's MVD colleague Viktor Yerin, who became a first deputy minister of security and internal affairs. KGB Maj. Gen. Anatoliy Oleynikov, who served as deputy chairman of the Inter-republic Security Service under Bakatin, was also named first deputy minister in charge of state security. Russian Federal Security Agency (AFB) Director Ivanenko now reported to him. Not only was an MVD general now in charge of the chekists, but the MVD also had access to the KGB files.

Yeltsin's intent was to try to control KGB internal security by placing it under the command of the militsiya. The MBVD did not reabsorb all the functions of the former KGB. Foreign intelligence remained independent, as did government communications, presidential security, and border guards. The USSR and Russian Ministries of Internal Affairs were merged. All personnel of the affected institutions were permitted to remain until 1 July 1992, after which the MBVD would dismiss large numbers of ineffective, unneeded or unwanted personnel.[11] Overlapping jurisdictions between the MVD and state security were to be removed.[12] Barannikov went to work immediately, ordering the mergers to take place not only at the top but on the oblast and kray levels as well. He issued a series of directions, including Order Number Five, a measure to create "rapid deployment squads" to put down the unrest that was expected following price liberalizations.[13]

Numerous reports leaked by state security officials alleged that, immediately after the merger, MVD personnel rifled and destroyed large quantities of KGB files on corruption within the police forces. The reports made sense. The year before, of 830 members of organized criminal gangs whose files the KGB had submitted to the Procuracy, 190 had turned out to be MVD personnel.[14] Citing an unnamed official close to the president and confirmed by anonymous high-ranking AFB sources, TASS was the first to report that the files had been destroyed. The television program "Vesti" followed up on the story with an unidentified AFB staffer who stated, "The elimination of corruption files is of selective character—it is [the] face of only high-ranking *militsia* officers that is being saved." These were Barannikov's men. Within days, the reports were being denied.[15]

It is possible that the story could have been disinformation—or facts—circulated by chekists upset with the new arrangement. Bakatin, who had no personal stake in the matter, said that the reports were "absolutely a lie."[16] Nevertheless, while the KGB had the authority to investigate MVD corruption, the reverse was not true. No one could investigate the KGB, and it stands to reason that corrupt MVD leaders would have wanted to get their hands on any compromising files. No concrete evidence has surfaced to substantiate or disprove either assertion.

Mysterious Circumstances Surrounding the Merger

Coming so soon after the first decisive steps to dismantle the KGB, the 19 December decrees were puzzling because they posed such a sudden and uncalled for reversal of the decentralization process. The circumstances surrounding the merger were mysterious, indicating that it did not originate in Yeltsin's office and was not a product of his reformist legal advisers. Yeltsin's closest aides, Gennadiy Burbulis and Sergey Shakhray, knew that Barannikov was preparing something and had tried to convince the president that issuing the decrees would be a mistake. They apparently did not expect him to sign, and Shakhray was away from Moscow when the decrees were issued.[17]

No one in Yeltsin's inner circle but Barannikov was aware that he was to sign when he did.[18] Presidential security adviser Yuriy Skokov, who had been one of the most hard-line communist members of the USSR Supreme Soviet, said he learned about it in the newspaper.[19] No one in the office of the president was available to talk to journalists about the matter.[20] When asked for comment, Shakhray's staffers said they did "not know what [was] going on."[21]

The Russian Supreme Soviet leadership was kept in the dark as well. First Deputy Chairman Sergey Filatov, a key Yeltsin ally, said, "I don't know how this decree appeared and consider it a very big step backward. Especially in terms of democracy."[22] Committee on Legality, Law and Order Chairman A. A. Aslakhanov, an MVD general, commented, "The decree was drawn up without taking account of the opinion of specialists, without taking account of the opinion of committees and heads of committees and members of the Supreme Soviet Presidium."[23]

Committee on Defense and Security Chairman Sergey Stepashin should have been one of the first to know, as he was also the Yeltsin-appointed head of the USSR state commission to propose security and intelligence reform and was a deputy chief of Russian state security. One of the accompanying decrees named Stepashin a deputy minister of the MBVD. That almost no one but Barannikov seemed to know in advance about the decrees indicates that Barannikov sought to create a security empire for himself before others would have the chance to question him or weaken his powers.

One account has it that the decrees originated in the leadership of the Russian MVD, indicating the involvement of Barannikov's longtime subordinate Yerin.[24] Later reports stating that Barannikov, whose loyalties were to Russia and not the Union, drafted the edicts himself were bolstered by the fact that one of them named him as chief of the new ministry.[25] Barannikov never consulted with Bakatin when drawing up the merger, and failed to show Bakatin an advance draft.

Bakatin, however, attributes this not to treachery but to haphazard decisionmaking, which was the norm at such a chaotic moment. He believes that once Russia had taken control of the bulk of the USSR KGB Second Chief Directorate, Yeltsin let Barannikov know that he wanted a strong service that would defend his government from possible chaos and hard-line reaction and that would be positioned to crack down on criminal elements taking advantage of the confusion. The 19 December decree creating the MBVD was poorly written, reflecting a lack of careful planning. "It was a typically Russian decision," Bakatin believes. "Yeltsin just signed when Barannikov said, 'Let's go and get this done.'"[26] This view is somewhat supported by Yuriy Shchekochikhin, who sat in the USSR Supreme Soviet at the time and was one of the most vocal liberal critics of the MBVD. He said that he did not believe that government's failure to inform the public on the matter was intentional: "Anybody who knows anything about present Russian structures would agree with this. This is simply the result of a failure to ensure that the decisive actions now being taken are always thought out and, most important of all, prepared properly. Not all members of the government service are sufficiently competent."[27]

Another mysterious aspect of the merger was the timing. A week before, Yeltsin had submitted a written request to the Supreme Soviet asking that it pass a new Law on Security calling specifically for separate state security and internal affairs structures. Committee on Defense and Security Chairman Sergey Stepashin held hearings on the law at about the same time.[28] Both chambers passed the law on its first reading on 18 December, but were not prepared to enact it on a second reading.[29]

Barannikov submitted his hastily written decrees to Yeltsin the very next day. He then moved with unusual speed to implement them, literally while the president was airborne for the Rome summit with Western leaders. Just days later, the presidents of the eleven republics were scheduled to hold a summit in Alma Ata to create the Commonwealth of Independent States. With the president out of the country and the rest of the government dispersed between Italy and Kazakhstan, Barannikov's window of opportunity was perfect.

Why did he act with such urgency? Some Russian commentators believed that turmoil in the Yeltsin administration allowed the organized nomenklatura to reassert itself and that the MBVD decree was a power grab on the nomenklatura's behalf. According to one commentator, "When fundamentally important government decisions are insufficiently prepared and supervised, a vacuum of authority always forms. Other forces increasingly take over real power—for instance, the gray army of untalented bureaucrats which has grown unbelievably stronger in recent months."[30] The Communist Party and the Soviet Union would collapse, but the security organs and nomenklatura would not.

Criticism of the MBVD

Criticism of the MBVD was widespread but varied. An *Izvestiya* commentator voiced support for the MBVD if it would "break up the former KGB system of agent support," but he found himself opposed to the decree creating the ministry. He called it "a mechanical merging of two monsters" and lamented, "there will be no one to continue what Vadim Bakatin began—the destruction of the totalitarian KGB from within. It seems to me that they are today trying to hide the old KGB from the eyes of the public behind the signboard of the Ministry of Security and Internal Affairs."[31] Even Bakatin, who voiced support for the decree as a more efficient way to combat organized crime, cautioned of a "potential possibility of its turning into an uncontrollable body."[32]

Other critics such as Shchekochikhin, the journalist-lawmaker, were harsher: "It seems to me that this is a colossal mistake. Seven different organizations in the United States are engaged in the battle against the mafia; in our country, this will be in one person's hands. This is the path toward colossal corruption."[33] Yevgeniya Albats, an investigative reporter with *Moscow News* who is considered one of Russia's top civilian experts on the security services, commented, "We have the following: a major structure of the old oligarchic regime that has not only not diminished in size, but has acquired a new cadre as personified by the militsia, has preserved the old cadre, structures and functions, lives on and operates under the same lawlessness."[34] Aleksandr Tsopov, chairman of the Moscow City Council anticrime subcommission, said, "The setting up of this monster was aimed at monopolizing the law-enforcement effort and played into the hands of the underworld and the corrupted nomenklatura."[35] Russian Justice Minister Fedorov also criticized the merger.[36]

Most important, so did professional chekists. They surely were not pleased to have been merged with the lowly militsiya and placed under the command of one of its generals. One news account reported: "The overwhelming majority of the employees of Russian state security appreciate negatively the decree on setting up the Russian Ministry of Security and Internal Affairs."[37] Spot reporting from chekists in the Russian hinterlands reflected this report.[38] State security employees in Moscow and St. Petersburg threatened to resign en masse.[39]

President Yeltsin, Supreme Soviet Chairman Khasbulatov, and AFB Director Ivanenko reportedly received protest telegrams and declarations voted upon by individual state security subdivisions in Arkhangelsk, Yekaterinburg, Chita, Izhevsk, Kyzyl, and Yuzhno-Sakhalinsk. A journalist who examined the messages reported that the chekists believed that "the monopolization of internal affairs and state security organs could lead to the reconstruction of a punitive system after the model of the People's Commissariat for Internal Affairs [NKVD] and to the collapse of the established system of agent support for counterintelligence and the fight against organized crime." They also expressed fear that "the merger of the departments will lead to the amalgamation of their information systems and materials, including those concerning high-ranking statesmen charged with corruption."[40] No statements of support for the MBVD by state security personnel, aside from MBVD First Deputy Minister Oleynikov, could be found. MVD personnel, however, reportedly were less opposed to the merger or even supportive of it.[41]

Some democratic Yeltsin loyalists tried to warn the president about the strength of the opposition in a memorandum circulated to the press analyzing the first months of the post-putsch Russian government. The memo concluded, "Old nomenklatura structures within the President's administration are strongly opposed to democratic reforms, with divisions among the politicians and bureaucrats in the presidential entourage coming to a head." The document accused presidential chief of staff Yuriy Petrov of personally blocking Yeltsin's restructuring directives and of withholding certain reform documents from the president. Liberal presidential decree drafts, such as those promoting reformist officials in the bureaucracy, were "lost" in the presidential Secretariat, only to be "found" at the insistence of pro-western Premier Yegor Gaydar. Presidential Secretariat chief Viktor Ilyushin and Petrov reportedly were "active supporters of nomenklatura-dominated provincial administrations."[42]

"The impression one gets," said the memorandum, "is that a deliberate attempt is being made to impede the government's normal functioning, bring about its downfall and install political figures suitable to the nomenklatura."[43] The words were prophetic. Purges of reformist officials and the installation of functionaries identified with the military-industrial complex began within months.

Apparently Yeltsin failed to consult his close aide and legal affairs adviser, State Counsellor Sergey Shakhray. Loyal to his boss, Shakhray tried to defend the MBVD in a televised interview two weeks after the decrees were signed. He nevertheless raised important points that signaled his own opposition to the merger. He called for the Internal Troops to be "removed from the jurisdiction of this ministry" and placed under direct presidential control. He also noted "professional incompatibility" between the chekists and the militsiya, observing, "Professionals from the state security organs will find it very difficult to work together with officers from the internal affairs bodies." As his logic progressed, he voiced more criticism, coming finally to the problem of corruption: "It is no secret that the internal affairs bodies, and partly the security bodies, have been penetrated by the rust of corruption, and it is very dangerous to merge this at the present time."[44]

Barannikov and his deputies apparently did not appreciate the level and scope of discontent and waited five days before making official statements to the press. First Deputies Oleynikov and Yerin told journalists at a 24 December news conference that all fears were unjustified and that the public should be supportive because now the state security and internal affairs services could pool resources and talent in the fight against crime and corruption. Concentration of resources, they said, would not lead to concentration of power; to the contrary, they would lead to more effective conditions for combating crime and espionage.

Yerin said personal experience had taught him that law enforcement organs were not a place to foster competition. Three or four subunits had a "clear professional direction," but abut twenty other subunits duplicated the MVD's work, he said. This disingenuous logic ignored the painful truth for every militsiya officer that there was always intense competition and suspicion between the pampered and all-powerful KGB and the much maligned and poorly equipped MVD.

Yerin and Oleynikov also said that Russian taxpayers should support the merger of the two services because it would save money. They tried to portray the MBVD as analogous to agencies in the United States, France, Italy, and Germany—as well as the evolving services in

Central and East Europe—which they said had single institutions that combined law enforcement, counterintelligence, and other security functions.[45] This argument, too, was inaccurate. None of the established democracies mentioned had a single, monopolistic security service like the MBVD.

The official theme was that the MBVD was created not to replicate Stalin's NKVD but to "protect the population."[46] Barannikov took to the airwaves to unveil "a whole package" of crimefighting measures.[47] He assured the public of strict civil control with unprecedented transparency: "This transparency has reached such a high degree since August that no usurpation of power is conceivable."[48] Yet creation of the ministry occurred in a more opaque environment.

Barannikov's arguments won few converts. The Supreme Soviet, careful not to call for a reversal of the absorption of the USSR MVD and the Inter-republic Security Service, passed a resolution on 26 December calling on President Yeltsin to declare invalid the section of the decree that concerned the merger of the MVD and the Russian Federal Security Agency (AFB). Only one of the 246 deputies dissented. Yeltsin and Barannikov ignored the resolution. The matter was then taken up by the new Constitutional Court, which declared the merger unconstitutional and ordered the government to rescind it. This historic decision marked the first successful challenge to the executive branch.[49]

On 16 January 1992, the president relented. He repealed the relevant section of the decree, thus disbanding the MBVD, though it is doubtful that he would have done so had the chekists backed the merger in the first place. In separating the super-ministry he established a much larger Ministry of Internal Affairs and an internal security service carved from the KGB called the Ministry of Security.

Ministry of Security (MB)

Accompanying the undoing of the state security-MVD merger were two key personnel decisions that strengthened MBVD Minister Barannikov's hand even as he lost his new empire. The first dismissed career KGB officer Viktor Ivanenko as director of the Federal Security Agency (AFB), which had been created from the KGB internal security organs. The second named Barannikov to replace him and assigned Barannikov's longtime deputy Viktor Yerin as new minister of internal affairs.[50] The AFB was maintained as a standby for a week until the Ministry of Security (Ministerstvo bezopasnosti, MB) could be established. The ministry was created "on the basis of the abolished

RSFSR Federal Security Agency [AFB] and the [USSR] Inter-republic Security Service," according to its founding presidential decree.[51] The MB was set up with eight deputy ministers (up from seven deputy chiefs for the AFB) and a seventeen-man collegium of top officials.

A ministry public relations spokesman said that the core of the organ consisted of several former KGB directorates: the Second Chief Directorate (counterintelligence); the Third Chief Directorate (military counterintelligence); the Chief Directorate for Combating Contraband and Corruption; the Internal Security Directorate, the Sixth Directorate (economic and industrial security); and the Directorate for Combating Terrorism (the euphemistic name of the former Fifth Chief Directorate for political enforcement).[52] The almost candid admission that the Ministry of Security absorbed the KGB's dissident-hunting office as part of its core contradicted earlier official statements from the Gorbachev government that the unit had been dissolved and dispersed and corroborated findings from a parliamentary commission led by progressive democrats that the remnants of the Fifth remained.[53]

The way the MB was created in the wake of the MBVD uproar indicates that the merger of the chekists with the militsiya continued in flagrant violation of policies set by both the Supreme Soviet and the Constitutional Court. Barannikov proceeded to build the armed bureaucracy into his personal feifdom. A clause in the MB's founding decree allowed him to name his own subordinates and thereby circumvent the ban on merging MVD personnel (but not structures) into Lubyanka. Such physical pairing of ministry bureaucracies could enable him to create a transministerial power base of his own.[54] This action also violated a previous agreement with the Supreme Soviet stipulating that high-level personnel decisions would be made in conjunction with a special legislative personnel commission.[55]

Maj. Gen. Oleynikov, the KGB veteran who served as first deputy minister of security and internal affairs responsible for state security matters, was retained for the moment as first deputy minister of security. Apparently owing to his association with Bakatin he was given few if any duties and was removed within months.[56] Other leading officers of a slight reformist bent were fired even sooner, including Ivanenko, his first deputy chairman Vladimir Podelyakin, and Deputy Director General for Personnel Valeriy Yampolskiy.[57] Barannikov replaced Ivanenko with himself and rapidly promoted hard-liners to other positions. A former MVD man named Trubin, who openly supported the August putsch, was now in charge of personnel, replacing Yampolskiy.[58] Vladimir Rubanov, one of the most liberal-leaning officers and head of the KGB Analytical Directorate under Bakatin, was also shown the door. Others, discussed below, followed.

The Personnel Numbers Game

After a transitional period to end on 1 July 1992, Ministry of Security personnel officially was to total no more than 137,900, including 2,800 for the central apparatus but not counting support and maintenance staff and guards.[59] About 400 positions were reported to have been abolished, and the generals who headed those posts were supposedly fired or retired.[60] In reality, the Russian government was playing a numbers game to convince the public that the Ministry of Security was a harmless organization. It is not possible to determine the exact size of the MB relative to the elements of the KGB that it absorbed.

The real size of the KGB's staff was never conclusively established, so one is left to rely on estimates that vary significantly and on conflicting official figures. According to Bakatin, the KGB (exclusive of Border Guards, agents and informers, civilian staff, and reserves) was almost 480,000 strong by August 1991.[61] The total given by Barannikov, with the same exclusions, was higher at 513,000.[62] An additional 240,000 served in the Border Guards.[63]

Even if they wanted to function as an efficient authoritarian force, the security organs had to undergo substantial cuts because they were too large, unwieldy, and wasteful. The KGB was a severely bloated bureaucracy.[64] The internal security services of the USSR contained substantial numbers of officers who performed no useful functions and could be furloughed without damage to the chekists' effectiveness. One officer near retirement age told Bakatin that in retrospect he had wasted his career chasing phantoms. Bakatin recalls the officer as saying, "I am going to retire, and there is nothing to remember, life passes for nothing. Moreover, we do not catch anybody. I ran all the time for nothing and I run not even knowing for whom."

Bakatin himself remarked that the system in that respect was a "waste [of] time and personnel."[65] He said that he found that in the KGB Investigation Department, each investigator had a caseload of 0.5 cases per year, while each investigator in the analogous Ministry of Internal Affairs unit on average had more than sixty cases annually.[66] In his words, "The KGB grew fat and its staffs were artificially swollen, which in no way positively influenced the quality of its work."[67] The situation was similar in foreign intelligence. A top espionage officer commented that he found a surprisingly large number of what he called "idlers and parasites."[68]

The bureaucracies of the former KGB had to make significant staff cuts if they were to function efficiently and effectively under their new names. The Ministry of Security announced that most of its cuts would be made through attrition, and *Izvestiya* reported that no particular furloughs were envisioned and that dismissals would primarily affect "only security officers of pensionable age, for whom it is time to stop working on the invisible front anyway."[69]

Unanticipated reductions also occurred. They involved the more talented and outgoing officers, especially the more reformist younger personnel, who would have been an asset to the service.[70] Lucrative business opportunities attracted some of the KGB's best human resources. So many officers were leaving for the private sector in late 1991 when the organs failed to meet payroll that the government was prompted to decree a special salary increase in a bid to entice them to stay. Even those who went into the private sector did not necessarily leave the organs, but remained on duty as members of the "active reserve," a new status created to allow retired officers to maintain their operational affiliations.[71] Many continued to work at their old professions while in business with Western firms—gathering intelligence, assessing potential human assets, raising hard currency, gaining access to needed technology, and reaping other benefits from their new partnerships with foreigners that would have been impossible had they remained on active duty. Numerous KGB generals received lucrative positions as officers or consultants, either to major firms run by the state or newly privatized to the nomenklatura or to new companies involved with trade and banking.[72]

Barannikov's attempts to show how small the MB supposedly was becoming relative to the USSR KGB were inadequate and misleading. In publicizing the disparity in personnel strength between the two, Barannikov did not account for the fact that some former KGB organs functioned separately from the Ministry of Security. The question to be answered was not whether the MB was smaller than the KGB but whether it was smaller than the KGB components it absorbed. Changes in staffing levels could indicate the direction of reform, or lack thereof, taking place in the Soviet security apparatus. Because the Ministry of Security offered no means of measuring those reductions and refused to provide information about its structure or force levels,[73] one must rely on guesswork. It is possible to arrive at a rough estimate of real staff cuts and thereby make a general conclusion about whether or not the chekist omnipresence was meaningfully reduced under President Yeltsin in his first two years as leader of post-Soviet Russia.

To estimate the Ministry of Security's relative strength, one may proceed from the USSR KGB level of 513,000 offered by Barannikov, exclusive of Border Guards. This figure is unsatisfactory because it is neither substantiated nor verifiable, but it may be taken as the official size. Add to this Bakatin's official estimate of 240,000 Border Guard troops and the total is 753,000 KGB personnel (nearly ten times the size of all U.S. federal intelligence, law enforcement and security services combined[74]). The difference between 753,000 and the 137,900 staff members allowed in the MB's founding decree leaves more than 615,000 chekists. Of the largely conscripted Border Guards, approximately 180,000 remained under Russian Federation command by mid-1992,[75] leaving roughly 60,000 divided among the other republics or lost to attrition, desertion, or failure to report for duty. "Tens of thousands" of KGB special troops that had been transferred from military and MVD units in the 1980s (including the 103rd Airborne, the 117th Narosomensk regiment, and the Pskov, Ryazan and Tula units) were returned to those services, according to Bakatin.[76] Numbers are not known, but "tens of thousands" conservatively would be no less than 20,000 troops.[77]

Thus, total KGB personnel (753,000), minus Border Guards (240,000) and special troops (20,000 at minimum), leaves at least 493,000 personnel. Bakatin reports that 90,000 USSR KGB staff members were transferred to the jurisdiction of the non-Russian republics in which they served,[78] leaving a balance of 403,000. Another 12,000 to 16,000 were employed by the First Chief Directorate and transferred to the Russian External Intelligence Service (SVR), bringing the difference to 387,000.[79] About 85,000 "troops and civilian staffers" were reportedly transferred to what became the Federal Agency for Government Communications and Information (the former KGB Eighth Chief Directorate, the Sixteenth Directorate and Communications Troops) and the Main Guard Directorate (the former KGB Ninth Directorate, the Alfa Group of the former Seventh Directorate, and the 500-man Vympel spetsnaz forces from the former First Chief Directorate).[80] More personnel may have been employed in the communications and electronic intelligence services, which consumed one-fourth of the entire USSR KGB budget.[81] The balance is now about 302,000, which by deduction should approximate the size of the Ministry of Security, exclusive of Border Troops.

This was more than twice the amount (137,900) permitted by the Ministry of Security's founding decree. Even if the estimate is tens of thousands off, given the unsatisfactory numbers available to reach the conclusion above, no evidence has been offered to suggest that anywhere near half the MB's personnel strength was cut, especially since the stated policy was to realize most staff reductions through attrition. The largest set of announced firings occurred under Bakatin, and these numbered no more than a few score.[82]

No independent verification was possible. Members of the Supreme Soviet with jurisdiction over the security organs said in mid-1993 that they had no way of knowing the staffing or budget levels. One lawmaker reported that in every village in his region remain small contingents of state security officers with nothing substantive to do, an observation supported by three of his colleagues.[83] Therefore, one must conclude that the pre-putsch KGB cadres were largely intact, and that the Ministry of Security, scattered in every town and village across eleven time zones, is far larger than the Russian government announced it would be. When one considers the several hundred thousand MVD Internal Troops still standing by 1994—troops which receive guidance, intelligence and "political security" from the chekists[84]—the former KGB internal organs remained a formidable potential coercive force.

Yeltsin Repeats the Mistakes of Gorbachev

As he crafted the first policies of an independent Russia President Yeltsin repeated the mistakes that Gorbachev had made: He relied almost unconditionally on the chekists as a pillar of power and initiated economic reforms mortgaged on a security apparatus that was unfettered by civilian oversight or checks and balances.[85] Barannikov began the process of reversing some of Bakatin's 1991 reforms. His first and most obvious move, as noted, was to convince Yeltsin to elevate state security from an agency to a ministry. Second, he acted quickly to prevent the transfer of military counterintelligence, the former USSR KGB Third Chief Directorate, to the Commonwealth of Independent States military General Staff. At his prompting, President Yeltsin signed a decree on 24 January 1992 which formally transferred military counterintelligence from the CIS General Staff to the Ministry of Security.[86] In reality, the previously announced physical transfer from state security to the military had never taken place (Bakatin had changed his mind), but the decree officially barred the change from occurring.[87]

These moves were accompanied by obligatory public statements calling for parliamentary controls over the apparatus.[88] Barannikov oversaw authorship of the Russian Federation's Law on Security, the fundamental base upon which all other national security legislation would be built. This law, discussed in detail in Chapter 6, sharply expanded the definition of "security" as well as the scope of the security services themselves.

More major structural changes in the Ministry of Security came in June. This time, Yeltsin and Barannikov did not even obtain symbolic Supreme Soviet approval. On the eve of Yeltsin's trip to Washington for a summit meeting with President George Bush, Barannikov drafted a number of decrees for the Russian leader's signature. The first decrees ordered the removal of four MB generals and about eighty other officers, many of them financial managers alleged to be "corrupt."[89] Despite the reported commission of such crimes, none of the officers was known to have been arrested, tried or punished.

Concurrent with the mass firings—characterized by one critic as a "public cleansing" of reformers[90]—the resignation of First Deputy Minister Oleynikov, the KGB careerist and former Bakatin ally, was announced. "Poor health" was the reason cited. A more credible rationale became apparent 17 June, when Oleynikov's replacement was announced: Deputy Security Minister Nikolay Golushko, a hard-liner who recently had quit his post as chief of the Ukrainian state security service.[91] Golushko had served as Ukrainian KGB chief from 1987 to 1991 and had taken allegiance to an independent Ukraine when the country became independent. Elsewhere, the shift would have been viewed as a defection, but Ukraine made no issue of it, even though Golushko reportedly took his archives with him.

A thirty year KGB veteran who had headed the Fifth Chief Directorate subunit to combat ethnic and nationalist sentiment, Golushko rose in stature as Barannikov settled into position, becoming MB chief of staff while retaining his new first deputy minister rank.[92] Other casualties included Counterintelligence Directorate chief Viktor Klishin, who left in disgrace amid unsubstantiated charges of corruption and was replaced by Viktor Zorin.[93] In addition, Border Forces Director Kalinichenko was also removed and replaced by Lt. Gen. Vladimir Shlyakhtin.[94] Almost simultaneously the MB absorbed the Border Forces, which had been an independent service since the putsch.[95] Barannikov also elevated the status of training facilities, renaming the former KGB Higher School to the more grandiose Academy of State Security.[96]

The security minister's stature grew a month later, when he and Defense Minister Pavel Grachev reportedly were decorated with "marshal's stars" in an official ceremony with President Yeltsin.[97] This award was unusual because the rank of marshal had been abolished. The presentation puzzled some former KGB officers who were interviewed; even as an unofficial symbol, it struck some Russian authorities as absurd. The event marked the first time a state security chief had been awarded such a high military rank since early 1941, when Stalin promoted NKVD Chief Lavrenti Beria to the marshal-equivalent rank of commissar general of state security. Beria formally was awarded the title "marshal" in July 1945.[98] The decoration of Barannikov, if inexplicable, is significant given what it represented.

Barannikov ensured that his Ministry of Security would enjoy extremely broad powers. The MB had absorbed no fewer than seventeen major KGB units, including those responsible for counterintelligence, border protection, military and MVD counterintelligence, nuclear weapons storage, security of subways, railroads, shipping, and the state-owned Aeroflot airline political repression, economic and industrial security, counter-organized crime, counternarcotics, surveillance, security of bunkers and most government buildings, analysis, military construction, technical laboratories, mail interception, archives, wire-tapping, investigations, and training.

The Ministry of Security was also responsible for monitoring state, cooperative, and private businesses in the transportation, industrial, and communications sectors (while many of its officers used their positions to help businesses they were running on the side), monitoring the mass media, analyzing social and political affairs, and protecting patents.[99] The only major responsibilities of the former KGB that the MB lacked were foreign intelligence, codes and ciphers, signals intelligence, communications troops, and presidential guards. The responsibilities and duties of the MB were codified by law in August 1992.[100]

Barannikov's Quest for Legitimacy

Like the KGB under Kryuchkov, the Ministry of Security under Barannikov and his successors considered crimefighting to be a major function.[101] The ministry's Economic Security Department, the former KGB Sixth Directorate, conducted economic counterintelligence and selectively investigated corruption. Economic Security agents arrested senior officials of the Russian Ministry of External Economic Relations' Spetsvneshtekhnika firm for taking bribes from foreign firms in October 1992.[102] The former Sixth Directorate, however, engaged in corruption on its own, including manipulation of the exchange rate.[103] The MB also had a Chief Directorate for Combating Contraband and Corruption.[104]

Fighting rampant corruption is by any standard a pressing priority for Russia. Nevertheless, it seems more likely that MB officials embraced anticorruption more as an excuse for the MB's continued existence than as a means of improving societal ills. (Furthermore, there is no organ in Russia that independently investigates corruption within the security service—another sign of chekist supremacy.)

In 1991, Barannikov scored the KGB for having become involved in crimefighting, saying the job was not for chekists but for the uniformed militsiya police. Compared to the large crimefighting apparatus of the MVD, state security's anticrime directorate was "insignificant," according to former MVD and KGB Chief Bakatin.[105] One of Barannikov's justifications for designing the December 1991 merger between state security and the MVD into the Ministry of Security and Internal Affairs was to remove duplication of duties. As MBVD minister, he derided the KGB's crimefighting functions as Kryuchkov's excuse to keep chekism alive and busy:

> The *militsia* waged a struggle against organized crime and the KGB waged a struggle against organized crime. As though two types of organizers of criminal communities are operating in our country. This is absurd! . . .
> But why, it seems to me, did the KGB get involved in this problem at all? Its leaders simply felt that sooner or later they would be asked for concrete results, for something real done in the state's interests. But what could they reply? Remember the achievements of the "political" main administrations? Or of the Sixth Administration, which "protected" the economy. . . . You cannot report back that you have been combatting dissidence in politics and in the economy. And so crime was needed.[106]

Barannikov's quick change of heart was significant given his unexpected loss of control over the MVD's crimefighting machinery when the MBVD was split. His struggle against crime, not unlike that of Kryuchkov, Chebrikov, or for that matter, Andropov in the last years of the Brezhnev regime, was part of an image-making effort to provide state security with a popular raison d'etre that it lacked and a political tool with which to ruin opponents in and out of government. Yet corruption within the Ministry of Security was rampant even at the highest levels. Barannikov distanced himself from Yeltsin and tried to act neutral in the president's conflict with the Supreme Soviet. Gradually it became clear that Barannikov actually sided with Khasbulatov.

As he prepared to dissolve the Supreme Soviet, Yeltsin dismissed Barannikov in July, using as a pretext the minister's alleged corruption and the failure of the MB Border Troops to prevent the entry of Islamic guerrillas from Afghanistan into Tajikistan. It was rumored that a real reformer would be named his successor, but after a few weeks the dynamics within the Kremlin became clearer when Golushko was formally appointed. Golushko's career in fighting nationalism—even the type of Russian nationalism now embraced by Rutskoy and Khasbulatov—meant the president would have to rely on the chekists more than ever, as long as he had the unchallenged power to name who would lead them.

Conclusions to be drawn about the Ministry of Security, given the evidence, are grim. The ministry was not significantly smaller than the KGB components that it comprised, nor were its functions much less extensive. Senior officers committed to even the mildest political reforms, including Yampolskiy, Ivanenko, Podelyakin, Oleynikov, and Stepashin, were removed. Yampolskiy was succeeded by the putschist Trubin. Ivanenko was replaced by Barannikov. Podelyakin was ousted in favor of Oleynikov, who was removed only to be replaced by dissident-hunting chekist Golushko. Golushko eventually took Barannikov's seat as minister. Stepashin, who headed security in St. Petersburg, was ousted in October 1992 and replaced by Viktor Cherkesov, a former interrogator of dissidents in the KGB Fifth Chief Directorate.[107]

A year later, after the armed confrontation at the Supreme Soviet in which the Ministry of Security played a key role, Stepashin became Cherkesov's boss as first deputy minister of security. He quickly disappointed reformers by announcing that the ministry's powers had to be expanded. By late 1993 the Ministry of Security was actively seeking new roles, especially in the area of economic security and countering organized crime, to protect its positions in Russian society. It continued to observe chekist traditions, including the seventy-sixth anniversary of the Cheka's founding.[108] After suffering enormous political losses in the December elections for a new parliament, Yeltsin utilized the broad presidential authority granted by the new constitution to reshuffle his state security apparatus and placed Stepashin in charge. The MB was renamed the Federal Counterintelligence Service.

Federal Counterintelligence Service

Stung by his political losses in the December 1993 parliamentary elections yet taking advantage of the slim margin of public support for his new constitution, President Yeltsin moved immediately to consolidate the chekists further under his personal control, but to weaken their ability to challenge him by splintering them into separate, smaller agencies. The changes, which came in the wake of his televised complaints that the Ministry of Security had insufficiently supported him during the October confrontation at the Supreme Soviet, indicated that the president was more concerned with political loyalty than professionalism.[109] He may also have been angry at chekist backing of hard-line candidates and parties during the election, not only for ultranationalist Vladimir Zhirinovskiy,[110] but for those representing Communist and other non-reformist blocs.

Yeltsin and his top aides recognized that the main problem of the security organs was their chekist nature. Remarked presidential confidant Gennadiy Burbulis, "The results show that we made a mistake when we did not disband the state security agencies after August 1991."[111] The president was even more specific. On 21 December he issued a decree to abolish the Ministry of Security, calling the organ "unreformable." In a remarkable admission, Yeltsin's decree recognized the continuity with chekism and the shallowness of all previous reforms:

> The system of bodies of the VChK-OGPU-NKVD-MGB-KGB-MB [All-Russian Extraordinary Commission to Combat Counterrevolution and Sabotage (Cheka)-United State Political Directorate-People's Commissariat of Internal Affairs-Ministry of State-Security-Committee for State Security-Ministry of Security] has proved unreformable. The attempts at reorganization that have been made in recent years were basically superficial and cosmetic. Up to the present moment the Russian Ministry of Security lacks a strategic concept of ensuring Russia's security. Counterintelligence work has deteriorated. The system of political investigation has been mothballed and could easily be recreated.
>
> Against the background of the democratic and constitutional transformations taking place in Russia, the existing system of ensuring Russia's security has outlived itself; it is ineffective, burdensome for the state budget, and a restraining factor in the implementation of political and economic reforms.[112]

Changes had been planned within the Ministry of Security for months, but like Russia's absorption of the Soviet organs in 1991, the new change came as a complete surprise to the chekist leaders and even the president's inner circle.[113] The MB's legal successor was called the Federal Counterintelligence Service (Federalnaya sluzhba kontrrazvedki, FSK). Yet despite the wording of the decree, the FSK maintained the continuum with the past. Yeltsin named not a reformer to head the new service, but the same notorious dissident-hunter who headed the MB, Nikolay Golushko.

Although the FSK chief retained his status as minister, the internal security organs were lowered in the bureaucratic hierarchy from ministry to a service directly under presidential control. At the same time Yeltsin reorganized much of the government, including the defense ministry, to concentrate controls in his own hands. Yeltsin strengthened his power in outlying regions of Russia, created the post of National Security Adviser so he would have someone in his apparatus with day-to-day administration of the "power ministries," and created new bodies to supervise the country's increasingly critical news media.[114] According to Oleg Lobov, secretary of the presidential Security Council, the FSK would be an instrument of presidential power. In his words, "This service must support the president. . . . The counterintelligence service is called upon to defend this new presidential rule."[115]

Yet Yeltsin had no game plan for reorganization; he left the details up to the chekists themselves. The changes were ordered in three initial decrees, two of which were public and one secret. The service's personnel strength would be limited to 75,000 officers, a 46 percent reduction from the official level of the MB, exclusive of clerical and support staff, academic and scientific personnel, military medical personnel, guards, and maintenance staff;[116] though some chekist veterans doubt that the number would be that low.[117] The vast majority of reductions were simple transfers of offices and personnel to the MVD and other security organs, so the actual reduction of chekists in government was negligible.[118]

To increase efficiency, some directorates were disbanded and others were merged where they duplicated or overlapped with one another.[119] The service remained top-heavy with more than 200 generals, some of whom were new promotions. Shortly before creating the FSK, Yeltsin had promoted twenty-seven chekists to general.[120]

Bureaucratically the FSK was led by a director who had one first deputy and five deputies, and who led the service's eleven-man collegium.[121] There were 227 departments and territorial organizations, all headed by generals; and 783 sub-departments.[122] The following Ministry of Security offices remained intact within the FSK: the Directorate for Counterintelligence Operations; the Directorate for Counterintelligence Provision for Strategic Installations; the Directorate for Military Counterintelligence; and the Directorate for Combating Terrorism. Virtually no staff cuts were envisioned for those organs either at the central or local levels. The Secretariat, the Material and Technical Services Directorate, and the Military Organizational Development Directorate were expected to suffer some reductions.[123]

Plans were reportedly made to cut the FSK central staff and strengthen its regional branches over a six month period; the central apparatus would be more than halved from 3,500 to 1,500 persons, with most of the reduction from management instead of operations.[124] A unit to fight corruption in the upper levels of government was also retained,[125] as was jurisdiction of the "active reserve" corps of chekists, which Golushko said would be attached to "ministries, departments, organizations, establishments, and firms."[126]

Cuts were planned for the Secretariat, the Material and Technical Services Directorate, and the Military Organizational Development Directorate.[127] The main FSK offices were moved out of the old Cheka headquarters at 2 Lubyanka Square to a neighboring and more modern building in the Lubyanka complex; the Border Troops moved into the old offices. While this was hailed as a great symbolic change,[128] in reality it meant that the border forces remained part of the chekist bureaucracy.

The problem of revanchist personnel was also addressed—at least for public consumption. A "certification commission" immediately was organized with a nine-week mandate to screen between 200 and 250 senior officers to determine the compatibility of their ideology with democracy, and their professionalism with the needs of a democratic society. Officers' political views were a major criteria in the screening process.[129] An encouraging sign that the commission would lead to an improvement in security personnel was the presence of human rights figure Sergey Kovalev on the panel,[130] but close associates of Kovalev in private dismissed his presence as window dressing.[131]

In the end, the certification commission rejected only thirteen of the 227 high-ranking chekists it screened, and said that none was rejected for having political views incompatible with democracy.[132] Several of the rejections were due to the advanced ages of the officers.[133] The commission seemed like more of a rubber stamp than a true body to screen undesirables from sensitive and powerful positions.

The staff cuts were not as drastic as anticipated. Although the announced cuts in FSK personnel would reduce manpower by nearly half, operational counterintelligence units would not be reduced.[134] Golushko himself denied from the beginning that the commission would carry out a "weeding-out process," and a top presidential security official said there would be no "purge" within the organs.[135] Substandard officers were promised new jobs in the MVD, the new tax police (headed by chekists), and the General Procurator's office.[136]

Yeltsin's strategy was to make the main internal security organ weaker politically, and to disperse the strength of the chekists by scattering them throughout the government. Although this may have served to reduce the chekists' ability to threaten the central regime, it also has the effect of bursting a fungus: The spores are no longer contained but distributed through the entire society. The FSK was to have lost the Investigative Department, which supposedly was to be transferred to the Office of the Procurator General (though 90 percent of the department's 500 investigators remained with the FSK, staffing operational departments);[137] the Department for Combating Corruption and Contraband, which along with other crimefighting units was said to be transferred to the MVD; and unspecified "special operations subunits" which were moved to the Federal Agency for Government Communications and Information. Economic security departments were said to be ordered to be placed under the Ministry of the Economy as its own economic counterintelligence directorate.[138] It was unclear whether the changes would be carried out, for the chekists resisted them strongly, and the presidential apparatus soon restored the FSK's mandate to fight ordinary crime.[139]

The facilities and personnel of the maximum security Lefortovo prison were placed under MVD supervision. Apparently the reason was that the chekists in charge balked at helping investigate Yeltsin's arch rivals former Vice President Aleksandr Rutskoy and ex-Supreme Soviet Chairman Ruslan Khasbulatov—who were imprisoned at Lefortovo for having incited violence and bloodshed while leading the October 1993 rebellion.[140]

Exacerbating the situation with the president was the February 1994 resolution by parliament which amnestied the October inmates. Golushko's support for the president during the October 1993 confrontation with the Supreme Soviet was said to have been lukewarm, and his failure to prevent Rutskoy, Khasbulatov and the others from leaving Lefortovo cost him his career.[141]

Stepashin became the new FSK chief. He soon disappointed reformist well-wishers who expected real change. His deputies included some of the worst figures from the KGB of old: Aleksandr Strelkov, who until 1992 was chief of a department responsible for the gulag system in Russia; Valeriy Timofeyev, former KGB chief of the city of Gorkiy where Andrey Sakharov was forcibly exiled; and personnel director Igor Mezhakov, previously of the KGB Fifth Chief Directorate.[142]

The internal security director openly challenged the plans to deprive the FSK of its crimefighting and economic capabilities. Stepashin said on national television, "I'll tell you straight that the special services will not go through another such perestroika or *katastroyka,*" making a pun on the catastrophic effects that restructuring was having on them. "I would like to stress once again—this is very important for those who hear me, for our colleagues—there will be no such perestroykas." He promised a public relations blitz to help the chekists block further reorganization: "Clearly, we should try and improve our importance and constantly say that we're necessary and important, not only and perhaps not so much by public statements, but by concrete actions and putting things into effect."[143]

Stepashin affirmed the FSK would "most certainly" keep the old agent networks, and was adamant that the identities of past KGB collaborators never be made public. He also said that his apparatus would continue to conduct domestic spying operations against Russian citizens based on their political views.[144] A journalist who interviewed internal security officers after Yeltsin's decree abolishing the MB reported, "As for the statement about political surveillance being stopped, people in the Security Ministry say that this is inseparable from the very existence of the state. . . . Therefore, nearly all Security Ministry officers say that the president's statement about stopping these actions in Russia are of a purely rhetorical nature. In all likelihood, all such services will be preserved and, possibly, reinforced.[145]

Though ostensibly aimed at potentially violent extremists, Stepashin's affirmation of political spying cast chills on many reformers, especially critics of the continued chekist nature of the security organs. He lashed out at "enemies" in the democratic movement and among journalists, even going so far as to call human rights activists "terrorists."[146] This stark change in rhetoric seems to reflect the influence of the hard-core chekists around him, placed there apparently in exchange for their unquestioning support of Yeltsin's powers.[147]

Other Security Organs

The collapse of the USSR left Vadim Bakatin without an official position. Yeltsin formally relieved him of his duties as the MB absorbed all structures of the Inter-republic Security Service (MSB) on Russian soil. Aside from the MB and its FSK descendant, four other security services emerged from the old KGB: the Federal Agency for Government Communications and Information, the Main Guard Directorate, Border Forces, and the External Intelligence Service. Additionally, the Supreme Soviet created new organs, probably at the instigation of the Ministry of Security, which broadened not only the definition of security but the number of organizations responsible for security operations. Confusion reigned; no coordinating mechanism was yet in place. Additional new security services were set up in early 1994 as Yeltsin sought to bring the organs under his personal control. Descriptions of the services follow.

Federal Agency for Government Communications and Information

Created on 28 December 1991, the Federal Agency for Government Communications and Information (Federalnoye agentsvo pravitelstvennoy sviazi i informatsiy, FAPSI) is endowed with both internal and foreign intelligence functions. It took over the responsibilities of the short-lived Soviet Government Communications Committee (KPS), which had combined the USSR KGB Eighth Chief Directorate, the 16th Directorate, and the Communications Troops. The agency, which has some of Russia's most gifted and skilled linguists and mathematicians, assumed control of Russia's physical communications system, including government telephone lines, high-frequency communication, and cryptography services that most other former Soviet republics are dependent upon.[148] FAPSI immediately sought to take control of government policy concerning information analysis.[149] The official announcement of its founding attempted to liken it to the National Security Agency of the United States.[150]

The agency operates the large signals intelligence-gathering facility at Lourdes, Cuba, per an agreement signed in Havana between Cuban Vice President Leonel Soto and Russian Deputy Prime Minister for Foreign Economic Affairs Aleksandr Shokhin on 3 November 1992.[151] Shokhin's signature on the accord indicates that the agency plays a major role in Russia's international business and trade and as such would be deeply engaged in economic and commercial espionage against the United States and Latin America to benefit favored Russian enterprises. Early statutes gave FAPSI the right to engage in the foreign telecommunications business. Its general director, KGB Lt. Gen. Aleksandr V. Starovoytov, announced that it would offer and solicit entrepreneurial ventures and would lease closed communications channels to financial and business groups.[152] The agency presumably monitors any information traffic on its open and leased channels.

Government agencies responsible for communications, reflecting the paranoia of the Soviet period, began to voice alarm in 1993 that computer networks and information systems in the country could not be controlled. Many of the Russian government's new IBM-compatible computer systems, installed in 1990, are effectively impossible for the chekists to regulate. The free flow of even nonclassified information posed a problem to Gen. Starovoytov and others.

Referring to information and communications systems as "society's strategic resource," Starovoytov deplored the proliferation of Western-installed systems and developed an initiative to increase "state control . . . over the information and communications sector." The initiative called for developing "the capacities of the existing communications systems [in a fashion] that will make it possible to switch to a system of confidential communications later on with minimum costs involved." This was not merely a plan to develop security for classified electronic data. It was a program to restrict the free flow of information and to enable state security to develop a monopoly over all electronic information, both government and private.[153]

Starovoytov complained that some "state-owned and commercial organizations" were acting "counter to this line" by developing costly systems of their own and by working in joint ventures with foreign firms "outside state control." Western communications companies, he argued, were "deliberately" introducing "into the Russian market such systems . . . that would enable [foreign intelligence] services to control information being processed and, if need be, to influence the situation in the country." Starovoytov's initiative was backed by the state Committee for Information, the Ministry of Communications, and the Ministry of Security. The Russian journalist who revealed the plan commented that the goal was "effectively to cut government agencies at all levels out of state-of-the-art information technologies and to bring all flows of information back to 'former KGB channels.'" She continued,

> The already substantial disinformation capacities of the Russian secret services will increase accordingly.
>
> At a time when super-confidential information constantly leaks from the presidential office under the very eyes of the secret services, the authors of the initiative are primarily preoccupied with the need to make secret the processing and analysis of open-source information. . . . Second, one can discern an attempt by the post-KGB structures to impose "on the sly" control over their "historical rival" in the confidential information area—the Main Intelligence Administration (GRU)—an attempt, it should be noted, that had never been allowed by the CPSU leadership for reasons of self-preservation.[154]

In early 1994 FAPSI won a year-long battle with the Administration for Information Resources of the presidential staff to control a "single information space" in the upper levels of governments of Russia and other CIS members. Although most of the administration's work was unclassified, FAPSI insisted on controlling all computerized communications in the Kremlin bureaucracy. The chekists prevailed by persuading President Yeltsin to abolish his own information administration and transfer its functions to FAPSI.[155]

Given the government's continuing imposition of state control over print and broadcast media, by means ranging from subsidies and licensing to tight regulation of paper supply, censorship, and even placement of state security officers or veterans on editorial boards, the plans of the Federal Agency for Government Communications and Information to control electronic communications lines show a concerted effort in Russia to control all forms of information.

Main Guard Directorate

The core of the Main Guard Directorate (Glavnoye upravleniye okhrany) is the former USSR KGB Ninth (Guards) Directorate, which was removed from the KGB following the August 1991 putsch and placed under the joint control of the Soviet and Russian Federation presidents. Between the putsch and the Soviet collapse, the body was known as the USSR Protection Service. Headed by Lt. Gen. Mikhail Barsukov, the Main Guard Directorate has the status of a ministry and is responsible for the physical protection of Russian political leaders (including the mayors of Moscow and St. Petersburg) and foreign dignitaries, and protection of certain government buildings. Barsukov also holds the title of Commandant of the Kremlin.

The Directorate, with no clearly defined legal functions, is accountable to no one but the president. It is reported to be 25,000 strong, also containing the 5,000-man Presidential Regiment which was formerly part of the KGB Kremlin Guards;[156] its own intelligence and counterintelligence forces; and the Alfa Group, an elite KGB special operations commando unit formerly of the USSR KGB Seventh (Surveillance) Directorate.

Alfa was deployed in the 12-13 January 1991 armed repression in Vilnius, Lithuania, to seize the communications tower and crush civil unrest.[157] The Alfa unit won international fame during the Moscow putsch, when it was widely reported that its men refused to attack the Russian Supreme Soviet building.[158] As a reward, Yeltsin made Alfa an autonomous presidential guard unit. Apparently he did not appreciate that Alfa was not trained or configured for such a function. It was later argued that the Alfa commandos' failure to attack the Russian parliament was not necessarily an act of rebellion against coup leaders; they simply had not received an attack order.

A second highly trained KGB force in the Main Guard Directorate was the Vympel spetsnaz troops. Vympel's multilingual personnel, all of whom are officers, specialize in combat, sabotage, and infliction of mass terror and chaos behind enemy lines in time of war.[159] Created in 1979, Vympel served as the shock force prior to the invasion of Afghanistan. In its first foreign operation, Vympel commandos stormed the presidential palace in Kabul and assassinated the inhabitants, including Afghan President Hafizullah Amin and seven of his children.[160] This allowed Amin's successor, Babrak Karmal, to "invite" the Soviet army to intervene in his country. Vympel forces also saw combat in Angola, Mozambique, Nicaragua and Vietnam.[161]

After Vympel, in a joint operation with Alfa, refused to shoot when it was deployed to take over the Russian Supreme Soviet building during the October 1993 rebellion, President Yeltsin ordered the force transferred to the MVD. Its members quit in droves. One report said that of its 500 members, 320 moved to other agencies and 120 quit.[162] Another report stated that 110 of 180 operational officers resigned almost on the spot.[163] Many former Vympel men organized a support fund and went into business; some trained illegal paramilitary groups.[164] Those who remained were assigned to combat nuclear terrorism.[165]

The directorate wields political patronage by controlling many perks of power, including the government limousine fleet, health facilities, stores, tailor shops, special communications installations, and other services. Control of these privileges alarmed the acting chairman of the Constitutional Court, Nikolay Vitruk, whose concerns were summarized, "On the one hand Minister Barsukov is supposed to take orders from the premier and his vice premiers. But on the other, it is on himself that all of them depend."[166]

Yeltsin also transferred the RSFSR MVD parliamentary guards unit, led by its chief, Aleksandr Korzhakov, to the Main Guard Directorate. This unit, now an "autonomous subdivision," provided for Yeltsin's personal security when he was president of the RSFSR Supreme Soviet.[167] In November 1991, Supreme Soviet Chairman Ruslan Khasbulatov, a Yeltsin ally who was on the way to becoming his most potent rival, created a new parliamentary guard force from an MVD unit, removing the personnel from MVD jurisdiction and placing them under a new parliament-controlled Directorate for the Protection of Organs of State Power. Their leader, Ivan Boyko, reported directly to Khasbulatov. However, the officers continued to wear the MVD uniform and insignia. The force recruited more guards from the MVD until it reached 5,000 in strength. The guards were financed from the

Supreme Soviet's operating budget. Yet people's deputies were not aware of the changes for months.

Furthermore, Khasbulatov directed the unit to guard seventy-five other facilities, including Ostankino state television, the Foreign Ministry, the Ministry of Justice, the Supreme Court, the Procuracy, and the State Committee for Statistics, in an apparent bid to expand his ability to control government institutions. Igor Nikulin, a subcommittee chairman in the Committee on Defense and Security responsible for drafting legislation on guarding the Russian political leadership, said that the whole arrangement was illegal. The directorate was formed without parliamentary approval, and the guards' removal from MVD command was apparently secret from the lawmakers themselves. Nikulin said, "I am sure that the majority of deputies do not even suspect that at the entrance to the White House their passes are checked by men who are not militsiamen, although they wear the uniform." The parliamentary guard unit was not subject to oversight by the Committee on Defense and Security, and was answerable to no one but Khasbulatov.[168]

A law on the guards service was passed by both houses of the Supreme Soviet in November 1992 making the Main Guard Directorate responsible only for the security of the president, the Supreme Soviet, and the Constitutional Court and subordinate to and controlled by the president of the republic, who would appoint its general director.[169] The law also required Khasbulatov-controlled guards of other buildings and ministries to return to the MVD.[170]

The Main Guard Directorate took on so many functions, including security of the Rosvooruzheniye state weapons export firm, that the president created a separate Presidential Security Service headed by KGB veteran Aleksandr Korzhakov, who had been Yeltsin's personal bodyguard since 1986.[171]

Federal Border Service

The Russian Federation Border Forces officially assumed responsibility for guarding not only Russia's land frontiers and points of transit but also the perimeter of the Federation coastal waters and the Continental Shelf. With 180,000 troops in early 1993, the forces were smaller than the USSR KGB Border Troops Chief Directorate, which had performed the same duties with 240,000 troops.[172] A Commonwealth of Independent States border force was originally envisioned under Russian domination with headquarters in Mensk, Belarus, but the idea was scrapped as unworkable when Ukraine swore in its own border guards, effectively assuming control of the frontier structures on its territory.

A survey of border guard troops throughout the CIS in January 1992 found that they were distrusted and ignored by locals in the turbulent Caucasus and were being "quietly" expelled from the three Baltic states. Command and discipline had completely broken down along the periphery. According to the survey's conclusion, border guard activity "in its previous form has lost all meaning since it is not clear what a Ukrainian serving in a Maritime Kray or a Kazakh serving in the Baltic should do and whether Uzbeks can decide autonomously to serve in the Far East or come home." Furthermore, "No one is answerable for the results of guarding the border. The Border Guard Committee . . . is waiting in vain for the leaders of the sovereign states to finally reach some agreement and say what the troops should do. Officers at outposts and detachments are waiting in vain for their leaders in Moscow to prove that they are on the job."[173]

Security Minister Barannikov quickly brought the independent Russian Border Troops under MB tutelage in June 1992. Under the Ministry of Security they ceased to be an independent service and expanded their role in supporting pro-Moscow regimes elsewhere in the CIS, such as Tajikistan, which has no common border with Russia. As noted above, Lt. Gen. Ilya Kalinichenko, who had been commander of the USSR KGB Border Guards, was retained until June 1992, when President Yeltsin issued a decree authored by Barannikov to fire him. He was replaced by his own chief, Lt. Gen. Vladimir Shlyakhtin.[174] Yeltsin fired Shlyakhtin in July 1993 for the Border Troops' inability to stop Islamic guerrilla groups from infiltrating into Tajikistan from neighboring Afghanistan, and he removed Barannikov days later on a similar pretext. Border troops were removed from the MB and made a Federal Border Service in the January 1994 reorganization of the federal government and internal security services. The Federal Border Service's new chief was not a chekist but an army officer, Col. Gen. Andrey Nikolayev;[175] his position probably gave the military substantial influence over the border troops.

Security Organs in the Civil Sector

The 1992 Law on Security authorized the government to create apparently independent security departments within state enterprises, nuclear power stations, and the transportation sector and mandated the establishment of agricultural and ecological security inspectorates.[176] The extent of chekist co-optation of these security services is unknown, but the MB wrote the actual draft law and most of the country's experienced personnel in these sectors are from the state security apparatus. One may deduce that the degree of co-optation was high. The Law on Foreign Intelligence, passed the same year, allows for foreign intelligence units of "ministries and departments" to be established throughout the government. As noted above, the Procuracy, Ministry of the Economy, Ministry of Internal Affairs, Ministry of Justice and other agencies absorbed partial or entire chekist units that had been part of the KGB and Ministry of Security. As the definitions of state security and state secrets broadened under Yeltsin, so did the authority of government agencies. Prior to the Soviet collapse only five or six bureaucracies could impose secrecy, but since that time the authority has expanded to approximately thirty government organizations.[177]

President Yeltsin also named a chekist, Anatoliy Kruglov, to head the Federal Customs Service, an agency not technically part of the organs, but one which had been led by KGB generals Vitaliy Boyarov and Nikolay Yermakov during the Gorbachev period.[178]

Russia's tax enforcement organ, the Department of Tax Police of the State Tax Committee, were also staffed by chekists from the Ministry of Security, External Intelligence Service, FAPSI and Main Guard Directorate, and headed by Maj. Gen. Sergey Almasov, who had been KGB chief for the closed city of Gorkiy (now Nizhniy Novgorod).[179]

External Intelligence Service

Russia's central foreign intelligence organ, the External Intelligence Service (Sluzhba vnesnhey razvedki, SVR), based at Yasenevo just outside of Moscow, is the former USSR KGB First Chief Directorate. Due to its size, the special nature of its work and its ramifications on international relations, and the quantity of information available, the SVR merits a detailed description. See section entitled "External Intelligence Service," which appears below the next section.

Services that Did Not Originate in the KGB

Security and intelligence services that were not bureaucratic offshoots of the KGB, such as the Ministry of Internal Affairs (MVD) uniformed police force and the MVD Internal Troops retained essentially the same functions and names as they had under the Soviet system and maintained their own chekist iconography.[180] So did the Main Intelligence Directorate (GRU), the military intelligence organ of the former Soviet General Staff, which was transferred not to the CIS General Staff but to the new Russian General Staff.

Col. Gen. Yevgeniy Timokhin, who headed the GRU until his removal in mid-1992, said that the service would discontinue operations in CIS states apart from Russia, but denied that its overseas operations would be curtailed. He told *Krasnaya zvezda* that the GRU was organized into three main parts: Strategic Intelligence Services, Technical Services, and Operational Intelligence Services in the army, air force, and navy.[181] Timokhin's successor, Lt. Gen. Fyodor Ivanovich Ladygin said when asked if the structure of the GRU would remain the same, "The old structure proved its worth, and so there is no reason to change it radically."[182]

Both the MVD and the GRU continue to be co-opted by the chekists in the Federal Counterintelligence Service (FSK), which controls counterintelligence for both bodies. The MVD's elite Dzerzhinskiy Division is believed to be under FSK operational control. The MB also retained military counterintelligence that penetrates the GRU; in late 1993 there was much renewed talk of returning that function to the armed forces, but the change did not take place as of mid-1994.

External Intelligence Service (SVR)

Like the Ministry of Security and Internal Affairs (MBVD), the SVR was established by decree effective 20 December 1991, the seventy-first anniversary of the founding of the Cheka foreign intelligence service, and the seventy-fourth anniversary of the Cheka itself. President Yeltsin was out of the country at a G-7 summit in Rome and thus had to have signed a postdated decree so that its official establishment would fall on the Cheka's birthday. Thus the "new" intelligence service represented not a symbolic break with the past but a continuum. This point is important because the SVR has taken pains to distance itself from the KGB publicly, especially among intellectual and political elites in the West, and has wooed Western secret services for mutual cooperation.

According to the decree, the SVR would "organize intelligence activity in the interests of Russia's security and supply the bodies of state authority and administration with information." The decree stated that within a month of issuance, all property, buildings, databanks, and documents of the USSR Central Intelligence Service (TsSR)—the renamed KGB First Chief Directorate—would be passed to the SVR under the supervision of a "special commission."[183]

The Russian government took actual control of Soviet foreign intelligence on 26 December, the day after the USSR was officially abolished. President Yeltsin paid an official visit to SVR headquarters outside Moscow at Yasenevo for the occasion.[184] There he signed a decree designating Yevgeniy Primakov, who had served as Soviet foreign intelligence chief, as SVR director general.[185] According to Bakatin, Yeltsin retained the Gorbachev confidant against his own personal judgment. Bakatin said that during the visit to Yasenevo, Yeltsin met with about 300 officers and asked for a vote of confidence in Primakov. When the overwhelming majority showed their support, Yeltsin agreed that Primakov would stay on as director.[186] Primakov easily won Yeltsin's confidence.

The other members of the Commonwealth of Independent States (CIS), with the possible exceptions of Belarus and Ukraine, which had nominal spy agencies of their own, did not receive portions of the former Soviet foreign intelligence service, although Russian officials stated that they would provide intelligence to fellow commonwealth members and would help certain "close neighbors" to set up their own services.[187] Most CIS members signed an intelligence cooperation agreement in April 1992.[188] The SVR says that it does not conduct intelligence operations against other members of the CIS (presumably this job is left to the internal security organs, which inherited the other KGB units and archives pertaining to this function), but specifically implies that it does operate against Estonia, Latvia, and Lithuania, which are closely tied to Western democracies. Formal KGB internal structures were withdrawn from the Baltic states in late 1991.[189]

The SVR initially played less of a role in the Russian decision-making process than the KGB First Chief Directorate had. Given Moscow's desire for more western aid and trade, many key decisions were based on the recommendations or perceived wishes of the western industrialized democracies. Yeltsin gave foreign intelligence relatively low bureaucratic status. He elevated the former KGB's internal security functions to cabinet level as the Ministry of Security, but he created the SVR as an autonomous "service" ranking in the fourth echelon of the bureaucracy (after ministries, state committees, and committees). The SVR chief reports directly to the president, but unlike ministers and state committee chiefs, he is not an ex officio member of the government.[190] He does, however, sit on a special Interdepartmental Foreign Policy Commission within the presidential Security Council, which formulates foreign policy and instructs the foreign minister, who also sits on the commission.[191] Primakov's personal profile rose in 1993, and he was rumored to be destined for more visible posts under Yeltsin. Similarities and continuities between Russian foreign intelligence and its parent Soviet service indicate that despite some bureaucratic shuffling, for all practical purposes little more than the name of the organ has changed.

SVR Leadership and Personnel

Unlike the economic team of former Acting Prime Minister Yegor Gaydar—which was composed of reformers with an instinctive trust and sympathy toward the West and its institutions—Russia's civilian and military intelligence services contain no proven liberals among their leaders. SVR Director Primakov was the only top-echelon holdover from the former Soviet government by late 1993.[192] With this single exception, President Yeltsin made a clean sweep of the first and second tiers of leadership throughout the Soviet state bureaucracy as it was absorbed by the Russian Federation.

Primakov, a former top official in the USSR Supreme Soviet and a member of Gorbachev's Security Council, was appointed chairman of the USSR KGB First Chief Directorate in September 1991. He remained chief when the directorate was made independent of the rest of the KGB and renamed the USSR Central Intelligence Service (TsSR), and was retained by Yeltsin when the TsSR was brought under Russian control and re-named the SVR. His lengthy background as a KGB collaborator and as an architect of the destructive and destabilizing pre-Gorbachev Soviet policy of backing terrorist states in the Middle East and his shameless support for the Soviet invasion and occupation of Afghanistan, were cited earlier.

Primakov's deputies in the SVR have similar political tendencies but are career chekists. SVR First Deputy Director Vyacheslav Trubnikov is a KGB lieutenant general; little is publicly known about him, but he did not distinguish himself as a spark for reform.[193]

Deputy Director Ivan Gorelovskiy, appointed in January 1991, is a career KGB officer who was chairman of the Azerbaijan KGB during the center's murderous provocations at Sumgait and during its January 1990 crackdown in Baku to suppress the Azerbaijani Popular Front. In the latter action, 130 demonstrators were killed and more than 700 wounded. An Azerbaijani parliamentary commission later found that Primakov, who was then Gorbachev's chief adviser on Islamic affairs and chairman of the Council of the Union chamber of the USSR Supreme Soviet, was the "main organizer" of the repression.[194] (Bakatin says that USSR Supreme Soviet Chairman Lukyanov gave the order to fire on the crowds, but most sources say the order was issued by USSR Defense Minister Dmitriy Yazov.[195]) After Sumgait, Gorelovskiy was transferred to the CPSU Central Committee staff and later to Gorbachev's presidential apparatus.[196]

The chief of the old chekists surrounding Primakov is retired Lt. Gen. Vadim Kirpichenko, who serves as his Consultants Group chairman. Kirpichenko's career spans more than four decades and goes back to the Stalin period. Thus he represents an even stronger link to the past. An Arabist like Primakov, Kirpichenko served five years as deputy head of the KGB First Chief Directorate and twelve years as first deputy head under Vladimir Kryuchkov.[197] Earlier, from 1974 to 1979, Kirpichenko was chief of Directorate S (also known as the "Illegals" Directorate responsible for deep-cover agents abroad), a position he held simultaneously as deputy head of the First Chief Directorate.[198] Within Directorate S was Department Eight, once known as Department V for "wet affairs." Department Eight was the KGB operational unit which actually trained, equipped, and otherwise supported terrorist organizations abroad, and which carried out political assassinations outside Soviet territory.[199]

Given the intense Soviet involvement in arming, training and funding Arab and other terrorist groups and regimes during their worst excesses in the 1970s and 1980s,[200] and Kirpichenko's immediate responsibility for Department Eight, it appears that the top adviser to the "new" Russian intelligence services was more than casually involved in attacks on American, Israeli, and other Western targets. One is compelled to doubt the SVR's sincerity in making proposals for cooperating with the West in the fight against terrorism.

The top leaders of the SVR, then, are hardly reformist. They do not share the democratic, pluralistic worldview of individual rights and free enterprise that their western counterparts generally espouse. Although their rhetoric has mellowed and their style has changed (see Chapter 8), their attitudes and practices have not. Rank-and-file officers also remain imbued with chekist ideology. Nearly all are unwilling or unable to come to terms with the fact that they served Communism. They do not seem to understand the gravity of their service to destroy the Western way of life they are now coming to embrace. They would rather have the world forget the past and include them in the future.

Yet they are selective in putting the past behind them. They cannot reconcile with their former colleagues who broke with the Communist system early by defecting to the West.[201] The grudge against defectors is not for having betrayed the Communist Party or even the Soviet state but, in the words of one sympathetic source, for having "betrayed above all the service in which they worked." To chekists, Cold War defectors "gave away not only state secrets, but also the secrets of the intelligence service."[202] Betrayal of the state is a secondary crime.

SVR Structure

As with the internal organs, no desovietization has taken place in the foreign intelligence service. The SVR has seen no dismantling of the old KGB First Chief Directorate systems and structures, no significant removal of old-thinking personnel, and no noticeable infusion of new, more forward-thinking staff. The likes of Oleg Kalugin, the former foreign counterintelligence chief who has publicly denounced some KGB excesses while remaining loyal to the Soviet Union and Russia, are anathema to the SVR. Kalugin's name is greeted with contempt and even hatred by SVR leaders.[203]

Unlike Bulgaria, which cashiered 10 percent of its diplomatic corps for having served Communism as spies, Russia did not remove diplomats who had spied for the KGB.[204] No more than a token few documents were released to the public concerning Soviet international abuses. No KGB officer was tried publicly for criminal activity. Espionage against the West continues virtually unabated, and new intelligence agreements have been forged with hard-line Communist regimes in the People's Republic of China and in Cuba. Intelligence ties with Beijing, which had been severed in 1959, were secretly reestablished in September 1992 through an agreement authorizing the SVR and the GRU to cooperate with the Military Intelligence Department of the People's Liberation Army.

Unlike the SVR's propagandistic statements which hail the slightest meeting with leaders of Western intelligence services, no official announcement was made of the Chinese and Cuban relations. The pact was made public by a leak from U.S. intelligence; a major American concern is that the SVR and GRU are joining forces with Chinese espionage to steal Western weapons technology.[205] At the same time, the SVR has tried to portray itself as a normal, Western-style intelligence service completely different from the KGB, as Chapter 8 discusses.

By the terms of its founding decree, the SVR was virtually identical to the former KGB First Chief Directorate (at the time known as the Central Intelligence Service, TsSR).[206] The name change represented the Russian Federation's seizure of the agency.

Most old First Chief Directorate services and directorates were maintained, and the only real reorganization occurred below, at the department level, according to a former First Chief Directorate officer, who added that the departmental changes were to increase efficiency and had little to do with the SVR's mission or methods.[207] The reasons for many of the decisions remain unclear. Although the transfer of the Vympel spetsnaz units to the Main Guard Directorate and ultimately the MVD may have been positive signs, the continued existence of Directorate S, which handles "illegals," assassins, and terrorists, is disturbing.[208] It shows a continued dependence on deep-cover agents abroad. Gen. Kirpichenko affirmed as much when he said, "we are maintaining our illegals. We need them. Our country is in very bad shape and we need our illegals."[209] Before the KGB was partitioned, the decision was made under Bakatin to increase attention to "illegals" planted abroad under nondiplomatic cover.[210]

No decrees abolishing Service A (responsible for covert political operations or "active measures") are known to have been published; in contrast, the purported abolition of other infamous units (such as the Fifth Chief Directorate) has been well publicized as representing meaningful breaks with the past. However, lack of CPSU control naturally meant a reduction in active measures as they applied to traditional Communist Parties, international front organizations, revolutionary groups, and left-wing movements. Although SVR leaders take pains to say they have abandoned "active measures,"[211] it was reliably reported that the foreign intelligence organs absorbed the active measures machinery of the CPSU International Department.[212]

These instruments are not, as far as is known, being employed at the present while Russia seeks foreign aid and hard currency, but this does not mean that they will not be employed at some point in the future. Indeed, recent SVR themes show that active measures continue in order to discredit defectors, to promote the idea of Western intelligence cooperation, and attract additional trade and more sophisticated technology from the West. Furthermore, although he said that Service A had been abolished, SVR spokesman Col. Yuriy Kobaladze admitted in a discussion that his service would continue to practice disinformation abroad as a "very important tool."[213]

The SVR had other reasons to reorganize parts of its structure to adapt to its environment without changing its essence. Shortly after the Russian government took control of the apparatus, it was announced that the intelligence presence in embassies abroad would be "slimmed down to minimum levels required to maintain state security."[214] Well-publicized attrition took place from December 1991 to July 1992. Bakatin already had planned a 30 percent staff cut, with a 50 percent reduction in personnel abroad,[215] reasoning that foreign intelligence no longer had to serve a political party with a globally offensive foreign policy heavily backed by covert operations or "active measures." The KGB First Chief Directorate had spent most of its resources to satisfy the desires of the CPSU International Department, which Bakatin described as the intelligence service's "main consultant and client."[216] Much of its presence abroad was completely unnecessary for the needs of the state. Bakatin commented,

> The activities of the FCD [First Chief Directorate] were indeed distinguished by a global and total nature. The secret agencies actively functioned and recruited agents in all, without exception, corners of the world, even in those countries whose names the average Soviet person had never heard and where the interests of the state security of the USSR were, mildly speaking, poorly distinguished.
>
> In accordance with party decree, the FCD was forced to be occupied not so much with the collection of significant intelligence information . . . as with providing the propagandistic aim of the CC CPSU, which had little in common with the actual state interests of the Soviet Union. The secret service was able to "yawn" at some of the most important events of international politics, but made up for it by regularly reporting to the center the reaction in various countries to the recurrent speeches of the Soviet leader or about the squabbles in the diminutive Communist Party of some African country. . . .
>
> As is now known, much data, which was yielded as a result of the secret service operation, was in fact drawn from the mass media and was prepared in order to humor the center. The disproportionately inflated staffs of the embassy secret agencies in no way corresponded with the actual results of the work.[217]

Far-flung outposts in small Third World countries with little or no strategic value were an unnecessary strain on resources. SVR leaders make a point of stressing that between thirty and forty intelligence outposts in minor Third World countries were closed down as a cost-cutting measure, but they decline to name which countries, so as not to risk offending local leaders by implying that they are not important enough to merit Moscow's continued attention, or so they say.[218] Reductions were also made in major posts such as Washington, where the SVR presence was said by U.S. counterintelligence in early 1993 to be about 25 percent lower than in December 1991, down to about forty agents.[219]

This cut was not at the expense of espionage potential and may even improve the SVR's effectiveness. A significant minority of SVR officers apparently were not worth the investment, especially those children of the Party elite who had joined the espionage service mainly to travel abroad. Others, such as those involved in support of Communist parties and fronts, were no longer needed. Remarked a top intelligence officer, "We will not support idlers and parasites abroad on our money."[220]

With the completely changed political and economic conditions between Russia and the West, it was no longer necessary to station many officers abroad whose responsibility was to recruit and run their foreign agents. Frequent trips to Russia no longer raise suspicions in the West. Instead of servicing agents in hard currency countries where the counterintelligence threat is greater, the SVR could now meet their foreign assets in the much more secure environment of Russia, where the agents were less likely to be monitored by their own country's security services. Indeed, since Moscow's opening to the West in the late 1980s, it has become easier, safer, and cheaper for the SVR to handle its foreign agents on Russian or CIS territory than it was abroad as older practice dictated.[221]

SVR Personnel

Other personnel reductions were carried out mainly by attrition by July 1992. The publicly stated goal, almost certainly for propaganda purposes, was 50 percent,[222] though the Supreme Soviet was never able to determine exact figures. Increased defections also forced some reorganization.[223] However, none of these changes make the SVR fundamentally different from the old First Chief Directorate. There has been no equivalent of the Halloween Massacre that decimated the operations directorate of the Central Intelligence Agency and demoralized much of the U.S. intelligence community under the Carter administration, though there are yeoman attempts to draw other parallels between the two services for propaganda purposes.

Personnel quality is mixed. During his fifteen years as KGB chairman, Andropov attracted the Soviet Union's most skilled young people to staff the organization, especially in the area of foreign intelligence. Extremely motivated and talented officers were the rule. Like with the rest of the CPSU, however, the KGB suffered from cronyism. Some of the most superior officers often found themselves working with the most substandard. Even in some of the most important posts abroad, the quality of officers or their work was at times extremely varied.[224] Shortly after becoming intelligence chief, Primakov complained of "little personal initiative" in the service.[225]

Several key officers abroad defected—at least ten between April 1991 and September 1992, according to the SVR,[226] and more since that time. These defections helped Western counterintelligence uproot important and highly productive espionage networks, which must have been humiliating and demoralizing to SVR personnel (although the chekists were jubilant when Aldrich Ames was exposed, allowing them to gloat in public about their skill). Successful agents in Belgium, France, Italy, the United States, and elsewhere were thus lost, and officers under diplomatic or journalistic cover were compromised.

Commercial Espionage Offensive

Some of the best and most experienced officers have been leaving security and intelligence, at least formally, to apply their knowledge and skills to more lucrative careers in business. Numerous officers from all KGB branches either have set up firms of their own or joined new Russian companies created by fellow chekists, nomenklatura members, and Party managers to take advantage of economic reforms and opportunities. These companies began to appear in observable numbers around 1988 and multiplied rapidly in the months following the 1991 putsch. Most were in search of Western partners.[227] The law conveniently required all Western firms seeking business in Russia to have a Russian partner.

Demand for Russian experts in other languages and cultures, for well-connected professionals with strong analytical or operational backgrounds, is strong among both domestic and foreign partners of joint ventures, and for those with special contacts and skills in getting things done in an environment where intimidation, bribery and extortion are the law. The relatively high pay in hard currency reportedly has lured some of Russia's most talented intelligence officers to the private sector. Western companies have hired KGB intelligence officers such as former First Chief Directorate head Leonid Shebarshin as consultants to perform due-diligence investigations of prospective business partners or to help open doors to local industry and government. Others have created joint ventures with Russian firms staffed by ex-KGB personnel. According to one report, chekists are involved in 80 percent of all joint ventures.[228]

In some bizarre cases, former American intelligence officers, viewing the chekists as "fellow professionals," even teamed together to do business in the former Soviet Union. A Maryland firm called Parvus Co., led by former National Security Agency assistant director Gerard P. Burke, signed a partnership with the Moscow-based Association for Business Security, a consortium of more than forty chekist-affiliated companies which is headed by retired KGB Maj. Gen. Viktor Budanov, former chief of foreign counterintelligence.[229]

Many of these new businessmen do not make the pretense of a cover story. They acknowledge and even advertise their previous careers and usually finding acceptance of their expertise, experience, and access. They can help Western businesses cut through endless bureaucracy, and they possess contacts and skills that make money. In interviews, ten out of thirty KGB businessmen freely admitted that they use "every means which he enjoys as a former KGB officer to neutralize any obstacle in their business no matter where they come from."[230] SVR officials have complained loudly about the apparent drain of experienced officers and staff. Said Primakov's press officer:

> Whereas previously, apart from all other considerations, competent and intelligent young people tried to get into intelligence for the high salaries and the opportunities for foreign travel, now commercial structures can offer the same thing with greater success and without tremendous risk. There are not that many people who see romance in intelligence work or people who feel a vocation for the work.[231]

Yet the complaints may not be as serious as they might seem, considering the SVR's new emphasis on economic, commercial, and industrial espionage. (One of those complaining most loudly was SVR public relations bureau chief Col. Yuriy Kobaladze, who by early 1994 was considering early retirement for a job with a Russian bank.)[232] It is difficult to believe that many chekists-turned-businessmen have actually left their old duties for good, although presumably some have. By permitting talented personnel to profit from career opportunities in the private sector, the SVR can penetrate that sector and make money as never before. Once in private business, intelligence officers then bring in more of their colleagues.[233] Russian intelligence is moving its spy methods from traditional official cover and taking advantage of the new business climate to have its personnel operate unofficially under cover as legitimate managers, employees, and consultants in a new and unchecked espionage offensive.

French counterintelligence has noted the presence of "former" KGB officers and agents who are now managers or representatives of numerous Russian companies and joint ventures that deal with French enterprises, and is reported to be watching them closely.[234] The caution, which is ridiculed by many Westerners, is judicious: some of the new chekist *biznismen* acknowledge that they "enjoy the assistance of colleagues who are still working in their former office" who provide inside information, counterintelligence, and other forms of help.[235] Despite reports of corruption within the SVR, such assistance appears to indicate the existence of a quid pro quo arrangement as part of a formal operational offensive to infiltrate the international business community.

The importance of this offensive should not be underestimated. As one former KGB general noted, "intelligence is playing a considerable role in science and technology and in obtaining new markets, even among friendly nations." One of the battlegrounds, he said, is Central Europe, a traditional market for Soviet products. He offered a hypothetical example:

> We learn that Hungarian-French talks are being held on the supply of certain products, while there is also a competitive Russian offer in that area. In that case, it is in our interest to discover the financial conditions offered by the French in order to lower our price and obtain or preserve our market positions.[236]

The question of which Russian companies would benefit from such intelligence has not been broached officially, though logic dictates that the net beneficiaries would be businesses owned or run by the nomenklatura and the chekists, at the expense of independent entrepreneurs.

Preservation of CPSU "State Secrets"

Russia continues to treat the secrets of the CPSU and the USSR as its own state secrets. They are protected by a presidential decree issued on 20 January 1992 and by a law adopted in its first reading in early 1993. A later law extended the holding period for classified documents from thirty years to fifty years (at the same time the U.S. government proposed a maximum life span of ten years for top secret information).[237]

Many Soviet-era secrets are understandably vital for a democratic government. However, it is unlikely that most of Russia's "state secrets" are directly related to the country's legitimate security needs; rather, they preserve the old ties, contacts, and operational networks of the Communist Party, the nomenklatura, and their chekist enforcers. Laws drafted by the chekists and enacted by the Supreme Soviet created the legal base. The 1992 Law on Foreign Intelligence and the 1993 Law on State Secrets make it a crime to publicize certain criminal activity of the Soviet period unless the release of that information has been specifically authorized.

Thus Russia has chosen again neither to make a clean break with the past nor to come to terms with its recent history. Government treatment of many Soviet files is handled by a state Commission for the Transfer-Reception of Archives, directed by a reformist military historian, Col. Gen. Dmitriy Volkogonov. The commission had early possession of most of the CPSU archives and made many files public, although some researchers complain of excessive selectivity in their release. The commission did not make public material from the CPSU International Department and did not have access to KGB archives.

No one outside the organs has such access. The SVR is of a mind that it, not civilian authorities, should determine which documents are released and when, and it has taken this privilege to an extreme. Some documents are selectively released—either to individuals or in the form of books sold in the West—for political purposes or for hard currency which is pocketed by SVR officials. Yet the numbers and circumstances are few. With the exception of completely innocuous material or occasional revelations for calculated purposes, the SVR will not consider the release of even the most dated documents. When asked by a scholar when the SVR would declassify documents on Soviet industrial espionage of the 1930s, SVR spokesman Kobaladze hedged and, after some prodding stated unequivocally, "Never."[238]

In addition to all the KGB First Chief Directorate archives and many CPSU International Department documents, Moscow retains immense files from the internal informant and agent networks and human assets of the Communist parties and secret services of the former Warsaw Pact states. A Polish parliamentary investigation found that throughout Central and Eastern Europe, security and intelligence service documents were destroyed at about the same time in 1989, as if coordinated from above. The documents were surreptitiously microfilmed or otherwise copied prior to being destroyed, and evidence suggests that the copies and many original files were shipped to the Soviet Union.[239] A Czechoslovak parliamentary commission also found that many missing documents were copied by unknown agnets prior to being destroyed.[240]

The Soviets maintained a central database of dissidents and other "enemies" within all Warsaw Pact member states. Joachim Gauck, chief of the German government's commission to process the archives of the defunct Stasi, reported that the internal security services of Soviet bloc governments

> formed a single system, which operated under the name SOUD—Interlinked System for Recognizing Enemies. Its headquarters were in Moscow. Information concerning anything that qualified as a threat to the system was sent there and investigated. Particular cases were analyzed and appropriate tactics were devised for them. It was enough for someone to be considered—only potentially—an opponent of the system, and the appropriate actions were initiated: he was put under surveillance and

information was collected on him. . . . and his case would end up in headquarters in Moscow.[241]

The SVR has indicated that it will not cooperate with former Warsaw Pact countries to help uncover the Communist agents and spies, suggesting that it plans to maintain those networks. Nor has it turned over the files to the Russian state Commission for the Transfer-Reception of Archives or to the relevant parliamentary security committees or commissions. In response to a journalist's question about this issue, Primakov responded, "The intelligence service does not intend to provide former socialist countries with lists of its agents who worked there."[242]

The reason is apparent: Russia would continue the KGB's Cold War spy games. German counterintelligence found that Russian operations in the Federal Republic were on the increase by mid-1992, thanks to the Stasi networks that survived the collapse of the East German government. Chief Prosecutor Alexander von Stahl noted that Russian espionage was in the process of "widening" its German network and "reactivating" an estimated 400 former East German Stasi officers and agents. The SVR is also reported to have recruited "a large number" of past members of the former East German Chief Intelligence Directorate (Hauptverwaltung Aufklärung, HVA).[243]

Many of the increased espionage activities are staged from former Soviet military installations in the eastern part of the country. These installations are served from Russia by Ministry of Security/Federal Counterintelligence Service-administered troop trains that, according to Bonn's agreements with Moscow for Soviet troop withdrawal, are not subject to inspections by German authorities. Russian military intelligence has also markedly increased its German operations since the collapse of the Soviet Union, von Stahl said.[244] There was "no noticeable change" in intelligence gathering from former Soviet military bases such as the headquarters of the Western Group of the CIS Joint Armed Forces in Wünsdorf outside Berlin.[245]

Russia also continued to use the intelligence services of former Warsaw Pact nations and other allies. Bonn formally notified President Lech Walesa's Polish government that its intelligence organs—largely unreformed and outside civil control—were still operating against Germany.[246] Authorities in Denmark complained that Polish and Russian "spy ships" continued to "patrol as before in the seas of Kattegat, Skagerrak and the Baltic."[247] Portuguese counterintelligence also noted continued East European espionage operations within its country's borders.[248] Spain expelled the Cuban consul in Madrid in 1993 for his part in a high-technology theft ring that probably was not limited to the spy services of the impoverished island regime.[249] Given the new intelligence cooperation agreements between Moscow and Havana, and Russia's continued attempts to give preferential trade to the Castro government, it may be surmised that the Cuban General Intelligence Directorate (Dirección General de Inteligencia, DGI) service is still working with or for its Russian counterparts.

The preserved networks are not only for economic or commercial espionage but represent clear and present dangers to the new democratic governments in Europe. In the Czech and Slovak republics, investigators found active penetrations of their governments by the old security and espionage structures and networks. Jiri Ruml, chief of the parliamentary commission to probe the former Czechoslovak StB, said that his investigation found that "former collaborators of the StB are still continuing their activity, and their network reaches into the new parliament."[250] Files on more than 10,000 agents and informants are missing from Czech archives. The only existing copies are reportedly in the hands of the former KGB.[251]

Those with access to the archives have the potential to undermine democratic gains in Central and Eastern Europe, subvert present and future democratic governments there, and renew regional espionage and political influence networks for operation in third countries, including established industrialized democracies. Because Moscow maintains such extensive files on present and potential future leaders of Central and Eastern Europe, it has the ability to blackmail or otherwise coerce and manipulate such figures well into the twenty-first century, thus compromising the newly found independence of these nations and complicating their relationships with the West.

Espionage, 1992-1994

Intelligence and counterintelligence officials from the United States, the European Union, and elsewhere indicated through 1993 and into 1994 that Russian operations against the industrialized democracies have continued roughly at the same levels as in the Soviet period. A decrease in personnel did not necessarily alter the level of espionage, western counterintelligence agencies believe, and the United States and Germany have reported a marked increase in combined GRU-SVR operations in their countries.[252]

The nature of Russian espionage, however, has changed. SVR operations were reported to have declined abroad (although the FBI and its Western counterparts would have little way of knowing whether the operations had been moved beyond their reach to former Soviet territory), but GRU operations sharply increased in the West. Moscow's shift toward stealing economic and technological proprietary information which began in in earnest in the mid-1980s,[253] has sped up as military tensions between the superpowers have eased, according to the FBI and French and German counterintelligence.[254]

These reports support the conclusion that the exodus of SVR officers into private business may be part of a new espionage offensive instead of a brain drain. Central Intelligence Agency Director Robert Gates said in March 1992 that despite political changes, "the interests of the Russian intelligence service in Western technology continues." He told a congressional committee, "We've seen relatively little change in the Russian intelligence service's operations in the United States," and added that the Russians' "first priority is still the United States and that their first priority in that context is still the acquisition of technology and high-technology equipment."[255]

The spate of defections in 1991 and 1992, which apparently continued into 1994, exposed large Soviet/Russian economic and technological espionage rings, resulting in their disruption or destruction and forcing the SVR to reorganize its operations.[256]

Gates and FBI counterintelligence agree that the GRU has also shifted its focus to commercial espionage, especially the search for "stealth" and communications technology and computer software. GRU officers in 1991 and 1992 were increasingly discovered posing as tourists and businessmen.[257] FBI Director William S. Sessions told a congressional panel, "Russians do not have the currency to pay for advanced business systems and designs, so they will steal them or obtain them through other, illegitimate means."[258] Western military technology remains a target because the Russian military industry could use it to upgrade its own weaponry as well as to manufacture arms specifically designed for competition on the international market. Arms exports remain an increasingly important source of hard currency for Russia, whose sagging military industry—the largest and most viable manufacturing and export sector—must stay competitive.

Russian intelligence officials on occasion have acknowledged their new emphasis on stealing technological and economic secrets. Foreign intelligence chief Yevgeniy Primakov announced that his service would engage in "economic intelligence" but merely as a defensive measure to prevent foreign business from "robbing" Russian enterprises.[259] Bold image-making efforts, described in Chapter 8, attempted not to deny but defiantly to justify certain forms of espionage giving notice that Russia would continue to operate aggressively. At the same time, technological competition gives the chekists a new excuse to justify their perceived need to remain well-funded in a time of severe economic hardship—despite reports of massive corruption at the top of the SVR, where hard currency earned from front companies and joint ventures was being diverted to build homes for top active duty and retired intelligence officers.[260]

Even before CIA turncoat Aldrich Ames was identified as a Russian agent, official statements, arrests, and expulsions in Western Europe showed that Russian espionage continued as aggressively as ever. Active Russian spy rings were discovered or agents expelled by Germany, Sweden, Belgium, France, the Netherlands, Finland, Denmark, Norway, and Turkey. So chronic were continued operations against Germany that Bernd Schmidbauer, the state minister responsible for intelligence in the chancellery, was moved to comment, "The new spirit of cooperation is hardly noticeable in the intelligence services of the former east bloc."[261]

The German Federal Office for the Protection of the Constitution found in April 1992 that the intelligence work of the KGB's successor services "continued unabated" in Germany and that Moscow had maintained much of the Stasi framework in the former German Democratic Republic to carry out intelligence work and to set up new "networks of sources."[262] Later that year, Schmidbauer officially complained to the Russian government that Russian espionage continued against economic, military, and political targets in Germany. Nevertheless, Bonn simultaneously began a process of mutual cooperation with Moscow when it opened a Federal Intelligence Service (BND) liaison office in the Russian capital.[263] Germany deported GRU Col. Viktor Sherdev that autumn after he had been arrested, convicted, and handed a three-year sentence for espionage and corruption.[264] A federal report issued in August 1993 showed that, despite Bonn's new intelligence cooperation with Moscow, large-scale espionage against Germany continued.

Russian intelligence officers were expelled from Belgium, France, the Netherlands, Finland, and Denmark. A series of dawn raids across Belgium on 10 April 1992 resulted in the arrests of three Belgian businessmen, a journalist, a civil servant, and others who had participated in a KGB spy ring operating since 1967. Four Russian intelligence officers in Brussels, two posing as diplomats and two under trade delegation cover, were expelled. The espionage ring, exposed by a defector to the United States, which in turn alerted Belgian authorities, was made up of more than two dozen people including Belgian military personnel, and stole advanced aeronautical technology from western governments and businesses. Foreign Minister Willy Claes angrily stated that the spying jeopardized relations between the entire European Community and Russia.[265] French counterintelligence broke up a related ring after being alerted by the CIA and later expelled agent Sergey Zhmyrev and three others. The ring was betrayed by a double agent, Viktor Oshchenko, who had been recruited by British intelligence.[266]

Meanwhile, three active SVR agents working under cover as journalists with ITAR-TASS and *Komsomolskaya pravda* were reported to have been expelled from the Netherlands.[267] The same day, two Russian citizens, a male and a female, were detained at Vantaa Airport in Helsinki. They were holding forged British passports and DM120,000 ($72,000) in cash. Finnish security chief Eero Kekomaki diplomatically said, "They were sent to Finland by a foreign intelligence service." The couple, identified as Igor and Natalya Lutskov, received a sixty-day suspended sentence and was deported back to Russia.[268]

Denmark was also troubled by continued Russian espionage. A Danish counterintelligence official reported in May 1992, "Spies from Russia and the other states of the CIS are still operational in the country . . . [and] involved in military and industrial spying." Copenhagen expelled a Russian diplomat and arrested one of its own officials suspected of passing "secret information" to help provide false identities to Russian agents in the country.[269]

Sweden's reports added to the trend. Security chief Mats Börjesson indicated problems in early 1992 when he told a newspaper that his service would not help Russia try to stem illegal proliferation of nuclear weapons until it ceased espionage activities against his country.[270] He stated half a year later that the SVR was "again" recruiting agents there.[271] The Swedish military has also reported continued covert incursions into its coastal waters by Russian mini-submarines that crawl along the ocean floor on treads. Japan experienced the same problem. Officials in Stockholm theorize that the operations could be carried out by a super-secret military intelligence organ of the former Soviet government that is not controlled by the current Russian regime.[272]

Some of the most reformist Russian figures defend economic and commercial espionage against the West as a means for the country to recover from its ruined state. Many in the West agree. They note, as does the SVR, that Belgium, France, Israel, and Japan, among others, run aggressive economic and business espionage operations against the United States while remaining friends and allies.[273] Even many

Americans agreed with Moscow after revelations of the far more serious Ames case that chekist operations against the United States should not affect bilateral relations; after all, they reasoned, the CIA operates in Russia.

The comparisons are inadequate. Even with the end of the Cold War and the demise of the Soviet Union, Russian espionage against the West is far different from the economic or technological spying some Western governments wage against fellow industrialized democracies. Most Russian economic and industrial spying appears to be aimed at enriching companies owned by the nomenklatura and KGB generals themselves, not to help Russia recover from its self-inflicted mess.

Furthermore, Western democratic institutions are stable and well established. Military, security, and intelligence services in the democracies are under varying degrees of civil control and are largely accountable to elected leaders and the courts, and often are subject to intense media scrutiny. Western services embrace no violence-based cult which glorifies past internal repression and external aggression.

Conclusion

Russia inherited a KGB that was reorganized and renamed but not reformed. Instead of starting anew and ridding itself of the chekist legacy or shunning it as a threat to democratization, the Russian government chose to embrace it and rely upon it as a pillar of stability and a starting point for future society. Russia's leaders have gone along with the fiction that the KGB is gone and have pretended that the post-Soviet security organs have become similar to those of the West. Yet even a cursory examination shows that today's internal security organs are merely the old internal security arm of the KGB. The size of the services are still unknown, but their authority and networks remain throughout the Federation and the rest of the former Soviet Union. There has been no influx of reformist personnel or exodus of hard-liners. To the contrary, veterans from the political police section of the old KGB have been promoted to the top.

No appreciable changes have been made to the former KGB Border Troops, which are deployed far from Russia's borders in Tajikistan to prop up a staunchly Communist regime, and stationed elsewhere in countries like Georgia where they are not wanted. Their new headquarters occupy the KGB's main office at 2 Lubyanka Square. The KGB units responsible for signals intelligence and secure communications were merged into the Federal Agency for Government Communications and Information (FAPSI). Before it was a year old, FAPSI extended its lease on the KGB offensive signals intelligence facility in Cuba. In conjunction with the internal organs, and as its own name suggests, FAPSI initiated a program to take control over all electronic communications and information in the country.

The KGB Ninth Directorate, which once protected the Politburo, now protects the post-Soviet Russian leadership under the new name of the Main Guard Directorate, and merged with two notorious KGB shock units: Alfa, the "antiterrorist" team designed to storm government buildings and which murdered unarmed demonstrators in the Baltic states; and (until it was transferred to the MVD) Vympel, the former KGB First Chief Directorate spetsnaz force which assassinated the president of Afghanistan and slaughtered his seven children.

Although it no longer serves the Communist Party, the External Intelligence Service (SVR) maintains the basic structure and personnel of the First Chief Directorate of the KGB, practices similar methods, and safeguards and utilizes the same agent networks and databases. Most secrets of the Soviet Communist Party, including agent networks abroad, are now the state secrets of the Russian Federation. The SVR is still led by career anti-Westerners from the old school who were operationally responsible for terrorism and murder. Not only has the SVR failed to promote more reformist officers; it has purged and publicly excoriated them. It has yet to put its knowledge and resources to good use by helping other countries expose and dismantle old Soviet intelligence and informant networks, and indeed has stated its refusal to do so.

No meaningful civil controls have even begun to be implemented over any of these services. Russian civilian leaders in government and parliament have been unable to determine the actual size of the bureaucracies or their budgets. Laws that on the surface govern the security and intelligence services actually codify most of the organs' old functions and enshrine their maintenance of KGB informant networks and repressive mechanisms with the legitimacy of a democratically elected government. The political system overall remains penetrated at all levels by informants and covert agents who are not free to break with the past. They remain vulnerable to blackmail and coercion because the security organs own their files which the subjects are not free to see. With few practical exceptions, little more than the names have changed.

5

Civil Controls over the KGB in the Perestroika Period

The democratic renewal of the country has not changed the place of the KGB in the political system. This committee exercises all-encompassing control over ministries, it is clearly placed above the state, being subordinate only to a narrow group in the apparatus.

—Yuriy Vlasov, USSR Supreme Soviet member,
31 May 1989.

There was almost no public discussion of civil controls over the KGB until 1989, when Gorbachev reorganized Soviet political structures to create a standing parliament-like body and the position of a state president. Even then, the discussion was not at his initiative. Democratic members of the new Supreme Soviet legislature took advantage of an unprecedented public forum of live, nationally televised legislative proceedings and debates viewed by practically the entire population to stage the first open political attacks on the KGB, demanding that the secret services be held accountable for past crimes and that they be brought under strict parliamentary control.

The KGB and its supporters in the Supreme Soviet leadership acted quickly to co-opt the reformers' arguments by imposing the checks and processes insisted upon, but placing Party loyalists in charge of them. Although the checks and balances were only cosmetic, they marked an historic turning point. No longer was the KGB immune to public challenge. From that point forward, the chekists would have to subject themselves to some form of public scrutiny. With each new revelation chipping away at their previously impenetrable armor, the state security organs at least had to go through the motions of answering to the public.

In an attempt to undermine its critics and take control of the unwelcome situation, the KGB waged a public relations campaign to show how much it was supposedly reforming. For the most part, the USSR Supreme Soviet moved quickly to satisfy public demands by creating new oversight structures but ensured their ineffectiveness by stacking them with lawmakers friendly or beholden to chekism. The whole process to thwart the democratic reformers had an unintended effect. It left the KGB so powerful vis-à-vis a weakened Communist Party that the Party leadership, especially Gorbachev, ultimately lost all power. This trend culminated in the KGB's attempted coup of August 1991. At the same time, the process set the stage for the oversight structures adopted by the legislature of the Russian Federation after the Soviet collapse.

Civil control of Soviet security and intelligence organs during the Gorbachev period was the sole purview of the CPSU Central Committee, as it had been under all his Soviet predecessors. What made Gorbachev's rule significant was that CPSU control eroded as the Party itself fractured and lost direction. This development allowed the security services to exert more power on their own and enhanced their political prestige and influence. Gorbachev failed even to attempt to create the framework for democratic institutions that could bridge a transition between totalitarianism and democracy. Instead he created a central power vacuum, which made the KGB accountable to no one at all, not even to himself.

Gorbachev attempted to maintain Party control over the KGB throughout his six years as Kremlin chief, though it became apparent by 1990 that control was slipping away. He made no attempt to open the service to non-Communist personnel. With the repeal of Article 6 from the Soviet Constitution, the Party's main control mechanism was severely weakened and the system became disoriented.[1] Thus, although the security machinery was completely staffed and administered by Party members, the lines it followed were no longer clear. Several active and former KGB officers began to speak out critically of the Party and the organs.[2] Vadim Bakatin, who was Soviet interior minister at the time, recalled, "Before the abolition of Article 6 of the Constitution the USSR Interior Ministry worked under the direct control of the Politburo and General Secretary of the Communist Party, but after the Constitution had been changed, the Ministry could no longer wait for instructions from top Party officials." He was adamant that until Article 6 was lifted, the Party controlled the KGB "and not the other way around,"[3] although that view is not universally shared.

As he went on with his reforms, Gorbachev substantially downsized the rubber-stamp USSR Supreme Soviet legislature as part of a larger radical restructuring of the power and administrative apparatus that he elaborated at the 19th Party Conference in 1988. His plan was to fold Party structures into those of the Soviet state, transferring political power from the CPSU apparatus while ensuring that Party members occupied all major state and government positions. Whereas the Party and state technically had been two separate structures with interlocking leaderships, he merged them into one. Shifting formal "legislative" power from the Party Central Committee to the state "parliament," Gorbachev created a Congress of People's Deputies to be elected partly by multiparty balloting as the USSR's supreme legislative body. The Congress would meet twice a year, choosing from its ranks a day-to-day standing "parliament," which was the new, smaller Supreme Soviet.

Although these changed added to the regime's legitimacy by providing for freer elections and a modicum of public debate, the system was rigged distinctly to ensure Communist Party domination. Unwieldy at 2,250 members, the Congress reserved 750 seats for representatives elected from territorial districts, and 750 for representatives from various nationalities elected in competitive balloting; and 750 for representatives elected from Party organs and social organizations.[4] The first Congress of People's Deputies was elected in March 1989. Though 88 percent of its members belonged to the CPSU, a number of liberal and radical reformers were elected to office, several of whom were Party members.

The new parliament was never designed to challenge central power. A prearranged slate ensured that the 542-member bicameral Supreme Soviet remained under Party discipline. Its members were chosen from among the people's deputies, and all committee chairmen who formed the Presidium were Party members. CPSU General Secretary Gorbachev doubled as president of the Presidium and therefore as state president.[5] Since service as a people's deputy even in the Supreme Soviet was a part-time job for the rank and file, members held their permanent positions in the government and Party apparats. Under this arrangement, they maintained a certain sense of loyalty to the status quo and remained unable to focus all their attention on politics and policy. Their nuisance potential vis-à-vis the CPSU leadership was minimized. Meanwhile, the KGB operated to ensure its own active participation in the new political process and to institutionalize its own presence in the legislatures. A KGB Collegium order in October 1989 instructed all personnel to work closely with people's deputies by offering privileged political and economic information about the constituencies they represented. The KGB actively infiltrated all political blocs, especially to disrupt unity among democratic lawmakers.[6]

Despite the arrangement to give democrats the short shrift, the Soviet leadership was compelled to contend with new players and voices such as reform Communists, untamed non-Communists, and even anti-Communists, some of whom, like physicist Andrey Sakharov, had been victims of Party persecution carried out by the KGB. As a result, like other Gorbachevian half-measures, the Party-guided legislative reforms had their unintended consequences. By including open opponents of the CPSU leadership or of the Party as a whole in the new parliaments, Gorbachev gave reformers the public platform they needed to demand powers that they had been deliberately denied. Sakharov's very presence in the Supreme Soviet was a constant reminder of the KGB's existence and the need to control it. Something had to be done.

Meanwhile, the Supreme Soviet saw the need for some sort of structure to create the illusion if not the reality that democracy was spreading to the state security pillar of Soviet power.[7] As a gesture to indicate measures toward civil control over the security, intelligence, and military services, the Supreme Soviet leadership formed a Committee on Defense and Security ostensibly to act as a Western-style parliamentary oversight body. The conditions for this logical outgrowth of glasnost and perestroika were ripe following a massacre of unarmed demonstrators in Tblisi, Georgia, a month before the opening of the Congress and Supreme Soviet. A mass outcry arose against the massacre, but the Soviet leadership emerged cleanly from the disaster it had wreaked by acting as though the security organs had acted on their own. The oversight body was touted as a bold legislative reform. (What the lawmakers failed to understand at the time was that the armed crackdown, in which security forces attacked protesters with sharpened sapper shovels and poison gas, was requested by the Georgian Party first secretary and approved by the CPSU Politburo.[8]) Reformist critics recognized the oversight system as little more than a Politburo attempt to project the image of pluralism while maintaining tight control.

On 31 May, four days into the nationally televised proceedings, deputies discussed nationality questions, credentials, employment and economic reform in what appeared to be an uneventful series of floor speeches. Then two members, in historic acts of courage, lashed out at the KGB and at the reorganized Supreme Soviet itself. The first was

Boris Yeltsin, the rebellious Communist functionary whom Gorbachev had ousted as a candidate Politburo member and Moscow Party chief two years before. In an attack on the legitimacy of the Supreme Soviet, Yeltsin accused the Gorbachev-led "parliament" of becoming an "apparatus or semi-apparatus" of the Communist Party. He spoke about the lack of accountability over the recent killings in Georgia:

> The Congress's plenary prerogatives regarding the formation of the supreme organs of power are extremely narrow. . . . The Soviet people's faith in real results of perestroika is waning. . . . One year after the party conference, which established a course toward democratization, we have been hitting at meetings and demonstrations with one decree, hitting at glasnost with another, and permitting the use of Special Troops against our own people. And, of course, there is the ill-starred Art. 11 [decree], the author of which has not yet proved possible to find but who may possibly be among us. It is precisely in an atmosphere of such prohibitory legislation, and especially recently, that such crimes as those in Tblisi become possible. . . . The people must be told . . . who it was, ultimately, who made the decision at the Center, about which the leadership knows.[9]

Later in the day, another deputy took the floor as the proceedings were broadcast live. Yuriy P. Vlasov was a fifty-three year-old former Olympic champion weightlifter. He had become famous for denouncing the Soviet sports establishment for tolerating the use of drugs, including amphetamines and steroids, to enhance the national team in athletic competitions. Taking the rostrum, he distanced his colleagues from what he was about to say. "No one arranged my speech," he began. He issued a list of demands for government accountability, read an appeal from his constituents to locate and establish memorials for victims of past state terror, and called on the KGB to release its archives. Then he uttered a demand that electrified the nation: "In order to limit the will of the apparatus, it is necessary to place one of the powerful foundations of its viability under the people's control." His words, even at the height of the glasnost era, were shocking. Singling out the KGB, he declared, "Even in our day the threat to democracy cannot be considered mythical." The athlete-turned-politician, whose father had disappeared at the hands of the chekists in 1953, went on:

> When the first steps are being taken on the path of democratization and at the same time there is a desire to crush it, a force such as the KGB takes on special meaning. After all, the KGB is subordinate only to the apparatus, the KGB has been removed from the control of the people. This is the most closed, the most clandestine of all state institutions. . . .

> The deep secrecy, explained by the specific nature of its activities, ensures a de facto absence of control over the KGB, although its actions are sometimes quite dubious. It is dangerous to look for it. To this day, manipulations involving alleged psychological abnormality can threaten people who are dangerous to the apparatus.
>
> The democratic renewal of the country has not changed the place of the KGB in the political system. This committee exercises all-encompassing control over society and over ministries, it is clearly placed above the state, being subordinate only to a narrow group in the apparatus. The appointment of the Chairman of the State Security Committee [KGB] should go through the Congress of People's Deputies. The People's Deputies should know the size of this organization and demand an accounting for all violations of legality, and they should know what its budget is.[10]

In retrospect, the words seem mild, even unremarkable. But they were radical for the time; no one had ever said such words before such an audience, let alone on national television. Free debate in the Supreme Soviet was so new, on TV no less, that a very large segment of the national population was glued to the proceedings. An American journalist covering the session captured the moment: "Never before had such severe criticisms been directed at the KGB from an official rostrum, and Mr. Vlasov's boldness drove hundreds in the hall to rise in thunderous applause, while others—including [KGB Chairman Vladimir] Kryuchkov—sat in startled silence."[11] Vlasov continued,

> It would be best to move KGB headquarters from Dzerzhinskiy Square. . . . For decades, orders for the annihilation or persecution of millions of people were issued from that building. This service sowed grief, lamentation and torture on our soil. In the bowels of this building, people were tortured—people who were, as a rule, the best, the pride and flower of our peoples. Then there is the very complex of these buildings, which are so unaccountably and monumentally immense, as if to indicate to whom power in the country really belongs. . . . The KGB is not a service but a real underground empire that has still not yielded its secrets, except for the graves that have been discovered. And despite such a past, this service retains its special, exceptional position. It is the most powerful of all the existing tools of the apparatus. It has no equal in terms of effectiveness and smoothness of operation. There is a proposal in the Supreme Soviet for a Commission on Defense and State Security. One assumes it will deal with the activity of the Ministry of Internal Affairs and the KGB. . . . This commission must be filled with new content, and it must exercise effective control. . . .[12]

For the first time in Soviet history, the KGB's power was publicly challenged from within the Kremlin itself in full view of the entire nation. At this point, the Soviet leadership seemed to realize that it would have to work hard to try to legitimize the KGB. Kryuchkov had to placate demands for real controls and develop a public relations campaign immediately. He responded as Vlasov's challenge gained momentum. Like Gorbachev, the KGB chairman, who had been appointed in October 1988, would have to comply with a new law requiring all top appointments to be reviewed and confirmed by the Supreme Soviet. Kryuchkov submitted a report to the Committee on Defense and Security, and he appeared before the Supreme Soviet on 14 July on live national television. The situation posed both an historic challenge as well as an unprecedented opportunity to give the KGB a new look.[13] Armed with the unanimous endorsement of the Committee on Defense and Security, Kryuchkov faced the full Supreme Soviet.[14]

Gorbachev, wearing his Supreme Soviet president hat, directed the meeting. Kryuchkov's appearance was scheduled late that Friday afternoon, near the very end of a long agenda. The deputies were looking forward to leaving Moscow for the weekend.[15] It was not to be a confirmation hearing, but more of a ritual to ratify a fait accompli. No pretense of scrutiny was expected. Gorbachev introduced Kryuchkov to the deputies, his words underlining the historic importance of the KGB chairman's appearance and hailing it as yet another sign of fundamental reform:

> Esteemed comrade deputies, recently the KGB Chairman has given, for the first time, a report on the work of the state security bodies to the USSR Supreme Soviet Committee for Defense and State Security. This was the first case of giving a public account; no such body simply existed before. This is the first time that the KGB head is speaking, today, addressing the USSR Supreme Soviet as a candidate for this post. . . . It is evident from this alone that the state security bodies, too, have found themselves within the orbit of perestroika.[16]

Kryuchkov began by announcing that he had already submitted to the Committee on Defense and Security "a report on the work of the state security bodies." He celebrated the report and his presence on the rostrum as historic firsts and summarized the document before a spellbound audience, explaining in basic terms the functions of Soviet foreign intelligence, counterintelligence, military counterintelligence, communications, and border guards. Yet to the Western observer, his remarks contributed nothing new to existing basic knowledge about the KGB. The speech was peppered with self-congratulatory rhetoric about KGB officers' "selfless and difficult struggle," and it stressed that "the Soviet people can, with complete justification, think of them with pride."[17]

As encouraging as Kryuchkov's speech may have seemed at the time, it was little more than doublespeak, another attempt to deceive the lawmakers, the Soviet population, and the world at large while protecting what KGB leaders saw as their own personal and institutional interests. Much of what Kryuchkov stated was clearly false; other comments were later proven untrue. Kryuchkov offered a series of what he touted as new themes that supposedly marked significant breaks with the discredited practices of the bygone Age of Stagnation. Although some of his themes were indeed new, many were recycled from the past. In attempting to distance himself from that past, he said that the KGB was now a force to undo the crimes of old; it was becoming a legitimate, Western-style service, and its roles and missions were being redefined. The new KGB would help society by fighting organized crime, terrorism, and nuclear proliferation, and by protecting individual rights.[18] It would need public support to carry out its new democratic functions, and as such the public had a "right to know" its workings.[19] Archives containing the dark secrets of the past would be opened.[20] The democratic KGB felt an "utmost need of a law" to govern its actions[21] and needed to be placed under strict parliamentary oversight.[22] This last theme, a direct response to the demands of Yeltsin, Vlasov, and other outspoken reformers, was another empty gesture. The parliamentary oversight committee was not an independent monitoring body but an artifice to project the image of oversight without the substance.

In another historic first, with millions of Soviet citizens watching in fascination, lawmakers directly questioned Kryuchkov from the floor. Some challenged the veracity of his speech as well as his answers. If some democratic people's deputies chafed at these responses, Gorbachev chafed at the questions. He tried to adjourn, interrupting the KGB chief and asking if the deputies had heard enough. They shouted him down, voting by a wide majority to have Kryuchkov continue.[23] This was an historic time for the deputies, too, who for the first time ever were embarking on a campaign to impose reform on the KGB.

Politically, Kryuchkov had no choice but to continue. He went on reading questions submitted by Deputy Marju Lauristin of Estonia: "Do you consider it possible to preserve the Stalinist-Brezhnevite structure of surveillance of Soviet people's thoughts? If not, then why is the present structure being maintained?" He answered in all seriousness, "No, comrades. The structure is not being maintained, and the subdepartment you are thinking of virtually no longer exists."[24]

Shortly after, Gorbachev interrupted again. He called for an end to the questions and recessed the meeting. Kryuchkov had been speaking for 58 minutes, he said, and it was time to go. But the deputies wanted more and resolved to reconvene. In the lobby with journalists during the break, Yeltsin fumed about Kryuchkov: "I don't believe him."[25] Reluctantly calling the session back to order, Gorbachev then recognized lawmakers friendly to Kryuchkov, calling on one, Britvin, who said he wanted everyone to vote to confirm the KGB chairman. The Soviet leader then called on Deputy Fominykh, who marveled that he had learned more about the KGB in the past hour than ever before. Deputy Lauristin was not satisfied, and demanded recognition from the floor. She thanked Kryuchkov for his answers and urged the KGB to dispose of its Stalinist legacy. Addressing her colleagues and the television cameras, she challenged the chekist chief:

> In my opinion, I nevertheless do think that there was no point in telling us that the KGB does not make use of secret informers. As a university lecturer, personally I simply know many students at home in Tartu, and I do not think that is an exception . . . when they failed exams and they were threatened with being thrown out of the university, and they got in a situation in which our local KGB body promised them help in getting back into an institute, university and so forth if in payment they would inform on their students, colleagues and teachers.
>
> That is a fact. These are facts of three or two years' standing. It is outrageous.
>
> However, such facts have still not been acknowledged so far and it was even considered criminal to speak of them. And in my opinion, it is now time to speak honestly of such things and renounce them. And in my opinion, the new chairman of the KGB, as he showed himself here to us, should, in my view, deal also with these methods of work of his bodies.[26]

In an unheard-of act for the time, she announced that she would not vote for Kryuchkov. Gorbachev searched the chamber for another deputy who would support his KGB man and called on reform Communist Anatoliy Sobchak of Leningrad. Sobchak prefaced his remarks by announcing that he would vote for Kryuchkov but followed with his own challenge to the KGB chairman's political power by calling for safeguards against abuses and for measures making it impossible for the KGB to be directed by the Communist Party.[27] Sobchak urged that statistics on the KGB's size and budget be published and said that local KGB offices should be moved from their "most architecturally striking and largest buildings" and "beautiful palatial buildings" into "more modest accommodation."

Gorbachev agreed on this last point then called on his main rival, Boris Yeltsin, whom he had tried to exclude from membership in the Supreme Soviet. The unpredictable Yeltsin, as was his manner, was blunt, launching a scathing attack against the chekists in general and pointedly rebutting some of Kryuchkov's key assertions.[28] Yeltsin had a number of complaints, and he took the opportunity to air them in front of Gorbachev and Kryuchkov on live television. He called for a "radical restructuring" of the KGB, noting, "Over these past four years [since Gorbachev has been in power] there has been no such radical restructuring, and today comrade Kryuchkov has made no mention of this restructuring."[29] He demanded that the KGB come forward with details on the mass repressions of earlier years and bare the facts of its seven decades of repression. He closed with what was at the time a radical proposal: division of the KGB into separate intelligence and counterintelligence organizations.[30]

The parliamentary session could not have concluded on a worse note for Gorbachev. It seemed as if no one wanted to speak. Then Vladimir Lapygin, chairman of the Committee on Defense and Security, took the floor to say how "impressed" he was by Kryuchkov's presentation. He obligingly voiced support for the KGB chairman's candidacy and reminded his colleagues that the committee had endorsed Kryuchkov unanimously.[31] The deputies then voted, in a lopsided manner that came to typify the voting patterns of both the USSR and Russian supreme soviets. Of the 542-member body, only six voted against Kryuchkov, and twenty-six, including Yeltsin and Lauristin, abstained.[32]

The national televised appearance before the Supreme Soviet set the tone of a KGB public relations campaign that would last for more than a year (described in Chapter 7). Amy Knight would later observe:

> In his numerous statements in the media over the past few months, Kryuchkov has demonstrated considerable adeptness at public relations. Portraying himself as a champion of perestroika and an ardent defender of human rights, he has managed to win over a large portion of the liberal Soviet establishment and to convince many Westerners that he is a man who can be trusted. But it is unlikely that Kryuchkov is any more disposed to significant reforms, particularly as they erode KGB powers, than are his KGB colleagues. Rather than opposing these reforms outright, KGB officials have developed a strategy of influencing the process of perestroika by initiating changes on their own. Not only has the KGB taken advantage of glasnost in order to conduct a sophisticated public relations campaign to enhance its public image, it has responded to demands for legal and institutional reforms by coming up with its own proposals, thereby undercutting many of its sharpest critics.[33]

Twenty-four hours after his appearance before the Supreme Soviet, Kryuchkov told Western journalists that parliament should have oversight of the KGB the same way the U.S. Congress has oversight of the CIA.[34] The great public relations game had begun.

The Supreme Soviet Oversight Mechanism

The USSR Supreme Soviet under Mikhail Gorbachev was never intended to be a meaningful check against executive power. As a part-time institution, the Supreme Soviet's effectiveness was limited from the start. Pay for a lawmaker was average by Soviet standards but nevertheless poor, about 800 rubles a month in late 1991, or less than $8.00 on the free market, but this was often a second income for the deputies.[35] Privileges of lawmakers were meager: Few but the highest Party officials had their own offices, and most had to share desks. Only the most senior members had assistants or secretaries of their own, and these members almost invariably were entrenched Party officials with vested interests in the status quo. Most deputies continued to hold their previous jobs, both for the stability and the income they produced. As a result, the majority of members logically focused first on their primary employment and second on parliamentary matters while the apparatchiks ran day-to-day operations.

Moreover, the CPSU Central Committee maintained control over all committee chairmanships and memberships, ensuring that non-Communists and opponents of Gorbachev within the Party would be denied important posts. The system of committee appointments was run by the top, with little input from the parliamentary rank and file. Secret rules for committee chairmanship selection made sure that non-Communist people's deputies would be unable to involve themselves in the process.

Supreme Soviet chairman and Politburo member Anatoliy Lukyanov, in consultation with Party technocrats and Central Committee leaders who chaired the parliament's two chambers (including Soviet of the Union Chairman Yevgeniy Primakov, who reliably is reported to have been a KGB "citizen agent" for more than thirty years[36]), formally chose each committee chairman. After the fact they presented a single candidate for approval by the full Supreme Soviet membership without prior screening, open competition with other candidates, or proper floor debate. Each candidate was introduced and an individual up-or-down vote was taken. The selection process for committee members was unclear, even to people's deputies themselves.[37] According to Jennifer Scheck Lee, an American with the nonprofit Global Outlook corporation who set up programs to advise the Supreme Soviet in military oversight, the committee chairman nominated committee members, who were then approved by the entire Supreme Soviet. The chairmen and deputy chairmen of subcommittees were approved by the full committee membership.[38]

In this context, the forty-three-member Committee on Defense and Security was created in May 1989 ostensibly for the Supreme Soviet to oversee the military, security, and intelligence services.[39] The concept of the committee was developed by liberal deputies who sought a mechanism to regulate the KGB, the armed forces, and the military-industrial complex. Yevgeniy Velikhov, the nuclear physicist-turned-lawmaker, was the reformists' choice to chair the committee; his vice presidency of the Academy of Sciences and his key role in the response to the 1986 Chernobyl nuclear accident gave him national stature, and his friendship with Gorbachev gave him access to the Soviet leadership. Velikhov reportedly expected the job and may have received signals from the Presidium to that effect, as he invited other reformist people's deputies to join him on the committee.[40]

However, Gorbachev, Supreme Soviet Chairman Lukyanov, and the Supreme Soviet Presidium all refrained from taking steps that might have enabled the committee to serve as a truly influential body. Two years before, Lukyanov had headed the Administrative Organs Department in the CPSU Secretariat, and he is believed, like Gorbachev, to have had "an association with the coterie of officials who worked with Andropov in the KGB."[41]

The military-industrial complex and the KGB won against reformers. Lukyanov appointed Vladimir Lapygin, a lackluster military-industrial careerist from the very sector the committee's intellectual sponsors had wanted to challenge. Seizing on the positive publicity over the revelation that the Supreme Soviet was apparently developing a mechanism to control the KGB, Chairman Kryuchkov touted the new Committee on Defense and Security as a means of transferring control from the Communist Party to the "parliament" and president.[42]

Like the majority of people's deputies, most committee members served only part-time. One senior Soviet military and diplomatic expert said that committee affairs took a "backseat" to deputies' professional careers, evinced by the relatively little time they spent on committee work.[43] Most Committee members held professions that presented fundamental conflicts of interests with their parliamentary work; no legislation forbade such a practice. Half of the committee's original 38 members were identified by one people's deputy as representatives of the military-industrial complex.[44] Another source said that of the 38, 2 were senior KGB officers, five were ranking Communist Party officials, 7 were active duty military officers, and 19 were military industry managers.[45] Of the eventual 43 members, 32 were, according to Mikhail Tsypkin,

> defense ministry executives, military officers, Party functionaries, and government officials, including three high-ranking KGB officers. The remaining minority are university administrators, industrial executives, and three intellectuals who might be less cooperative with the KGB than most of the other members of the committee: Belorussian writer Vasil' Bykov and two social scientists from Estonia and Lithuania, one of whom, Mecys Laurinkus, is a member of [the anti-Communist and pro-independence party] *Sajudis*.[46]

Observed Lee, "Members are subject to conflicts of interest in their duties, since the Committee largely consists of people who continue to build their careers in the very areas the Committee purports to oversee—the Soviet Ministry of Defense (MoD), the defense industries and the state security organs."[47] Committee members included Marshal Sergey Akhromeyev, former chief of the General Staff, who served as military adviser to Supreme Soviet Chairman Lukyanov.[48] A Russian security observer noted that of those members who were not part of the apparat, "quite a few had formal or informal attachments to the KGB."[49] This was also true with members of democratic, anti-Communist organizations and parties.[50]

Vladimir Lapygin, the committee's first chairman, provides a prime example. A rocket scientist who specialized in ICBM guidance systems, Lapygin represented the military-industrial complex. He may have also been co-opted by the KGB. Supreme Soviet Council of the Union Chairman Primakov remarked that Lapygin was chosen by the leadership "after a great deal of thought, after debates and so forth."[51] According to an exceptionally well-informed USSR people's deputy, Lapygin had KGB approval because of personal behavior that compromised his independence and effectiveness. The former lawmaker alleges that Lapygin was regarded as "obedient" because of a severe drinking problem: "This made him vulnerable to denunciation, with witnesses."[52] As such, according to this reasoning, the Ministry of Defense and security apparatus had their interests protected by Lapygin's chairmanship. The full membership protected these same interests.

Before committee work began, Supreme Soviet leaders quickly squelched objections to allowing conflicts of interests. They made their move during the June parliamentary debate which followed the formal announcement of leadership elections. Following debate the Supreme Soviet was to elect chairmen for the thirteen joint committees of the two houses of the Supreme Soviet, the Council of the Union and the Council of Nationalities. During the debate Supreme Soviet Chairman Lukyanov and Council of the Union Chairman Primakov had the floor.

Primakov announced the chairmen of each joint committee, including Committee on Defense and Security chief Lapygin.[53] Debate immediately focused on Defense and Security. The first deputy to take the floor challenged the conflicts-of-interests problem:

> I have calculated that a large part of this committee—19 out of 38 people—consists of representatives of the military-industrial complex. And as chairman of this committee we are being offered a pronounced representative of this military-industrial complex.... Therefore, I would like us to give very careful attention to the principles of the formation of the committees and their chairman, so it doesn't turn out that on the most important committees we have representatives who are not competent in the relevant field or, on the other hand, who have a stake in resolving questions in favor of the apparatus.[54]

A second deputy also addressed committee membership criteria, as did the third lawmaker, Igor N. Gryazin, department head of the Institute of Philosophy, Sociology, and Law at the Estonian Republic Academy of Sciences:

> We all understand that the very fact of the creation of a Committee on Questions of Defense and State Security is a tremendous step forward. ... Shouldn't we remove from the membership of that committee those professional military men who are on active duty and who are now working in the military-industrial complex? We need retired military professionals, of course, and if it's a matter of specialized knowledge, the committee can recruit them as experts. But in my opinion, military men who are on active military duty should not be members of the committee.[55]

Gryazin's words brought wild applause from the floor. Supreme Soviet Chairman Lukyanov, however, stopped such talk, arguing that if such individuals could not serve on the Defense and Security Committee, "the entire system of creating the committees would be disrupted. Then people working actively in agriculture couldn't be included in agriculture committees, and so forth." He allowed no room for making exceptions to the very special situation of Defense and Security, claiming that it would be "simply unconstitutional" to forbid such elected officials to serve on the committee. He did concede, "We must see to it that the military element does not dominate the committee,"[56] but these were mere words and no actions were taken.

Questions emerged from the floor indicating that the parliament as a whole had no say in running the joint committees. One people's deputy asked how the committees were formed and what they would do; another inquired how their members were selected. Primakov's vague responses did little to illuminate the issue. He said that committee members were selected by "technical personnel, on the basis of the applications that were submitted." He did not indicate the positions of these personnel, nor did he reveal the identities of those who submitted applications. Growing defensive, he added, "You shouldn't suspect that the composition of the committees was handed down to us from higher-level organizations of some sort." Yet that was exactly the impression he left.

Then, like Gorbachev during Kryuchkov's "confirmation hearing," and Lukyanov during the debate about eliminating conflicts of interests, Primakov intervened when the deputies began to challenge him. When a voice from the floor called for creation of a committee of elected lawmakers instead of unelected "technical personnel" to choose committee memberships, Primakov retorted, "I believe that the existing situation is more progressive." He then called a recess.[57]

The maneuver failed to stop the momentum of discontent. Later that day Lukyanov reconvened, calling for votes on the candidates for committee chairmen. Noting that the Supreme Soviet leadership offered no alternative candidates, a deputy suggested that in the future, the parliament's rank-and-file be permitted to suggest candidate chairmen from below. Lukyanov entertained the motion, but it was too late for a serious nomination.[58] Lapygin was elected by voice vote, but an "obvious minority" voted against him and an "obvious minority" abstained.[59]

Aside from rubber-stamping Gorbachev's appointment of Kryuchkov as KGB chairman, the committee did no substantive work in the first four months of its existence. Nor did it have a staff.[60] None of its members or eventual staff members were legal experts. Reformist military officers elected to the Supreme Soviet tried to serve on the committee but were excluded; some complained that the body was "remote-controlled from above."[61] Work was largely done in secret, and no transcripts were kept. Since most of the committee's meager activity focused on the military, the KGB's work was allowed to continue unhindered. For that matter, the Defense Ministry was inconvenienced little by the parliamentary body. Several committee members requested details about the 1990 military budget to no avail.[62] They were denied even elementary data on such basic items as the costs of tanks and aircraft.[63]

In the first open hearings on KGB-related matters, the discussion centered on the nonsecret Border Guards. The proceedings were described by one observer as "dominated by the KGB,"[64] and there was little opportunity for the KGB to be challenged. The only publicly known hearings on intelligence or counterintelligence questions during Lapygin's year-long chairmanship took place in a closed session in April 1990. The session did not provide for oversight; rather, it was a secret KGB briefing on foreign intelligence operations against the USSR,[65] presumably to emphasize the chekists' importance.

Not surprisingly, the Committee on Defense and Security was of little value as a check against the abuse of executive power, a fact noted early by then-U.S. Congressman Les Aspin, chairman of the House Committee on Armed Services. Aspin, who sought to assist the committee by providing information about the process of civilian oversight of the military in the United States, led an Armed Services Committee delegation to Moscow in early August 1989 at the invitation of the USSR Supreme Soviet.[66] To help encourage his Soviet counterparts, Aspin reciprocated by inviting Chairman Lapygin and nine other committee members to the United States to view the process firsthand, which they did in February 1990. Aspin was not impressed. At a Soviet Embassy reception to conclude the visit, he commented, "I really don't know. These guys don't know a lot about their own system, let alone ours."[67]

Committee policy did not change significantly in June 1990 when Lapygin was replaced as chairman by Leonid Sharin, a career Party apparatchik from the Amur oblast in the Soviet Far East,[68] or after September 1990 when the Supreme Soviet membership held its by-elections. On the inside, it seemed for a while that Sharin was concerned about KGB abuses. Newly seated People's Deputy Oleg Kalugin, a former highly decorated KGB major general whose criticism of abuses, corruption, and incompetence within the security apparatus had prompted Gorbachev to strip him of his rank and awards, was asked to testify at a closed hearing on problems within the KGB.

The committee leadership gave Kalugin a detailed set of written questions in advance. He answered them extemporaneously in a two-hour meeting and was questioned further. Later he was surprised that the explicit and severe nature of his criticism failed to elicit any repercussions from the KGB. But his frankness led nowhere. The Committee did nothing to follow up, either with Kalugin or with the KGB leadership. After the hearing, to his disappointment, Kalugin was never given any subsequent questions or contacted for clarification of any points. Neither were there any attempts to discredit what he had said. It was as though he had never said anything.[69]

Nor did the committee ever confront the conflicts-of-interest problem. Focusing not on the KGB but on the military, Lee wrote shortly before the putsch,

> The [Committee on Defense and Security] has discussed a number of issues on this score: barring currently-serving military men from simultaneously seeking a legislative position; decreasing the number of members serving on the Committee [on] Defense and Security; and changing some of the functions of the Committee in order to decrease the rule of military structures in Soviet political life. Although the Committee has discussed these issues, such changes would threaten the status of the very people who serve on the Committee.[70]

Even Supreme Soviet Chairman Lukyanov, a hardliner who in June 1989 rebuffed deputies seeking a means to avoid conflicts of interest, acknowledged the situation, noting in an April 1991 interview that many committee members were there "to defend the interests of their own department."[71] Yet he never utilized his immense powers to take remedial action. As a result, the committee had little to show for itself. Its only achievements between its creation in May 1989 and the August 1991 putsch were the dissolution of military construction units and an increased budget to meet soldiers' social needs.[72] The KGB was untouched.[73]

Several observers, both Soviet and American, excused the conflicts of interest as necessary evils. The USSR had few if any independent civilian experts on defense, security, or intelligence. Nikolay Kapranov, an atomic physicist and former consultant to the Defense and Security Committee who later was critical of the conflicts of interest, said the committee depended on military experts. They had to be allowed to retain their old jobs so that they could be attracted to serve the committee at all, he maintained: "We must permit them to remain in previous positions. Otherwise, they will [leave] the Supreme Soviet."[74]

This argument failed to consider the need for a well-paid professional committee staff that would not have to live on two incomes. The committee in 1991 had no restrictions on the number of employees it could hire but had a total staff budget of only 400 rubles ($4) a month.[75] A staff was out of the question. The budgetary problem could have been solved at the pleasure of the Supreme Soviet leadership, though inexperienced junior lawmakers confessed that it did not occur to them to introduce an appropriations bill to fund a full-time professional staff.[76]

Soviet analyst Georgiy Sturua added another dimension. He asserted that the "holiest of holies" would never cooperate with outsiders, that is, citizens who were not somehow connected with the military-industrial complex or the KGB.[77] Though this argument may be true, it fails to consider that the Committee, co-opted as it was from top to bottom, failed to elicit even the most elementary information from the KGB and had no impact whatsoever on any state security or intelligence policy. Furthermore, such noncooperation should have been answered by stiff sanctions against the apparat. The committee's response was submissive. It was unable to learn the number of employees in the KGB, the KGB budget, or the KGB structure—the latter of which was public knowledge in the West. Nor did the KGB provide data on its nonsecret components, such as the Border Guards.[78]

The Law on State Security Organs

Indeed, the Committee on Defense and Security served as a rubber-stamp for the KGB. It provided Chairman Kryuchkov with a means of preserving the structure and authority of the chekist apparatus. With much fanfare, in 1991 the committee considered a Law on State Security Organs. Despite its historic importance as the country's first openly published law on state security, the legislation was little more than a propaganda exercise to appease democrats who demanded civil control over the special services and to prove that perestroika was truly moving the country toward a law-governed society. No reformist legal scholars authored the legislation; instead, it was drawn up by the KGB itself and may have been based on a draft prepared but never completed during the Brezhnev era.[79] Although passage of the law seemed to mark an official end to the KGB's extralegal activities, it actually marked the legalization of criminal actions. The 1991 Law on State Security Organs, instead of being a reformist document for which Gorbachev could take credit, was a totalitarian law for which he had to take blame.

Since 1959, when Khrushchev reorganized the Soviet security and intelligence services, and for that matter since the Cheka was founded in 1917, the KGB's missions and methods had been legalized, in the Soviet context of the term, by secret laws and decrees. According to a ranking KGB official, the chekist apparatus by 1991 was regulated by eight laws and more than 800 governmental (or Party) acts, all of which were secret.[80] A public law governing the activities of the KGB reportedly was initiated as early as 1977 by KGB Chairman Andropov, but it was never enacted.[81]

Impetus for the 1991 law, flawed as it was, came not as a forward-thinking part of Gorbachev's perestroika strategy but as a belated response to public pressure. The Soviet leader made no attempt to initiate debate or legislation to exercise civil control over the activities of the KGB until well after he was pressured by the angry confrontation between parliamentary democrats and Chairman Kryuchkov in July 1989. Waiting an additional year before approving a draft law, Gorbachev turned not to reformist legal scholars or human rights advocates, or even to the Supreme Soviet Committee on Defense and Security (a move that would have been at least procedurally correct if substantively meaningless). Instead, he asked the KGB itself to supervise the draft.[82]

Gorbachev and the KGB failed to subject the draft law to proper legislative review from the beginning, ensuring that reformist voices would play no role in formulating the basic philosophy or approach to the glasnost-era definition of "state security." The important point is not that the co-opted Committee on Defense and Security would have made a difference in how the law redefined state security but that the Gorbachev government imposed the old CPSU definition rather than developing a more liberal concept consistent with the stated intents of his initial political liberalization. Therefore the architects of perestroika sponsored as public law the abusive and discredited chekist status quo. To make matters worse, the Soviet leadership camouflaged the law's abusive core with language promising commitment to individual rights.

Prior to its submission to the Supreme Soviet, according to a KGB Inspection Directorate official, the draft law was sent for multiple reviews throughout the KGB bureaucracy and then to the USSR MVD, the Procuracy, the Supreme Court, the Ministry of Defense, the Ministry of Foreign Affairs, and the Ministry of Justice. Members of the Supreme Soviet Presidium were then solicited for their views, as were officials of "all" republican governments.[83] The draft was also sent for initial consideration to the USSR Academy of Sciences Institute of State and Law, where reformist (if not completely independent) legal experts were sharply critical. Yet the legal scholars themselves did not feel free to speak their minds, even though glasnost by that time had entered its sixth year. Institute Professor V. M. Savitskiy, one of the critics, indicated his own apprehensiveness in challenging the KGB despite the chekists' invitation that he critique the draft legislation:

> My telephone at home started ringing. I picked up the receiver and heard: "The KGB is calling." The voice was distinct, there was a pause after every word. And although I have nothing to hide, my heart simply stood still; the fear was somehow unaccountable. And the voice continued: "We would like to invite you to come down." Pause. I could feel sweat pouring down my back. "Could you spare some time to deliver a lecture to us?" Before saying yes, I had to catch my breath.[84]

Savitskiy was one of the few academy scientists to criticize the KGB publicly before it became socially acceptable to do so. Before the draft law was submitted to the Supreme Soviet, he said that contrary to popular belief, the KGB had not changed. Its personnel had not changed, its ideology and broad powers had not changed, and the removal of Article 6 from the Constitution had no meaningful effect on the chekists:

> The same structures and functions still remain. And the main thing is that in the KGB there are no nonparty members, even in the least significant little job. . . . Therefore the KGB inevitably sees a threat in the representatives of other parties that have just appeared. . . . The KGB is still a secret institution for us. We do not know about its staff or budget. The fear generated by its existence remains. And it will remain until we see changes in this department.[85]

Savitskiy called for a prohibition against "political surveillance," which he described as "the total invasion of state and social structures and personal life," and said that the Soviet Union should have laws similar to those in the United States which protect individual citizens against government intrusion and provide for judicial recourse. The Soviet government, Savitskiy said, "must cut off the giant tentacles of this unseen octopus which pervades all spheres—without exception!—of our domestic life." Only a parliamentary act, he maintained, could accomplish such an objective. He continued, "We must free our life of the degrading suspicion that your colleague is watching your every step and reporting on you. . . . Until we take apart this system of surveillance and universal reporting we will not be able to create a civil society and we will not be able to create a rule-of-law state."[86]

Shortly after Savitskiy's remarks were published, the draft law was presented to the Supreme Soviet presidium, dominated by Gorbachev. Though ready for submission to the Congress of People's Deputies on 3 December the draft was not actually delivered until 28 February 1991. A day later it was officially presented to a socio-economic commission of the Supreme Soviet.[87] This lag coincided with Gorbachev's 3 December removal of reformist Interior Minister Vadim

Bakatin in favor of former Latvian KGB Chairman Boriss Pugo, and the subsequent armed crackdowns in Lithuania and Latvia in which unarmed protesters were beaten, shot, and in one instance, crushed to death by a tank. No attempt was made to conceal the law's origin: The bill was presented to the Supreme Soviet by USSR KGB Deputy Chairman Valeriy Lebedev, who hailed the historic moment as marking the first time the state security organs would be regulated by public law.[88] Fewer than six months later, Lebedev became one of the plotters of the failed attempt to overthrow the government.

The KGB was not content to part with its offspring upon Lebedev's introduction, and the vast majority of legislators did not seem to think this unusual. Chairman Kryuchkov officially unveiled the draft law in a speech before a joint session of both houses of the Supreme Soviet during the bill's first reading on 5 March. Amid his words of lofty optimism and not a little self-congratulation for the historic reforms the law supposedly promised, Kryuchkov indicated the context in which the law would function: It would strengthen "the place and role of the state security bodies in the mechanism of a socialist, law-governed state." The Law on State Security Organs, he said, was the first step in a long process, the core of what he envisioned as a years-long endeavor upon which more specific laws would be built, as in the West. The law, he said, was akin to those in the world's freest societies, such as Great Britain, Germany, and the United States. It was to be the cornerstone of KGB reform under perestroika.[89]

To the inexperienced lawmakers who had never been exposed to genuine civil control mechanisms in established democracies, Kryuchkov's promises that the bill meant fundamental and permanent reform sounded convincing. To Party stalwarts the words were reassuring. Only a few deputies came out in opposition. Anatoliy Sobchak, Yuriy Ryzhov, Irina Andreyeva and others voiced strong objections and asked that the legislators carefully study and debate the issue. Several maneuvers shepherded by Marshal Sergey Akhromeyev (a member of the Committee on Defense and Security) and Committee on Legislation Chairman Yuriy Kalmykov kept the bill from being subjected to critical scrutiny. Submitted just days before it was considered, the long and complicated law was not published and therefore was initially insulated from independent analysts and journalists. Neither Gorbachev nor the Supreme Soviet Presidium so much as suggested that the country rethink its fundamental chekist approach to state security. Several lawmakers complained that they had little chance to study or debate the document. Natalya Gevorkyan, who covered the proceedings for *Moscow News*, reported, "The draft law had not been discussed, as prescribed by the procedure, at all the committees and commissions of the Supreme Soviet." Most important, as Ryzhov observed, no debate was allowed on "the general concept of state security"; if the law was to be the base for all future security legislation, surely the lawmakers should discuss principles and goals before discussing regulations. Then the Supreme Soviet leadership called a vote on the first reading to approve its general provisions, and the bill passed overwhelmingly.[90]

Many members of parliament expressed dissatisfaction with the way the law was presented and voted upon. Commented Gevorkyan, "The legislators who voted 'for' did not fully understand the nature of the vote since the draft circulated among them, as announced in the conference hall, did not contain the latest changes and addenda, i.e., it was simply incomplete."[91] A small group of thirty-two democratic people's deputies worked on an alternative bill of their own but got nowhere.[92]

With the initial draft approved, the bill was revised over the next two months. According to acting Committee on Defense and Security Chairman Leonid Sharin, the process was open to any lawmaker,[93] although the entire process was strictly controlled by the leadership. The final version was approved on 16 May with Kryuchkov present to offer his imprimatur in a celebratory speech. A Western correspondent who covered the session reported that the KGB chief "thanked legislators with untypical passion after they passed the bill."[94]

Provisions of the Law

What was it about the law that made the dour Kryuchkov so passionate? The law did not split the KGB into separate services for intelligence, counterintelligence, internal security, presidential guards, border guards, and the like but preserved it as a single, all-encompassing agency. It made the KGB responsible for "state security" without defining the term. Bowing to nationalist awakenings in the periphery, it did call for some decentralization by converting the KGB from an all-Union to a Union-republican service, giving more responsibility to individual republic KGB structures while keeping their subordination to the center. Other minor adjustments were made, such as formally removing the KGB from Party control, to make the organization's status consistent with previous perestroika legislation and decrees. Words pledging protection of individual rights, appeals processes, and other liberal guarantees were added to the law, but in substance such measures would not necessarily be observed, as the August putsch proved.

Thus the law offered no substantive change. Indeed, the law helped ensure the KGB's independence from the Soviet political leadership. Not only was Gorbachev's control as CPSU general secretary legally broken following the unilateral repeal of the Communist Party's monopoly of power, but his control as state president was officially weakened. At the same time, the hard-line Supreme Soviet enjoyed greater influence over state security on paper, though not in practice. A month after the law was published and officially in force, Kryuchkov attempted to use the Supreme Soviet to topple Gorbachev in a legal coup. Only after this effort failed did the KGB stage the August putsch.

For the purpose of this discussion, I shall focus on those sections of the law that enabled the KGB to maintain its abusive potential and the absence of measures mandating civil control and oversight.[95] Some of the law's major flaws follow.

KGB Structure and Authority Preserved. The new law preserved the old KGB structure and lines of authority yet did not define KGB personnel duties and did not include measures for penalties for abuse of authority.[96] Prior to the law's enactment, the KGB's most noxious structures had assumed new names; the Fifth Chief Directorate, which carried out political repression, for example, reappeared as the Directorate for Protection of the Constitutional System. Yet in praising the new law, acting Committee on Defense and Security Chairman Sharin hailed the official "establishment of a directorate within the KGB for the protection of the constitutional system" as a "new" security function that had been absent in the past and was therefore a positive development that would help safeguard human rights.[97]

Politicized Controls Preserved. The law stipulated that the KGB was "not bound by the resolutions of political parties." This wording, however, according to Yasmann, was "taken directly from the Institutions on the Work of CPSU Organizations in the Armed Forces" published in March 1990 and was consistent with a subsequent Gorbachev decree that made the military, the MVD and the KGB subordinate to the CPSU-run state government rather than to the CPSU Central Committee.[98] There was no innovation here, merely an attempt to remain consistent with earlier presidential decrees. The entire KGB staff maintained CPSU membership and discipline. Officers who broke with Party discipline were punished.[99]

Powers over Republican Legislatures. The law made it "obligatory for ministries, state committees, departments, enterprises, institutions, organizations, and public associations' bodies to fulfill . . . acts [on state security issued by the KGB]."[100] Therefore the law positioned the KGB to issue legally binding orders to civilian bureaucracies and nongovernmental organizations. Even if the orders themselves were not established by law, they would have to be followed. The power of the KGB would thus supersede that of republican legislatures.

Total Investigative Power. The law authorized the KGB to monitor all state entities, including the Interior Ministry (MVD), which controlled the police, as well as the Defense Ministry, the military, and "organs of public associations."[101] There would be no counterweight to the KGB, and no institution to monitor its activities or to investigate alleged crimes carried out by its personnel.

Secret Informer Networks Maintained. The law authorized the KGB to continue its extensive use of secret informers, and, though it stipulated that recruitment be voluntary, it imposed no definitions of voluntarism or restrictions on recruitment methods.[102] In the past, the KGB recruited informers through blackmail. This law, providing no measures to the contrary, apparently permitted continued "voluntary" use of informers who had been recruited against their will or who had "volunteered" out of fear. The law also charged the services to "provide protection against public disclosure of information concerning a citizen's confidential assistance to the security bodies."[103] In theory, this clause allowed the KGB to act against individuals or media outlets exposing collaborators.

The Right to Wiretap and Open Mail Without Judicial Order. No independent judiciary existed in the Soviet system, and the law did not envision one. It merely stipulated that the prosecutor be notified after the fact when the KGB conducted wiretapping or mail interception. It provided no deadline for notification, nor was there any provision in the event a prosecutor might reject such intrusions. The law did not delineate the powers of the prosecutor, and it did not address the problem of abuses of power.[104]

Deprivation of the Right to Travel. The law permitted the KGB to restrict an individual's right to travel abroad, granting the service sole power to determine who had "access to facts that are state secrets in connection with their departure abroad and application to give up USSR citizenship."[105] What constituted a state secret was not defined.

No Freedom of Information. The law did oblige state security organs to "give explanations at the request of a citizen as to the reasons for them restricting his rights and liberties," but little else. The law permitted the KGB to maintain criminal records and lacked provisions for the periodic expunging of files, correction of erroneous information, overturning of convictions, and other considerations.[106] It made no provision for, or recognition of, an individual's right to inspect his file. On a broader scale, the law allowed the KGB to "provide information to state bodies, working collectives, public associations, and media on the questions of insuring state security," but it provided for no declassification or freedom of information procedures. As the post-putsch discovery of KGB wiretap transcripts in Gorbachev's office proved, a section of the law barring disclosure of "information concerning the private life, honor and dignity of the citizens which has become known to the state security bodies" was not observed.[107]

Control over all Aspects of Secrecy. The law granted the KGB complete authority to control all files concerning state security.[108] It did provide for the KGB to establish a system of "registration, storage and use" consistent with future laws. However, Russian Supreme Soviet human rights staff expert Ernst Orlovskiy noted that the KGB was legally "absolute master of archive documents concerning its activities. . . . It makes it the master independently determining the procedure for recording, storing, and using them. The law does not provide for any time limit for transferring these documents to state archives. It turns out that the KGB is free either to conceal these documents forever, including from the Supreme Soviet, or to destroy them as itself sees fit."[109]

Economic Functions. The KGB's monopoly on investigating crimes involving hard currency or salable goods was retained; it was also expanded to include the monitoring of commercial information and telecommunications and the administration of Soviet satellite telecommunications, which were deemed critical to the country's economic and industrial modernization.[110] Again, there was no measure preventing selective enforcement of economic crimes to the benefit of the nomenklatura and chekists who were actively engaged in illegal business practices. This law ensured that no other agency would have the authority to investigate the KGB's own front companies.

Political Harassment. The law made no provision to protect the individual from being harassed by the KGB. Observed a reformist lawmaker, "There is a need for clockwork regulation for the use of the network of agents and human rights guaranteeing society against the special services being turned into a political police."[111] The law provided for no such regulation.

Force Against Political Demonstrations. The law specifically permitted the KGB to use force against political demonstrations by authorizing personnel to use riot-control gear as well as "combat fighting techniques," "armored cars, other modes of transport, and service dogs," as well as "other special means," not only against armed situations but to "halt mass disturbances" and to "detain lawbreakers showing disobedience and resistance." Because the terms were not defined, the law left their interpretation up to the KGB. The law also left open the question of which civil authorities would authorize such action—or whether the KGB could act on its own in such instances. Even in the event it was subject to civilian direction, no parameters were set to indicate when the services had to refrain from using force against a demonstration or act of civil disobedience.[112] This provision legalized deadly crackdowns like the one against unarmed demonstrators in Tblisi.

Warrantless Searches. The law permitted the KGB, without the authority of a judge or even a prosecutor, to "have unimpeded access at any time of day or night for the purpose of directly stopping crimes . . . or in pursuing persons suspected of committing such crimes, where there are exceptional circumstances that threaten state security, to enter housing or other premises belonging to citizens, and the grounds and premises of enterprises, institutions, and organizations, and inspect them."[113] The prosecutor would be notified up to 24 hours after the fact, but there was no provision whereby a prosecutor could deny the KGB's authority to make such a search. Again, neither this nor any other Soviet law defined "state security," making it impossible for the citizen engaged in nonviolent opposition to the government to know whether his activity was legal.

Arrest and Detention. The law granted the KGB the authority to detain citizens held by the police, prosecutors, and courts.[114] The KGB maintained its own prisons and detention centers apart from the civil penal system.

Right to Shoot an Individual. The law restricted the right of a state security officer to use a firearm or "special means" against an individual, with one large loophole: An officer could shoot "To detain a person . . . caught red-handed committing a crime."[115] Since the type of crime was not defined, and since criminal behavior at the time included certain unauthorized political expression such as criticism of the president, the restriction was especially ominous, giving the KGB the right to shoot demonstrators.

Protection from "Insults." Although the law in reality did little to preserve the rights of Soviet citizens, it went to unusual lengths to preserve those of KGB personnel and dependents. The law ratified earlier presidential decrees that made it a crime to "insult" or impinge upon the "honor" or "dignity" of a KGB officer or family member.[116] This clause, which included revelations of wrongdoing, severely restricted free speech and conceivably allowed KGB personnel to use force in response to public insults or criticism.

Civil Control. Only two paragraphs of the law were dedicated to civil control over the KGB. On the republican level, the KGB was accountable both to "the highest bodies of state power and government of the corresponding republics" and to the USSR KGB. The activities of the USSR KGB, in turn, would be "monitored" by the USSR Supreme Soviet, the USSR president, and the USSR Cabinet of Ministers. The Procuracy would ensure that KGB activity was lawful—a moot point given that the Procuracy was penetrated by the KGB, and more important, that the law authorized the abusive measures of the past. However, the law made all procedures and types of information necessary for oversight and control the exclusive domain of the USSR president.[117] Thus, the nominally elected Supreme Soviet surrendered all meaningful oversight matters to the presidential apparatus. There was no perestroika in the security reform law of perestroika. Soviet President Mikhail Gorbachev signed the law in the Kremlin on 16 May 1991.

It was subsequently reported that, unknown to several democratic people's deputies, the law contained a series of classified amendments granting the KGB extraordinary powers of internal security. These amendments, according to one Russian human rights monitor, took the form of "decrees in the USSR Supreme Soviet Presidium, resolutions and ordinances of the USSR Government, and also normative acts promulgated by the KGB itself." In November 1990, just a month before the draft law was finalized, the USSR Constitutional Oversight Committee had ruled these same measures unconstitutional, but they were submitted and enacted nevertheless.[118] The classified amendments included one granting the KGB broad and publicly unknown powers through 31 December 1992.[119]

The vagueness of Soviet laws stifled dissent by encouraging self-censorship and permitted authorities to crack down at any time, as they had on numerous occasions in 1990 and 1991. With a nebulous legal definition of "terrorist" or "criminal" behavior, no definition of "mass disturbance" or "disobedience," and no definition of "state secret" or "state security," the law permitted Soviet authorities arbitrarily to take action against legitimate political, cultural or business activities. The new law authorized the KGB to fight "terrorism and organized crime affecting state security interests," yet it did not define these offenses. Though the law mandated that detentions be carried out only "in cases provided for by the law," the unknown amendments made it impossible for the public to know whether a given action was legal.

KGB and MVD leaders, including Kryuchkov, denounced the actions of democratically elected parliaments in independence-minded republics as "terrorist" and "criminal"; the vagueness of the law technically allowed the KGB henceforth to combat those local parliamentary actions with the full authority of the USSR Supreme Soviet.[120]

Despite the official repeal of Article 6 of the Constitution, which gave the Communist Party its political monopoly, the USSR Law on State Security Organs did not ensure that non-Party members would be given equal protection with Party members when it came to internal security matters. The Party elite, or nomenklatura, in effect would remain outside the purview of KGB surveillance. Former KGB Maj. Gen. Oleg Kalugin, a ranking counterintelligence officer in Leningrad during the first four years of the perestroika period, alleged that the KGB still maintained a "list of 'untouchables'" in the nomenklatura who were generally off-limits to investigation unless they fell into political disfavor. Said Kalugin, "Special lists . . . protect 'special people' from unpleasantness," but more important, "The main thing is that everyone is by no means equal under law."[121]

Conclusion

Although the KGB in the year before the coup was more accessible and outspoken than ever, the organization remained closed to scrutiny for continued and past abuses. As it drew up legislation, surrounded Gorbachev with co-optees, and expanded its own powers, the KGB opened public relations centers in Moscow and in the capitals of the republics, held news conferences, participated in seminars, and provided information to journalists. Although much of this information revealed the mechanics of the state security apparatus or helped to rehabilitate victims of repression during the Stalinist period, the KGB fundamentally remained impervious to the sunshine of glasnost and diverted attention from that fact.

Ultimate responsibility belonged to Gorbachev. Not only did the Soviet leader give Kryuchkov virtually free rein; in his quest to create a more liberalized society without true liberalism, to expand political freedoms without freeing them, and to control the process from above without meeting needs and aspirations from below, he had to preserve the very machinery of control. Gorbachev created not a real parliament but a phony one; he proposed not real structures to check the KGB's powers but cosmetic ones. In so doing, he not only cheapened his perestroika and glasnost hallmarks; he showed that despite the historical advances he had permitted, he could not bring himself to allow forces of democracy to run their course.

These were personal decisions and actions for which he cannot avoid responsibility. Nowhere was his conscious attempt to smother real reforms more openly and shamelessly exhibited than in the summer of 1989 when he and his toady Primakov personally tried to thwart democrats on the floor of the Supreme Soviet in their challenge to Kryuchkov and the cult of chekism. Only later did he go through the motions to project the image that state security was being overseen by elected officials; behind the scenes he allowed the KGB to proceed as it pleased.

Then came the putsch, which not only destroyed Gorbachev politically but smashed his cherished Communist Party (against which he would refuse to testify) and Union of Soviet Socialist Republics. Only when the hermetic seal around his inner circle was broken did the truth start to emerge. Documents began to reveal the personal complicity of the great world leader in the most unstatesmanlike, petty, and totalitarian decisions and actions against his own people. Russian parliamentary investigators who sifted through documents from the KGB and from Gorbachev's office reported:

> We studied carefully the correspondence between the president of the USSR and the leadership of the KGB during the '80s and '90s. Our conclusions: Attempts to exert pressure upon the democratic forces, attempts to remove the democratic forces from the political arena, were being hatched by the Committee for State Security in the autumn of 1990. Kryuchkov repeatedly sent letters to Gorbachev, the aim of which was the introduction of a state of emergency and the use of acts of force and repressive actions against the democratic forces. We found all the correspondence that preceded the use of troops in Vilnius. It was addressed to Gorbachev directly by leadership of the Committee. We found letters calling for acts of force against the Russian Parliament in March of [1991]. . . .
>
> We found a mass of documents containing evidence of anticonstitutional activity by the Committee for State Security. And in fact, Gorbachev, the president of the USSR, was informed about this work and Gorbachev took no steps to halt this anticonstitutional activity by the Committee for State Security.[122]

The Soviet leader was indeed a deliverance from the nightmare of communism-as-usual and a major catalyst for change in the world. Any objective assessment of his place in history, however, must be made not only in the context of his reforms but in the light of his dogged attempts to keep reforms from going to their logical conclusion, which was liberal democracy. Gorbachev shines in comparison to his predecessors, but he pales when compared to the leaders of Western democracies who at times seemed to accept him as one of their own—and often as superior. No Western leader, even in France where political black bag jobs are not uncommon, or in Israel, whose very survival was threatened daily by hostile neighbors who denied even its right to exist, would have permitted the uncontrolled excesses perpetrated systematically by the security services with the support of the head of state and government.

6

Civil Controls in the Russian Federation

A draining battle with the security forces is not part of anybody's political strategy.

—Aleksandr Kichikhin,
former colonel, KGB Fifth Chief Directorate, 1993[1]

Some [political] parties should be under constant surveillance. We have to determine now which parties should be controlled.

—Nikolay Golushko,
Minister of Security, October 1993[2]

Following the 1991 putsch, the Russian government developed state mechanisms to control the security and intelligence services it had inherited from the Soviet Union. These controls changed at least three times between December 1991 and June 1992, reflecting political infighting within the top echelons of government over who would influence the direction of reforms. Eventually those most closely allied with the entrenched military-industrial and security interests prevailed, but the exact dynamics of control were never understood, even by some of the country's political leaders.

A judicial review mechanism, the Constitutional Court, was created in 1991. A year before, when Russian lawmakers had first conceived of the court, most had thought it would be little more than a ceremonial body. Immediately following the Soviet collapse, however, the Constitutional Court proved its intention to be much more than symbolic and made a key decision that successfully challenged one aspect of the executive's unchecked control over the state security organs. The court's powers, suspended by presidential decree in late 1993 to await implementation of a new constitution, are still uncertain. Although the court has been heavily politicized, the foundation for a functioning judiciary, however small, has been set.

Until its dissolution in September 1993, the Russian Supreme Soviet, the standing "parliament" elected in 1990 in the image of its USSR counterpart, was likewise dominated by Communist Party holdovers and representatives of the vast bureaucracy and military-industrial sector infiltrated from the beginning by the KGB. Prior to the 1990 elections for the congresses of people's deputies in Russia and other republics, from which each respective Supreme Soviet was chosen, the KGB set up special task forces to organize and manipulate the electoral processes. It conducted training courses in political organization for KGB-backed candidates, and provided those candidates with privileged political and economic information concerning their constituencies. Open KGB officers—2,756 in all—ran in the federal, regional, and local parliamentary races in all fifteen republics, and 86 percent of them won in the first round. In Russia, 57 percent of the 630 overt KGB officers who ran won the first round.[3] Several of them took prominent positions in the federal Supreme Soviet.

Immediately following the 1991 putsch, it appeared as if the Russian Federation Supreme Soviet was taking steps to help break apart the theretofore impenetrable armor of the KGB and bring some of its grim secrets to light. The executive and legislative branches subsequently seemed to devote much time and energy to bringing the organs under the control of law and making them accountable to elected institutions, but initial hopes that the controls would be meaningful were soon dampened by the realization that Russia's post-Soviet leaders wanted to use the Soviet security system for their own purposes. A series of laws to control the organs, publicized with much fanfare, in reality granted the security forces many of the abusive powers they had enjoyed when they were known collectively as the KGB. As with the USSR Law on State Security Organs of 1991, these laws were not imposed by lawmakers but initiated by the chekists.

The core law, based on the above Soviet statute though somewhat less draconian, is the Law on Security of 1992. It supposedly established strict controls by the executive branch, the legislative branch, and the state prosecutor. More than a year after its enactment the actual mechanisms of control were unclear.[4] Many of the 6,000 secret regulations governing the KGB were still in force by 1993, according to one observer who noted, "No one seems to have a very clear idea of how the [Ministry of Security's] day-to-day activities are in fact monitored."[5]

New Definition of Security

Russia's break from the Soviet center began in earnest in 1989 when Boris Yeltsin, as a member of the new USSR Supreme Soviet two years after his expulsion from the Politburo, publicly challenged the authority of the KGB and the CPSU. The break widened the next year when Yeltsin demanded a separate state security apparatus for the Russian Federation. By this time he was echoing the demands of his staunchest supporters in the anti-Communist Democratic Russia movement, many of whom were former dissidents and political prisoners. He repeatedly called for an end to the machinery that Kremlin elites used to subjugate the population. The KGB was the subject of withering attacks from Democratic Russia, reformist journalists and cultural figures, and disgruntled KGB officers themselves. It therefore stood to reason that, following the 1991 putsch and the Soviet collapse, the leaders of the Russian Federation would attempt to redefine the concept of security consistent with democratic and liberal ideals.

But reason does not always stand. Although the Russian government ascended in political stature and strength after the coup attempt, it rapidly lost momentum, internally divided as it was between young, pro-Western reformists like Prime Minister Yegor Gaydar and his economic and legal progressives, on one side, and nomenklatura and in the intellectual, state, industrial, military, and security sectors, on the other. Economic change was given to the Gaydar team, but security matters were left to the chekists. Few if any officials outside KGB and militsiya circles would play a meaningful role in reforming Yeltsin's concept of the organs of security.

The KGB took the initiative. It was the organs themselves—not democratic reformers—that initiated discussion and offered the first new definition in a draft Law on Security introduced in early 1992. On the surface, the debate presented an opportunity for Yeltsin and his allies to attack the foundations of chekism from above as well as from below. In May the Supreme Soviet passed the law, which offered a new, official definition of security. Article 1 defines the "concept of security and its objects" as follows:

> Security is the situation whereby the vital interests of the individual, society, and state are secure from internal and external threat.
>
> Vital interests are the combination of requirements which are reliably satisfied by the existence of and opportunities for the progressive development of the individual, society, and state.

> The following are ranked as fundamental objects of security: the individual—his rights and freedoms; society—its material and spiritual assets; the state—its constitutional system, sovereignty, and territorial integrity.[6]

This attempt to redefine security suffers from several fatal flaws. First, it is sufficiently vague as to permit even the most ardent chekist to agree and to continue his work accordingly. Second, nowhere in Russian jurisprudence does there exist the equivalent of a bill of inalienable rights; hence, there are few "fundamental objects" of individual security for the state to protect. The state is placed on par with the individual—a dangerous equation in a society in which the state always wins. The statement about protection of the "material and spiritual assets" of society may be taken as authority to control not only property but conscience, an intolerable mandate in any democracy that is all the more disturbing because the organ empowered to "protect" spirituality is precisely that which persecuted people for their consciences not many years ago. Finally, a fundamental object of state security—the constitution—is explicitly defined.

Yet neither the old Brezhnev-era RSFSR Constitution of 1978 still in force, though amended more than 300 times through 1993, nor the new Constitution voted upon at the end of the year protects inalienable rights according to international standards of liberal democracies. The security services can thus operate constitutionally under most of the terms of the old regime. The state still reigns supreme in practice. To do so, it requires a powerful "state security" system.

Russian political culture, still grotesquely disfigured from decades of one-party rule, is such that even democratic legislators approved of the new security concept and voted for the law, which announces in its preamble that it "enshrines the legal foundations of the security of the individual, society, and state." Therefore, subsequent legislation based on the principles laid down therein, presents the chekist apparatus with the legal authority to survive and operate without significant modification.

Presidential Mechanisms to Administer the Security Organs

Executive mechanisms to administer and control the security and intelligence organs are not well understood even by many Russian insiders. A succession of new presidential offices and mechanisms to run state security, confusion about their legal status, and conflicting reports about their official and actual functions indicate that the civil government exercises very little real control and that the security organs operate with few real checks and balances.

Until May 1991 the Russian Federation had no need of a political control structure for security and intelligence services, because it had no such organs aside from a relatively new Ministry of Internal Affairs. As the erosion of central Soviet authority quickly accelerated prior to the putsch and Yeltsin succeeded in establishing a minuscule but symbolically important Russian KGB, his government began to conceptualize a presidential apparatus with which to administer the services.[7] In the months following the putsch, with broad executive powers granted by the country's Congress of People's Deputies to absorb the Soviet services, Yeltsin was still without such a mechanism until late December 1991 or early January 1992.

Initially, the security services (officially at least) reported to one of the most reformist members of the Yeltsin government, Sergey Shakhray, vice premier and state councillor for legal policy.[8] It was the loyal Shakhray who had forcefully if reluctantly defended the formation of the immensely unpopular Ministry of Security and Internal Affairs (MBVD). Under his direction the government had developed a new mechanism for administration of the security organs, the Presidential State and Legal Administration (Gosudarstvenno-pravovoye upravleniye). The MBVD had been assaulted from all sides for resembling Stalin's NKVD; the unfortunate acronym for this new organ, GPU—the same as that for the renamed Cheka that had preceded the NKVD—only heightened criticism in the Supreme Soviet. Yeltsin gave the GPU broad powers to coordinate the Ministry of Defense, the Ministry of Justice, the Procuracy, and the MBVD, as well as bureaucracies concerned with nationalities, citizenship, and civil defense,[9] and formally gave administrative authority to Shakhray.[10]

Despite his impassioned defense of the MBVD before the Supreme Soviet and the Constitutional Court and his noteworthy personal fidelity to Yeltsin, Shakhray saw his authority quickly dwindle; he was not able to exercise the administrative powers over the ministries that he and his GPU had been given on paper. Too serious a legal reformer to let the new concentrated security apparatus stand unchallenged over the long term, Shakhray was likely viewed by the organs as more of a threat than an ally; he was too independent to allow himself to be co-opted, though it could be argued that he had seriously damaged himself politically in defending Yeltsin's authorization of the new MBVD, even though the objective was to subdue the chekists. Shakhray was also overextended personally. In addition to his two major government posts he was an active member of the Supreme Soviet. By spring 1992, Gennadiy Burbulis, who was given authority to supervise foreign operations, had eclipsed Shakhray and managed to acquire his authority to supervise the security and intelligence organs. However, Burbulis's triumph was short-lived. Lacking an effective apparatus, he proved unable to take charge of the internal security services.[11]

The organ chiefs themselves were able to circumvent Shakhray and Burbulis by taking their cases directly to the president on a regular basis. Until he was fired in July 1993, apparently for playing a double game with Yeltsin's archrival, Supreme Soviet Chairman Ruslan Khasbulatov,[12] Security Minister Barannikov was able to go over the heads of the reformist presidential assistants and induce Yeltsin to approve his own empire building within the security apparatus. Barannikov quickly consolidated his own personal power and those of the institutions he led. His rushed presentation of the decree creating the MBVD on the tarmac as Yeltsin boarded his plane to Rome—in time for the Cheka's anniversary—is a case in point.

Shakhray's quixotic public defense of the megaministry after it had been established behind his back and against his advice cannot have helped him earn much of the security minister's esteem even if it did support him politically. By mid-1992, having thoroughly removed even the most moderately reformist top officers in Lubyanka, Barannikov's control over the Security Ministry appeared strong. Until he tried to double-cross Yeltsin, he reportedly enjoyed access to the president matched by only two other members of the government: Burbulis and presidential secretary Ilyushin.[13] Shakhray, who was replaced as GPU chief by former army political commissar Lt. Col. Aleksandr Kotenkov, was significantly marginalized, though he remained in the loop if not the innermost security circle. Minister of Justice Yuriy Kalmykov was unlikely to intervene. After all it was he, as chairman of the Committee on Legislation of the USSR Supreme Soviet, who had helped maneuver the passage of Kryuchkov's 1991 Law on State Security Organs.

Security Council

A presidential structure to coordinate policies related to state security was authorized by the Supreme Soviet in its May 1992 Law on Security.[14] The structure, known as the Security Council, had been conceptualized for about a year, but Yeltsin appeared to be in no hurry to make it a reality despite the void created by its absence. Described as "the fourth pillar of presidential power" in the Russian Federation (the other three being the State Council, the Council of Ministers, and the Council of the Federation and Territories), the idea of a Security Council was first discussed shortly before the August 1991 putsch when the Yeltsin government was asserting itself at the expense of the Soviet center. As originally envisioned for a Russia that remained part of the USSR, the Security Council would liaise with security services on the all-Union level and coordinate responses to crisis situations, such as natural disasters and ecological problems.[15]

Formed and administered by presidential decree in accordance with the Law on Security, the Security Council of the post-Soviet Russian Federation apparently had a much more powerful function than originally intended by lawmakers. The Supreme Soviet gave the Security Council a range of responsibilities that significantly broadened the new definition of security:

> The Russian Federation Security Council is a constitutional organ which prepares decisions of the Russian Federation president in the spheres of ensuring security.
>
> The Russian Federation Security Council examines questions of the Russian Federation's domestic and foreign policy in the sphere of ensuring security and strategic problems of state, economic, public, defense, information, ecological, and other types of security, public health protection, forecasting and prevention of emergencies and elimination of their consequences, and the ensuring of stability of law and order, and is accountable to the Russian Federation Supreme Soviet for the state of protection of the vital interests of the individual, society, and the state against external and internal threats.[16]

However, the Supreme Soviet did not endow the Security Council with real powers. It had authority under the law to do no more than "prepare decisions" for the president and "examine questions." It was to be "accountable" not to the president but to parliament. Yeltsin signed the law but proceeded to make the Security Council much stronger than envisioned by his legislative rivals.

Security Council sessions, held weekly and usually on Wednesdays, are closed. The first meeting took place on 20 May 1992 and was chaired by President Yeltsin. An *Izvestiya* correspondent was told that the main agenda items, which were not officially made public, included the concept of Russian security, the Security Council structure, the statute on the Security Council, and the structure of the Defense Ministry and Armed Forces General Staff.[17] Decisions, determined by a simple majority of permanent or ex officio members, may be implemented by presidential decree.[18] Original permanent members included the president (Boris Yeltsin), the vice president (Aleksandr Rutskoy), the first deputy chairman of the Supreme Soviet (Sergey Filatov, an opponent of Khasbulatov), the chairman of the Council of Ministers or premier (acting Prime Minister Yegor Gaydar), and the Security Council secretary (Yuriy Skokov), as well as nonvoting members who include the ministers of security, internal affairs, foreign affairs, justice and defense; the director general of the External Intelligence Service; and certain state committee chiefs. Burbulis and Shakhray were notably absent. Filatov remained on the Security Council after he was removed as Supreme Soviet first deputy chairman, though he surrendered his right to vote on council matters to his replacement, Yuriy Voronin.[19]

Yeltsin publicly stated that he envisioned the body as having only a small working staff because such an arrangement would prevent it from being used illegally to seize control of the government.[20] At the same time, however, the president made high-profile statements and personnel appointments that indicated a reversal of reforms to placate pro-Communist and extreme nationalist elements.[21] One of the casualties was Vice Premier Sergey Shakhray, who was relieved of his duties as state councillor.[22] Shakhray warned publicly that precisely the Communist/nationalist elements, some of which had sympathizers, such as Rutskoy and Skokov, in the Security Council membership, would usurp the president's powers in a "collective leadership."[23] Shakhray was given new duties far from Moscow as a troubleshooter in the volatile Caucasus and was made chairman of a State Committee for Nationalities Policy.

Soon, however, the Security Council began to draw criticism from pro-Yeltsin reformers and neo-Bolshevik adversaries alike, first in response to a presidential decree dated 7 July that greatly centralized the body's powers. The decree, "On the Procedure for Implementing the Russian Security Council's Decisions," instructed all top officials of federal ministries and departments and of local state management offices to prepare extensive measures of compliance with Security Council decisions and to report fortnightly to the council.[24] In another presidential bow to the military-industrial lobby, the decree also granted hard-line Security Council Secretary Skokov extraordinary powers to coordinate all government organs to carry out council decisions. The terms of the decree entrusted Skokov, a career manager in the military-industrial sector who had served as RSFSR deputy prime minister in 1990, with "monitoring the realization of Security Council decisions and Russian Federation presidential decrees on questions of security" and, even more significantly, with "coordinating the activities of organs of executive power in the process of realizing adopted decisions."[25]

Following the 7 July decree, President Yeltsin's hard-line opponents in the Supreme Soviet tried to block creation of the Security Council by adopting a new "Law on the Protection of Constitutional Organs of State Power," which forbade the executive to add new structures to existing constitutional bodies.[26] This bill may have been more an expression of Supreme Soviet Chairman Khasbulatov's attempts to encroach upon Yeltsin's turf than it was an attempt to protect constitutional organs, as the Security Council had been authorized by the Supreme Soviet just two months before. What had not been authorized was the authority that Yeltsin had given the new office. In any case, Yeltsin ignored the law.

Security Council voting members almost immediately took a tough stance against reformists. At their 8 July meeting—a day after the official date of the presidential decree empowering Skokov and while Yeltsin was away at a G-7 summit in Munich—they recommended that Foreign Minister Andrey Kozyrev and First Deputy Minister Fedor Shelov-Kovedyayev be removed. Yeltsin retained his top diplomats but failed to take action against the wayward council members.

Democrats, including Shakhray, were alarmed at the Security Council's rapid accumulation of powers. In August, Shakhray accused the Security Council of operating like the CPSU Politburo: "This club possesses an exceptionally wide sphere of interests, and there is no effective form of control on its work."[27] Given the nature of the Supreme Soviet under Khasbulatov, the Security Council might have been the right prescription for Russia's ills, enabling the reformist president to bypass the troublesome legislature. A strong central council might have been justified as a counterweight.

It soon became apparent, however, that the Security Council had become the vehicle by which the security and military services could implement their own policies. One high-level Security Council official said that Yeltsin paid little attention to security policy, indicating that decisionmaking in this area was left to others, presumably the council or the security chiefs themselves.[28] It was reported in early August that the Security Council had appointed, without Yeltsin's support, hard-line General Aleksandr Lebed, an Afghanistan veteran who had urged employment of military force throughout the territory of the former USSR, to be commander of the 14th Army in Moldova, which was actively supporting a secessionist movement there to create a Russian-speaking Trans-Dniester Republic.[29] The president is not known to have fought the appointment, which he could have stopped by decree, nor is he known to have made a public statement on the matter.

The authority of military-industrial interests within the Security Council grew by late 1992 following a stormy Congress of People's Deputies session that succeeded in ousting State Secretary Burbulis and Prime Minister Gaydar and demanded the removal of Foreign Minister Kozyrev. Yeltsin yielded. He removed Gaydar as acting Premier and replaced him with Viktor Chernomyrdin, a veteran of the oil and gas industry and part of the nomenklatura ruling class. A presidential decree formed an "Interdepartmental Foreign Policy Commission" within the council to coordinate foreign policy decisions over the head of Kozyrev. The decree named Skokov as commission chairman.[30] By early 1993, Russian political observers termed Skokov the "second most powerful" figure in the country after Yeltsin.[31]

Although they continued to have Yeltsin's ear, Russia's reformists were outnumbered in the presidential apparatus responsible for administering the security and intelligence services even though Shakhray had been appointed to the Security Council. Apparently Shakhray's main duty was to formulate policies for contending with unrest among ethnic minority groups in Russia, as he retained the chairmanship of the State Committee for Nationalities Policy.[32] He was not positioned to challenge Skokov, who came to identify openly with Supreme Soviet Chairman Khasbulatov by the time of the March 1993 Congress of People's Deputies session. At that point, Yeltsin fired Skokov. He later replaced him with former Commonwealth of Independent States Joint Armed Forces Commander-in-Chief Yevgeniy Shaposhnikov.

Some doubt remained as to the actual authority of the Security Council on state security matters. Vadim Bakatin argued that the Security Council's powers were exaggerated by critics, explaining that by September 1992, the organization was not fully functioning and still lacked the necessary staff and office space.[33] If this early assessment is accurate—and given the Security Council's broad jurisdiction it appears that a sufficient staff would have to be rather large—it indicates that the special services may have retained a significant degree of autonomy from the president or that their leaders remained able to circumvent presidential structures such as the Security Council and appeal directly to Yeltsin without the benefit of a policy discussion.

Shaposhnikov revealed nearly a year later that the Security Council was becoming irrelevant as a shaper of policy and implied that the ministers of security, internal affairs, and defense, as well as the reform-oriented minister of foreign affairs, wanted to abolish the body altogether.[34] He later resigned from the body prior to a new round of reshuffling of its members. By late 1993 new Security Council Secretary Oleg Lobov began plans to expand the staff and influence in anticipation of a new parliament and a constitution giving the president broad and virtually unchallenged powers.[35]

With a narrow mandate for his constitution but facing defeat in the parliament, Yeltsin wasted no time building the Security Council as an active administrative body. He also created the post of national security adviser, an individual who would have direct day-to-day supervision of the security, intelligence, police and military organs. The actual authority of both the Security Council and the national security adviser remained in a state of flux, though it appeared that there was significant cooperation with at least some of the organs. Security Council Deputy Secretary Vladimir Rubanov, a career KGB officer who had been expelled by Kryuchkov for being too reformist, maintained an active and effective daily relationship with the organs, whose officers viewed him as a colleague, yet who remained staunchly and outspokenly committed to bringing the security apparatus under civil control.[36] In practice, civil control was far from assured.

Judicial Controls

Having emerged from a system that did not recognize the principle of an independent judiciary, Russia has no purely judicial oversight or controls over the security intelligence services. Its legal system rests mainly in the hands of the state prosecutor. A separate judicial entity, however, the Constitutional Court, surprised almost everyone when it successfully compelled the government in January 1992 to reverse the merger of state security with the MVD into the Ministry of Security and Internal Affairs (MBVD). Conceived in 1990 but not created until October 1991, the Constitutional Court had little more than "symbolic" significance as far as most lawmakers were concerned.[37]

Executive power on security matters was successfully challenged for the first time in Russian history. Outraged democratic forces managed to leverage the dissolution of the MBVD shortly after its formation. But the victory was not theirs. The reasons for the Supreme Soviet's virtually unanimous opposition to the MBVD differed sharply among deputies. Democrats feared the resurgence of a new Stalin-like MBVD that would crush newly won civil liberties; the coalition of authoritarian reformers and old-line Communists led by Khasbulatov denounced not so much the fact that an NKVD was being resurrected as that it would be Yeltsin's NKVD. Others voted as they did because they were professionally or personally beholden to the organs, especially to the chekists, who were also against the merger because they were now under the militsiya.

Opposition to the MBVD marked the first-ever emergence of the seedling of an independent judiciary in Russia. A group of fifty-one reformist lawmakers petitioned the Federation's new Constitutional Court, a body endowed with no real powers or even much respect, to examine the constitutionality of the merger decree. Court Chairman Valeriy Zorkin, a former law professor, then called on the president immediately to suspend—but not revoke—the decree until it could be studied by the justices. Yeltsin's administration was silent.[38]

The new thirteen-member court quickly arranged hearings to determine the legality of the MBVD. These attracted a high-level audience, including Supreme Soviet leaders, the minister of justice, and Supreme Court Chairman Vyacheslav Lebedev. Yeltsin's office issued a surprise appeal as Zorkin opened the hearings, calling to adjourn the examination of the case sine die. Zorkin rejected the appeal, observing that the president had been informed and invited in advance to attend the session.

Then came the arguments for and against the MBVD. Mikhail Mityukov, chairman of the Russian Supreme Soviet Committee on Legislation, analyzed the 19 December decree from a constitutional and legislative position, citing the Concept for Juridical Reform approved by the legislature. Shakhray, ironically Mityukov's predecessor as committee chairman, argued on behalf of the government. *Izvestiya* described his presentation as "less cogent in form" than that of Mityukov, reporting that it revealed "traces of uncertainty. . . . It was felt that Shakhray was in fact opposed to the MBVD but that duty compelled him to defend B. Yeltsin's viewpoint." Shakhray was cut off when he tried to accuse the court of political bias. Outside experts testified that the MBVD could jeopardize constitutional order and human rights and as such "should be deemed inconsistent with the constitutional duty of the president."[39]

Appearing as defense witnesses, MBVD first deputy ministers Viktor Yerin and Anatoliy Oleynikov, under a "formal pledge to speak the truth and nothing but the truth," evaded answering direct questions and denied that the merger decree was being carried out. Neither would answer the question, "Exactly who prepared the draft decree?" Both said that the merger would not proceed at a local level; Oleynikov claimed that "nothing special" had happened in their departments since 19 December and added that there was "no likelihood" of merging local state security and militsiya bodies.

Other witnesses from the security services contradicted them, speaking of specific plans to merge state security with the MVD at the central and local levels.[40] Court Chairman Zorkin noted the conflicting testimony and accused the MBVD chiefs of "attempts to mislead the Court."[41] A ranking state security officer alleged that Barannikov had made a veiled threat against those opposing the merger. Aleksandr Yurchenko, a deputy department chief of the AFB Main Directorate for the Struggle Against Organized Crime, revealed the existence of Order No. 5 to set up units to crush protesters. He also said that Barannikov had told a 27 December conference of MBVD officers, "The people are sick of perestroika. The president's only support in the current conditions comes from the Armed Forces, and the security and internal affairs organs . . . I shall deal with the lobby opposed to the merger and the fulfillment of the presidential decree."[42]

The court's decision was immediate and unanimous: The 19 December decree was unconstitutional and declared null and void. The 14 January 1992 decision was unequivocal:

> After examining in open session the case relating to verifying the constitutionality of the Russian president's Decree "On the Formation of the RSFSR Ministry of Security and Internal Affairs," the Court resolved: to adjudge this decree inconsistent with the RSFSR Constitution from the point of view of the division of legislative, executive, and judicial powers within the republic, as well as the demarcation of competence among the higher organs of state power and management enshrined in the Constitution. The said resolution is final: It is not subject to appeal, and will come into force immediately after its proclamation. In legal terms, this means that the Russian president's decree on the formation of the MBVD and all other normative acts and their individual clauses based on or derived from it lose juridical force and are considered invalid. All juridical relations based on the said decree revert to the status they possessed before the adoption of the anticonstitutional decree.[43]

This conclusion was a milestone. More important, both sides of the conflict abided by the decision. Neither the executive nor the legislative branches of the Russian government had had any regard for the authority of the new Constitutional Court, but both had turned to the justices to decide a critical issue over which the two branches were at odds. Justice Zorkin's leadership challenged the system and won new respect both from sympathizers in the Supreme Soviet and from the Russian government.

The Constitutional Court solved other crises, such as a major dispute between Yeltsin and the Congress of People's Deputies in December 1992, and was viewed by some to be the nucleus of a third independent branch of government. The court's authority, structure, and actions, however, were severely flawed in many ways, opening it to criticism that it was more of a political than a judicial entity.[44] And yet, the assertiveness of Chairman Zorkin and some other judges was credited as making the body "an aggressive tribunal determined to safeguard the emerging Russian democracy."[45]

New laws formally make the security and intelligence services answerable not only to the president and the Supreme Soviet but also to the state prosecutor or procurator general, as well as to specially authorized prosecutors, to ensure the legality of operations and actions.[46] In practice, such controls remain to be seen. A sobering aspect of the Constitutional Court's decision is that, although it successfully challenged presidential power, it did not challenge the chekists. A more reliable test of its authority would be a ruling that conflicted with the interests of the former KGB. Such a test would determine the real independence of Russia's judiciary.

Parliamentary Controls

Impediments to Meaningful Parliamentary Oversight and Reform

The accomplishments of Russia's legislative branch in the country's first year of independence—its use of the Constitutional Court to block the attempted merger of state security and the militsiya and its passage of laws laying down the fundamentals for security and intelligence—were milestones for the development of civil control and oversight of the country's special services.

These accomplishments, however, were not as impressive as they might seem. First, the victory for the democrats was paradoxically a victory for the hard-liners and the KGB. The Congress of People's Deputies and its standing Supreme Soviet subsidiary did not challenge chekism or the pervasive powers of the organs. As noted above, creation of the NKVD-like Ministry of Security and Internal Affairs did not seem to disturb parliamentary leaders as much as the fact that Yeltsin had control of it. Khasbulatov made common cause with the democrats and the chekists for the severance of state security from the MVD, but the two groups had radically different reasons for their actions. The Supreme Soviet majority was engaged not in a struggle with Yeltsin about the nature of the security and intelligence services, but in a struggle about control over them.

This point is illustrated by Khasbulatov's closure of a special commission he himself had created during the post-putsch excitement to investigate the former KGB. The commission issued damning revelations about past KGB behavior in the service of the Soviet leadership. Several months into the probe, however, Khasbulatov disbanded the investigators after consultation with Yeltsin's intelligence chief and ranking state security officers, as will be discussed below. Meanwhile he began a cooperative relationship with the leaders of the special services to formulate the basic laws by which they would operate but attacked the president's powers to administer the services.

One of the major hurdles in the way of parliamentary democrats who sought to break with the chekist legacy and create a Western style security and intelligence apparatus was that the Supreme Soviet found itself in conflict with such goals from the beginning. The assembly was a surviving structure of the Gorbachev era, and as such it was not created to encourage true pluralism. It was not a real parliament in the Western sense. Its 252 members were chosen from the 1,041-member Russian Congress of People's Deputies and had been elected to a five-year term in March 1990. Ninety percent of the Congress, or 912 members, consisted of former Communist Party members, and although many were quite reformist, the majority was not. By 1993, the single largest bloc of the Congress consisted of an alliance of 355 ideological Marxist-Leninists and extreme nationalists; the smallest bloc was made up of 107 members sympathetic to democratic principles and free-market reforms. The remainder consisted of two "centrist" coalitions (i.e., representatives of the bureaucracy and the military-industrial sector) 357 members strong and a grouping of 222 others, nearly all of whom had a vested interest in the status quo.[47]

The Supreme Soviet membership profile was similar. To make matters worse, chekists and their allies who were elected to parliament with the help of the special KGB task forces quickly assumed sensitive posts. Yevgeniy Kim, a deputy representing Ulyanovsk, had resigned from the Party in 1990, but after the putsch he had led a campaign to discredit democratic lawmakers by exposing their alleged and real affiliations with the KGB. Kim himself was later identified as a KGB agent.[48] Gen. Filipp Bobkov, a coup conspirator who was KGB first deputy chairman under Kryuchkov, kept his position attached to the Supreme Soviet leadership. General Ivan Fedoseyev, a former head of the Irkutsk KGB who later became deputy head of the Fifth Chief Directorate, was by 1993 a deputy secretary of the Supreme Soviet Constitutional Commission.[49]

Compounding the democrats' difficulties as a minority faction was the composition of the committee responsible for security and intelligence concerns. That body, the Committee on Defense and Security, like its defunct Soviet counterpart, was dominated by lawmakers who were professional officers in the MVD, the armed forces, or the former KGB or who had ties to the military-industrial complex. Key committee members are described below.

A third factor complicating prospects for legislative reform, alluded to earlier, was the fact that a number of legislators from the democratic faction had been co-opted by the KGB and were thus disinclined to risk exposure by challenging the security apparatus. A decision was made at the highest level of the Soviet government to compromise reformist Russian people's deputies when the new legislative system was created in 1989 and 1990.

There were some overt placements of "dissident" KGB officers among the reformers, such as the four regional KGB chiefs who joined Democratic Russia.[50] Other placements or co-optations were covert. According to Col. Aleksandr Kichikhin, formerly of the Fifth Chief Directorate, "[KGB Chairman] Kryuchkov told us to recruit agents from the democratic faction of the Russian parliament." Recruitment of lawmakers who were already Communist Party members, Kichikhin said, was not needed as they were already co-opted.[51] A ranking state security officer confirmed the story: "There are quite a few of our people among the parliamentarians!" [*sic*].[52]

Lawmakers aligned with Democratic Russia acknowledge the same; some have stated that they have determined the identities of some of their colleagues who worked for the KGB as informants or agents.[53] Defense and Security Committee Chairman Sergey Stepashin, a moderate reformer disinclined to pose a serious challenge to the status quo, concurred, saying that he had information on KGB penetration of democratic organizations and of the Russian Supreme Soviet. He said that it would be "technically impossible" to determine who the agents were, adding ominously that it was "not politically expedient" to try.[54]

Discovery of agent identities might not be as difficult as Stepashin asserted. A prominent leading democratic lawmaker, Lev Ponomarev, did not quibble about the political inexpediency of tracking down agents but insisted that it was technically possible to do so. A few members of the Russian parliament—including members of the most democratic factions—were identified by former KGB officers and parliamentary investigators as KGB agents and informants, but no action was taken against them.[55]

Ponomarev led a parliamentary team of investigators who discovered the existence of what he called "an intact file listing the names of all agents throughout the time Soviet organs of repression have existed." He added, "It is therefore, for example, no problem identifying which Russian deputies are KGB staffers." He proposed that, rather than exposing them in public, a law be passed to disqualify former KGB collaborators from holding high office.[56] His idea got nowhere, although later some of his compatriots drew up such a draft law.[57]

Revelations in some of the Baltic republics indicate that key legislative leaders there were co-optees or agents of the KGB. In late March 1992, after painstaking study, the Lithuanian Supreme Court ruled that a prominent member of Sajudis, the powerful movement that led Lithuania's independence drive in 1991, was a long-time KGB agent whose cryptonym was "Juozas." The agent, according to the ruling, was Virgilius Cepaitis[58] who had been one of the most influential members of the republic's parliament as leader of the majority coalition and chairman of the Independence Party. "Juozas" was also chairman of the Permanent Parliamentary Commission for Human Rights and Ethnic Affairs and was regarded as one of the most radical members of the legislature.[59] A Lithuanian-American woman who served as parliamentary press attache admitted that she informed for the KGB from 1986 to 1990 but said that she was a double agent for the FBI and the new Lithuanian security service.[60]

Later in 1992, the Lithuanian Supreme Court ruled after a long investigation that former Prime Minister Kazimiera Prunskiene, who chaired the Lithuanian Council of Ministers during the critical months of independence from March 1990 to January 1991, worked "deliberately" for the KGB.[61]

A Short-Lived Challenge: The Ponomarev Commission

For a while after the putsch it seemed as though the Supreme Soviet was intent on reaching into the bowels of the KGB and pulling out the innards. During the excitement of late August 1991, the legislature established an investigative body to probe CPSU and KGB abuses. The action held great promise for future reforms. Headed by physicist Lev Ponomarev, a lawmaker from the Democratic Russia camp, the Commission to Investigate the Causes and Circumstances of the August Putsch was formed at about the same time as the USSR state

Commission to Investigate the Activity of the Security Organs (the Stepashin Commission described in Chapter 4, not to be confused with the Russian Supreme Soviet Committee on Defense and Security, which Stepashin also chaired). Ponomarev quickly expanded the scope of his commission from investigating the sources of the putsch to investigating all Communist Party abuses, especially financial improprieties and political crimes committed through the KGB.

Commission members and investigators pored over KGB and CPSU files, compiling data for an official Supreme Soviet report. Significantly, they were not permitted physical entry to KGB archives and storerooms. Instead, they were fed files and documents by KGB officers. Although some of this material was compromising and much of it quite scandalous, the net result was that little crucial information was granted to parliamentary investigators. Ponomarev commented,

> From the outset our commission's powers were not clearly designated. Therefore to obtain access to archives—the CPSU Central Committee and KGB archives—we had to write letters and obtain authorization. But once they had breached this wall, our experts were able to work in the early stages. They were not helped, but neither were they hindered. Recently, however, when certain results of our labors became known, we did start feeling mounting resistance from the Russian Ministry of Security leadership. Our experts have been denied access to the archive at Lubyanka several times. The warrant officer at the entrance states that he has received an order not to let us in. From whom? Naturally, it is impossible to find out. After we tried to gain access to the [former KGB] First Main Directorate archives, [foreign intelligence chief] Yevgeniy Primakov himself came to the White House [parliament building] and sidestepped the whole Supreme Soviet leadership. As a result those archives have simply remained inaccessible to us.[62]

Another member of the investigative commission concurred. Deputy Aleksei Surkov commented on how the foreign intelligence service blocked access to files concerning KGB distribution of CPSU funds abroad to foreign Communist parties, front organizations, and terrorist and guerrilla groups:

> The fact is that the leaders of the investigations group have twice sent official requests to the SVR [External Intelligence Service] for access to all the necessary materials. The answer is known. Yet the investigation knows very well that it is impossible that there are no documents in the SVR

> archives showing specifically how the Politburo's instructions were carried out, in what accounts the money was kept, in what countries, and who controls them now.[63]

It seemed as if the KGB and its successors released small amounts of damaging information about areas where abuses were well known, such as infiltration of the church, as well as relatively minor secrets as a kind of preemptive damage control. The organs could appear to be forthcoming with key information but could regulate the content and flow. However, the flow could not be completely controlled. Individuals from the apparat were interviewed by investigators and apparently revealed damaging information on their own, although chekist pressures won out in the end. Ponomarev said that "dozens of people, maybe even hundreds" within the military and state security forces, as well as former Party officials, suffered "persecution" from the apparat for having attempted to provide information to the commission.[64]

Supreme Soviet Chairman Khasbulatov permitted the commission a mere seven minutes to present lawmakers with the findings of five months of investigation and forbade distribution of the commission's 1,000-page report.[65] When the commission began revealing internal agent identities, Khasbulatov shut it down at the urging of public figures who were both reputed covert agents and officials of security and intelligence organs. In addition to SVR chief Primakov, these individuals reportedly included Patriarch Aleksi of Moscow.[66] Said Ponamarev, "Ruslan Khasbulatov terminated our commission unilaterally, and he didn't give any explanation. He said he didn't need a commission whose chairman criticized the chairman and Presidium of the Russian parliament."[67] The commission's report, though not classified, was not officially published or abstracted for the public.[68]

The security organs threatened to retaliate. In June 1992, Security Minister Barannikov announced plans to ask the state prosecutor to indict Ponomarev and fellow commission member Gleb Yakunin, a Russian Orthodox priest who had spent five years in Lefortovo Prison and the Perm 37 labor camp and more than three years in internal exile for dissident activities under the Soviet regime, for willful exposure of "state secrets." No immediate police action took place, but the threat served notice that publication of the past KGB crimes of a defunct Soviet regime would not be tolerated even from elected members of parliament.

Standing Committees

Officially, Russian legislation enacted in 1992 empowers standing commissions and committees to oversee the security and intelligence services. The primary responsible parliamentary body was the Committee on Defense and Security,[69] though the Supreme Soviet created or empowered other commissions of either chamber, or other joint standing committees, to monitor the security services.[70] Committees and commissions could hold hearings, interview officials, and receive written reports from the respective agencies. In the case of the External Intelligence Service (SVR), the Supreme Soviet directed the Commission on the Budget, Plans, Taxes and Prices of the upper house, in conjunction with the joint Committee on Defense and Security, to "review the estimated costs of maintaining foreign intelligence agencies and present the estimates to the Russian Federation Supreme Soviet; [and] supervise the expenditure of funds allocated to foreign intelligence agencies by these agencies and hear the reports of the heads of these agencies on the expenditure of these funds."[71] However, members of these two bodies stated a year after the law went into effect that they were unable to ascertain the budgets of the security and intelligence services.[72]

Committee on Defense and Security

The Committee on Defense and Security was the permanent Supreme Soviet body responsible for security matters on a day-to-day basis. It served as the parliament's official liaison with the military, the Ministry of Security, the External Intelligence Service, and other organs and carried out a semblance of oversight functions. The committee was the Russian parliament's equivalent to the committee of the same name created in 1989 in the USSR Supreme Soviet. It contained at least four subcommittees: on defense, security, internal affairs, and intelligence.

The committee membership precluded the possibility that a fundamental reformer could emerge and challenge the chekist apparatus. All members were carefully chosen. Differences of opinion did exist, and some steps toward reform were taken, but the Committee on Defense and Security was in fact a "kept" organization because it was dominated by active and former KGB, MVD, and military officers who were elected to their legislative posts as well as politicians with a political base in the large and unreformist military-industrial enterprises. According to one committee member, the majority of those on the committee held the rank of colonel.[73] Key professional staff were also drawn from the military and chekist bureaucracies.[74] Committee leaders held dual positions as members of the security services. They included the chairman, Sergey Stepashin; the first deputy chairman, Boris Bolshakov; and the chairman of the Subcommittee on Security, Nikolay Kuznetsov, among others.

Stepashin was a career officer in the MVD and a moderate in that context. The policeman was elected to the Supreme Soviet as an active-duty lieutenant colonel from Leningrad. Following the August 1991 putsch, President Yeltsin transferred him to the KGB and promoted him to the rank of major general at the age of thirty-nine, naming him deputy chairman of the RSFSR KGB and chief of state security for St. Petersburg city and oblast. The well-regarded Stepashin was also named chairman of the USSR state Commission to Investigate the Activity of the Security Organs, the body that advised Bakatin on how to divide up the USSR KGB. He retained his rank and position in the security apparatus when the Russian KGB was re-named the Federal Security Agency (AFB), the Ministry of Security and Internal Affairs (MBVD), and the Ministry of Security (MB).[75] Stepashin attempted to resign as committee chairman in October 1992, but the resignation was rejected by Khasbulatov. Instead, Security Minister Barannikov, who was gravitating politically toward Khasbulatov, removed Stepashin from his post as deputy minister and chief of state security for St. Petersburg and replaced him with a hard-line KGB veteran from the Fifth Chief Directorate.[76]

First Deputy Chairman Boris Bolshakov was elected from Ivanovo, where he was an oblast KGB officer with the rank of colonel. Bolshakov believed that the country's crisis could be solved not by introduction of market forces but through "the rallying of all the workers around the ideals of socialism in their original form," though he voted in favor of a draft decree to condemn the use of force in the Baltic states in January 1991. Bolshakov was also deputy chairman of the Committee on Law, Order, and the Struggle Against Organized Crime; the chairman of this committee, A. A. Aslakhanov, was a general in the MVD.[77]

Committee member Nikolay Nakolayevich Kuznetsov, another KGB careerist, was chairman of the Subcommittee on Security. The young, energetic, and tough officer was instrumental in removing from the USSR state Stepashin Commission its most articulate anti-KGB member, journalist Yevgeniya Albats. At a conference in early 1993, Kuznetsov gave insights into KGB intervention in politics when he said the KGB had "assigned" him to run for a seat on the Supreme Soviet.[78]

Kuznetsov became committee secretary by early 1993.[79] (After the legislative body was dissolved in September, Kuznetsov was named deputy chief of the State Tax Police, where many officers from the Fifth Chief Directorate had been reassigned.)

The Supreme Soviet Presidium and the Committee on Defense and Security worked in partnership with the Ministry of Security and the intelligence organs to develop laws. In 1992, original drafts of basic laws on security and intelligence were actually authored within the organs and then submitted to the Committee on Defense and Security for consideration. The only noteworthy friction was the organs' reluctance to share certain information with the committee, which never was able to ascertain the SVR budget, according to a committee member. The committee tolerated the services' refusal to provide budget figures and never allowed the situation to sour overall cooperation.[80]

The committee conducted elementary oversight functions such as hearings, though of limited scope, and called security and intelligence officials to testify. Most if not all hearings were closed. Although some members advocated reform and civil control, none went on record as supporting fundamental reorganization of the organs, or called for for a break with chekism. Intelligence subcommittee chairman Yevgeniy Kozhokin went so far as to claim after an investigation that the SVR was "a new service with new traditions and ideologies," as if there had been a major change with Primakov at the helm.[81] The committee seemed more interested in preserving the apparatus than in challenging its essence to make it consistent with a democratic, pluralistic society. Thus the legislative process in post-Soviet Russia as it pertained to state security was not fundamentally different from that of the USSR when the KGB wrote its own reform law.

This is not to say that Committee on Defense and Security leaders were opposed to certain needed reforms. Chairman Stepashin visited Washington in autumn 1991 specifically to solicit advice on the principles and intricacies of legislative oversight (including from the CIA)[82] and welcomed the support of private American groups in providing expertise and establishing ties with congressional experts.[83] The committee had a number of exchanges with the intelligence and armed services committees of the U.S. House and Senate.[84] In December 1992 the committee held a well-publicized roundtable on "Parliamentary Control over Intelligence and Security Services" and invited experts from West European countries and the from United States.[85] More exchanges were planned for 1993 but later canceled when the Supreme Soviet was abolished.[86] As a reward for his support during the crisis that followed, President Yeltsin made Stepashin the first deputy minister of Security.

Relations Between Security Organs and the Supreme Soviet

Although institutional tensions were reported to exist between the Supreme Soviet and the services, they were by no means as pronounced as those between the parliament and the government itself. Indeed, legislative/security service relations could be described as quite cordial overall, albeit complicated. Given the KGB's strong effort to get its own people elected to the Supreme Soviet and placed in critical positions, it is difficult to determine where the former KGB ended and the civilian legislature began.

Chekist co-optees in the Supreme Soviet were independent of any political leader. Their attempts to establish parliamentary controls over the services were criticized by both reformers and hard-liners like Khasbulatov, who once branded the Committee on Defense and Security and the Committee on Legality, Order and the Struggle Against Crime (headed by MVD General A. A. Aslakhanov) as tools of the security organs.

The Committee on Defense and Security suffered from another institutional weakness unrelated to those discussed above and found itself at loggerheads with Khasbulatov on more than one occasion. Despite repeated attempts, for example, it was unable to obtain answers about an illegal armed guards unit that Khasbulatov controlled outside the authority of the organs. Seeking his own armed force, Khasbulatov, with First Deputy Chairman Filatov, had decreed in November 1991 that a Directorate for the Protection of Organs of State Power be established. The directorate's officers and men consisted at first of the MVD parliamentary guards unit, which Khasbulatov transferred from the state to his personal control. Despite the change, many lawmakers were under the impression that the guards remained under MVD command because the personnel retained militsiya uniforms and insignia.

Khasbulatov gradually usurped more duties of the Russian MVD by maneuvering for the transfer of MVD guards of seventy-five key state institutions, including the Foreign Ministry, the Ministry of Justice, the Supreme Court, the Prosecutor's Office, Ostankino television, the State Committee for Statistics, and scores of other bureaucracies, to his personal control. The size of his force eventually reached 5,000. When the Committee on Defense and Security attempted to determine the guards' status, guard commander Ivan Boyko refused to cooperate.[87]

Committee on Defense and Security member Igor Nikulin, a career KGB officer, reported in October 1992, "However we have tried to investigate this, however many times we have appealed to Boyko, we have been unable to ascertain with complete clarity how the directorate puts buildings and establishments under its guard." He added, "Back in February [1992] we sent letters to Yeltsin, Khasbulatov, and [Constitutional Court Chairman] Zorkin requesting an investigation into who was protecting whom, what service was involved and on the basis of what laws." Only then did the Supreme Soviet leadership attempt to draw up legislation on the security of "supreme organs of state power." Nikulin concluded, "Society is not protected from any abuses and violations of legality: A subunit dressed in militsia uniform but is not subordinate to the MVD, there is no departmental control over it and as far as I know there is no prosecutor's office supervision."[88] It was established that the use of the MVD uniforms was illegal,[89] as was the status of the force itself. The MVD advocates prevailed, and Khasbulatov lost his praetorian guard.

Other Commissions

The Russian Supreme Soviet Presidium organized temporary commissions to assist the Committee on Defense and Security with its legislative work concerning the security organs and to serve as liaison.[90] These commissions, about which little has been reported, were made up of lawmakers from different standing committees to approach the issues of security law from various perspectives. Members of the commissions were drawn from the Committee on Defense and Security, the Committee on Communications and Mass Media, the Committee on Law and Order, and the Committee on Legislation, all of which were joint committees; as well as the Commission on the Budget, Plans, Taxes and Prices of the Soviet of the Republic chamber and other parliamentary bodies. The commissions were also to have overseen personnel and other policies of the security organs but were reportedly ignored.[91]

Committees in the Federal Assembly

The Federal Assembly, the new parliament elected in December 1993, has a slightly different oversight structure. The lower house, or State Duma, has a Committee on Defense and a separate Committee on Security. When the various political blocs made deals to determine who would chair what committee, a democratic Russia's Choice lawmaker received chairmanship of the Committee on Defense, while a hard-line Communist Party member became chairman of the Committee on Security. The security committee has four deputy chairmen, each of whom represents a different political faction. According to one of the deputy chairmen, there are fewer conflicts of interest on the Duma Committee on Security than on its Supreme Soviet predecessor.[92]

A Committee on Defense and Security has oversight duties in the upper house, the Federation Council. The committees were just beginning to organize their political agendas as of this writing, and their power and influence remain to be seen.

Security and Intelligence Laws of 1992 and 1993

The new Constitution proclaims the sanctity of individual rights but does not view them as inalienable. The document empowers the government to curtail rights severely without need of constitutional amendments.[93] Thus the old KGB structures are constitutional bodies. Moreover, laws enacted well before approval of a constitution ensured the chekists' place in society. Rather than being saddled with laws imposed by the Supreme Soviet, the security organs took the initiative to author the "oversight" legislation themselves and submitted draft laws to the Supreme Soviet for approval. Thus the chekists determined how they would be regulated under the law.

Security Minister Barannikov, like KGB Chairman Kryuchkov in the USSR Supreme Soviet before him, demanded that parliament immediately pass specific laws governing the special services. An interim decree was drafted by the MB and issued by President Yeltsin. Barannikov then gave what he called a "package of laws" to the Supreme Soviet for elaboration and passage, and he was adamant in a February 1992 statement to lawmakers that the drafts be enacted.[94] Descriptions of the main laws submitted by the MB and the SVR and enacted by the Supreme Soviet follow. They are the Law on Security, the Law on Federal Organs of State Security, the Law on Operational Investigative Activity, the Law on Foreign Intelligence, and the Law on State Secrets.

Law on Security

Like the Soviet Law on State Security Organs of 1991, the Russian Federation Law on Security of 1992 enshrines the legal basis for abuse of individuals by the state. This is a critical issue because the new law was designed as the foundation on which all other security legislation would be built. Despite many new themes, such as protection of the rights of the individual, the law reflects Soviet-style legalistic thought by containing enough qualifications and exceptions to permit continued state-sanctioned abuse of power.[95]

The war between Yeltsin and Khasbulatov for control over the services is strongly evident in the law, even though Yeltsin's hard-line (and ultimately double-dealing) Security Council Secretary Skokov played a major role, along with the Ministry of Security, in its drafting.[96] Although the president signed the legislation, legal power shifts decisively away from the president in favor of the legislature. Perhaps this explains why Yeltsin sought to make the Security Council much stronger than legally allowed.

According to the law, the legislature sets security priorities, develops security legal framework, establishes procedure for the organization and activity of security organs, "exercises control" of personnel policy, determines security organ budgets and appropriations, and "ratifies and denounces" international accords on security matters.[97]

By contrast, the executive is to ensure that security laws and normative acts are executed, "organize the elaboration and implementation" of state security programs, "implement a system of measures to ensure the security of the individual, society, and the state within the limits of their competence" and "formulate, reorganize, and abolish state organs for ensuring security" consistent with law. The president must issue a report on security to the legislature on an annual basis.[98] The president is also granted the right to exercise "overall leadership of state organs for ensuring security," to head the Security Council, to determine strategy for internal and external security in conjunction with the legislature, to monitor and coordinate the activity of the security organs, and to make operational security decisions within limits set by law.[99]

The law also lists the responsibilities of the judiciary, which, though no longer guided by ideology and therefore less subjective than before, has not evolved meaningfully from its kangaroo status of the Soviet period. Judiciary responsibilities, according to the law, are to ensure and be guided by the constitution, to dispense justice in security-related cases, and to "ensure the legal protection of citizens and social and other organizations whose rights have been violated in connection with activity to ensure security."[100] This last point is encouraging, but it remains to be seen how it will be carried out over time.

The text of the Law on Security begins with the vague legal definition of security discussed earlier in this chapter. Nowhere is the type of society to be protected or the inalienable right of the individual defined. A short set of "principles of ensuring security" is also inadequate: "legality; observance of the balance of the vital interests of the individual, society, and state; mutual responsibility of the individual, society, and state in ensuring security; [and] integration with international security systems."[101]

The law's definition of "threat to security" is equally amorphous: "A threat to security is a combination of conditions and factors that present a danger to the vital interests of the individual, society, and state. A real and potential threat to objects of security from internal and external sources determines the substance of activity to ensure internal and external security."[102] The legal definition of "vital interests" is likewise vague: "Vital interests are the combination of requirements which are reliably satisfied by the existence of and opportunities for the progressive development of the individual, society, and state."[103]

Thus the law is useless as a basic legal charter for reform. It provides no indication of who is responsible for deciding whether something is a vital interest, nor does it provide any criteria for making such decisions. Since the law grants the organs of the former KGB the power to carry out security functions, it does not consider the chekist apparatus a threat to society but the guardian of society. By implication, a citizen or organization that works to weaken the powers or integrity of the chekist apparatus might be considered to be threatening the country's vital interests and therefore could be dealt with in the name of "state security." The Law on Security is riddled with other major flaws; some loopholes are of sufficient size as to permit the security organs to operate as before if so ordered or permitted. These flaws include those listed below.

No Provision to Break with Chekist Legacy. The basic law assumes that the chekist apparatus is sufficient to provide proper security for Russia. There is no provision or statement of principle that the historic and cultural nature of chekism is inconsistent with democratic pluralism and human rights, no repudiation of Dzerzhinskiy or apology for the past, and no recognition that perpetrators of state crimes under the previous regime occupy posts at all levels of the security and intelligence apparatus. The law is content with the chekist status quo.

Scope of Entities Performing Security Functions. Not only does the law provide security functions for the chekist apparatus, police, and other agencies, but it expands the "security system" to include social and nongovernmental groups: "The security system is formed by the organs of legislative, executive, and judicial power, state, social, and other organizations and associations, and citizens participating in ensuring security in accordance with the law as well as by legislation regulating relations in the security sphere."[104] A further clause identifies security organs more specifically.

In addition to the military, state security, internal affairs, foreign intelligence, and other "traditional" organs, the law includes "organs ensuring the secure running of operations in industry, power engineering, transportation, and agriculture," as well as "services ensuring the security of means of communication and information, customs services, nature conservation organs, public health organs, and other state organs for ensuring security which operate on the basis of legislation."[105] Nearly every aspect of society and daily life, then, may be part of the new state security system.

Continued Protection of Informants. The law stipulates, "The state provides legal and social protection for citizens, social and other organizations and associations which assist in ensuring security in accordance with the law."[106] No distinction is made between informants who report on political "criminals" and those who report on real criminals. The implication is that past, present, and future informants, regardless of the nature of their work, may be paid and given all necessary means of assistance by state security, as was the case under Soviet rule. Thus the political informants of the past may continue to receive benefits courtesy of the Russian taxpayer, and the state security organs may maintain their networks of agents and informers planted throughout society.

Extrabudgetary Financing of Chekist Organs. The law stipulates that the organs shall be financed not only by the governments of the Russian Federation, republics within the Federation, krays, oblasts, and other local regions but through an additional source called "extrabudgetary funds."[107] This item appears to support the hypothesis that the Russian security and intelligence organs are financing operations via front companies and other co-opted firms, and businesses run by officers in the active reserve. Following the putsch and the dissolution of the CPSU, many of the Party's holdings, including legal certificates and bearer bonds, were transferred to the KGB to KGB operatives.[108] As of November 1991, such properties were "actively involved in commercial operations in domestic and foreign markets" and exceeded official figures, according to the Congress of the Stock Exchange.[109] Not only were these properties used to finance security and intelligence operations internally and abroad, but they were employed after the putsch to subsidize hard-line antidemocratic media, including *Pravda* and *Sovetskaya rossiya*.[110] A conclusion that one can draw is that the budgets of the organs by law are not intended to be under strict civil control and that the special services are legally allowed significant extragovernmental autonomy.

Human Rights. The Law on Security guarantees citizens' rights and freedoms—unless the situation makes it necessary to curtail them. According to the law, "In ensuring security limitation of citizens' rights and freedoms is not permitted, with the exception of cases for which the law makes direct provision."[111] Therefore, all laws pertaining to security may, if passed by parliament, permit potentially massive and systematic abuses of the citizenry. This is not beyond the realm of possibility. Citing the need for decisive reforms following the 1991 putsch, the Russian Congress of People's Deputies set precedent for giving the president the power to rule by decree, a power that Yeltsin used extensively until the December 1992 Congress, which failed to renew his emergency authority. The 1993 Constitution gives the president extremely strong powers and permits basic human rights to be curtailed by presidential decree or a simple act of parliament.

Law on Federal Organs of State Security

To complement the Law on Security, a Law on Federal Organs of State Security was passed in July 1992. The law, in the words of its preamble, "defines the function, tasks, legal foundations, principles of organization and activity, duties and rights, and resources of the federal organs of state security and also the kinds of control and supervision over their activity."[112] As such, the "federal organs of state security" are defined as "organs of executive power." They are meant to "provide for the security of the individual, society, and the state, and engage in work to detect, prevent, and cut short intelligence and subversive activity by foreign intelligence services and organizations, and also unlawful encroachment on the constitutional order, sovereignty, territorial integrity, and defense capability of the Russian Federation."[113]

The law makes a sharp distinction between "organs of state security" and "organs of internal affairs." According to the law, state security duties include traditional functions such as intelligence, counter-intelligence, counterterrorism, border security, and provision of information to the Russian leadership as well as law enforcement functions that are relatively new for state security: combating organized crime, corruption, and drug trafficking, plus investigation, detection, prevention and stoppage of other crimes as specified by law.[114]

These duties, previously under the purview of the MVD, were first enunciated by KGB Chairman Viktor Chebrikov. Kryuchkov later expanded them during glasnost in an attempt to give the KGB new legitimacy.[115] Indeed, before Viktor Barannikov relinquished formal control of the MVD to head the Ministry of Security, he sharply criticized Kryuchkov for encroaching on MVD territory and for trying to find new excuses to keep the KGB in operation.[116] Barannikov soon found himself echoing Kryuchkov's stated needs to involve the KGB in crimefighting, and the law seems to reflect his conversion.

The law repeats earlier rhetoric about upholding the principles of "legality," "respect for human rights and the rights and freedoms of the citizen," "humanism," and "accountability and control by higher organs of state power and management."[117] Yet this law too makes "exceptions." It also gives formal legal status to the old KGB internal security structures from the federal to the village levels.

Legal Recourses Against Abuse. An individual who feels he has been victimized by the security organs is granted the right to "complain" to the government and the courts and to "demand compensations for damages" caused by illegal state security activity. Significantly, the law holds state security officers who exceed their authority or abuse their powers to be liable to disciplinary, administrative, criminal, and other action.[118]

However, since the Law on Security allows the organs wide latitude in conducting surveillance and other operations against citizens and keeps the bureaucratic structures and identities of certain personnel secret, it legalizes numerous KGB-style practices that are forbidden in democratic societies and makes it difficult for a citizen to make his case. Moreover, state security officers do not wear visible name tags or numbered badges, so a citizen cannot identify the officers they accuse. To make matters even more difficult for the victim, Russia's judicial system, beyond dysfunctional, is structured and indoctrinated so that it is more a tool of state power than a check against it; hence, the right to legal recourse in the theory of the law is effectively denied in practice.

Centralized, Top-Down Internal Structures. The law defines the "organs of state security" as an all-encompassing bureaucracy "in the republics making up the Russian Federation and in the krays, oblasts, autonomous oblasts, autonomous okrugs, and the cities of Moscow and St. Petersburg," as well as within the Armed Forces (military counterintelligence), and as border guards. Defined subdivisions include "engineering and construction, medical, material-technical, financial, *and other*" (emphasis added).[119] This is essentially the structure of the Ministry of Security as it was inherited from the KGB and allows for expansion.

State Security Penetration of Public and Private Institutions. The Law on Federal Organs of State Security preserves the old KGB powers to penetrate any and all public and private entities to carry out its work. Aside from a provision allowing for an undefined "procedure" established by the government,[120] and a prohibition in the Law on Security against political manipulation, there are no restrictions. Therefore, the law permits continued infiltration of newspapers, churches, nonviolent political movements, and human rights groups to conduct intelligence activities.

"Security" for Religious, Social, and Political Groups. Although the chekist organs may infiltrate religious, social, and political groups and still control the Soviet-era surveillance files, they may also "provide security for sociopolitical and religious events" in Russia.[121] No reason is offered to explain why this is not assigned to the MVD, which bears primary responsibility for guarding certain buildings and foreign missions. One can deduce that this provision was designed to enhance the chekists' ability to monitor events that may be attended by people who do not necessarily support the government and who often associate closely with foreigners.

Restrictions on Freedom of Speech and of the Press. The law empowers the security organs to restrict freedom of speech and freedom of the press by using the amorphous "state secrets" rule. Not only does the law give state security the responsibility of protecting secrets within government entities and among government employees, but it allows the chekists to "exercise control over their safekeeping . . . at enterprises, establishments, and organizations regardless of form of ownership, and in the organs of public associations."[122]

This provision was invoked in September 1992 when state security agents raided the editorial offices of *Moscow News* and *Izvestiya,* which had run an article and an interview, respectively, with two chemists who spoke of continued production of new generations of binary chemical weapons.[123] The Ministry of Security also used the law in January 1993 to arrest Sergey Mikhailov, a reporter for *Biznes novosti* in Saratov, who committed the crime of reporting a local city council member's public statements concerning the area's secret chemical weapons laboratories. The city council member, Vladimir Petrenko, was a former military decontamination expert who was secretly poisoned in a chemical weapons test. Because of his immunity as an elected official, he was not immediately prosecuted.[124]

The law might also apply to foreigners who visit Russia, even if the "secret" information in their possession did not originate in the country. Upon arriving in the Russian Federation or any other member of the Commonwealth of Independent States, foreigners must sign a customs declaration in which they surrender their right to the privacy of all their documents and recordings.[125]

Criminalization of "Insulting the Honor or Dignity" of Chekists. Buried in a clause that protects state security personnel from those who would impede their service duties, resist arrest, issue threats, use force, or make attempts on their lives, health, or property is a statement which makes "insulting the honor or dignity" of security personnel a crime. Another section of the same article protects the "honor and dignity" of family members of state security personnel from the public.[126]

Authority to Confiscate Communications Equipment. State security may confiscate privately owned "communications" equipment or facilities in time of "emergency," according to the law, which stipulates that the seizures must be for "service purposes" and that the owners may be compensated upon request. The law does not define "communications" or "emergency," leaving open the possibility that the former KGB may be able to seize any and all forms of communication, such as radios, telephones, and computers.[127] Reports that the Ministry of Security and the Federal Agency for Government Communications and Information (FAPSI) were planning in late 1993 to take control of electronic communications and information in Russia indicate that the organs have very set ideas about the direction the chekists wish to go with this clause. Technically, the chekists' confiscation of computer equipment from the Moscow offices of human rights figure Sergey Grigoryants on 21 March 1994, prior to an important international seminar he was organizing on civil control and oversight of security services, may have been legal under this part of the law. The computer equipment contained records of Grigoryants's activities to promote reform of the security organs, transcripts of proceedings of previous related events, and international correspondence.[128]

Entry of Premises. Security personnel may enter any home or premises at any time without a warrant or the permission of the occupant in the course of "interdiction of crimes whose investigation has been transferred to the federal organs of state security, and to pursue persons suspected of having committed them in cases in which delay could pose a threat to the life and health of citizens." The law requires state security to inform a state prosecutor within 24 hours of entry but does not require the prosecutor to approve the action and makes no provision for him to block entry. The prosecutor may be informed after the fact. There is no requirement for the approval of a judge. This part of the law also contains a number of large legal loopholes concerning what constitutes suspicion and what determines a threat to life and health and thus could be abused for political purposes.[129]

Militsiya or Military Searches or Detention of Chekists. The law protects chekist personnel from the MVD and military by stipulating that a state security employee may not be detained, held, or searched in the course of carrying out official duties unless another chekist official is present.[130] No similar protections could be found for MVD or military personnel.

Chekists' Role in Time of War or State of Emergency. The law specifically charges the state security organs with the "duty" to "provide for the security of control points of the state and the Armed Forces of the Russian Federation in wartime and under conditions of states of emergency, and their ability to function."[131] Thus the former KGB is to be in a position to run the country during a state of war, or more disturbingly, if the government declares a state of emergency such as that which took place in Moscow on 4 October 1993.

The Supreme Soviet passed the Law on Security and the Law on Federal Organs of State Security by very wide margins. Even many of the most pro-Western reformers voted to enact the laws. Some may have done so under the impression that the legislation represented a meaningful step forward. According to former RSFSR KGB Chairman Viktor Ivanenko, though, when the draft legislation was discussed, lawmakers were quite conscious of the flaws, but voted for the bills because they feared what the chekists would do to them if they did not.[132]

Law on Operational Investigative Activity

The Law on Operational Investigative Activity, published in May 1992, was analyzed by lawyer Sergey Zamoshkin in a critique for *Moscow News*.[133] Key areas of concern follow.

Entry of Premises. The law permits security personnel to enter a premises without a warrant "in the line of duty" to question and interrogate individuals, to seize property, including documents; and to spy on individual citizens without authorization of an independent judge.[134]

Mail Interception and Electronic Surveillance. Mail may be intercepted and telephones tapped with permission from the state prosecutor (not a judge), but permission is not needed if "inaction under the circumstances may result in a terrorist or subversive act." A warrant may be obtained retroactively within 24 hours, the assumption being automatic approval by the prosecutor. Because the law does not stipulate how searches, mail intercepts, or electronic eavesdropping must be conducted, the implication is that witnesses need not be present; thus, agents could easily plant "evidence" in order to incriminate an individual, as it did under the old regime. Subjects of surveillance must be suspected of involvement in a crime, though the law does not differentiate between a potential suspect and a potential witness and opens both to legal violation of civil rights.[135] Furthermore, nothing in the law or criminal code defines "terrorist" or "subversive."

Continued Potential to Frame an Individual. The law also leaves citizens open to being framed by the chekist apparatus. It allows the former KGB to begin a criminal investigation based on planted evidence or on accusations by anonymous sources. An awkwardly worded clause states that the security organs may conduct intrusive surveillance of an individual if it suspects "an illegal deed being prepared, being executed or already having been executed, which necessitates a preliminary investigation in the absence of evidence that this is a crime." Western societies, including the United States, have seemingly similar laws under "probable cause," but Russian laws are quite different. The Law on Security ensures government protection for anonymous informants, but in Zamoshkin's analysis, "The law . . . gives a great deal of power to writers of anonymous letters, to those seeking revenge, and to political provocations."[136]

No Right to Face Accuser. Like the Law on Security, the Law on Operational Investigative Activity appears progressive because it grants the individual the right to demand written explanation of the reason for the infringement of his or her rights and the right to appeal in court. The law, however, also states that the organs must provide the explanation "within the limits of classification," a publicly undefined criterion that effectively denies the right of the accused to face his accuser, since the accuser may be an informant, and every informant's identity by law is a state secret.[137] Nor is there much assurance that an affected individual will have a meaningful chance to prove his innocence in court, since the Russian judiciary is not independent, presumes guilt before innocence, and maintains a tradition whereby the judge often defers to the prosecutor.[138]

Civil Institutions and Churches. Security personnel are prohibited from "secretly taking part in the operation of bodies of representative or judicial power, as well as of duly registered public associations and religious organizations" if "the objective is to influence the nature of their activity." However, if the objective is not an influence operation, there is no legal prohibition.[139] Other laws discussed above contain similar provisions.

Law on Foreign Intelligence

The cornerstone Law on Foreign Intelligence was enacted in July 1992 to govern the External Intelligence Service (SVR) and all other agencies that conduct intelligence activities abroad.[140] The law is important because it is the first public legal basis for Russian intelligence, and is a cornerstone of the SVR's public relations campaign to show how reformist it supposedly has become. The law contains wording to keep foreign intelligence services separate from other security organs and makes them subordinate and accountable to the "supreme legislative and executive authorities of the Russian Federation."[141] It gives the executive branch the power to "create, reorganize, or dissolve" foreign intelligence units in any given ministry or department as well as to approve the units' statutes and appoint their leaders.[142] It also empowers the president to administer, supervise, and coordinate foreign intelligence organs and activities independently of the legislature but requires him to work with the legislature to define intelligence strategy.[143]

The law forbids foreign intelligence services to carry out activities against Russian citizens on Russian Federation territory,[144] although one could argue that this point is moot because the SVR is not configured to run domestic spying operations; this duty is reserved for the Federal Counterintelligence Service. Legislators, judges, and prosecutors at every level of government may not be asked for "confidential assistance" (i.e., to serve as agents, informants, or provocateurs) by the foreign intelligence services.[145] The legislation specifically states that intelligence personnel are obligated to obey all laws,[146] but again, the laws are quite permissive in what they allow the chekists to do.

Some portions of the Law on Foreign Intelligence, though positive, are apparently being violated. An example is the clause that states, "The methods and means of intelligence activity must not jeopardize human life and health or the environment."[147] Presumably, this statement would mean that the intelligence units responsible for political assassinations and for training and supporting terrorists would be banned. Yet six months after the law went into effect, a top SVR official confirmed that the former KGB Department S, which housed those units, was still in existence and would continue to be. He did not acknowledge that the department, also known as the Illegals

Department, contained subunits responsible for assassinations and terrorism.[148]

Any positive aspects of the Law on Foreign Intelligence are neutralized by language that protects the legacy of the KGB from public scrutiny, endows the foreign intelligence agencies with specific missions detrimental to Western business and industry, permits abuse of power and funds so that the chekists may enrich themselves, and imposes extreme restrictions on the freedoms of speech and of the press. Here, the hand of the SVR leadership, which played a major role in writing the law, becomes evident. SVR Public Relations Director Yuriy Kobaladze admitted that Primakov signed his approval of the draft before it was submitted to the Supreme Soviet for consideration.[149] Sections that preserve the old KGB legacy include the following.

Citizenship to Foreigners Who Spied for the KGB. Russian citizenship is granted to foreigners who served the Communist Party of the Soviet Union as assets for the KGB, according to the law, which also provides for "social protection," presumably living quarters, health care, and a stipend or pension calculated by the duration of collaboration. The specific clause applies also to foreigners who assist the current Russian intelligence services:

> Individuals who are giving (or have given) confidential assistance to foreign intelligence agencies and are not citizens of the Russian Federation may be granted Russian citizenship. The cooperation of these individuals with foreign intelligence agencies will facilitate their naturalization as citizens of the Russian Federation.[150]

Foreigners naturalized under the law will receive the same benefits as professional intelligence personnel. Those not naturalized will enjoy benefits calculated under a special presidential procedure.[151]

Theft of Economic, Scientific, and Technological Secrets. While the United States, after much debate, has opted not to use its intelligence services to spy on behalf of American companies, the Russian law provides the SVR, the GRU, and electronic intelligence agencies carte blanche to steal business secrets from Western countries to benefit their partners and competitors in Russia. The law specifically authorizes the services "to promote the economic development and scientific-technical progress of the country by means of the acquisition of economic and scientific-technical information, including embodied information, by foreign intelligence agencies and the provision of government bodies defined by the president of the Russian Federation with this information."[152] It also specifically allows the GRU to conduct "military-political, military-technical, and military-economic" activities abroad.[153] The law legalizes monumental conflicts of interest by permitting active-duty (and presumably active reserve) intelligence personnel to gather, analyze and disseminate intelligence for the benefit of companies in which they or their colleagues have a financial stake. Given this fact, the Law on Intelligence is a legal mechanism for chekists to enrich themselves personally by using the resources of the state espionage services for private business and possibly criminal activity.

Surveillance of Russian Citizens Abroad. The law authorizes the intelligence services to "safeguard the security of . . . citizens of the Russian Federation who are working on assignments abroad and have access to state secrets in their professional capacity."[154] Although this phrase may be intended to protect Russians traveling on official business, it could be used as before to justify spying on émigré communities or on citizens traveling on private business. The definition of "state secrets" is so broad[155] that almost any engineer, scientist, former government official, veteran, or even journalist or environmental activist could be termed as being in possession of such information and would therefore be subject to surveillance. The Russian government continues to deny certain individuals, such as certain dissident scientists, the right to travel abroad because of the knowledge they possess.[156]

Weak Budgetary Controls. The law provides for the weakest of budgetary controls over foreign intelligence and effectively prevents the legislature from monitoring the budgets closely. By contrast, in the United States there are oversight committees with audit staffs that can monitor any aspect of the intelligence community at any time and that in fact routinely inspect intelligence budgets line by line in heavily detailed Congressional Budget Justification Books. The Russian Supreme Soviet effectively denied itself similar powers. It empowered itself to "review" the "estimated costs of maintaining foreign intelligence agencies" and not grant itself jurisdiction over actual costs, to say nothing of specific line-items, missions, operations, or even structures.[157]

Penetration of Legislative and Judicial Institutions, Public Organizations, and Churches. Like other legislation, the foreign intelligence law forbids the penetration of "representative or judicial bodies or . . . public associations and religious organizations in the Russian Federation" if the goal is to influence their activities. It does not forbid, and thus permits, the penetration of those institutions for other purposes.[158] Internal security organs are subject to a similar rule.[159]

Prior Consent. Another dangerous section of the Law on Foreign Intelligence is a clause that in effect requires journalists to submit their articles about foreign intelligence to the intelligence services for prepublication review, comment, and authorization. Although submission of such articles prior to publication is voluntary, a journalist or news organization can be held criminally responsible if the story results in "moral or material damages" to intelligence personnel or to the intelligence services themselves. This direct attack on freedom of the press holds news organizations and individual journalists criminally liable for revealing information that the government does not specifically approve. Forbidden information is not narrowly defined and includes much more than just agent identities or nuclear weapon designs. As before, the all-purpose "state secret" is invoked. The clause in question reads:

> If materials [in the news media] on foreign intelligence are not sent to the agencies for an expert ruling or if a ruling ascertains the presence of information constituting state secrets or other secrets protected by special laws, the publication of these materials in the media and the consequent disclosure of these secrets and infliction of moral or material damages on foreign intelligence agencies and their personnel will incur the criminal and civil penalties envisaged by law.[160]

Since almost everything the Russian government does not want the public to know is officially a state secret, including information about Soviet industrial espionage in the 1920s and 1930s,[161] journalists and scholars have little freedom (without fear) to write about Soviet intelligence. Similarly, it is apparently a criminal offense to report revelations by former intelligence officers or to print articles about past operations that cast the SVR or KGB in a negative light. The relevant clause of the law was not known to have been invoked by early 1994, but it can be enforced at any time.

Law on State Secrets

The Law on State Secrets, adopted in August 1993, is so fundamentally flawed that no amount of reworking could make it compatible with pluralistic democracy. It approaches the issue of secrecy from a decidedly totalitarian perspective. It does not specify what information is classified; instead, it specifies what information is not subject to classification. The military magazine *Krasnaya zvezda* approvingly reported that the category of nonsecrets includes "information about accidents and disasters threatening people's safety and health, about privileges, compensation, and benefits given to citizens and officials, about cases of violations of human rights and freedoms, and about senior Russian officials' state of health."[162] The law is a fundamental threat to freedom of speech, the press, and expression and effectively denies the citizen the right to be informed about his government's activities and the right to expose abuse of power and other government wrongdoing. In an extra bid to prevent the public from learning the crimes of the Communist past, the Supreme Soviet passed a law to keep intelligence documents classified beyond the established thirty-year limit to fifty years.[163]

Other laws and practices exist that are designed to allow the government to curtail severely the free flow of information, as does the 1993 Constitution, which guarantees freedom of the press but allows for the government to impose "forcible suspension or termination" of a publishing or broadcasting enterprise.[164]

Conclusion

Even as it was being parceled into separate services, the KGB after the 1991 putsch took the initiative where the Yeltsin government paused and in so doing blunted any attempts by democrats to bring it under control or even do away with its chekist essence. The KGB infiltrated political parties, helped its own people get elected to parliament, and ensured that it was well-represented in crucial legislative posts. State security officials drew up and shaped the basic laws by which the KGB's constituent elements would be defined, structured, controlled, and overseen. Lawmakers were too fearful to vote against them.

The chekists determined their own missions. They left no room for their dissolution or even for basic reforms. Executive mechanisms to control the security services shifted so often in so short a time that it is unlikely that the organs were ever under firm presidential control. The ever-changing Security Council, when it was at its strongest, had a hard-liner in charge of its meetings and actions. Democratic officials in the presidential apparat never exercised control, and it appears that in the case of internal security, Minister Barannikov circumvented all presidential structures and reported directly to the president (who concerned himself little with security matters) and played a double game with Yeltsin's bitterest foes in the Supreme Soviet.

Judicial controls—though successful in one instance when the Constitutional Court determined the illegality of the merger of the

MVD with state security—remained extremely weak and undeveloped and never challenged the chekists. Russia has no functioning independent judiciary.

The Supreme Soviet was led by individuals with vested interests in the preservation of the chekist apparatus. It willfully rigged an oversight system that performed little oversight but instead worked in collaboration with the unenlightened security and intelligence leaders to codify the most important methods and means of old into law. The few liberalizations that were enacted did little to curb the abusive powers of the state security organs. The incestuous relationship between lawmakers and chekists, and the fear that many lawmakers have of the secret services, preclude the immediate possibility of meaningful reform under present circumstances and make a mockery of claims that the organs are subject to the rule of law.

7

KGB Public Relations During Glasnost

Our major secret weapon is to deprive you of an enemy.

—Georgiy Arbatov,
Director, Institute on the USA & Canada,
to an American audience, 1988[1]

I think the 'secret war' can be ruled out today, even at the level of the intelligence services.

—Vladimir Kryuchkov,
Chairman, USSR KGB, 1989[2]

At critical periods in history when political expedience so dictated, the Soviet state security organs made highly publicized breaks with their past and tried to show the public and the world how much they had "changed." In an effort to distance themselves from the old KGB, the Russian Ministry of Security and the External Intelligence Service in 1992 launched image-making campaigns that on the surface made the agencies seem new. A close look at their efforts, however, reveals a high degree of congruence between post-Soviet public relations and the KGB propaganda of the glasnost era, 1985-1991. In drawing parallels between the public relations campaigns of the new Russian organs and those of their immediate KGB ancestors, one finds once again that the reports of Russian-American journalist George Popoff, who observed the transformation of the Cheka into a new service seven decades ago, remain relevant to yet another transition.

When the Cheka was declared "dissolved" on 6 February 1922 largely owing to its terrible reputation and the Kremlin's need for internal and external support, a "new organ," the State Political Directorate (Gosudarstvennoye politicheskoye upravleniye, GPU), was created. Popoff's firsthand account of the transformation, which he called "play-acting calculated to influence public opinion and the world," is again instructive to understanding the nature of the image-making campaigns of the post-Soviet instruments of state power:

> What did the theoretical dissolution of the Tcheka amount to? It took place under the influence of the so-called New Economic Policy, when for some months Moscow seemed seriously to intend to change its course. The Bolsheviks wished to trade with foreign countries, to get credits, etc., and recognized quite reasonably that this aim could never be attained unless the chief obstacle, the Tcheka, were removed. The first measures were taken as follows: Dsershinsky left the Lubjanka and became Minister of Communications. He was replaced by Unschlicht, the Commissar for Refugees, a man generally known throughout Moscow as "humane" and "good-natured." At the same time a decree was issued abolishing the death penalty (once more!). . . . The words "Extraordinary Commission" [part of full name of Cheka] were abolished and the "new" institution received the harmless-sounding name "State Political Direction". . . . That was what was done in theory.[3]

The journalist continued,

> How completely convinced the Tcheka was that, in order to influence foreign countries, it was quite enough formally to declare the Tcheka dissolved and announce the fact in the Press, without having the remotest intention of doing so in reality, is proved by the fact that it was not even considered necessary to change either the abode or the personnel of the Tcheka. Here, too, everything remained as it had been; not a single Tchekist stirred from the Lubjanka. The only changes that I could discover were new notices on the outer doors and in the inner rooms of the Tcheka. But even this was mere cynicism and comedy. In the interior of the Tcheka administration placards were to be seen over every door bearing the name of the section to which the room belonged in finely printed letters. . . . The change, the only change, which was made after the publication of the famous dissolution decree was the following. Small white labels were everywhere pasted over the letters "Tche-Ka" and "G.P.U." written on them in ink. The other designations remained untouched.[4]

Of course, many personnel and structural changes did take place in the course of developing the post-Soviet security and intelligence organs of Russia, and the Marxist-Leninist ideological base was gone. Popoff's basic premise in 1922, however, retained much of its meaning in the glasnost years and beyond. There was no break with chekism, and the essence of the services did not change.

Glasnost and "New Thinking"

Gorbachev's reforms could not help but have a disruptive effect on the KGB. They opened state security to new and embarrassing revelations, new criticisms, and open questions about its history, current practices, and role in a future society. The Soviet leadership compensated by proceeding with internal and external publicity campaigns to admit well-known concerns about Stalin-era repression and by releasing some documentation about abouses of the period while distorting reality by portraying the KGB as reformed, progressive, and benevolent.

The image-making efforts were conducted in the context of larger traditional and nontraditional domestic and international "active measures" (aktivniye meropriatya) operations designed to promote Gorbachev's agenda through the CPSU and to discredit the policies of the United States and its allies abroad, on the one hand, while promoting mutual cooperation on the other. The campaign introduced independent and semi-independent actors to promote glasnost and perestroika in an effort to induce Soviet citizens to work harder and to attract Western technology and hard currency. Gorbachev correctly reasoned that he could win substantial support and goodwill merely by allowing relatively free speech to exist, if not flourish.

At the same time, Gorbachev relied heavily on the KGB for detailed intelligence on his domestic opponents and on international public opinion. A rare insight into Gorbachev's internal motivations, the KGB's role in helping him develop his image as a humanitarian, and the cynicism with which decisions were made can be found in one of the few stenographic notes to emerge from the Politburo archives. Those notes cover the top-level debate about whether to allow Yelena Bonner, the wife of dissident Andrey Sakharov, to leave their imposed exile in the closed city of Gorkiy to travel to the United States for badly needed eye surgery. Persecution and petty harassment of the Sakharovs during the early Gorbachev era is well documented, as are the attempts by the KGB to use the physicist for propaganda purposes.[5]

It is now known that Gorbachev personally knew of these attempts and made the decision to let Bonner visit the United States for political, and not humanitarian, reasons, while at the same time he sought to isolate Sakharov from the rest of the world.

The transcript of the Politburo meeting of 29 August 1985 proves that persecution of the couple under perestroika was not a rogue operation or inertia from the past; bugging, forced internal exile, and denial of medical attention occurred with the express personal approval of the Soviet leader. It also shows how Gorbachev tried to figure a way to silence the dissidents, indicating the level of obsession among the Soviet leadership with people like Sakharov, whose very existence threatened the image-making campaign the Politburo was so carefully trying to craft. KGB Chairman Viktor Chebrikov dominated the discussion:

Gorbachev: Now a few words on a different subject. At the end of July I received a letter from the famous Sakharov. He requested that authorization be given for his wife Bonner to travel abroad for medical treatment and [to] see relatives.

Chebrikov: This is an old story. It's been going on for 20 years. . . . The appropriate measures were taken with respect to Sakharov himself as well as Bonner. . . .

As far as Sakharov is concerned, he's virtually lost all significance as a political figure and recently he's been saying nothing new. Possibly we ought to let Bonner go abroad for three months. According to the law in force, it is possible to interrupt a term of exile for a specific period of time—and Bonner, of course, is in exile. Naturally, once she's in the West, she may make statements, or be given an award, and so on. . . . If Bonner were given authorization to travel abroad it would look like a humane step.

In the future, she may behave in one of two different ways. One — she goes back to Gorkiy. Two — she remains abroad and starts to raise the issue of reuniting her family, i.e., Sakharov's being authorized to emigrate. In the latter case, the result may be that government figures in Western countries make appeals, some representatives of communist parties may do so too. But we can't let Sakharov go abroad. The Medium Machine Building Industry [responsible for nuclear programs] is opposed to this—it's against it since Sakharov has a detailed knowledge of the entire development of our nuclear weapons. The experts believe that if Sakharov were given a laboratory, he would be able to continue his military research. Sakharov's behavior reflects Bonner's influence.

Gorbachev: There's Zionism for you.

Chebrikov: Bonner has 100 percent influence on him. We are relying on the fact that without her his behavior may change. He has two daughters and a son from his first marriage. They are behaving well and they may have a definite influence on their father.

> **Gorbachev:** Couldn't we arrange for Sakharov to write a letter saying that he understands that he cannot go abroad? Can't we get a statement to this effect from him?
>
> **Chebrikov:** It seems to me that we need to decide this question right now. If we make a decision either just before or else following your meetings with Mitterrand and Reagan, it will be interpreted as a concession on our part, which would be undesirable.
>
> **Gorbachev:** Yes, we need to make a decision. . . . What is going to involve greater cost—authorizing Bonner to go abroad, or not permitting it?
>
> **Foreign Minister Eduard Shevardnadze:** Of course, there are serious doubts about authorizing Bonner to go abroad. Nonetheless we would profit from it politically. We need to make a decision right now.[6]

Other Politburo members, including Defense Minister S. L. Sokolov, V. V. Kuznetsov, G. A. Aliyev, P. N. Demichev, and I. V. Kapitonov, participated in the discussion, indicating the Kremlin's concern with the international political consequences of allowing Sakharov's wife to leave the Soviet Union and its fixation with trying to alter Sakharov's own behavior. Gorbachev finally concluded,

> Perhaps we'll take the following action. We'll acknowledge receipt of the letter [from Sakharov], say that it has been reviewed and follow-up instructions have been given. We should indicate that we may be forthcoming with respect to the request for Bonner to be allowed to go abroad, but everything will depend on how Sakharov himself behaves, and also on what Bonner does while she's abroad. For the time being it makes sense to limit ourselves to this.

Sakharov's forced exile was a constant headache for Gorbachev. It was a serious obstacle in his efforts to cultivate support for perestroika among non-Communist intellectuals and Western leaders. Bonner and later Sakharov were both eventually released. In his sympathetic biography of the Soviet general secretary, journalist Dusko Doder said that after a year as CPSU chief, Gorbachev increasingly "began to regard public opinion as a basic element of power. The liberation of Sakharov brought him more international goodwill than any other single act; he had been repeatedly placed on the defensive when meeting Western leaders who raised the unpleasant issue of human rights violations in his country and invariably brought up Sakharov's name."[7] Sixteen months passed from August 1985, when the Politburo first deliberated the release of the dissident physicist's wife, to

December 1986, when international pressure finally succeeded in setting Sakharov free as well.

Gorbachev expanded his political base beyond the Party and its co-opted intelligentsia, institutes, and media and extended it to completely independent, even anti-Communist actors who would see him as the only force standing between tyranny and freedom. Along with the genuine, if limited and controlled, lifting of curtailments on free speech and expression came some official admissions of past wrongdoing. Never before had such forthrightness been heard from the Kremlin. In retrospect, most of this frankness was simply belated statements of the obvious, or confirmation of what was already known in the West, but at the time it marked a radical shift from past ideological drivel and outright lies.

Methods and Themes Under Gorbachev and Chebrikov, 1985-1988

The Gorbachev period, like the Khrushchev period, saw official denunciation of past abuses and experimentation in various degrees of liberalization in order to reinvigorate the Party and the system; however, it went much further. By the 1980s the Soviet Union was part of an increasingly interdependent world and was subject to much more foreign influence than before. Communications technology, Radio Liberty, and popular culture pierced the smothering veil of censorship. The time had come for the Party to reassess its well-trod path of waste, abuse, and excess in favor of another route to progress. As the old guard with institutional memory of Stalin died off, new leaders emerged from within the Party who espoused new thinking.[8] Gorbachev surrounded himself with them to review the Party's failures and to chart the course of perestroika and glasnost in every sector of society—politics, law, economics, agriculture, industry, journalism, academia, and culture—every sector, that is, except state security.

The chekists had no use for new thinking, at least as far as their role in society was concerned. Some mid-level and many junior officers did see a real need for reform, but few dared voice such opinions; to the KGB leadership, new thinking was a way to improve the system's efficiency while extracting the most possible financial assistance from the West. Gorbachev could have set the pace for fundamental change by appointing a "new thinker" to replace Viktor Chebrikov, whom Andropov had chosen as KGB chairman.

This was not to be. Chebrikov's support was critical to Gorbachev's rise as Party general secretary. Although Chebrikov did not quite fit in politically with Gorbachev's inner circle, he dutifully included the glasnost and perestroika themes in his speeches. As chronicled by Cambridge scholar Richard Popplewell, Chebrikov broke with Andropov's publicly ideological approach, favoring instead cooperation with the West and eschewing Andropov's rhetoric, which acknowledged few societial problems (aside from the corruption of the Brezhnevites) and spoke of overtaking the West.[9] Chebrikov's image making was chiefly in the form of speeches and other public statements. He was the first KGB leader to call for international cooperation on areas of common concern such as terrorism, drug trafficking, and fighting organized crime, subjects that became public relations staples to confer legitimacy upon the organs. He also initiated overt cooperation with the reformist Soviet press. In April 1988, *Argumenty i fakty* began publishing a column for a domestic audience called "The USSR KGB Informs and Comments." A surveyor of the column observed,

> The column seeks to justify the very existence of the KGB in the age of glasnost. That it appears in *Argumenty i fakty* also suggests that the column is to be used by the CPSU's propaganda workers in defending the activities of the KGB at home and abroad. While in general the Soviets are trying to present an atmosphere of a new detente abroad, the Soviet active measures apparatus is trying to keep the perception of an imperialist threat alive in the Soviet Union.[10]

As the unintended consequences of glasnost began to challenge Soviet power, Chebrikov departed from the "new thinking" line and blamed foreign subversion for the country's increasing internal conflict. He claimed,

> Imperialism's special services are trying to find new loopholes through which to penetrate our society and are exerting targeted, differentiated influence on various population groups in the USSR with the aim of instilling in Soviet people a bourgeois understanding of democracy, removing the process from increasing the working people's socio-political activeness from the party's influence, splitting the monolithic unity of party and people, and installing political and ideological pluralism.[11]

The KGB chairman made similar remarks in other speeches, going so far as to dismiss Western concern with human rights as a provocation by intelligence services. As Popplewell noted, such talk did little to enhance the image of Gorbachev's government. One of Chebrikov's last public statements as KGB chief took place just as the World Psychiatric

Association was considering readmission of the Soviet Union amid opposition by human rights and Jewish groups.

The opponents charged that the individuals and institutions who had locked dissidents in psychiatric hospitals were still in power. At the worst possible moment, Chebrikov said that dissidents should be so confined because the KGB was obligated to prevent antistate crimes by "helping the deviant to shed his delusions."[12] Such remarks were extremely embarrassing at a time when the Politburo needed to impress the West in order to receive the massive aid, credits, and loans it needed to finance perestroika. Chebrikov made few public statements of note during most of spring and summer 1988, and in October he left the KGB to become chairman of the Commission on Legal Affairs, which administered state security for the CPSU. Whether this reassignment was a demotion or a promotion remains a point of controversy.

In any case, the event marked Gorbachev's second opportunity to announce dramatic reforms in the KGB, and once more he passed, naming foreign intelligence chief Vladimir Kryuchkov instead of a reform Party official as the replacement. With his international experience in both espionage and active measures, Kryuchkov understood the need to impress the world if Moscow was to continue to enjoy Western support for perestroika and the billions of dollars in aid and credit that would accompany the accolades. Here was another non-reformer, a product of the cult of chekism, who could appreciate the need to massage international public opinion skillfully—the ideal candidate for a service that wanted to project the image of reformation without actually doing so. Immediately Kryuchkov began a lengthy campaign to portray the KGB abroad as just another intelligence service that could make common cause with the West.

Methods and Themes Under Gorbachev and Kryuchkov, 1988-1991

Because the KGB was still actively operating internally and in the West and would continue to do so, the Soviet government had to sell the idea that it was a legitimate service carrying out legitimate activities. Under Kryuchkov an international active measures drive was begun in 1988 to utilize the traditional instruments of the CPSU,[13] while elaborating new methods and fine-tuning the messages. Kryuchkov revolutionized the political and social promotion of the KGB. As the first chairman to wage a comprehensive image-making campaign to promote the KGB overtly to a foreign audience, he abandoned the old rhetoric against "imperialism" and amplified calls for increased international cooperation. (The Cheka had carried out some changes for foreign public relations purposes when Lenin needed international support, but the publicity campaign at the time was not comprehensive.)[14] Former KGB foreign intelligence officer Stanislav Levchenko, who specialized in influence operations, observed in 1989:

> The two major goals are to help promote a positive image of the Soviet Union throughout the free world, and to drive a wedge between the United States and its allies by attempting to discredit U.S. foreign and domestic policies. Moscow wants to improve its foreign image and to reinforce the impression of "economic reliability" (for the purpose of attracting Western credit); to diffuse western perception of the Soviet military "threat"; to direct attention to domestic policy shifts on human rights and religious freedom; and to persuade the West that an expansionist Soviet Union, along with the global export of its Communist ideology, is a thing of the past.[15]

Perestroika's unintended consequences were transformed into enlightened grand strategy. Moscow was losing control of its Eastern European military alliance, the Warsaw Treaty Organization, which was collapsing from within, but Gorbachev claimed credit for "letting" it dissolve and for "helping" the West maintain regional stability. At the same time the Warsaw Pact was unraveling, Gorbachev tried to split the NATO alliance from the United States by proposing a pan-European (and therefore Moscow-inclusive) Common European Home.[16] Meanwhile, he sought to attract hard currency through "appeals for loans, credit, and joint trade and industrial ventures."[17]

Events in Eastern Europe, especially the impending collapse of the German Democratic Republic, clearly influenced Kryuchkov, as evidenced by his statements and actions, which Popplewell surveyed.[18] The KGB chairman, who had once been in charge of services in the bloc, became extremely conciliatory, on the surface, toward reform Communists like Boris Yeltsin and even anti-Communist figures in Soviet politics, as well as to the United States. He even received dissidents for face-to-face discussions.

The new approach came in response to the direct public challenge to the KGB's authority at the new Congress of People's Deputies and Supreme Soviet. Live television broadcasts of the floor proceedings when the legislature opened in May 1989, a national sensation in their own right, were made even more controversial by the stunning denunciations of the KGB by people's deputies Boris Yeltsin, Yuriy Vlasov and others. The KGB had to respond by appearing more reformist than the reformers. It was no longer invincible. The people were beginning to lose their fear. The revolutions to the west also inspired the emerging opposition groups of the USSR, which in the autumn of that year organized the first of several demonstrations at KGB headquarters in Moscow.[19]

The campaign to save the KGB from internal and international opprobrium was a subtheme of the overall perestroika image-making effort. Kryuchkov worked to hide the fact that the KGB had not changed and would not change. Levchenko added in his 1989 observation:

> General Kryuchkov is now aggressively implementing a new active measures campaign which, in his view, will influence foreign public opinion of the KGB. This campaign pointedly ignores the fact that one of the major functions of the KGB, to protect the Soviet socialist system from dissent and opposition, remains the same, although it is being implemented differently for tactical reasons. It also conceals the fact that the KGB's secret police operations have not changed in any fundamental way, although some changes on the surface are striking. Skillfully using glasnost, Kryuchkov pretends that the new leadership of the largest secret police force in the history of civilization is reviewing its history critically and is building a much more benign organization. One of the weakest points of this operation is that General Kryuchkov and other KGB propagandists never specify what kind of enemies their organization has been fighting for the past seventy years, and exactly why in the era of glasnost they still have at least one quarter of a million officers and soldiers in the KGB.[20]

The resultant public relations campaign touting civil control of the KGB created the image of true reform consistent with larger themes of glasnost, perestroika, and the "law-governed state." Many of the early international themes were identical to those for domestic consumption, and all sought to portray the KGB as a democratic, Western-style institution that protected individual rights and freedoms.

Kryuchkov previously had been head of the First Chief Directorate in charge of foreign intelligence operations and was keenly aware of the need for active measures to influence the policies of foreign governments by shaping the attitudes of their citizens and leaders. Noted former First Chief Directorate officer Levchenko, "Kryuchkov demonstrated a deep understanding of the importance of secret active measures in furthering the foreign policy goals of the Soviet Politburo."[21] The KGB chairman also understood the need for active measures domestically. His approach was simple: acknowledging the obvious and joining his critics in demanding strict civil controls. Departing sharply from the policies of his predecessors, Kryuchkov maneuvered to legitimize the unreformed KGB in an unprecedented way.

The effort began in earnest immediately after Gorbachev's more reformist opponents took their stand in the new Supreme Soviet in June 1989. The Yeltsin and Vlasov speeches may have been infuriating, but the KGB chief recovered quickly to address the concerns raised and to preempt broader criticism by anticipating and publicly agreeing with the opposition's demands and by suggesting proposals and "reforms" of his own. First, he shaped his own personal image, taking advantage of a new law requiring that the KGB chairman and other high government officials appear before the Supreme Soviet for questioning and a vote of confirmation. Given the way the new "parliament" was rigged in favor of the CPSU, the result was preordained.

The confirmation proceedings would give the opposition a chance to challenge Kryuchkov, but they also presented the KGB with the opportunity to sell itself to the public. A formal vote was scheduled for July. In preparation, Kryuchkov arranged a television interview, in which he spoke in a very personal fashion by Soviet standards. He attempted to cast himself as a man of culture, commenting on his "love" of theater and opera; as a flesh-and-blood Soviet citizen of working-class origin who served in the Great Patriotic War; and as a warm family man with a sense of humor. Elsewhere he expressed fondness for Bellini's opera *Norma* and for the pianist Van Cliburn.[22] This was nothing new, as his predecessors had done the same: Unschlicht, who succeeded Dzerzhinskiy; Shelepin, who under Khrushchev imaged a break with Stalinism; and the jazz-loving "closet liberal" Andropov, when he became CPSU general secretary. Kryuchkov would go further and personalize the entire KGB leadership before the public. It would be chekism with a human face.

KGB officers who worked with him at Yasenevo recall a different man from the one portrayed on television. A former high-ranking intelligence officer describes Kryuchkov as a "humorless" workaholic with little time for family or entertainment.[23] Vadim Bakatin, who as Soviet Minister of Internal Affairs worked with Kryuchkov and ultimately succeeded him after the putsch, remembers him as a "stern, cold intriguer."[24] Christopher Andrew writes about defector Oleg Gordievsky's view:

> Kryuchkov's personal photographs, in which the corners of his mouth turn decisively downward, show a tough, unsmiling Tartar exterior thinly concealing a tough, unsmiling interior. Throughout his years in the FCD [First Chief Directorate] he displayed enormous energy, single-mindedness, and self-confidence, combined with administrative skill and political flair. In Gordievsky's experience he never strayed from his prepared texts at FCD

meetings, never tried to coin a striking phrase, never showed any sign of a sense of humor.[25]

Having tried to establish a pleasant public persona, Kryuchkov prodded the Supreme Soviet to "be engaged in daily, constant supervision of the work of state security bodies."[26] He laid down his themes in the 19 July nationally televised speech before the Supreme Soviet. Prior to being questioned by deputies he called for civil control of the KGB consistent with Gorbachev's slogans. In reality, the campaign was a reaction to demands of Yeltsin, Vlasov, and other reformers. It served not to fuel a real movement for reform, but to preempt, frustrate, and contain the democrats. With the strong support of the machinery and the leadership of both the CPSU and the Soviet state under Gorbachev's personal guidance, as well as the collusion of Communists who dominated the USSR Supreme Soviet, Kryuchkov became the single most outspoken state security reform advocate in the government.

Methods and Themes After the Supreme Soviet Challenge

Kryuchkov's methods and themes, driven by challenges from the few vocal reformers in the Supreme Soviet, stressed that the KGB had already made many reforms, that it was no longer in a position to abuse the population or cause mischief abroad, and that it was playing an aggressive role in perestroika. In fact, the campaign tried to make the KGB look like a service found in any Western democracy. Journalists, foreigners, and even Soviet citizens were given unique access to KGB officials. KGB leaders set up a new public relations office, made appearances on television talk shows, and suggested proposals for collaboration with their Western colleagues. Examples of Kryuchkov's main themes follow.

KGB Reforms. Kryuchkov claimed that his service was undergoing substantial reforms on its own. Soon after his controversial confirmation appearance before the Supreme Soviet in July 1989, he announced that the dreaded Fifth Directorate, created by Andropov in the 1960s to root out and repress ideological dissent, had been abolished. The announcement also followed a highly publicized confession in *Ogonyok* by Yaroslav Karpovich, a former Fifth Directorate officer who had persecuted dissidents and said he felt compelled by guilt to describe his crimes.[27] With such attention directed at the Fifth, and a vocal minority in the Supreme Soviet demanding that the KGB be reformed, Kryuchkov said that the machinery of political repression was no more and that in its place was a new Directorate for Defense of the Constitutional System, designed as "a fundamentally new directorate to protect Constitutional rights."[28] This ploy, it was later learned, was only a name change, a deception reminiscent of the paper cards of the GPU pasted over the old door plaques of the Cheka in Lubyanka, a move to placate critics and to impress the West. Kryuchkov repeated the theme for months.

The KGB at the Forefront. His KGB, Kryuchkov said, was not only subject to civil control but was so progressive that it helped write the glasnost-era legislation on "the work of law-enforcement organs."[29] Although such words were designed to impress, they really showed that the legislation coming from Gorbachev's new Supreme Soviet had the imprimatur of the chekists before leaving committee.

KGB Initiative. Kryuchkov credited not Gorbachev with the "reforms," but the KGB itself. He told *Izvestiya* in October 1989:

> In accordance with a government resolution the Directorate for the Defense of the Soviet Constitutional System has been set up within the KGB. I will not be giving any secrets away if I say that it was the security officers themselves who initiated the formation of this subunit within the system of the state security organs. The same decision abolished the Fifth Directorate of the USSR KGB, which was formed in 1967 and had the task of combatting enemy ideological subversion. The organizational changes are very principled in nature.
>
> We see this as one component in the substantial *perestroika* in the activity of state security organs.[30]

KGB Principles and Ideals. Only officers of the finest moral fiber could join the new KGB, Kryuchkov said, making the same groundless boast that a number of his predecessors had made:

> I must say that the moral makeup of KGB organs' personnel is very important for all its components, irrespective of the tasks they perform. We keep a close eye on it. The words of Feliks Edmundovich Dzerzhinskiy, that a security officer must have a "cool head, a warm heart, and clean hands," are not an empty slogan as far as our personnel are concerned. We make sure we get rid of anyone who could be a stain on their purity.[31]

Kryuchkov's invocation of Lenin's security chief was intended as an idealistic reference but should have been a warning of how removed the KGB really was from reform.

KGB Protection of Human Rights. Protection of human rights was a new theme for the KGB. In a broadcast to North America, Kryuchkov said, "The methods we use should not violate human rights. On the contrary, our staff must safeguard human rights and act exclusively within the framework of the law."[32] When asked if the KGB maintained secret files on private citizens, he responded, "You might find such things in other countries, but not here."[33] As if these assertions did not strain credibility, Kryuchkov told a European newspaper, "Violence, inhumanity and violation of human rights have always been alien to the work of our secret services."[34] Even inmates lived rather well at the KGB's Lefortovo prison. One propaganda video showed the new KGB public relations chief sampling the prison swill and remarking, "My wife can't make kasha like this. I have a taste for it, back from my army days. Can I have some more, please?"[35]

The KGB and Public Welfare. The KGB had difficulty accepting the reality of market reforms, and in a bid to polish its tarnished image, it attempted to show the public that it was helping to ease the hardships caused by socialism and the economic transition. During a brief period in late 1990 and early 1991, the KGB waged a publicity campaign against "economic sabotage." It staged high-profile raids of cooperatives and food storage centers to search for those responsible for slack food production and empty shelves. Thousands of officers from the Second Chief Directorate and the Fourth (Transportation) Directorate investigated warehouses and shops, at times with television cameras bearing witness, to uncover evidence of skimming and illicit storage of canned and other goods. The sight was intended to arouse public gratitude toward the KGB for its diligence to alleviate food shortages.

Officially, investigation of such theft was the jurisdiction of the MVD, which maintained large structures and staffs just for that purpose. By comparison, KGB crimefighting units were "insignificant," according to Bakatin, who had led both security services.[36] Well before glasnost, the KGB stressed how foreign intelligence operations benefited the population. Although many Soviet citizens deplored the KGB for its penetration and manipulation of society and for internal repression, a substantial majority polled felt that its foreign intelligence work, even without scrutiny, was important to the well-being of the country.[37]

Strict Civil Control. Several new KGB themes were initially surfaced through the Italian Communist Party newspaper *L'Unita,* whose publishers were receiving covert Soviet backing. Kryuchkov's first interview with a foreign journalist was a two-hour exchange with *L'Unita* correspondent Giulietto Chisea, published on 19 August 1989. In that interview, Kryuchkov explained the civil control structure over the KGB as if it were subject to the same checks and balances as services in the West:

> Today the principal control is exercised by the highest organs of state power; the Congress of People's Deputies, the Supreme Soviet of the USSR, both directly and through the Committee on Questions of Defense and State Security, the Constitutional Control Committee (from the moment of its institution), the USSR Council of Ministers. Control functions are also carried out by the Procurator's office, in the realm of its functions, by the Ministry of Finance and other departments. Control of the state security organs, at least in the last two decades, developed in many directions: financial activity is controlled rigorously by the Ministry of Finance, the Council of Ministers monitors us in individual questions, organizes commissions and summons us to meetings. There is a very strict party control. For example, the removal, the dismissal of an official are possible only in the bounds of the law and the smallest element of arbitration is excluded. Likewise, the KGB's building activities are controlled, the training and selection of cadres. I do not think there is any state institution as strict as the KGB towards its employees. I will tell you that at one of the first meetings of the committee of the Supreme Soviet we very soon took up the problem of control.[38]

Civil control was a staple of the larger "law-governed state" motif of the latter Gorbachev period. Counterintelligence chief Viktor Grushko later echoed that the KGB was "subordinate only to the Congress of People's Deputies, the president, the Supreme Soviet, and the Council of Ministers of the USSR. We continuously send information to these organs on all questions that fall within the jurisdiction of the KGB, and we report regularly to the USSR Supreme Soviet Committee on Defense and Security."[39] A KGB spokesman even apologized to journalists for not being more forthcoming with information, saying that he would provide the facts if only the Supreme Soviet would let him: "Had it been in my hands, I would have disclosed the figures in the KGB budget. . . . However, I have no right to do so. This is a state secret. It is not a KGB secret. It is a matter within the authority of the parliament."[40] In truth, as discussed earlier, the Supreme Soviet had no access of its own to the KGB budget because the KGB would not give it; the Committee on Defense and Security was powerless even to learn the size of the Border Guards or the price of an army tank.

Unique Role for World Security. The theme of the KGB's fight against "nuclear terrorism" surfaced in public statements after Kryuchkov's July speech to the Supreme Soviet. Ukrainian KGB Chairman Lt. Gen. N. M. Golushko said in early September 1989 that the KGB guards against "the real danger of nuclear terrorism, attacks on nuclear plants, and crimes committed using radioactive materials."[41] This was a unique role to enhance world security, especially in light of international pressure for the Soviets to safeguard their poorly constructed and maintained nuclear power plants in the wake of the 1986 Chernobyl disaster in Ukraine. A new unit was reportedly created to confront the problem.

An Equal Opportunity Employer. After a KGB major general was embarrassed by a television interviewer's question about the role of women in the state security apparatus (he admitted that women were limited mostly to clerical work),[42] the KGB attempted to compensate by bringing a female employee, Lt. Katya Mayorova, into the limelight. Instead of being presented as a professional officer, she was cast as a pistol-packing beauty queen with the title "Miss KGB." The presentation failed to have its desired effect when she modeled for photographers wearing body armor.[43] Later, after the KGB's post-putsch reorganization, the foreign intelligence service was represented to the press by a woman, Tatyana Samolis, even though few advances had been made in bringing women into responsible posts in the intelligence apparatus. Samolis did not advance through uniformed KGB ranks but was hired in October 1991 from the KGB-affiliated institute that new intelligence chief Yevgeniy Primakov had previously directed.

KGB Mistakes. Upon admitting historical "errors," KGB leaders conceded that chekists are only human and therefore make mistakes, adding that the mistakes would be corrected and that the (murdered) victims of the Stalin era would be "rehabilitated."[44] Anti-Stalin themes became prevalent in anticipation of the fiftieth anniversary of the Molotov-Ribbentrop pact of 1939 and to blunt the impact of the increase in independent revelations about state crimes committed during that period. The KGB continued to feign inability to locate archives concerning the massacre of 15,000 Polish officers at Katyn forest in Smolensk during World War II, although the files were later made available intact to a journalist.[45] In private many chekists—even those who trained new recruits—continued to defend the Katyn massacre. The chairman of the KGB Higher School examination commission asked a graduate from Smolensk, "How could you people in Smolensk allow the Katyn affair to be brought to light?" A colonel intervened: "Comrade general, our president apologized for Katyn to the president of Poland." The irritated general shot back, "Nonsense! Let him know that they shot only spies and wreckers there."[46]

Defectors. The KGB was no longer a vindictive, cutthroat organization, according to Kryuchkov in an international broadcast, who said that any officer who had defected to the West could safely return and "always count on his homeland's mercy."[47] This was also a lie. Death sentences imposed in absentia on defectors to the West remained in place not only through the Soviet collapse but beyond, according to Levchenko, who as of 1994 was still under sentence to be executed.[48]

A Partner with Western Intelligence Services. Departing sharply from the incendiary rhetoric of the past, Kryuchkov rhetorically changed the KGB from a rival of Western intelligence services to an ally. He portrayed his service as becoming a member of the international community, referring to officers of the long-demonized CIA as "colleagues." He spoke positively about antinarcotics cooperation with the British and Canadian services in a widely publicized August 1989 article in *New Times*.[49]

This theme was actually initiated by Chebrikov in 1987, when the Soviet government, faced with internal political violence, asked France, Great Britain, and West Germany for counterterrorism assistance. The hijacking of a Soviet domestic airliner to Israel in December 1988 prompted Moscow to cooperate with Western services, including the CIA and Mossad, to resolve the crisis. Kryuchkov's deputy, Vitaliy Ponomarev, stated in an interview on Radio Peace and Progress that the KGB was willing to cooperate with American, British, and Israeli secret services in combating terrorism.

The next month, unofficial Soviet-American meetings commenced to discuss common means of fighting terrorism. The meetings were initiated by the Soviet Peace Committee, an active measures apparatus under the direction of the CPSU International Department.[50] They resulted in a commercially published book, *Common Ground on Terrorism*,[51] which was reviewed as "shy[ing] away from the history of Soviet support for terrorist groups" and as portraying the USSR "first and foremost as a victim of terrorism" in the Middle East. A reviewer could find only one "meek sentence" in the book's 183 pages hinting of Soviet support for terrorism: "There were instances when the Soviet Union was accused of allegedly supporting and thus being involved, if only indirectly, in activities of terrorist groups in the region."[52] Party documents made public in 1992 by the office of Russian Information Minister Mikhail Poltaranin, and obtained by unofficial means, showed that Soviet support for international terrorism was approved at the highest levels.[53]

In a three-part broadcast to North America in October 1989, Kryuchkov cited a new "mutual understanding" that allowed the KGB to cooperate with Western services in "assuring the security of foreign nationals and officials in one country or another." Fighting terrorism was a theme; the Soviet Union, like much of the rest of the world, was also a victim of terrorism. The KGB, he said, could work with Western services as a humanitarian force for good:

> There have been precedents of the intelligence services of a given country acting on humanitarian grounds and issuing a warning about plans for terrorist attacks. And the same goes for combatting smuggling and the drug business. Terrorism respects no territorial boundaries. Regrettably the recent wave of terrorist attacks has not spared the Soviet Union. In the circumstances intelligence services in many countries can have common interests. And that leads them to planned contacts to the benefit of citizens and states.[54]

Helpful Chekists. The enemy image of Western intelligence services was gone; Kryuchkov now called them good company. An official 1989 pamphlet in his name about the "new KGB" was published and distributed with the clumsy title, *The KGB Must Abide by the Interests of the People.* It contained photographs of helpful chekists guarding borders, rescuing a stricken boat, battling terrorism, capturing a gangster, and fighting drug smugglers. Kryuchkov wrote, "At the basis of all our efforts we have placed two criteria—legality and truth." Almost in passing, the pamphlet noted that the KGB also performed intelligence and counterintelligence functions. Overall, it portrayed the KGB as a service "like every country had."[55]

Glasnost and Security. Kryuchkov explained that glasnost would actually help state security do its job, for only through glasnost would the public know about the KGB and its contribution to society. On one occasion he said:

> Naturally, there is an inherent contradiction between such categories as *glasnost* and secrecy, and this contradiction is present in the work of any special service because of the very nature of their work. It is like fire and ice. However, despite certain costs, which will undoubtedly be incurred, there are also certain pluses. Therefore we are taking rather bold steps in this direction. The more Soviet people know about the security organs, the more understanding they will be about our work, and this will lead to a strengthening of our position in society. Law enforcement organs cannot work without citizens' support; in order for this support to be active and, even more importantly, effective, people must possess certain volume of information.[56]

One domestic theme was downplayed for foreign audiences. Although Kryuchkov implied in a Radio Moscow broadcast to North America that Western intelligence was behind inter-ethnic unrest in the USSR, he did not make it an issue.[57] However, the charge did become a theme for internal audiences, apparently to offer one more reason for the KGB's ubiquity. In late October, KGB officials discussed perestroika with experts at the Institute of the Far East of the USSR

Academy of Sciences. Several of the themes described above appeared, as well as the assertion that Western intelligence activity was "on the rise" and that "Western special services are stepping up attempts at recruiting Soviet citizens. These attempts are facilitated by the expanding international contacts."[58]

New Methods

New public relations methods quickly developed. Initially, Kryuchkov's image-making drive relied on television and the print media to spread his message, which, with the single exception noted above, was essentially the same for domestic and foreign audiences. In 1988 *Argumenty i fakty* started a column called "The USSR KGB Reports and Comments." *Moskovskaya pravda* followed by featuring a regular pro-KGB column in September 1989 called "Letters from Lubyanka." The purpose was to clear up "distortions and rumors" about the KGB and to "remove the veil of secrecy from their difficult and courageous work."[59]

KGB officials conducted face-to-face public diplomacy, a practice that Shelepin had begun during the Khrushchev period, to visit the common citizen. In one instance in August 1989, KGB officers met for three hours with space technology factory workers, "discussed their work, demonstrated models of certain technical devices used by western special services to gather secret information, and answered numerous questions." They also showed a promotional video.[60]

Kryuchkov and other senior officers gave extensive interviews on Soviet and foreign television and radio programs, including Radio Peace and Progress (Radio Moscow), and to the print media. Though the interviews contained few revelations, Kryuchkov impressed journalists as well as the public with the KGB's new "openness." These methods were inexpensive or free for the KGB and required little preparation. Hence Kryuchkov was able to convert demands for reform to suit the KGB's purposes by echoing the anti-Communists' appeals, thereby confusing the issue to his advantage. That the first major wave of KGB reformist propaganda did not commence until after Kryuchkov's July appearance before the USSR Supreme Soviet indicates that the image-making campaign was a response to calls for change rather than an initiative of perestroika.

The KGB's public relations themes grew in sophistication and diversity. Its methods expanded in 1990 and 1991 as vocal opposition to the KGB intensified. The campaign crafted a permanent message and structure. Although officials hailed a new chapter in the history of chekism and cited the new openness as proof that glasnost and perestroika were genuine, Kryuchkov's public statements and real policies became completely contradictory. When he spoke for domestic or foreign public audiences, he was generally conciliatory and reformist. The following quotation is characteristic: "Perestroika is being carried out in the KGB. It has affected the structure of the subunits and virtually all avenues of operational activity."[61] Yet when he addressed Party cadres, the words were reminiscent of the pre-Gorbachev period. For example, in June 1990, he revealed that he would tolerate freedom only up to a certain point:

> The attempt to exploit the crisis phenomena in the economy, the desire to earn political clout exclusively from positions of confrontation with the CPSU have led some sociopolitical organizations to rally on strictly anti-Communist bases. . . . The establishment of a multi-party system cannot be allowed to aggravate the situation in the country still further.[62]

In July he argued against depoliticization of the KGB, urging maintenance of Communist Party control.[63] These statements occurred at approximately the same time that he began planning for a state of emergency.[64] Meanwhile, he expanded the KGB's public image-making campaign.

Public Relations Office. To polish its image and engender public confidence, the KGB opened a Public Relations Center in September 1990. After opening the public relations office, the KGB directed reporters and television cameras to its "brand new" suggestion box in the hall.[65] In addition to issuing communiques, producing videos, and speaking with reporters, the Center arranged for senior officers to grant interviews.[66] Yet from day one of the Center's existence, it was engaged in disinformation. At its opening ceremony, Public Relations Director Aleksandr Karbainov crassly told journalists that the KGB did not play a role in persecuting dissidents and was not involved with sending Vladimir Bukovsky, Pyotr Grigorenko, and Leonid Plyushch to psychiatric hospitals.[67] Karbainov's office denied revelations that the service had been behind the 1978 murder in London of Bulgarian dissident Georgi Markov and threatened to take legal action against the main accuser, Oleg Kalugin, who sat in on the planning meetings when he was chief of foreign counterintelligence and who implicated Kryuchkov and others.[68]

Karbainov was not a career KGB officer, but he knew much about hunting dissidents. A Party apparatchik, he became knowledgeable about the chekists when serving with the Administrative Organs Department of the CPSU Central Committee. Sometime during the

Gorbachev years, he had been transferred to the KGB Fifth Chief Directorate, which was responsible for political persecution of Party adversaries.[69] His deputy in the Public Relations Center was Col. Aleksey Petrovich Kandaurov.

They disappeared from public view during the August 1991 putsch, failing either to support or denounce the action. When it was clear that the putschists had been defeated, they went back to work. Karbainov confessed to *La Repubblica* on 23 August, "I did nothing, I did not say a word against the coup. My heart was as heavy as a stone. It was all so difficult, complicated, horrible. But I lacked the courage. I carried on my job as though nothing had happened."[70] He called for a "reformed" security service, washing his hands and those of his colleagues of any culpability: "Of course we have our faults and our responsibilities. But we ordinary aides of this committee were dragged into this terrible business by the KGB chiefs, without ever having made any decision, without ever having been consulted, and in many cases without agreeing with the decisions that were being made."[71]

Karbainov and Kandaurov survived the post-coup purge, and continued making absurd statements. Karbainov told a German newspaper in late 1991, "We no longer serve a party today, but our work is exclusively devoted to human rights."[72] Inexplicably, KGB Chairman Vadim Bakatin ignored warnings to remove Karbainov and did not dismiss him until November of that year, more than a month after the KGB was dismembered.[73] Karbainov's dour and nervous deputy, Kandaurov, remained in the new Russian organs and was promoted to major general as public relations chief at the Ministry of Security. He retained his position after the reorganization of the internal security service in 1994 when the MB became the Federal Counterintelligence Service (FSK).

New Public Journals. The KGB published several classified journals, one of which was issued in unclassified form to the public. The professional publication *USSR KGB Digest* became available for general circulation in May 1990. The first issue featured the "exceptional devotion to the motherland and high patriotism" of the secret services during World War II but said nothing of its other services to Stalin.[74] By mid-July 1991, the KGB had issued a second public journal, *Kuryer sovetskoy razvedki* (Courier of Soviet Intelligence), aimed at a more popular readership. Its editor, Sergey Tolkunov, wrote in the preface of the premiere issue, "We see our aim as offering readers a chance to become acquainted with documents and other materials on the role of intelligence in the various periods of our state's history, the victories and the inevitable losses and defeats in every battle. The authors of almost all our publications are professional intelligence agents."[75]

Videos. The KGB public relations office produced its own video programs, including a "documentary" entitled "The New KGB." Complete with its own disco soundtrack, the video reflected the service's new crimefighting, intelligence, counterterrorism and anti-narcotics themes and showed Karbainov sampling the swill at Lefortovo and asking for more.[76]

Comparisons to Formerly Taboo Institutions. The KGB continued to compare itself favorably to Western institutions that until recently had been openly regarded as the enemy. The Eighth Chief Directorate for cryptography, previously unknown to Soviet citizens, was likened in a *Pravda* interview to the U.S. National Security Agency.[77] Not only was the KGB like the British MI-5, MI-6, and GCHQ and the American FBI, CIA, and NSA; its most despised elements, the *stukachi*, or informers, now found their roots in the Bible. KGB Colonel of Justice Semen Yenkovich Martirosov of the Inspection Directorate commented on the KGB's "secret helpers" within the USSR and said that their counterparts of old could be found in the Old Testament:

> Twice during the Exodus of the sons of Israel from Egypt the kings resorted to the help of secret "spies." On prompting from the Most High, Moses sent 12 of his helpers on a secret reconnaissance to the land of Canaan and Joshua the son of Nun sent two spies to Jericho. It was with the help of the local woman Rahab that they obtained extremely valuable information on the mood of the residents of Jericho. What is most interesting, the acts of their secret helper subsequently were given high marks by the evangelists—the apostles of Jesus Christ.[78]

One of the problems with this argument is that Moses never sent people to inform on fellow Hebrews, nor did the Apostles spy on other Christians.

Demystification. To illuminate the shadowy and intimidating image of the KGB in the public eye, chiefs of main directorates and their lieutenants granted exclusive interviews to Soviet print and electronic media to describe their bureaucracies and how they worked. These appearances began in September 1990 and continued through turbulent December, when Foreign Minister Eduard Shevardnadze resigned amid warning of a coup. Meanwhile the security services were preparing for violent crackdowns in the Baltic and the Caucasus, and for a state of emergency throughout the Soviet Union.

Through the Public Relations Center, the KGB granted the controlled newspaper *Pravda* unusual access to the Eighth Chief

Directorate in charge of cryptography and signals intelligence. The lengthy two-part article, billed as the first public look, termed the directorate the "Holy of Holies of Security." The Eighth's director was featured in a very personal profile, and its battles against the American National Security Agency were recounted. As a bonus, the Eighth even provided *Pravda* with a coded message and a key for readers to decipher it.[79]

Kryuchkov gave a long interview to *Soyuz*, published in late November, outlining the KGB's function in society.[80] In an interview with *Argumenty i fakty* in early December, Second Chief Directorate head V. Grushko explained in broad and innocuous terms the function of his state security division.[81] First Chief Directorate leader Lt. Gen. Leonid Shebarshin, "whose name until recently was a secret," according to TASS, appeared on Soviet television on 16 December to explain the role of the foreign intelligence service.[82] Intelligence Analysis chief Maj. Gen. E. N. Yakovlev was interviewed in *Pravda* on 20 December. He described the sources and personnel in his unit. The interview's publication date occurred on the seventy-third anniversary of the founding of the Cheka, which was also the seventieth anniversary of the founding of the first Soviet intelligence service.[83] At least one republic security chief joined the campaign. Moldova KGB Chairman T. L. Botnar discussed the changing roles and functions of the KGB in the republics, coming across very personably in a front page *Pravda* story published in February 1991.

Public Relations During Baltic Repression. Kryuchkov was the only KGB figure to become strident in official appearances as the armed actions against the Lithuanian and Latvian governments were prepared in December 1990. On 11 December he issued an unscheduled speech on live television, the first time a KGB chairman had ever made such a presentation. Speaking in the name of President Gorbachev, Kryuchkov pledged that the secret services would wage battle "with all the means at their disposal" against "anti-Communist" forces that threatened central power within the USSR.[84] Gorbachev never rebuked him. The next day, *Pravda* interviewed the KGB chairman; the transcript of the interview was published the following morning under the rubric "response to readers' reactions" to the 11 December television appearance.[85] On 15 December, *Izvestiya* published a "more detailed" interview on "economic sabotage," a follow-up to Kryuchkov's televised speech.[86]

As the crackdown date loomed closer, Kryuchkov resumed his moderate persona. He was a special guest on a live television talk show on 12 January 1991 to address citizens' concerns. Apparently to protect the KGB chief from embarrassment, viewers were allowed only to state their questions to an operator, who wrote them on cards. At the end of the interview, Kryuchkov was shown a batch of questions submitted over the phone. He promised to answer them all, "some by letter, some orally if, of course, we can get to the authors of these letters. I think they will not remain without an answer."[87]

The KGB suspended its public relations work during the Vilnius repression but resumed it immediately thereafter, though clearly on the defensive. Kryuchkov held a public question-and-answer session in Moscow, and recorded excerpts were broadcast by radio. He brushed off a very moderately worded remark about Lithuania by one questioner, saying that the crackdown occurred in response to the "infringement of human rights."[88] Using xenophobic rhetoric he tried to justify what had just occurred in Vilnius and Riga. To "illustrate the intrigues of enemy special services," a public exhibition was sponsored by the KGB at the House of Political Education in Moscow within days of the crackdowns. Kryuchkov personally attended the event, which apparently failed to convince a skeptical and alarmed public.

According to Soviet television coverage of the exhibition, guests appeared less concerned with how the KGB was supposedly protecting them from "enemy special services" and more interested in how it was abusing them. Commented the correspondent, "It seems to me, the audience was more interested to find out how the KGB is doing in its capacity of the sword, and questions asked were mostly about the possibility of retribution. . . . The main subject discussed, naturally, was the events in Lithuania." He continued, "Here in the hall one can feel how stirred up and how worked up society is." The clumsy public relations attempt was made all the worse for the KGB when Kryuchkov publicly praised the behavior of the security forces in Vilnius. He said, "Our lads . . . have behaved as they were supposed to. They were not the ones who fired the first shot. They used blanks."[89]

By that point, public relations mattered little. Kryuchkov had already made up his mind to impose a state of emergency. The United States and most of its major West European allies deplored the violence, but convinced of the need to "save" Gorbachev they responded mildly to spare him from embarrassment. The Soviet public seemed powerless to resist.

Conclusion

Chekism perpetuated itself throughout the glasnost and perestroika period while the KGB went to extraordinary lengths to persuade domestic and international opinion that it was really reforming into a Western-style security and intelligence service. The first image-making campaigns were initiated by the Communist Party or the KGB itself; the new Congress of People's Deputies and Supreme Soviet, which first convened in 1989, permitted independent voices on national television to excoriate the organs and demand that they be brought under civil control. From that point, the KGB tried to defeat the opposition by joining it, and formally requested the Supreme Soviet to place the special services under immediate parliamentary oversight. By 1991 the KGB had dusted off a draft law authored years before by Chairman Andropov, modernized it, submitted it to its allies on the parliamentary Committee on Defense and Security, and shepherded it through to final enactment as the USSR Law on Security. Now officially under civil control in the law-governed state of glasnost, the KGB was legally endowed with most of its powers of the past; meanwhile, it tried to convince the world that it had reformed.

8

Chekist Public Relations, 1992–1994

Why did the KGB get involved in [fighting crime] at all? Its leaders simply felt that sooner or later they would be asked for concrete results, for something real done in the state's interests . . . and so crime was needed.

—Viktor Barannikov,
Minister of Security and Internal Affairs, 1991[1]

The endless use of the Russian secret services as an enemy image is tiresome for the public. . . . The best way is for the public to regard its secret services as a guarantor of law and democracy.

—Col. Aleksey Kandaurov,
Deputy Chief of Public Relations,
Ministry of Security, 1993[2]

Weeks after the KGB was divided into components and turned over to the Russian Federation, a public opinion poll previously commissioned by Bakatin was conducted in Russia and eight other republics of the Commonwealth of Independent States. The poll was intended to measure public attitudes about the KGB. Among its findings was that public opinion was remarkably uniform throughout the CIS. Differences of opinion emerged not by region but according to whether the security organs had directly affected the respondents' lives.[3]

Seventeen percent of those surveyed were described as KGB "advocates." Twice as many were considered "antagonists." Three in ten said that their relatives had suffered at the hands of the KGB or its predecessors, and one-fourth said they had been "supervised" or monitored by the secret police. Of the most educated respondents, 35 percent with higher education and more than 50 percent with advanced degrees said their lives had been monitored.

But there was good news for the chekists. Of the total surveyed, 45 percent saw the KGB officer as a "person of duty," 46 percent viewed him as a "strong person," and 64 percent considered him a professional. A third perceived Western intelligence services to be a "tremendous threat" to their country. The same percentage said there should be no reduction in the state security budget. Nearly a quarter thought highly of Stalin, and fully 40 percent said the KGB should battle "ideological diversions." Overwhelming majorities felt that state security still had legitimate duties: 82 percent said the chekists should fight organized crime, drug trafficking and terrorism; 75 percent said state security should guard military installations and protect "state secrets"; and 73 percent said—despite the KGB's leadership in attempting the August putsch—that state security should prevent military coups.[4]

One can conclude, if the data are accurate, that in early 1992 the chekist organs had strong support from about one-third of the population, that supporters outnumbered opponents, and that a vast majority of citizens felt that the chekists had legitimate functions in post-Soviet society. This wide level of support no doubt reflects the totalitarian political culture, which had never truly experienced democratic pluralism and accepted the KGB as a normal if not necessarily revered part of daily life.

For the chekists, the polling data must have been encouraging, especially with more than eight out of ten citizens endorsing their new anticrime, antitrafficking, and antiterrorism functions. The image-making campaigns conducted from 1992 were remarkable in their similarities to those waged by the KGB between 1988 and 1991. New themes emerged in the process, especially after the Soviet collapse as the services attempted to distance themselves as far as possible from the KGB, at least in their public appearance. These attempts were intended to mask the continuum of the chekist legacy.

Outward signs of this continuum can still (as of 1994) be seen in downtown Moscow at state security headquarters at Lubyanka Square. On the black granite street-level façade of the main building is a rectangular mark where a plaque was once set honoring former KGB Chairman Yuriy Andropov. The plaque was removed by demonstrators in the euphoric aftermath of the 1991 putsch. The looming statue of Dzerzhinskiy that dominated the traffic island in front was toppled by the same demonstrators with the help of a crane from the Moscow city government. Restoration of Dzerzhinskiy Square to its original name came at the initiative of the city council.

All the chekist icons that were out of reach were preserved. Whereas the white, blue, and red tricolor replaced the red banner with a hammer and sickle, and Soviet-era placenames across Russia were discarded to varying degrees, the security organs themselves preserved the symbols of their peculiar culture. Long after the supposed break with the KGB, the cast bronze coat of arms depicting a Communist hammer and sickle upon a chekist sword and shield adorned the perimeter of the main building at 2 Lubyanka. Even the brass door handles at the back entrance bear the chekist crest.

Busts of Lenin and Dzerzhinskiy remain on display within; a marble sculpture even stands near the door to the chekists' discotheque, and a portrait of the Cheka founder hangs religiously in nearly every office. A great red marble wall with the names of chekists killed on duty inset in bronze remains in a main lobby, with an eternal flame afire below.[5] Dzerzhinskiy portraits still hang in the interrogation room of Lefortovo Prison.[6] In the foreign intelligence service, too, Dzerzhinskiy remains a revered figure. A huge bust remains at SVR headquarters in Yasenevo. Questions about the crimes committed under his command provoke emotional defenses from the highest ranking intelligence officers.[7] So ingrained is chekist tradition that the founding of the Cheka on 20 December 1917, and of the Cheka's foreign intelligence service on 20 December 1920, are still commemorated; in fact, intelligence officers continue to be paid on the 20th of the month as they have since Dzerzhinskiy's time.[8]

Internal Security Image-Making Campaigns

Like Vladimir Kryuchkov, who attempted to portray the KGB as a new and completely reformed organization, Minister of Security Viktor Barannikov and his successors attempted to show the country and the world that their organization was thoroughly different from the discredited KGB. Most of the internal security image-making campaign themes were identical for internal and foreign audiences, with the exception of an internal theme stressing protection against foreign intrigues. Similarly, aside from a concerted effort to distance itself from the KGB, the Ministry of Security has echoed and expanded upon themes set by KGB Chairman Chebrikov in 1987 and 1988 and by Chairman Kryuchkov between 1988 and 1991. Spokesmen stressed over and over again that the Ministry of Security—and now the Federal Counterintelligence Service—is a new and benign service committed to protecting human rights; that it performs functions useful to society, such as combating corruption, organized crime, terrorism, drug trafficking, and smuggling; that it is similar to Western security services; that it wishes to cooperate with the West; and that the West is still not sincere about full cooperation. Examples of the main themes follow.[9]

Themes

Break from the Discredited Past. The Ministry of Security was portrayed as something new, a break with the past. In his first television interview as minister, Barannikov discussed the organ's newness: "The system of the ministry should move from being the party's armed detachment to being a constitutional body for the firm defense of Russians, first and foremost, of their rights and freedoms, of the security of the state, and of the territorial inviolability of our country."[10] The MB leadership, he said, was selected through an internal "democratic process." Moreover, the security professional of the new Russia "should like people."[11]

One top ministry official said that the MB was completely different from the KGB:

> What is left is the professional core of counterintelligence agents and specialists in combatting crime, contraband and in ensuring economic security. The staff that headed services was changed practically completely. The old personnel have been replaced with well-trained and professional people who never took part in political gambles or fulfilled the will of some other politicians.[12]

As Chapter 4 shows, the MB absorbed most of the KGB's internal structures and personnel, and relatively few officers were removed. Furthermore, the official who made the above statement, First Deputy Chairman Oleynikov, was soon sacked for being too liberal. He was replaced by hard-line dissident-hunter Golushko. The Security Ministry middle leadership was stuffed with Barannikov loyalists from the MVD. The Ministry of Security continued to idealize the noble chekists. In an interview with *Krasnaya zvezda*, the minister commented about the younger officers rising up through the ranks: "They are the new face of the Russian security service. To all appearances, an honest and courageous face."[13]

Idealizing the chekists as superhuman has not been a prominent theme, however. Continuing where Kryuchkov left off, the MB tried to display the human side of its officers but went even further to show their frailties and other shortcomings. In the same interview, Barannikov discussed at length the low morale of state security cadres, the concern and uncertainty they shared with the average Russian for the future, and the difficulties they had making a living.[14] The ministry also announced instances of corruption, such as the alleged arms smuggling carried out by two presidential bodyguards from the separate Main Guard Directorate, and the criminal proceedings that followed.[15] The most important announcements of corruption within the Security Ministry were allegations officially leveled at four generals and eighty other officers purged in the process of Barannikov's power consolidation. These allegations must be considered in a political instead of a legal context because no announcement was made of any of the officers being prosecuted.

Corruption allegations—legitimate as they may be—are a time-worn power play to remove political or personal opponents. The KGB used them against Brezhnev and Chernenko loyalists prior to the successions of Andropov and Gorbachev as CPSU general secretaries. Corruption was one of the official reasons Barannikov himself was fired when his political intrigues lost favor with Yeltsin in July 1993.

President Yeltsin's December 1993 decree describing the MB as an "unreformable" lineal descendant of the Cheka and Stalin's secret police made the public relations work of the successor Federal Counterintelligence Service (FSK) quite difficult. Because Yeltsin created the FSK with the same leadership as the MB, the reorganization seemed like little more than a name change. The FSK, though silent for several days (as had been the Ministry of Security and Internal Affairs upon its sudden formation two years before) had to move quickly to show how different it would be not only from the KGB, but from the Ministry of Security. The FSK was immediately attacked by reformers. Parliamentary faction leader Grigoriy Yavlinsky dismissed the reorganization as being "of a purely propagandistic character." He noted, "Political surveillance can be conducted with the wish or the connivance of the country's leadership by any department, regardless of its name."[16]

Decrease in Power. To distance itself from the KGB, the Ministry of security claimed that it was not as powerful as the organization it succeeded and thus incapable of totalitarian actions. First Deputy Minister Oleynikov set the tone at the news conference in which the ministry made its image-making debut. Asked about guarantees that the MB would not "turn into a new monster," he replied that the ministry's "structure is quite different" from that of the KGB. "Many services have been taken away from us, including the government communication system, border guard troops and intelligence service."[17] In using the word "us" to characterize the Ministry of Security, Oleynikov let slip that in the minds of its leaders, the MB was the clear successor to the KGB. Within three months, the ministry reabsorbed the Border Guards.

Subsequent public presentations were more sophisticated. *Krasnaya zvezda* paraphrased Minister Barannikov: "The Ministry of Security has concentrated in its subunits only the potential necessary to combat espionage, terrorism, smuggling, and corruption. This has resulted in the abolition of many bureaucratic superstructures.[18]

A similar line was used to disguise the chekists' powers more than seventy years before. Amy Knight in 1988 observed from a historical perspective the 1922 transition from the Cheka to the GPU:

> On paper it appeared that the powers of the political police had been reduced significantly. The GPU did not have the emergency special status of the Vecheka but was a regular branch of the state, incorporated into the NKVD. . . . The GPU's jurisdiction was curtailed so that it was to be responsible only for overt threats to the state's security—counter-revolutionary activity, banditry, espionage, and smuggling—as well as for defense of Soviet borders and protection of railways and waterways. All other offenses previously handled by the Vecheka (such as speculation and bribery) were to be dealt with by Revolutionary Tribunals or courts. Moreover the GPU was to be subject to definite procedural requirements without the powers of summary justice that the Vecheka had enjoyed.[19]

Although the context of 1992 was different—the regime was no longer ideological or totalitarian—the point is the same. There was no break with chekism.

Internal Security Apparatus. Ministry of Security leaders frequently cited the fact that personnel was significantly reduced to support their claim that the MB was unlikely to become another KGB. According to an official summary of a statement by Barannikov in May 1992, "Approximately 400 generals' posts have already been abolished in the Russian Federation Security Ministry system, and the total number of direct employees of the security organs has been reduced from 513,000 to 137,900."[20]

The figure was misleading, as demonstrated by the rough calculations that appear in Chapter 4. Barannikov was referring to two different things: the USSR KGB, on the one hand, and a set of its components in the form of the MB, on the other. He did not try to explain where the other 375,100 officers had gone. Only a small proportion of the officers were actually lost to retirement or attrition. Most KGB officers were retained, either as active duty or active reserve. Thus Barannikov's claims of reductions were false.

Furthermore, the MB would not reveal its actual force and personnel strength or structure.[21]

Useful Role for Society. The Ministry of Security's myriad benefits to Russian society were so often repeated in 1992 and 1993 that the observer could predict the litany of advantages in a given interview or article. The series of benefits differed little from those cited by KGB officials under Kryuchkov: the strong counterintelligence to protect the country from foreign spies and conspiracies, strong antiterrorist forces, and ever-growing units and operations to fight corruption, organized crime, and smuggling of national wealth, narcotics, weapons, and radioactive material.[22] These themes had been set before the Ministry of Security was formally created.[23] (The chekists liked to say they performed other beneficial functions as well. On one occasion MB officials spoke of protecting Russians from AIDS-infected foreigners by maintaining a list of known carriers of the HIV virus so that the individuals could be denied entry to the country.[24])

Barannikov committed the same sin he had charged Kryuchkov with committing by engaging state security in the fight against organized crime. As head of internal affairs, Barannikov had accused Kryuchkov and the KGB of combating organized crime only as a cynical rationale for chekism's continued existence: "Why," he asked, "did the KGB get involved in this problem at all? Its leaders simply felt that sooner or later they would be asked for concrete results, for something real done in the state's interests. . . . And so crime was needed."[25] Only after he had left the MVD to take the reins of state security did Barannikov, too, "need" crime to justify his bureaucracy's existence. As insincere as the anticrime argument was, it made excellent politics because of the exploding crime rate. The chekists were needed again.

The FSK preserved the same principal themes, beginning with the press conference that announced its reorganization.[26] Spokesman Aleksey Kandaurov (who previously had been a top spokesman for the MB and the KGB before it) said that Yeltsin's decree abolishing the MB and creating the FSK "sets out the broad outlines of the functions and structures of the renewed special services—the struggle against the espionage and subversive activities of foreign services; the struggle against terrorism, against illegal armed groups, against movements with extremist leanings, against drugs and arms trafficking, and against corruption and smuggling."[27]

Strict Civil Control. Security Ministry officials continuously maintained that there was a need for strict civil control over their actions, even as Barannikov openly flouted the parliament's near-unanimous vote against merging the MVD with the chekists by transferring large numbers of militsiya officers into Lubyanka in December 1991 and January 1992.

Like Kryuchkov before him, Barannikov publicly urged that his service be under close Supreme Soviet supervision. "Activities of the state security bodies must be under the strict control of the parliament," he told the deputies after the MB was created. TASS reported that he "called for the soonest adoption of a corresponding law, the core of which should be the 'protection of the constitutional system of the state and our citizens.'"[28] The new chekists, he implied nearly three months later in his first televised interview, were not content with operating under presidential decree and were impatient to be governed by law. In the interview he noted that the lack of laws on security "to some extent . . . is disconcerting for the staff."[29] He said he envisioned for Russia "the kind of parliamentary control which exists today in the civilized countries [*sic*]."[30]

Strict adherence to law and constitution was the standard boilerplate that MB officials used to attempt to convince the public of their deep commitment to human rights. At times official statements bordered on the ridiculous. On one occasion, the first deputy minister of security allowed his professed enthusiasm for civil controls to jump ahead of reality. As he explained how the apparatus was carrying out a process to "remove" the organs from the "ideological sphere," an interviewer asked to where the organs would be removed:

> Q: "Remove where?"
> A: "Remove to the sphere of legality and constitutional compliance."
> Q: "But we still have no Constitution."
> A: "But we shall have a Constitution. Do you agree? We must not wait for it."[31]

Before the Supreme Soviet passed the Law on Security, the same official said that he was "disappointed" that "there was still no state security legislation to rely on."[32] After the Law on Security, drafted under Barannikov and introduced by chekists in the Supreme Soviet Committee on Defense and Security, was enacted and made effective in May 1992, the MB stressed the comprehensiveness of civil control over its activity. A ministry spokesman told *Pravda,* "The Russian special services' activity is now tightly regulated by the unequivocal laws 'On the Federal Security Organs' and 'On Operational Investigatory Activity.' Only a madman unafraid of prison could break these laws."[33]

Protection of Individual Rights. Further distancing itself from the KGB, the Ministry of Security portrayed itself as a protector of individual rights. Rhetoric to support this claim was enshrined in the

Law on Security, the Law on Federal Organs of State Security, and other legislation. First Deputy Minister Oleynikov said the purpose of the MB was "to protect our Constitutional system, the rights, freedoms and lawful interests of the individual."[34] On one occasion he expressed frustration that the line was not being universally accepted: "Nobody wants to realize that the Ministry of Security is a newly formed mechanism, intended to defend society as a whole, and each of its citizens individually."[35] Barannikov grandly told the Supreme Soviet, "I think it most important in the activity of the ministry and subordinate security organs as a whole to have reliable provisions for the defense of the person, his rights, and his freedom so that we could directly come to the realization of the principle, 'Government is for the person, and not the other way around.'"[36]

Yet a lawyer defending a government employee jailed at the MB's Lefortovo Prison on charges of accepting bribes said that the MB continued to seize the notes taken by lawyers who visit their imprisoned clients.[37] Even citizens not accused of criminal activity continued to face denial of some of their basic human rights, such as the right to travel. The *propiska* system, which required people to obtain a government permit to live in a particular city or town, remained in place. The Yeltsin government reinforced restrictions on travel abroad when Prime Minister Viktor Chernomyrdin signed a July 1993 decree instructing the ministries of foreign affairs and internal affairs to stamp Russian passports with the authorization "Permitted to leave until" a given date, "on the basis of existing agreements with federal organs of state security."[38]

A Force for Stability. With Russian society deeply concerned over economic ruin, political uncertainty, and ethnic unrest, the MB attempted to soothe popular anxieties with reassurances. A public relations office statement paraphrased by a news agency purported to summarize a meeting of the MB Collegium:

> Russia needs general national consent, consolidation of legislative and executive powers, and all progressive forces.
>
> The board believes that the most important task of the Security Ministry is to observe legality and stability in functioning of constitutional institutions of power. It resolutely rejects any attempts to use the system of federal security bodies as an instrument in political confrontations, and in satisfaction of separatists' ambitions.[39]

Reality dictated otherwise. The internal security agencies are permitted by the Law on Security and the Law on Federal Organs of State Security to penetrate civil institutions and run informants.

Furthermore, in replacing Barannikov in summer 1993, Yeltsin placed the country's top chekist authority on manipulation and suppression of ethnic and nationalist unrest in control of the main levers of state power. New Security Minister Nikolay Golushko, after all, had spent much of his KGB career in the Fifth Chief Directorate pitting ethnic groups against one another and repressing them all.

Repudiation of Old Methods. The MB frequently claimed that it abandoned old and feared KGB methods. Barannikov told the Supreme Soviet, "Reorganization of secret services has put an end to shadowing as a method of fight against dissidents."[40] However, the laws passed in 1992 legalized previous forms of surveillance. The MB also claimed that journalists would no longer be recruited as agents of influence. A ministry spokesman wrote an article in *Literaturnaya gazeta* in which he said that there was no practical reason to plant or recruit agents in the mass media, because the MB could make its concerns known by having its officers write openly in newspapers and magazines.[41] Yet major publications continued to accept MB officers as staff members in exchange for state subsidies.[42] Very few Russian journalists have conducted genuine investigative reporting on the state security organs, and even what little investigative reporting there was declined markedly between 1992 and 1994.

Openness. Ministry officials dropped bits of information or released files in a bid to show the openness of the service, and often to attempt to show that the ministry was more open than many western agencies. A case in point was the MB news conference of 27 February 1992. Several key themes were enunciated. Official statements revealed that the Soviets had shot down two American spy planes before downing pilot Gary Powers in 1960 and noted that the U.S. government remained silent about the incidents.[43] This observation put the U.S. government on the defensive, as it had not made any of this information public and remained reluctant to do so.

Mutual Cooperation with Western Services. Equating itself with Western counterintelligence and law-enforcement agencies was an important Ministry of Security motif. It differed from the KGB theme only by attempting to appear even more helpful to the West. Main themes stress the common struggle against terrorism, organized crime, and proliferation of weapons of mass destruction.[44] The MB publicly proposed to establish a joint Russian-American commission to probe the fate of U.S. military personnel "who for some reason were on Soviet territory during the Second World War or in the postwar period."[45]

The proposal coincided with hearings on the fate of American prisoners of war in the U.S. Senate and followed retired Maj. Gen. Oleg

Kalugin's controversial testimony in Washington affirming that the KGB interrogated U.S. POWs after the Vietnam conflict. (Oleynikov issued an official statement to contradict Kalugin.) Army Col. Gen. Dmitriy Volkogonov, a historian in charge of the Russian state committee on CPSU archives, was already cooperating with American investigators by the time the statement was made, so the MB "proposal" was nothing new.

Some cooperation has been real, to a limited degree, especially with regard to organized crime, smuggling, and terrorism. The MB, like Kryuchkov's KGB, publicized cooperation with Western governments to convince the world that the chekist organs were similar to Western institutions. On one occasion the MB announced in a low-key statement the success of a hostage-release operation in Russia carried out with the cooperation of the FBI, without emphasizing that it was a case of the FBI helping the MB, and not vice versa.[46] It seems that Lubyanka's post-Cold War politics are starting to bear fruit; the United States, Germany, and other major democracies are moving toward cooperation with the chekists without insisting first on true professionalization and transformation of the service. These developments leave the ever-maligned MVD—the closest thing Russia has to a legitimate police force—out in the cold.

Revival of Paranoia. At the same time that it publicized its desire to improve cooperation, the Ministry of Security implied that cooperation with the West would be held hostage until criticisms of the Russian organs ceased. In 1992 well into 1994 some official statements from the organs reverted to the paranoid pre-Kryuchkov themes. Barannikov accused Western intelligence services of fomenting organized crime in Russia.[47] Officials frequently denounced criticism of the service that appeared in the press, impugned the patriotism of the critics, and accused their contacts in the West of being spies, "enemies," and "terrorists" (see pp. 260-262).

Methods

Public Relations Center. The Ministry of Security took over the KGB Public Relations Center that had been created as part of Kryuchkov's image-making campaign. The chief of the center, Gen. Aleksandr Karbainov, was dismissed on 4 February 1992, the day Barannikov testified before a Supreme Soviet commission. Karbainov carried a great deal of political baggage, including a stint at repressing dissidents as an officer in the KGB Fifth Directorate and his failure to condemn the 1991 putsch. *Izvestiya* cited reports that "the general's fate was decided by Supreme Soviet deputies who deemed that Aleksandr Karbainov showed excessive zeal during the unlawful merger of the KGB and the Ministry of Internal Affairs [into the Ministry of Security and Internal Affairs (MBVD)]."[48]

More likely, Minister Barannikov simply wanted his own spokesman. He chose Andrey Chernenko, who had been chief of the MVD Public Relations Center. Chernenko billed himself as a professional journalist, but nevertheless held the careerist rank of colonel upon taking over the MB Public Relations Center.[49] He soon was promoted to general. Chernenko retained Karbainov's deputy, Maj. Gen. Aleksandr Gurov, an MVD officer and a Russian People's Deputy who had been transferred to the KGB in late 1991.[50] Another deputy chief, Col. Aleksey Kandaurov, was also kept in a post he had held since Kryuchkov was KGB chairman. Like Karbainov, Kandaurov failed to condemn the putsch in the three days it was in progress. He was promoted to public relations chief and to major general later in 1993.

Exclusive Interviews. A staple of any government agency, exclusive interviews to newspapers and television programs were a basic Ministry of Security public relations technique. A survey of interviews through 1992 shows that MB officials tended to prefer giving interviews to controlled or politically friendly publications such as *Krasnaya zvezda*, *Pravda*, and *Trud* rather than to more reformist papers like *Izvestiya*, *Komsomolskaya pravda*, and *Moscow News*. (Golushko promised to give an interview to *Izvestiya* but reneged.[51]) The MB was less adept at trying to disarm its harshest critics than was Kryuchkov's KGB. Whereas Kryuchkov received dissidents for well-publicized chats in his office, Barannikov and Golushko showed no penchant for such theater.

Symposia, Briefings, and Public Events. To announce positive developments, answer questions, and refute allegations, the MB and FSK took advantage of symposia, briefings and public events. When the newspaper *Kuranty* published an article stating that clicking sounds on a telephone meant that a conversation was being monitored, the Public Relations Center held a press briefing at which a Ministry of Communications specialist explained that the noise in Russia's antiquated lines is "a perfectly ordinary occurrence in telephone communications and that state security techniques are sufficiently sophisticated not to give themselves away."[52] MB officials also spoke at university functions and participated in national and international conferences on security. At the first Glasnost Foundation conference on the "KGB: Yesterday, Today and Tomorrow," held in February 1993 under the direction of former dissident Sergey Grigoryants, the officers were poorly prepared for the relentless criticism and handled themselves badly.[53] The MB sent an extremely polished representative to the second Glasnost Foundation conference three months later who announced that the ministry would sponsor its own conferences on security and civil control.[54]

The internal security organs refused to send official representatives to subsequent Glasnost Foundation seminars and conferences. Instead, they arranged their own conferences to be held two or three days before the Glasnost Foundation events. Glasnost's 9-10 April 1994 seminar on civil controls was preceded on 7 April by Lubyanka's own large conference on the same subject, with the same title, and with many of the same participants. The chekists even invited Greenpeace, but not their strongest critics.[55] Certain participants in the Glasnost seminar failed to show, having been confused by the similar dates and identical titles.[56]

Overt Internal Propaganda. Domestic KGB propaganda had a marked effect on public attitudes toward the chekists. A sociological study found that the average Soviet woman viewed the state security officer as "a type of superman. She is afraid of him, but he is strong. He is clever." The director of the study commented, "I believe the formation of such an image was influenced by Soviet feature films."[57] The MB continued the practice of producing such programs. A 10 July 1992 program entitled "Man and Law" was broadcast on state television to portray the organ in a positive perspective.[58]

As Russia's television medium grew, so did the organs' utilization of it. Not trusting the "ordinary journalist" but seeking to make use of their outlets, the MB set up its own television crew made up of officers from the press service and public relations center to videotape "operational events" for television news programs.[59] The MB launched a new public journal, *Problems of Security,* and ranking officials frequently wrote guest columns for newspapers and magazines.

Covert Internal Propaganda. The MB also may have conducted internal propaganda aimed at the domestic population. In one instance *Moscow News* stated that American-made TEC computers purchased by the USSR Aviation Ministry had been planted with a computer virus designed to disable the electronic devices a year after being installed. According to this story, the Aviation Ministry would then have to send for an American technician who in the process of repairing the computers would download all electronic data collected over the previous year. The MB claimed credit for discovering the plot.

Victor Yasmann of Radio Liberty, who has a background in electronics, observed, "The publication of this story by *Moscow News* seems to be part of a coordinated campaign to raise the morale and the image of the Russian secret service. It may also be a response to Western complaints about continued Russian espionage abroad."[60] (Subsequently it was revealed that the United States had issued several high-level démarches to Moscow in response to its aggressive spying.[61]) Soon after, TASS reported that a young Russian entrepreneur had made a formal complaint to U.S. Ambassador Robert Strauss because he and his company had begun to encounter difficulties in obtaining American visas and doing business in the United States after he refused to cooperate with the CIA. The U.S. Embassy dismissed the report as baseless and added that all eligible employees of the entrepreneur had received the visas they solicited.[62]

Accusations Against Critics. On several occasions, the MB issued official statements saying that Russian critics of the organs working with certain nongovernmental organizations from the United States and other countries were part of a plot by Western intelligence services to destroy the state security system. The theme began in spring 1992 but initially did not imply that the critics were part of a foreign conspiracy. Minister Barannikov told *Krasnaya zvezda* that attacks in the press were harming the morale of security personnel, noting, "There is a campaign to discredit the organs, even including attempts to destroy them completely, there is the desire to regard the work of agents and operatives as unlawful and immoral."[63]

The MB gradually increased the intensity of its commentary on critics in the wake of a campaign by hard-line Communist and ultranationalist elements who accused reformist Russian officials, as well as Yeltsin, Gorbachev, and glasnost architects such as Aleksandr N. Yakovlev, of being paid by the CIA. In an interview that appeared in the 30 September edition of *Pravda*, MB public relations chief Andrey Chernenko said that "rumors" criticizing the former KGB that had been published in Russian newspapers were "part of a carefully planned campaign to further discredit Russia's security, intelligence, and internal affairs organs." He called the criticisms "disinformation" that was "concocted by very experienced intriguers with knowledge of the specific nature of the work, specialized terminology, and so on" and stressed, "The campaign to discredit the security organs was planned by highly intelligent people, and we assume not on Russian territory." He further implied that the campaign was developed by "a foreign intelligence community" to bring about the "further and final collapse of the Russian special services."[64]

A second verbal assault took place 29 October, less than a week after Moscow State University hosted a small symposium on democratic control of security and intelligence services and the benefits that Russians might take from Western experiences. The event was co-sponsored by *Demokratizatsiya: The Journal of Post-Soviet Democratization* and organized in part by the author.[65] During a meeting with representatives of political parties, MB public relations chief Chernenko complained about American groups that work with Russians to challenge old Soviet structures. He did not name the conference organizers, but he did single out the Heritage Foundation, a privately funded policy organization in Washington, which he said "has prepared a memorandum for the administration with specific proposals which stipulate 'fully abolishing the internal intelligence service and the Security Ministry.'"[66]

Attempts to discredit those who questioned the internal chekist organs' legitimacy continued through 1994. Three weeks prior to the first "KGB: Yesterday, Today and Tomorrow" conference organized by former prisoner of conscience Sergey Grigoryants, Chernenko was far more critical. In a news conference to observe the first anniversary of the founding of the MB, he said that the service looked forward to cooperation with the CIA but added that relations were being "impeded by what you might call a pseudo-reformist wave, which aims at . . . the total dismantling of the law enforcement system." He attributed the campaign to U.S. intelligence services, saying, "We believe this campaign is pre-planned. . . . There are at least 10 foundations which have affiliates in Russia and which are run by former career intelligence officers."[67]

Chernenko singled out two groups in particular: the Heritage Foundation and the International Freedom Foundation,[68] the latter of which sponsored the author's work to promote oversight programs in Russia. The Security Ministry spokesman added, "We can see behind certain funds . . . a group of people who have been coordinating the activity of the CIA and FBI for a long time."[69] No proof was offered, and both organizations denied any such affiliations; IFF in fact was the only American organization which had been outspokenly critical of CIA and FBI cooperation with the chekists. The nonreformist and other news outlets affiliated with the organs hurled similar accusations at Grigoryants personally, implying that the human rights leader was an agent of a foreign secret service.[70] Official rhetoric became more extreme under FSK Director Sergey Stepashin. In 1994 Stepashin referred with irritation to democratic activists, former KGB officers, journalists and others critical of the lack of real reform among the chekists, calling them "enemies" and "terrorists."[71]

External Intelligence Image-Making Campaigns

Like the Ministry of Security and Federal Counterintelligence Service, the External Intelligence Service (SVR) has gone to great lengths to show how different it is from the KGB. Yet the more it has tried to convince Russians and Westerners that it has turned a new leaf, the more its actions have indicated a fundamental lack of reform within. From 1992 into 1994 the SVR stressed its desire to cooperate with the West, especially with its German and American counterparts, as if to say that it had joined the camp of civilized nations. At the same time, Russia turned back the clock by continuing to operate the KGB networks against the west and quietly signing new intelligence agreements with the Communist governments of China and Cuba.

Intelligence ties with Beijing which had been severed in 1959, were secretly renewed in September 1992 through an agreement authorizing the SVR and the GRU to share information and cooperate with the Military Intelligence Department of the People's Liberation Army. The pact became public by a leak from U.S. intelligence. A major U.S. concern is that the SVR and the GRU are joining forces with Chinese espionage to steal Western weapons technology.[72]

The new agreement with Cuba, signed in Havana on 3 November between Cuban Vice President Leonel Soto and Russian Deputy Prime Minister for Foreign Economic Affairs Aleksandr Shokhin, reportedly kept a Soviet-built electronic intelligence-gathering facility on the island under Russian operation and control.[73] The site, near the town of Lourdes, is believed to be run by the former KGB Eighth Chief Directorate, now the main component of the Federal Agency for Government Communications and Information (FAPSI). Shokhin's signature appears to mean that the facility plays a major role in gathering economic and commercial intelligence from the United States as well as from Russia's new trade partners in Latin America. The Russian government did not announce the agreement with Beijing, and it scheduled the low-key signing of the Cuba accord on 3 November, when it would be lost in the news of the U.S. presidential election, indicating that although Russian intelligence goes to great lengths to publicize its new ties with the West, it quietly continues and renews its old practices and relationships.

Themes

Image-making themes employed by the SVR from 1992 through 1994 are similar in most cases to those employed in the same period by the Ministry of Security/Federal Counterintelligence Service, and by the KGB from 1988 to 1991.

Break from Discredited Past. SVR Director Primakov represents the continuum from the KGB First Chief Directorate but has taken pains to distance the Russian External Intelligence Service from its Soviet origins. He was the final leader of the First Chief Directorate, continued as director when the organ became independent as the USSR Central Intelligence Service (TsSR), and was retained by Yeltsin when the Russian Federation took over the service and renamed it again. The day the SVR was officially founded, Primakov said in an interview that he was trying to create a "new image" for the organization "not associated with the KGB at all."[74] The SVR fed a number of Western correspondents with the line that the KGB had been "abolished," the implication being that its machinery and agents were no more.[75] Yet the SVR's celebration of its seventy-second—not first—anniversary on 20 December 1992 and a similar fete the following year indicated that it sees itself as a continuation of the chekist legacy.

SVR leaders have observed that the SVR no longer reports to a political party. The "enemy" worldview was also jettisoned, according to Lt. Gen. Vadim Kirpichenko, chief of the SVR Advisory Council, who has served in foreign intelligence since the Stalin era. He told scholars in Washington:

> The concept of our intelligence service went through a very noticeable change. We completely reject the concept of regarding some countries as adversaries or the main adversary. . . . We do not regard some countries as adversaries, but [regard as the new adversary] some things that threaten mankind, such as the spread of nuclear weapons, or crime, drug trafficking, terrorism.[76]

The SVR, the MB/FSK, and the Federal Agency for Government Communications and Information (FAPSI) constantly employed the theme of likening themselves to Western intelligence services, in the tradition that Kryuchkov had originated.[77]

Reduction in Personnel. SVR officials are fond of repeating that the organization is much smaller than the former Soviet foreign intelligence branch. The hard currency shortages and changed strategic priorities of the Yeltsin government did make the SVR's blanket presence abroad unnecessary. Announcements were made as early as

January 1992 that the SVR would reduce its personnel abroad by 50 percent,[78] although the reduction had been planned by Bakatin. By September, the intelligence agency stated it had closed at least 30 *rezidenturas,* chiefly in African and small Far Eastern countries of little strategic importance.[79] A November announcement again claimed that intelligence staff at remaining missions abroad would be slashed by 50 percent.[80] By January 1993, a spokesman for the SVR claimed that headquarters already had undergone a 30 to 40 percent cut in personnel, and that personnel abroad was reduced by "up to 50 percent," with "twenty to thirty stations closed."[81] This theme was exploited for its maximum publicity value, appearing again and again into 1994 and being treated as a news story seemingly every time.[82] American and West European counterintelligence indeed saw some reductions in SVR activities in their countries.

Several factors indicate that staff reductions approximate to those publicly announced would not have had a major effect on operational capabilities, had they been carried out. First, the Kremlin's foreign policy dramatically changed from systematic subversion abroad through Communist Parties, front organizations, and support for armed insurgent groups, as well as technical support, liaison, and oversight of the structures and policies of foreign ruling Communist Parties. Support personnel for such enterprises were no longer required. Second, as the SVR itself has noted, state policy lost interest in marginal parts of the world and the presence of intelligence officers in those places became unnecessary and wasteful. Third, as Primakov observed in his criticism of "parasites," and as defectors and former intelligence officers have reported, there was a significant number of unproductive officers and agents. Kobaladze admitted as much, saying, "We made it better. It was too bureaucratic." He added that many Soviet intelligence officers were more interested than traveling abroad than in practicing good tradecraft.[83] Budgetary constraints were a fourth reason.

Fifth, the huge influx of foreign businessmen and others to Russia, coinciding with Moscow's marked shift toward greater economic and commercial espionage, made it much safer, easier and cheaper for the SVR to recruit and service its foreign agents from Russian and other formerly Soviet soil than from abroad. Finally, given the large-scale KGB co-optation of young professional diplomatic and foreign trade officials at the early stages of their careers, the SVR has ample support staff outside its formal structures abroad. A former KGB intelligence officer reports that as of the late 1970s, up to 80 percent of diplomats were co-opted in this way.[84] Fifteen years later, these diplomats now occupy more prominent posts. There has been no indication that the practice has changed.

Useful Role for Society. In public statements and through politically reliable domestic media, the SVR has tried to show the Russian public that it performs a useful and indeed valuable role for society. The service did attempt to explain the normal functions of informing the political leadership, use as a foreign policy tool and the like, but most explanations were more propagandistic. The SVR claims to help the troubled economy. An unnamed active-duty Russian industrial spy told *Pravda*, "Business and intelligence work. These two professions are always side by side. Today they are becoming closer and closer together." He added that the profits to be gained by economic and commercial espionage were "far greater than that of scientific research institutes. So judge for yourself." A second active industrial espionage officer, described as "charming and educated," said, "My job is not just to find out the secret but [to] place it at the service of many people."[85]

The line for the West is different. Primakov's aide Kirpichenko, supported by SVR spokesman Kobaladze, claimed to American audiences that "scientific and technological intelligence is a priority" but only for "humanitarian" reasons: to verify arms control agreements and to protect mankind from proliferation of weapons of mass destruction. Kirpichenko said that the SVR does not steal secrets for Russian business, industry, or the military because "there is nobody to use the fruits of our work."[86] The SVR press office dismissed highly publicized reports in Belgium, France, and the United States of Russian industrial espionage as "forgeries" but did not comment on the expulsions of SVR officers from Brussels and Paris.[87]

Foreign intelligence operations carried out by the SVR can benefit the average Russian's daily life, according to one domestic propaganda film aired on state television. Some of the reasons given were legitimate, but others were preposterous. The SVR, according to the film, combats organized crime at home and abroad, ensures adequate counterintelligence, and fights smuggling, drug trafficking, and nuclear proliferation. There would be no such thing as arms control without a strong foreign intelligence capability to detect and verify violations or compliance. SVR First Deputy Director Vyacheslav Trubnikov went so far on the program as to claim that "even such a thing as finding yeast, which ensures that bread is of high quality, is also at times the task of the intelligence service."[88] What was not mentioned, of course, was the role of the SVR in making money for itself, its officers, and its allies by spying on Western business and industry and conducting its own activity through joint ventures, front companies, and business transactions abroad.

Strict Civil Control. Like the internal security organs, the SVR stressed the need in its image-making presentations for strict civil control over its operations, but the SVR was not as deferential toward civil authorities as the Security Ministry campaign was. This difference probably reflects the fact that the public fears internal security's abuses far more than it is concerned with what the services do abroad. Indeed, public support for the foreign intelligence service is quite strong, and was boosted by a national sense of elation when the United States announced that the SVR had penetrated the upper echelons of the CIA.[89]

Early in 1992 the SVR leadership practically pleaded with the Supreme Soviet for strict civil controls: "First [the SVR requests] the earliest adoption of a law on the intelligence service. The second request was that a special parliamentary commission on intelligence be set up that would be quite separate from the other commissions, particularly from the commission for security and others."[90] Primakov gave a major address on the virtues of parliamentary control later in the year.[91] (It will be recalled that Primakov, as a leader of the USSR Supreme Soviet, helped stack the oversight committee with chekists and quashed attempts by democratic law-makers to question the practice.)

In early 1994 the SVR appeared to want the new Duma to limit itself in exercising practical oversight. Primakov briefed the parliamentary chamber in a closed session. The contents of his presentation were not "state secrets," but were characterized as more of a "scholarly seminar," as if the SVR was cognizant of the likelihood that in briefing an entire house of parliament (rather than a small, select committee) the information would be leaked. Public relations chief Kobaladze told the press that having an intelligence chief brief a full house of lawmakers was "normal international practice."[92] Obviously it was not a standard practice. Kobaladze later complained that lawmakers could not be trusted to keep secrets, citing the fact that the contents of the Primakov briefing were immediately leaked to the press. His comment had the desired effect of prompting one Duma member to suggest that perhaps such briefings should be limited to only three or four lawmakers who would be entrusted with oversight responsibilities.[93]

In a propaganda film for domestic television, a leading SVR official called civil controls "sufficient" but said the area was "still almost uncharted." He noted that "public controls" also existed in the form of the mass media but remarked that media treatment should be "objective, sympathetic, and helpful to the intelligence services."[94] After passage of the Law on Intelligence, which the SVR largely drafted and which Primakov personally authorized prior to submission to the Supreme Soviet, intelligence officials explained its provisions to the public.[95]

In his public relations campaigns Kobaladze used the law as standard boilerplate in his statements, likening it to American and European legislation. He took pains to tout the law's Article 9, which gives journalists the "right" to have their articles about intelligence matters screened by the SVR so that no "state secrets" are revealed. He conveniently overlooked the following sentence in Article 9, which holds journalists criminally responsible if they fail to exercise that right.[96]

A Force for Stability. By virtue of its functions which are useful to society, such as curbing terrorism and weapons smuggling, and verifying arms control compliance, the SVR showed itself as a force for stability. This message was also carried directly to Washington by a visiting SVR delegation. Said Lt. Gen. Vadim Kirpichenko, who as chief of the Advisory Council is Primakov's top confidant, "In the post-Cold War world, intelligence can be a stabilizing factor" which helps "political predictability."[97]

Repudiation of Old Methods. Another staple theme is that the SVR abandoned the KGB's more unsavory methods. Active measures and interference in other countries' internal affairs, a spokesman said, are "out of the question."[98] Yet another spokesman acknowledged, when pressed, that the SVR would continue to use disinformation as a "very important tool."[99] A top SVR general told American scholars, "[The] work of intelligence agencies should be handled in a civilized way [and should eschew blackmail, coercion, or] different types of psychotropic means."[100]

The SVR would not rely on indoctrination to recruit its officers, Primakov told a group of foreign relations students at the Ministry of Foreign Affairs. According to a summary of his presentation, "People will now be admitted to intelligence in the spirit of the times—in accordance with their wishes."[101] Primakov announced in his first news conference as intelligence chief that although he would maintain diplomatic cover for officers abroad, he would do away with using the cover of journalists.[102] Yet the SVR continued to operate with journalistic covers. Three out of four SVR agents expelled by the Netherlands in April 1992, for example, were posing as journalists: Yevgeniy Kleskhov of TASS, Leonid Lipnyakov of Novosti, and Leonid

Chernushkur of *Komsomolskaya pravda*.[103] Two years later, the SVR was still saying that it would do away with using the cover of journalists.[104]

Openness. The SVR's sudden release of a relatively small quantity of selected documents, the existence of a public relations bureau, and unprecedented access of journalists to top officials caused the service to call itself in a domestic propaganda film "the most open in the world."[105] It would be more accurate to say that the SVR may be the most politically savvy secret service in the world. The reluctance of the CIA, Britain's MI-6, and other Western services to release old archives containing sensational material only served to reinforce the SVR's image-making efforts.

Mutual Cooperation with Western Services. Like the Ministry of Security, the SVR has issued statements touting its cooperation with Western intelligence services. Primakov, addressing a Moscow conference on "Transformed Russia in the New World," said that Russia's foreign policy would reject "confrontation" without moving away from defense of Russia's "national interests." Primakov gave a familiar list of mutual interests: "non-proliferation of vital technologies, combatting terrorism, and preventing regional conflicts from developing into global crises."[106] Counternarcotics was another favored subject of mutual cooperation that led to conferences with officials of Western secret services. Curiously, a CIA delegate to a joint 1991 conference on fighting drug trafficking was none other than Aldrich Ames.[107]

The theme continued through 1994. Primakov's top adviser, Kirpichenko, told a group of American scholars in early 1993, "As a soldier of World War II, we were allies, but somehow forgot about it. For me it's not part of history, it's part of my life. I hope that the developments in our countries will make us become allies again to mutually protect mankind."[108]

Four KGB First Chief Directorate veterans representing the Russian Association of Retired Intelligence Officers traveled the United States on a five-week tour that echoed all the official propaganda themes. The October-November 1993 tour, sponsored by associates of CIA defector Philip Agee,[109] attempted to place Western and Soviet intelligence on equal moral footing. Delegation leader Col. Yuriy Totrov began his presentations by eulogizing a slain CIA officer (Tucker Gougelmann, who was captured by the North Vietnamese when Saigon fell in 1975, and who died in captivity) and calling for a moment of silence to honor the American and "Russian" intelligence officers who died during the Cold War. Totrov and his three colleagues took pains to refer to their long careers in "Russian" intelligence, pointedly avoiding such terms as "Soviet," "communism," and "KGB." At their first public appearance the author asked Totrov why his group and their U.S. organizers criticized only the CIA while not one of them criticized the KGB, and wondered aloud why dissident former KGB officers like retired Maj. Gen. Oleg Kalugin were not members of their association. At the sound of Kalugin's name all four chekists grimaced, and one spoke for the group by denouncing Kalugin as "destructive."[110]

Curtailment of Spying Activity. Because it no longer served its "main client," the CPSU International Department, as well as for other reasons given above, the SVR found that its size had become a large drain on scarce hard currency reserves. It attempted to turn the necessary cuts to its advantage by implying that they were due to goodwill in the post-Cold War era. The West, by not curtailing its activities in a much more unstable and unpredictable Russia, was by implication unable to think past the Cold War and thus was behind the times. The SVR frequently commented on this theme until the exposure of the Ames operation in early 1994. On occasion the service named specific countries from which intelligence personnel were being withdrawn (Germany, Italy, Sweden, and the United States), without acknowledging that those countries had recently expelled Russian agents for espionage or were in the process of doing so.[111]

A spokesman for the SVR director responded to western pressure for Russia to reduce its spying abroad by saying that any reductions should be reciprocal.[112] In an interview with the *Sunday Times* of London, Primakov proposed a moratorium on espionage, offering to recall intelligence officers from countries that would do the same with Russia. This idea was originally floated in November 1991 by Georgiy Arbatov, director of the Institute on the USA and Canada and a longtime toady of the CPSU and KGB.[113] The theme was repeated in late 1992.[114]

Interestingly, Kobaladze once called CIA intelligence activity in Moscow a "stabilizing factor." The statement, which never became a theme for mutual cooperation, was made on 15 December 1991, while the country was in political turmoil and Russia was rapidly absorbing the Soviet government apparatus. Kobaladze told a domestic television program,

> American intelligence is interested in the processes which are taking place in our country. They really should know, in order to predict correctly, in order to give a correct evaluation and to forecast to its leadership, so that the leadership makes less mistakes. There is a kind of stabilizing factor in this. We should follow these processes.[115]

Personalization of Leadership. Twice in a three-day period during his debut as foreign intelligence chief in late September and early October 1991, Primakov told the press about his personal life, professing Western tastes and a fondness for John LeCarré spy novels.[116] The new approach was well received in the West. A search of the NEXIS electronic news database shows that the LeCarré remark was carried by no fewer than sixteen wire services and major metropolitan newspapers in the U.S. and Canada and was a headline item in the *Washington Post* and other leading papers. To the skeptics, the remark evoked memories of the image-making machinery that sought, first through Dusko Doder of the *Post*, to portray former KGB Chairman Yuriy Andropov as a Scotch-sipping "closet liberal" who relaxed with American jazz. Although he hinted that intelligence was not new to him, Primakov said he was not affiliated with the apparat.[117] His excellent English, affable style, and long contact with Westerners did much to change the public perception of the SVR abroad, especially among many Western diplomats and scholars who had known him professionally from before.

Methods

Public Relations Bureau. The SVR established a Public Relations Bureau similar to that of the KGB at a lavish building in downtown Moscow. Its chief, Col. Yuriy Kobaladze, styles himself as a professional journalist (as did his Ministry of Security counterpart, Gen. Chernenko), but in reality he was a KGB foreign intelligence officer who had worked under cover as a journalist in Britain. His deputy and consultant, Oleg Tsarev, was actually declared persona non grata for espionage in London.[118] Asked at a public conference if he would describe what it was like to work as a spy under journalistic cover, Kobaladze indignantly insisted that he had been nothing of the sort, and that he was a straight journalist. When pressed in front of a large audience and television cameras, he burst into an emotional denial, adding for good measure that Tsarev had not been expelled from the United Kingdom but had "left on his own accord."[119]

The SVR Public Relations Bureau holds news conferences and briefings, arranges for interviews and appointments with SVR officials, and responds to public criticisms and private queries. It openly solicits requests for information or comments from foreign academics and journalists.[120] Primakov maintains a personal press secretary, Tatyana Samolis, who gives frequent press briefings and issues official statements.

Exclusive Interviews. The SVR began its official existence with aggressive overt work in the press to rebut negative publicity. Primakov, a former journalist with experience in shaping public opinion, gave numerous interviews, as did his deputies and spokesmen. The SVR gives exclusives to a broad range of domestic and foreign news agencies and publications, with little regard to their political views or biases. SVR officials write commentary for newspapers in the same fashion as ranking Ministry of Security personnel. Examples are Kobaladze's commentary in *Izvestiya* which followed a translation of an article in the Stockholm newspaper *Svenska Dagbladet* on continued Russian spying in Sweden, and a lengthy article by SVR advisory council chief Kirpichenko on "Why We Need Intelligence."[121] The energetic and articulate Kobaladze is regularly available for interviews to almost anyone who seeks official comment, and he often goes on the offensive to seek out journalists and other writers.

Symposia, Briefings, and Public Events. On the eve of the official creation of the SVR, Primakov went about his "new look" campaign by receiving a delegation from NATO, meeting ambassadors and foreign journalists, and conversing with veterans of foreign intelligence services.[122] The SVR offered a special course on Russian intelligence services at the Moscow State Institute for International Relations of the Ministry of Foreign Affairs. The well-publicized course, which was welcomed as a sign of new openness, featured Primakov as its first lecturer.[123] Primakov and other SVR officials met with American students at Moscow State University, participated in a conference on "The Proper Role of an Intelligence Agency in a Democracy" sponsored by the Center for Democracy in Bulgaria, and spoke in a roundtable on civil control of intelligence sponsored by the Supreme Soviet Committee on Defense and Security.[124]

Overt Domestic Propaganda. Like the MB, the SVR produced at least one propaganda movie for domestic television broadcast. The program, "I Have the Honor—Intelligence Service," aired on 13 August 1992. The broadcast featured interviews with SVR leaders and officers as well as average Russian citizens who said the country needed a strong intelligence capability. SVR First Deputy Director Trubnikov spoke about the need for a powerful service in the post-Cold War era so that Russians could make high-quality bread with purloined yeast. He also reverted to familiar themes: "We are dealing with the issues of combatting organized crime, keeping an eye on . . . mafia structures—and foreign partners. We see how much specific deals may cost the state, and where the conditions are disadvantageous for the country." Trubnikov also said that the SVR was under firm civil control:

> Not only can society monitor the activities of its intelligence service, it should do so. You can hardly do that with someone else's intelligence service. For this, counterintelligence methods exist. As for our own intelligence service, a sufficient number of various kinds of control exist, which is how it should be. The main one is the law. Parliamentary controls exist, too. For us the process is still almost uncharted. We are beginning to enter a period in which intelligence services find themselves subject to ever more controls. There are also public controls in the guise of the mass media. . . . You know, it is a matter of honor in all civilized countries that intelligence services should be helped by the mass media, statesmen, and parliamentary structures.[125]

Yet media "help" is not welcomed if it is not authorized, as indicated in Article 9 of the Law on Foreign Intelligence, which, though not known to have been enforced, causes a chilling effect by making it a crime for a journalist to report anything about the SVR that is not officially sanctioned.

Russian newspapers and broadcasts are received throughout the former Soviet Union, but Moscow targets programming at the "near abroad" to promote its intelligence activity. Ten days after the Ames arrest, Radio Slavyanka began a series of programs on the SVR featuring Kobaladze for audiences in Tajikistan.[126]

Contracts with U.S. Publishers. The SVR signed an exclusive arrangement with Crown publishers, a subsidiary of Random House, to provide archival information to selected Western authors. A contract envisioned books on the Cuban missile crisis, KGB penetration of the British government and its intelligence services, KGB operations in Berlin, the assassination of Leon Trotsky, and the history of Soviet intelligence. The arrangement ensured that the SVR would control all information input and exercise heavy influence if not control of the literary products by making SVR personnel coauthors with the Western writers. Public Relations Bureau Deputy Chief Oleg Tsarev, who had served as an intelligence officer under journalistic cover in Britain, coauthored the first book in the series, *Dangerous Illusions*, with John Costello.[127] Independent authors are not afforded such access. Although the book contains interesting revelations, it also contains disinformation themes apparently intended to discredit past Soviet defectors. It reports, for example, that NKVD Gen. Aleksandr Orlov was not a real defector and that the information he gave the United States was worthless. The underlying theme, that the world cannot trust defectors, came at a time when the SVR was suffering from a hemorrhage of agents and officers to the West.

Assurance to Illegals Abroad. The SVR is maintaining its international network of "illegals," specially trained agents living abroad who assume the nationality of a westerner under a false identity. In an apparent subtle bid to reassure illegals that the KGB networks will be preserved, a former top illegals officer now highly placed in the SVR stated, "We are going to carry out our intelligence work when and wherever necessary."[128]

Disinformation. Although it has gone through a range of facelifts and has become far more public if not more open, the SVR continues to disseminate disinformation to deceive the West. While this conclusion may be reached by examining certain SVR public relations themes, it was confirmed by Kobaladze in a question-and-answer session with critics in October 1993.[129] The disinformation is different from that employed in the past. Though many traditional CPSU fronts such as the "peace councils" survive, they are discredited and poorly funded, playing no meaningful role as before. Since the SVR no longer reports to a political party, the disinformation is no longer ideological. To date, little of it has been offensive in nature to discredit the West. The SVR disinformation that has been detected has been defensive in nature to convince the West that the KGB is extinct and that the SVR is a completely new incarnation.

The first major disinformation campaign after the putsch was to convince the world that the KGB had been "abolished." Moscow's foreign intelligence service succeeded in helping plant that impression. An American journalist wrote a *New York Times Magazine* cover story of the dismantlement of the organs, misleadingly entitled "Closing Down the KGB."[130] Other press reports, some of which were objective but taken out of context by copy editors, also conveyed the image that the organization was really gone for good.[131] Still other reporting or commentary was sloppy and ill-informed.

Second, as part of the effort to distance the SVR from the past, on more than one occasion Primakov denied that he had had personal ties with the KGB during his long career in the Communist Party, as a journalist, and in the Academy of Sciences.[132] It was only after *Moscow News* quoted retired KGB foreign counterintelligence chief Oleg Kalugin as saying that he knew Primakov as a KGB agent with the cryptonym Maxim in the late 1950s did the SVR director acknowledge the relationship. Primakov testified to a Supreme Soviet commission about his KGB work as a *Pravda* correspondent in the 1960s, "I fulfilled many orders which came from my leadership. . . . And while complying with these tasks I supplied intelligence, supplied the *okhrana* [guard] with material along KGB channels." "But," he added, "that was all." He made it all seem innocent and said nothing of other allegations that he had served as a courier for KGB money to Palestinian terrorist leaders in the late 1960s.[133] Primakov sought to portray foreign intelligence as starting anew, free of KGB baggage. His assertions were not only for public consumption but for government officials as well.

A third example of SVR disinformation occurred in March 1992 when Primakov made a surprise public admission that stories about the AIDS virus being created at a U.S. biological weapons laboratory were actually fabricated by the KGB.[134] He could have ended there and convinced the skeptics that he was truly abandoning disinformation, but he did not; he followed by announcing that reports blaming the Soviets for complicity in the 1981 assassination attempt against Pope John Paul II were mere CIA fabrications, calling them a simple tit-for-tat retaliation for the AIDS disinformation.[135]

This assertion is untrue. Italian courts proved beyond reasonable doubt that the Soviets assisted Bulgarian agents in supporting the Turkish terrorist who shot the Pope.[136] Two thorough private American investigations, one by journalist Claire Sterling and another by retired CIA official and author Paul Henze, came to similar conclusions.[137] All three investigations were complete by 1983, when *Pravda* and the Soviet-funded Italian Communist Party newspaper *Paese-Sera* attacked the findings and blamed the CIA for the crime.[138]

Irrespective of whether one believes in the Soviet connection, Primakov was still wrong. The KGB's AIDS disinformation campaign did not begin until 30 October 1985, when *Literaturnaya gazeta* recycled a KGB-planted story in the Indian newspaper *Patriot* (a frequent practice) reporting that AIDS was a product of U.S. biological warfare engineering. This was two years after the results of the investigations of papal shooting had been made public. The *Literaturnaya gazeta* article was then was broadcast by Radio Peace and Progress and published in *Sovetskaya rossiya* before being picked up by the mainstream Western media.[139] Primakov's version of the sequence of events, and his justification for the AIDS disinformation, was accepted by the journalists who covered his comments.

Treatment of KGB Critics. Further evidence that the institutional interests of today's Russian SVR have changed little from those of the KGB is offered by SVR attacks against former Soviet intelligence officers who have criticized past actions. Following the putsch, Gorbachev rehabilitated former foreign counterintelligence chief Oleg Kalugin, who had been stripped of his rank, decorations and pension at the behest of USSR KGB Chairman Kryuchkov. The chekists in the SVR, however, were less forgiving and launched a personal attack against him for his testimony about KGB participation in the 1978 assassination of Bulgarian dissident Georgi Markov. Testifying in Sofia about the KGB's involvement in the infamous London umbrella murder, Kalugin—based on top-level KGB meetings in which he attended—revealed the names of at least ten Soviet officials whom he alleged had personal knowledge about high-level KGB complicity in the affair. In his position as foreign counterintelligence chief at the time, Kalugin would have known intimate details of the operation in advance, as it would have been his responsibility to ensure operational security. Two of the individuals he named were former USSR KGB Chairmen Viktor Chebrikov and Vladimir Kryuchkov.[140]

SVR public relations chief Kobaladze staged the attack on Kalugin, denying his accusations and questioning his motives. Kobaladze stated categorically, "The former and present KGB leadership has repeatedly stated that the Soviet intelligence service had nothing to do with Markov's murder." His words, quoted in English by TASS, were curious in that they contradicted the theme that the SVR was a completely new organization by referring to the continuation of a "KGB leadership." The rush to defend the KGB's honor, as well as the gaffe, reflected a lack of changed thinking.

More important, the attack on Kalugin misstated the sequence of events. The retired general, Kobaladze said, made "sensational" remarks in Bulgaria in order to salvage his reputation from controversial statements he had made concerning KGB interrogation of American prisoners of war in Vietnam.[141] In reality, Kalugin originally accused the KGB of involvement in the Markov murder in March 1991, well before speaking about its interrogation of American POWs. Likewise, the Bulgarian government officially had asked Kalugin to testify in Sofia before the Vietnam questions arose. (The hearings did not take place until afterward.) Kobaladze's attack was clearly an attempt to protect the reputation of the former KGB and to discredit—but not disprove—its critics.

Conclusion

Building on the themes begun by KGB Chairman Chebrikov, the Ministry of Security (MB), Federal Counterintelligence Service (FSK), and the External Intelligence Service (SVR) employed similar themes and methods in the course of their image-making campaigns of 1992 through 1994. Each service claimed to represent a break with the past, but none denounced or attempted to expose past abuses. They portrayed themselves as smaller and less powerful than the KGB and tried to show that they were benevolent without explaining the realities behind the reduced numbers and bureaucratic changes. They publicized the useful roles their services played for a democratic Russia and the world. They emphasized that they were not powers unto themselves but were under strict civil control and oversight. They called themselves forces for stability and stated that they had abandoned the methods of old. Both tried to show how open they were in comparison with the security and intelligence services of the West. Finally, they held open the possibility for mutual cooperation with the West but blamed the West for not making such partnerships immediately possible.

At the same time, patterns emerged to indicate that, as the continuity of the themes themselves suggest, there was no real break with the past. Neither the internal security nor foreign intelligence services attempted to expose or denounce past KGB crimes and transgressions. In fact, they attacked and impugned the motives of Russian citizens and Westerners who did. They were not frank about the nature of its personnel reductions or the personnel composition of their forces. They did not abandon the use of disinformation, and in fact used disinformation to distort the truth about the KGB.

Although their themes and methods generally were more sophisticated than those of the KGB, especially the SVR's rather successful efforts to influence the opinion of the Western public and elites, they did not, upon close analysis, reflect substantive change. To the contrary, when the personnel, culture, missions, and structural continuities of the services are taken into account, the image-making themes and methods of 1992 through 1994 strengthen the conclusion that Russia's security and intelligence organs today are merely extensions of the Soviet KGB.

Conclusion

Our nation hasn't undergone the process of penitence after the adoption of totalitarianism, and the predominant feeling is that all of us were victims of the regime.

—Galina Starovoitova,
former adviser to President Yeltsin, 1993[1]

In his 1990 analysis of changes in the Soviet Union, John Lenczowski argued that the sweetest fruits of glasnost and perestroika were their unintended consequences. He listed nine major categories and 121 subcategories and attempted to measure the degree of reform in each area. The main categories were: (1) regime adherence to Marxist-Leninist ideology, (2) existence of the internal security system, (3) monopoly of political power by the Communist Party, (4) absence of the rule of law and curtailment of individual rights, (5) central control over the economy, (6) central propaganda apparatus and monopoly of information, (7) military buildup and militarization of society, (8) erosion/elimination of islands of autonomy and competing authority, including attempts to substitute Party-controlled "mass organizations" for various institutions of normal civil society, and (9) maintenance of empire.[2] He studied a five-year period, 1985-1990, and measured whether there was a change for the worse, no change, minor change, partial change, or total change.

Lenczowski's measurements of the degrees of change in the internal security area as of perestroika's peak in 1990, were itemized with the caveat that most of the positive changes took place only in the large urban centers of Moscow and Leningrad. Lenczowski also noted that the situation was extremely fluid. Several conclusions can be drawn from his findings. On the positive side, totalitarianism, at least in the urban areas, had weakened considerably. Yet, as Lenczowski noted, almost none of the positive changes were irreversible. Furthermore, where the instruments of coercion were concerned in the chekist services, there was mostly either no change or change for the worse. Thus perestroika's continuities with the totalitarian past could be discerned, though few in the West cared at the time.

Perestroika preserved the cult of chekism. Indeed, the evidence suggests that the KGB under Andropov created the base for what became perestroika and glasnost and in the process helped to boost a circle of young Party leaders, ultimately led by Gorbachev, into the Party's highest echelons so that they could implement the reforms they felt were necessary to keep the system from perishing. Gorbachev remained beholden to the KGB up to the putsch of 1991. Party control over the security organs, formally removed through the elimination of Article 6 of the USSR Constitution, in practice continued to exist because all KGB officers had to be Party members and subject to Party discipline.

The new Congress of People's Deputies and its subsidiary Supreme Soviet, even with a Committee on Defense and Security, was never intended to exercise actual oversight of the KGB, which successfully ran and trained its own officers and collaborators as parliamentary candidates. The USSR Supreme Soviet, which contained a significant minority of non-Communist and even anti-Communist members, was tightly run by the CPSU from the top down with Gorbachev as Party chief, Supreme Soviet leader, and state president. Committee assignments were determined in secret by the leadership and a team of unelected apparatchiks, and the Committee on Defense and Security responsible for oversight was thus stacked with loyalists from the militsiya, armed forces and military-industrial sector, and chekist organs. Democratic reformers never had a chance to present a real challenge, and the committee was never granted access to even the most elementary information about the secret services.

The new legislature of perestroika, the Congress of People's Deputies, provided a nationally televised forum in which the few brave reformist members could question chekist officials and attack their institutions. The KGB responded by redesigning its image. The new strategy was to appear almost as part of the democratic opposition itself. The KGB leadership demanded public laws by which it would be governed, then wrote those laws themselves so that chekist powers could be preserved.

Meanwhile, as it spoke in favor of human rights, the KGB carried out a range of abuses in support of the Party and its own interests throughout the perestroika period. These included toleration and protection of mass corruption among the nomenklatura, repression of legitimate free market economic activity, maintenance of internal informant networks, continued persecution of dissidents and abuse of religious and social life; harassment of foreign residents and domestic critics, penetration of the new political system, illegal surveillance of political opponents, and destruction of evidence of illegal activity. The KGB also implemented what Helsinki Watch called the Gorbachev Doctrine to use deadly force to deal with nationalist unrest in Kazakhstan, the Caucasus, and the Baltic states.

The Soviet leadership also used the KGB to continue pre-perestroika-style operations against the United States and other industrialized democracies. It conducted espionage without a legal charter, civil controls or oversight; supported international political violence on three continents; and waged covert political warfare against the United States and its allies in the form of forgeries, disinformation, and funding of anti-Western or pro-Soviet groups and movements around the world. These activities were curtailed not as part of a perestroika grand strategy but in response to intense diplomatic and personal pressure from the United States and a desire for Western trade, credits, and aid.

Simultaneously, the chekists waged a deception campaign among Soviet citizens and the international community to convey the impression that the KGB had changed. Targets for deception even included the USSR Supreme Soviet. Perestroika did almost nothing to destroy the most noxious instruments of Soviet rule but merely relaxed the practices of those instruments. The reforms of Mikhail Gorbachev were never intended to be the great liberating force that they inadvertently became.

Through all this continuity amid change, the KGB began to split internally among the self-perpetuating chekists, the professional officers gravely shaken by the decay in their society and the KGB's complicity in promoting that decay, and a handful of officers who had not lost their human decency and were driven either to quit or defect. Not since the Stalinist purges had the security organs been so divided. When chekist leaders joined other Party hard-liners to save the crumbling system by launching the putsch of August 1991, the spark was struck that would propel both Party and Union to collapse. After recovering from the initial shock, and amid indecision among the political elites, chekism reasserted itself to serve and be served by the government that would inherit the bulk of its structures, resources, and personnel: the Russian Federation.

Even the most skeptical observer cannot deny that the Russian Federation has reformed remarkably compared to the Soviet system in each of the nine categories of the Lenczowski paradigm for measurement of change. Many of the reforms appear irreversible. The least amount of reform, however, has occurred in the category of internal security. Lenczowski uses two standards by which change must be gauged: comparison of the principal features of a totalitarian system with a democratic system and rhetoric versus reality. Now that the Russian Federation has made the transition from Communism and has publicly and repeatedly stated its intent to move toward a Western-style democratic system, Russia must be held not to its status in comparison to Communism but in comparison to the basic foundation of Western-style democracy. It is here that Russia fails the test.

Lenczowski measured the degree of change in the USSR over a five-year period as perestroika moved from absolute totalitarianism to something less closed. A similar measurement of change in Russia, however, cannot be conducted. To begin with, the time frame is too short. Second, Russian government policies and the people who set them have been erratic and contradictory in the brief period since the Soviet collapse. Although there has been little net change for the worse in the security organs in comparison to the KGB of August 1991, there have been significant changes for the worse in comparison to the organs in November of that year, when for a brief time, committed if outnumbered reformers were in positions of control. Although the reformers seemed on the verge of inflicting permanent damage on chekism, their changes were insufficiently comprehensive.

By mid-1992 those reforms for the most part had been reversed and the reformist personnel removed. The inherent repressive and aggressive structures and the old KGB officers who gave them their character remained. A third reason why degrees of change in Russia cannot yet be measured with any precision is that the political situation remains mercurial. There is uncertainty as to who is in control of the security organs and substantial evidence to suggest that the organs may be powers unto themselves. Fourth, it is clear that not all policies issued from the top are necessarily being carried out below and that many policies, as well as the inaction, are intended to preserve chekism. As with the Soviet Union, the Russian legislative system of 1990 to 1993 was designed to preserve the old Communist Party nomenklatura power structure.

Therefore, to help determine the extent of current change and the path of future reform in a democratic context, I have designed a more absolute method of measurement. Either the chekist power structure has been removed or it has not. Any half-measures cannot be considered a break with the machinery and psychology of totalitarianism. The table on the following pages is a series of criteria drawn from the text of this study. It is intended to help observers to project the future of democracy in Russia by determining the security services' present continuities with the past. Each item is offered so that its status in Russia as of mid-1994 may be compared with its status in the Soviet

Table 1 Changes and Continuities in the Russian Security Services, 1994

Category	*Status Relative to Soviet System*
Complete changes	
Demand for ideological conformity	eliminated
Party monopoly on communications and information	eliminated
Party control of chekist and police organs	eliminated
Restrictions on contacts with foreigners by ordinary citizens	eliminated
Continuities	
Institutions, officers, and personnel	
Maintenance of symbols, anniversaries, traditions, and worldview of chekism	continues
Official reverence to Feliks Dzerzhinskiy	continues
Prevalence of chekist identity over nationality among officers and personnel	continues
Concentration of internal security in a single powerful bureaucracy	continues
Expansion of role of state security organs in society	continues
Expansion of definition of "state security"	continues
Lack of distinction between chekist and law-enforcement organs	continues
Absorption of legitimate law-enforcement roles by chekists from police	continues
Training of new security recruits with old KGB texts and methods	continues
Domination of state security organs by unreformed KGB personnel	continues
Presence of top officials who ordered or engaged in repression of dissidents	continues
Presence of personnel who ordered or engaged in repression of dissidents	continues
Presence of top officials who ordered or engaged in atrocities against civilians	continues
Presence of personnel who ordered or engaged in atrocities against civilians	continues
Presence of top officials who ordered or supervised torture or murder	continues
Presence of personnel who ordered or committed torture or murder	continues
Large-scale corruption and extortion by top officials and personnel	continues
Lack of effective legal measures against corrupt security officers and personnel	continues
Inconsistency of broad chekist authority with democratic values	continues

(continued)

Table 1 *(continued)*

Informants and "state secrets"	
Arbitrary legal definition of "state secrets"	continues
Holding journalists responsible for protecting "state secrets"	continues
Requirement of journalists to vet articles on intelligence prior to publication	continues
Protection of past KGB political informants	continues
Maintenance of KGB political informant networks	continues
Maintenance of KGB surveillance files on private citizens	continues
Denial of the right of citizens to examine their files	continues
Protection of information on crimes committed by Cheka	continues
Protection of information on crimes committed by KGB	continues
Protection of secrets of the Communist Party of the Soviet Union	continues
Repressive activity	
Chekist infiltration of businesses	continues
Chekist infiltration of churches and other religious entities	continues
Chekist infiltration of social groups	continues
Chekist infiltration of political groups	continues
Chekist infiltration of news media	continues
Chekist infiltration of universities	continues
Official censorship	continues
Unofficial censorship by means of political, financial or other pressure	continues
Use of disinformation to influence citizens	continues
Use of domestic political propaganda to influence citizens	continues
Search without warrant	continues
Interception of mail without warrant	continues
Electronic surveillance without warrant	continues
Registration of citizens' handwriting samples	continues
Prosecution of critics under arbitrary "state secrets" rubric	continues
Denial of property rights	continues
Denial of writ of habeas corpus	continues
Denial of citizen rights to seek redress of grievances before an impartial court	continues
Denial of right to confidential lawyer-client relationship	continues
Denial of right of accused to face accuser	continues
Extraction of forced confessions	continues
Torture	continues

(continued)

Table 1 *(continued)*

RSFSR Article 64 on "high treason"	continues
Denial of freedom to travel for certain citizens	continues
Practice of *propiska* system requiring permits to reside in certain city or region	continues
Deportation of Russian citizens from areas within Russian Federation	continues
Criminalization of statements or actions which insult chekists	continues
Political surveillance of anti-government individuals and organizations	continues
Harassment and intimidation of critics of security organs	continues
Public defamation of critics of security organs	continues
Maintenance of empire	
Maintenance of KGB political informant networks in other republics	continues
Maintenance of archives of agents and informers in former Soviet and bloc states	continues
Maintenance of KGB agent networks in former Soviet and bloc states	continues
Concealment of information on crimes committed by KGB in other republics	continues
Subversion and destabilization of neighboring countries	continues
Civil controls and oversight	
Lack of working checks and balances among branches of government	continues
Lack of civil control of budget of security organs	continues
Lack of mechanisms for citizens to defend against abuse	continues
Self-funding of security organs via "extrabudgetary funds"	continues
Lack of independent judiciary	continues
Chekist infiltration of police (*militsiya*)	continues
Chekist infiltration of armed forces	continues
Chekist infiltration of bureaucracy	continues
Chekist infiltration of Procuracy	continues
Chekist infiltration of judiciary	continues
Chekist infiltration of local and regional elected government bodies	continues
Chekist infiltration of federal elected parliamentary body	continues
Illegal surveillance of reformist government officials	continues

Union as of August 1991 and is worded to show whether the Soviet-era policy has continued or has been eliminated in Russia today. The pattern that emerges indicates the extent or dearth of real reform in the Russian security and intelligence services.

Continuities vastly outnumber the changes both qualitatively and quantitatively. The KGB was disbanded in name only after the August 1991 putsch and preserved in smaller functional and territorial components endowed with similar powers. One could even go so far as to argue that the modest reforms carried out under Vadim Bakatin after the putsch had little practical long-term impact.

Civil oversight of the security organs in the Russian Federation, while structured formally between the Presidential Security Council and the new legislature, is likely to remain a point of contention between both branches of government as well as among outside observers. Yeltsin's first two ministers of security, though of different backgrounds, were representative of the Soviet old guard, especially Golushko who spent most of his 30-year KGB career hunting down dissidents; dissident-hunters remained in control of personnel and other key areas of the new Federal Counterintelligence Service.

The Russian Supreme Soviet did nothing that would alienate the chekists. A majority, including the leadership which strongly opposed the president, believed that the Security Council could be an advisory body only and that the special services should have reported primarily to the parliamentary leadership. The Supreme Soviet Committee on Defense and Security enjoyed a strong, incestuous relationship with the security organs. Many of its leaders were fellow chekists or militsiya officers with institutional conflicts of interest that ensured that the legislature would not mount a significant challenge to the sanctity of state security. Indeed, committee members complained that by the time of the Supreme Soviet's dissolution in 1993 they were still not able to obtain certain basic information from the organs and that the Supreme Soviet still lacked control of the purse strings.

Nevertheless, the Supreme Soviet passed a number of laws in 1992 and 1993 to govern the chekist apparatus while doing little to curb abuses and even legalizing some of the services' more excessive capabilities. At the same time, like Kryuchkov's KGB, the Ministry of Security, its successor Federal Counterintelligence Service, and the External Intelligence Service conducted impressive public relations campaigns domestically and abroad to convince Russia and the world that the KGB was gone forever and that something new and beneficial to mankind had been erected in its place. Future image-making campaigns should be studied with caution.

The uncertain and often chaotic political situation in which Russia found itself in 1994 made it impossible to determine which branch of government would prevail in the struggle between the presidency and the new parliament. The Yeltsin Constitution concentrates powers in the hands of the president, permitting few checks and balances, and discouraging the development of functioning institutions of government. Given that the most stable institutions in the Russian Federation were the security organs, it appeared that they were a force of their own well positioned to influence decisively the political and economic future of the country. Yet even the chekists were no longer unified. They had dispersed not only into separate services, but the networks of chekists penetrated every element of civil society, especially business, erasing the line between secret service and the outside world. Thus one is led to conclude that as Russia enters the second half of the 1990s there will be no foreseeable, meaningful civil control or oversight of its security and intelligence services.

The few restrictions imposed on the security services to date are fragile, and guarantees are few. In many instances, certain practices such as mass repression, stopped, but the structural, bureaucratic or legal mechanisms—as well as social attitudes—that made totalitarianism possible remained. Post-Communist societies, as Václav Havel observed of Czechoslovakia, are gravely ill and morally contaminated by generations of lies, mass collaboration with the regime, and the other dehumanizing effects of totalitarian rule on a defeated and demoralized people. Most of these societies have yet to confront themselves or their past, as Russian democratic leader Galina Starovoitova observed: "Our nation hasn't undergone the process of penitence after the adoption of totalitarianism, and the predominant feeling is that all of us were victims of the regime."

If all were victims, then who were the victimizers? Havel holds that even the victims were victimizers. Yet, however valid this argument may be, it should not be used as an excuse to allow the chekists and former Party leaders to escape blame and punishment for their very special roles. They were, before anything else, the victimizers. Aside from eastern Germany, of all formerly Communist countries it was Havel's Czech government that most aggressively has sought to identify former secret police personnel and bar them from key areas of public life. And it is Starovoitova who is among the more respected Russian voices calling for the equivalent of de-Nazification of the former Soviet Union, but few are rallying to her call.

In Russia and the rest of the Commonwealth of Independent States, the self-perpetuating chekist culture, financed independently by growing business and organized criminal networks and wielding unknown political clout, reinforces the bureaucratic and social culture that finds dictatorial or otherwise abusive practices acceptable and even standard operating procedure. The chekists are likely to grow in value to some of Russia's bitterly competing political and bureaucratic elites who will, as President Yeltsin did in his October 1993 battle in Moscow, rely on the organs' unchallenged strengths to realize certain individual and institutional ambitions. The price of such loyalty is unlikely to diminish the chekists' strength and possibly has enhanced it. Indeed, given the lack of meaningful controls over them, the security organs may be considered Russia's fourth branch of government if not its core.

The question of implementation of civil controls and oversight in Russia is not simply a domestic issue. It affects almost every country in the world. If strict constraints are not imposed on the country's vast and ambitious foreign intelligence service, the ramifications for other countries could be serious. Chekist actions could even be directed at undermining development of the internal democratic system itself. Therefore credible checks and balances against abuse, meaningful judicial redress of grievances by individual citizens, thorough screening or "lustration" of all government officials, and comprehensive overhaul and rigorous monitoring of all aspects of the security and intelligence services of Russia should be an international priority.

Vadim Bakatin, a product of the Party apparat who lacked the libertarian worldview to reinforce his reformist instincts and intentions, presciently observed days after the Soviet Union's dissolution that fundamental change would not be soon in coming. The erasure of chekism from the national psyche meant first a transformation of a political culture steeped in lifetimes of totalitarianism built upon centuries of autocracy. The reader may recall Bakatin's words after the Soviet collapse.

Looking back on his three months in Lubyanka and ahead at the new Russia being born, the KGB's last chairman sighed, "No one will ever turn the KGB upside down, at least not at present. . . . I am sure that in the future society will gradually rid itself of the chekist ideology, but that requires that it become a really democratic, civil society." Thus Russia's tragic paradox continues, for the question of when, how, or whether the society will become democratic and civil depends in no small part on the fate of the chekists.

Notes

Introduction

1. John Lewis Gaddis, "The Tragedy of Cold War History: Reflections on Revisionism," *Foreign Affairs*, Vol. 73, No. 1, 1994, p. 142. I thank Robert Turner of the American Bar Association Standing Committee on Law and National Security for drawing attention to the article in the *National Security Law Report*.

2. *Ibid.*

Chapter 1

1. "From Our Moscow Correspondent," *Novaya zhizn*, 9 June 1918, p. 4, signed by B. Rossov, from the Bertram Wolfe Collection, Hoover Archives, box 110, file 110-2, cited by John J. Dziak, *Chekisty: A History of the KGB* (Lexington, Massachusetts: Lexington Books, 1988), p. 13.

2. R. Ignatyev, "Perestroika in the KGB," *Izvestiya*, 27 October 1989, p. 3, trans. in Foreign Broadcast Information Service, *Daily Report-Soviet Union* (hereafter referenced as FBIS-SOV), 89-207, 27 October 1989, p. 67.

3. Lt. Gen. Vadim Kirpichenko, verbal exchange with author, American Bar Association Standing Committee on Law and National Security meeting, Washington, D.C., 13 January 1993.

4. For a study of the implementation and institutionalization of these systems, see Alexander Dallin and George W. Breslauer, *Political Terror in Communist Systems* (Stanford: Stanford University Press, 1970). For a perspective from a modern intellectual about the effects of Leninism on the human spirit, see Václav Havel, "New Year's Address," *Open Letters: Selected Writings, 1965-1990*, trans. and ed. Paul Wilson (New York: Vintage, 1991), pp. 390-396.

5. This theme was a constant motif of the Old Left in protest of FBI penetration of their organizations and was revived by the New Left in the 1960s. Numerous journalists, authors, activists, and politicians gathered examples of official abuses or actions that they felt were abuses, and arrived at the mistaken conclusion that the United States maintained a vast secret police apparatus to repress dissent. For a representative mainstream example, see David Wise, *The American Police State: The Government Against the People* (New York: Random House, 1976). Much of this dissent, it now emerges, was directed, funded, or otherwise influenced and inspired by the governments of foreign countries such as the USSR, Cuba, Libya, and Vietnam.

6. Two of the most influential books that helped fuel such impressions about the CIA, whose appearence coincided with the highly publicized Pike and Church Committee hearings in Congress, were authored by former CIA employees. See Victor Marchetti and John D. Marks, *The CIA and the Cult of Intelligence* (New York: Knopf, 1974); and Philip Agee, *Inside the Company: CIA Diary* (Harmondsworth, England: Penguin, 1975, and New York: Stonehill/Bantam, 1975). On page 639 of the British edition, Agee thanks "representatives of the Communist Party of Cuba" for their "important encouragement at a time when I doubted that I would be able to find the additional information I needed." Also see David Wise and Thomas B. Ross, *The Invisible Government* (New York: Random House, 1964, and Vintage, 1974). Senator Daniel Inouye took this to a more absurd extreme during the Iran-Contra inquiry of 1987 when he called the supply operation to sell arms to Iran in order to fund the Nicaraguan Resistance a "secret government."

7. Dziak, p. 1.

8. Amy W. Knight, *The KGB: Police and Politics in the Soviet Union* (Boston: Unwin, Hyman, 1988, 1990), p. xvi.

9. *Ibid.*

10. Merle Fainsod, *How Russia Is Ruled* (Cambridge, Massachusetts: Harvard University Press, 1967); Jerry F. Hough and Merle Fainsod, *How the Soviet Union is Governed* (Cambridge, Massachusetts, and London: Harvard University Press, 1979). Indeed, Hough's treatment of the Stalinist purges is so atrocious that it is even lower than the deliberately misleading official figures issued at the time by the Brezhnev regime.

11. Seweryn Bialer, *The Soviet Paradox: External Expansion, Internal Decline* (New York: Knopf, 1986), pp. 32-33, 42-43.

12. Raymond L. Garthoff, *Détente and Confrontation: American-Soviet Relations from Nixon to Reagan* (Washington, D.C.: The Brookings Institution, 1985), pp. 197, 208. By contrast, Garthoff paid considerable attention to the CIA in U.S. foreign policy.

13. Michael MccGwire, *Perestroika and National Security* (Washington, D.C.: Brookings Institution, 1991).

14. Coit D. Blacker, *Hostage to Revolution: Gorbachev and Soviet Security Policy, 1985-1991* (New York: Council for Foreign Relations Press, 1993).

15. Dziak, p. 2.

16. Sociology Institute of the Russian Academy of Sciences poll of 1,530 individuals in nine Soviet union republics, December 1991-January 1992. The poll was commissioned by the Inter-Republic Security Service, the last union-level state security organ of the USSR. Olga Kryshtanovskaya, "Advocates and Antagonists of the KGB," *Nezavisimaya gazeta* international edition in English, Vol. 4, Issue 4-5, August 1993, p. 3.

17. The best treatments of the development of the KGB are offered by Dziak and Knight in their respectively cited works.

18. For a study of civil oversight of the security organs in the Gorbachev era, see J. Michael Waller, *The KGB and Its Successors Under Gorbachev and Yeltsin: Russian State Security and Elusive Civil Controls*, Ph.D. dissertation (Minneapolis: University Microfilms, Inc., 1993) pp. 149-215.

19. The exception is Moscow state security chief Yevgeniy Savostyanov, a leader of the Democratic Russia movement who was appointed in September 1991 by Moscow Mayor Gavriil Popov. Previously the Moscow KGB chief was named by the Soviet Politburo. After the 1991 putsch, the Soviet and Russian leadership allowed the capital city and oblast security chief to be appointed by the mayor. Savostyanov was not able to bring in his own team, and his office was completely staffed by professional officers who were CPSU members. Savostyanov himself is believed to have been a lieutenant in the KGB academic reserve prior to his appointment.

20. See Chapter 4. Russia's new internal security chief, Sergei Stepashin, had the reputation of a politically tolerant moderate reformer, but he soon disappointed democrats by speaking and acting in true chekist fashion.

21. See J. Michael Waller, "Commonwealth of Chekists: Internal Security Organs in the Commonwealth of Independent States," paper delivered at the International Studies Association annual conference, Washington, D.C., 31 March 1994.

22. See Chapter 4.

23. Kirpichenko to author, 13 January 1993; Jeff Trimble, "New Act, Old Tricks," *U.S. News and World Report*, 8 February 1993, p. 42; author's conversations with chekist officers in Moscow, September and October 1993, and April 1994.

24. *Pravda*, 18 December 1927, p. 2, cited by Fainsod, p. 663n. A slightly different translation is provided by Simon Wolin and Robert M. Slusser: "(1) To hunt out and liquidate all counterrevolutionary [and] sabotage attempts and actions throughout Russia, no matter what their origin; (2) to hand over all saboteurs and counterrevolutionaries to the Revolutionary Tribunal and prepare measures for combatting them. . . ; (3) the Commission is to carry out preliminary investigation only, to the extent necessary for suppression." Simon Wolin and Robert M. Slusser, eds., *The Soviet Secret Police* (New York: Praeger, 1957), pp. 3-4.

25. *Pravda*, No. 33(259), 10/23 February 1918, p. 1, cited by Fainsod, pp. 425-426. An alternate translation is that the organ saw "no other way to combat counterrevolutionaries, spies, speculators, burglars, hooligans, saboteurs and other parasites than their merciless annihilation at the scene of the crime." Wolin and Slusser, pp. 4-5.

26. George Popoff, *The Tcheka: The Red Inquisition* (London: A. M. Philpot, Ltd., 1925), p. 232.

27. *Ibid.*, pp. 237-238.

28. Wolin and Slusser, pp. 4-5.

29. *Ibid.*

30. *Ibid.*, pp. 5-6.

31. Popoff, p. 233.

32. Quoted in "Information on Russia," *Senate Document 50*, 67th Congress, 1st Session, 1921, p. 64, cited by Fainsod, p. 426.

33. Minutes of the Second All-Russian Conference of Commissars of Justice, Moscow, 2-6 July 1918, trans. in James Bunyan and H. H. Fisher, *The Bolshevik Revolution, 1917-1918* (Stanford, 1934), pp. 580-581, cited by Fainsod p. 427.

34. W. H. Chamberlin, *The Russian Revolution, 1917-1921*, Vol. 2 (New York: 1935), p. 79, cited *ibid*, p. 427.

35. For greater treatment of the Cheka, see Christopher Andrew and Oleg Gordievsky, *KGB: The Inside Story of Its Foreign Operations from Lenin to Gorbachev* (New York: Harper Collins, 1990), pp. 38-64; Richard Deacon, *A History of the Russian Secret Service* (London: Frederick Muller Ltd., 1972. Dorset, 1990), pp. 195-222; Dziak, pp. 19-38; Ronald Hingley, *The Russian Secret Police: Muscovite, Imperial Russian and Soviet Political Security Operations* (New York: Dorset, 1970, 1990), pp. 117-132; and especially George Leggett, *The Cheka: Lenin's Political Police* (Oxford: Oxford University Press, 1981).

36. "From Our Moscow Correspondent," *Novaya zhizn'*, 9 June 1918, p. 4, signed by B. Rossov, from the Bertram Wolfe Collection, Hoover Archives, box 110, file 110-2, cited by Dziak, p. 13.

37. Leggett.

38. Fainsod, pp. 426, 663-664n.

39. Leggett, p. 467.

40. Robert Conquest, "The Human Cost of Soviet Communism," prepared for the Senate Committee on the Judiciary, Subcommittee to Investigate the Administration of the Internal Security Act and Other Internal Security Laws, Washington, D.C., 1971, p. 11, cited by Dziak, pp. 174-175.

41. One extrapolation of Bolshevik execution totals in 1920 calculates a daily average of five executions in each local unit of the Cheka, the Tribunals, the Military Tribunals and other "torture centers." Since there were about 1,000 such centers, by this estimate there would have been 5,000 executions daily, or 1.8 to 2.5 million executions annually between 1918 and 1923. Egeny [sic] Kominin, *Roul*, 3 August 1923, cited in S. P. Mel'gunov, *The Red Terror in Russia* (London: J. M. Dent & Sons, Ltd., 1926), furnished by Dziak, pp. 174-175. Comments Dziak, "This is the highest figure I have come across and it far exceeds the Deniken figure of 1,700,000," which is "no doubt exaggerated."

42. Popoff, p. 125.

43. Sergei Kovalev, chairman, Committee on Human Rights, Supreme Soviet of the Russian Federation, presentation to the first international conference on "KGB Yesterday, Today and Tomorrow," Moscow, 20 February 1993. Text of statement.

44. Wolin and Slusser, p. 6.

45. Dziak, p. 175.

46. *Ibid.*

47. Col. Peter S. Nikulin, former deputy director, Institute of Security Problems, Russian Ministry of Security, presentation at the Second International Conference on the "KGB: Yesterday, Today, and Tomorrow," sponsored by the Glasnost Foundation, May 1993, in E. Oznobkina and L. Isakova, eds., *KGB: Yesterday, Today, Tomorrow (Collected Reports)* (Moscow: Znak-SP/Gandalf, 1993), p. 143. Former Romanian intelligence chief Lt. Gen. Ion Mihai Pacepa described a similar system organized by Romanian Communist Party chief Nicolae Ceausescu to track down citizens who wrote letters to Radio Free Europe. See Ion Mihai Pacepa, *Red Horizons: Chronicles of a Communist Spy Chief* (Washington, D.C., Regnery Gateway, 1987), pp. 198-200.

48. Konstantin Simis, *USSR: The Corrupt Society* (New York: Simon and Schuster, 1982), p. 248.

49. Nikulin, p. 142.

50. Havel, pp. 391-392.

51. Vadim Bakatin, quoted by Will Stewart, "KGB Boss Fights to Guard Secrets," *International Express* (London), 23 October 1992.

52. Popoff, pp. 238-239.

53. *Ibid.*, p. 240.

54. Edward Crankshaw, *Gestapo* (New York: Pyramid, 1970), p. 7.

55. The secret services are known by their acronyms: VeCheka, Cheka, GPU, OGPU, GUGB, NKGB, GUGB again, NKGB again, MGB, KGB of the Council of Ministers, and KGB of the USSR, and in post-Soviet Russia the RSFSR KGB, AFB, MBVD, and MB. See Dziak, pp. 184-185. The MB was renamed and reorganized in December 1993, with its largest components becoming the Federal Counterintelligence Service (FSK).

56. L. A. Plotnikova, ed., *Chekisty* (Leningrad: Lenizdat, 1982), p. 501, cited by Knight, p. 160.

57. Vadim Bakatin, *Izbavleniye ot KGB* (Moscow: Novosti, 1992), p. 26.

58. After World War II, under Stalin, the device was removed and apparently discarded. Pyotr Deriabin, interview, Andrew and Gordievsky, p. 42.

59. Knight, p. 240.

60. *Ibid.*, p. 226. According to Dziak, the United State Political Directorate (OGPU), which was the Cheka's new name between 1923 and 1934, had a Dzerzhinskiy Division which engaged in combat against "kulak gangs." Dziak, citing I. G. Belikov, et. al., *Imeni Dzerzhinskogo* (Moscow: Voyenizdat, 1976), and I. K. Yakovlev, et al., *Vnutrenniye voyska sovetskoy respubliki 1917-1922 gg* (Moscow: Izdatel'svo 'Yuridicheskaya Literatura,' 1972).

61. All-Union Center for the Study of Public Opinion, poll of 1,848 individuals in seventeen regions of the USSR. Cited by Roy D. Laird, *The Soviet Elite* (Westport, Connecticut: Praeger, 1992), pp. 157-158.

62. *Ibid.*, citing *Pravda*, 11 September 1987.

63. R. Ignatyev, "Perestroika in the KGB," *Izvestiya*, 27 October 1989, p. 3, trans. in FBIS-SOV-89-207, 27 October 1989, p. 67.

64. Andrew and Gordievsky, p. 40.

65. *Ibid.*

66. Former high-level Russian intelligence officer, confidential interview with author, Moscow, October 1993.

67. RSFSR People's Deputy Nikolai Ryabov, deputy chairman, State Commission to Investigate the Activity of State Security Organs, *Rossiyskaya gazeta*, 18 September 1991, p. 1, trans. in FBIS-SOV-91-181, 18 September 1991, p. 25.

68. Russian Television Network, 2180 GMT, 19 September 1991, trans. in FBIS-SOV-91-184, 23 September 1991, p. 27.

69. Vadim Bakatin, in *Izvestiya*, 2 January 1992, morning edition, p. 6, trans. in FBIS-SOV-92-002, 3 January 1992, pp. 4-5.

70. Andrei Mironov, interview with author, April 1994. Mironov, one of the last to be convicted and imprisoned for political crimes under glasnost, was among the demonstrators who attempted to topple the Dzerzhinskiy statue. Mironov

recalled the genuine grief on the faces of chekists who watched the removal of the statue.

71. These observations are based in part on my own observations at Lubyanka when it was KGB headquarters (December 1991), Ministry of Security headquarters (May, September and October 1993), and Federal Counterintelligence Service headquarters (April 1994); and on several 1993 and 1994 conversations with state security officers and journalists who had recently visited Lubyanka.

72. See Vera Tolz, "Ministry of Security Official Gives New Figures for Stalin's Crimes," *RFE/RL Research Report*, Vol. 1, No. 18, 1 May 1992, pp. 8-10; and *idem*, "The Katyn Documents and the CPSU Hearings," *RFE/RL Research Report*, Vol. 1, No. 44, 6 November 1992, pp. 27-33.

73. Nikulin, p. 148.

74. In addition to his presentations at the Kennan Institute at the Woodrow Wilson Center, the American Bar Association, the Permanent Select Committee on Intelligence of the U.S. House of Representatives and elsewhere, Kirpichenko issued two papers during his 10-18 January visit: "Legal Basis for the Activity of Russian Intelligence" and "Intelligence in a Democratic Society." Both papers are in the author's collection.

75. Kirpichenko to author, 13 January 1993.

76. Minutes of the Second All-Russian Conference of Commissars of Justice, 2-6 July 1918, trans. in Bunyan and Fisher, pp. 580-581, and cited by Fainsod, p. 427.

77. Vadim Bakatin, interview with author, 19 September 1992.

Chapter 2

1. Gorbachev speech to Ukraine Communist Party Central Committee Plenum, 28 September 1989, trans. in FBIS-SOV, 29 September 1989, cited by John Lenczowski, *The Sources of Soviet Perestroika* (Ashland, Ohio: Ashland University, John M. Ashbrook Center for Public Affairs, 1990), pp. 2-3.

2. *Nezavisimaya gazeta*, 28 December 1990, cited by Dmitry Mikheyev, *The Rise and Fall of Gorbachev* (Indianapolis: The Hudson Institute, 1992), p. 155.

3. Lenczowski, pp. 4-5.

4. Gorbachev, cited in *ibid.*, p. 2.

5. *Ibid.*, pp. 2-3.

6. *Ibid.*, p. 3.

7. Long before perestroika, and even before Brezhnev had consolidated control, Merle Fainsod noted that criticism and competition within a totalitarian system can serve, if skillfully managed, to reinforce the regime. He wrote, "When discontent accumulates, 'loyalty' to the regime may be consolidated by providing scapegoats on whom frustrated aggression may exhaust itself. The shrewd totalitarian dictatorship may go further and permit ventilation of grievances of a nonpolitical and nonorganized character. It may even institutionalize such expression as the Soviet dictatorship does when it sanctions criticism of bureaucratic malpractice or inefficiency. Such criticism may play a constructive role in strengthening the regime since it accomplishes the triple function of

draining off aggression on the part of its subjects, prodding the bureaucracy to improve its performance, and sustaining the belief that the supreme leadership is genuinely concerned about popular complaints and vexations. Yet ultimately the totalitarian dictatorship must depend on terror to safeguard its monopoly of power." Merle Fainsod, *How Russia Is Ruled* (Cambridge, Massachusetts: Harvard University Press, 1967), p. 421.

8. Even these people had close ties to the security services and to repression. Shevardnadze was a particularly rough minister of internal affairs of the Georgian SSR before moving up the Party hierarchy to Moscow. Rev. Gleb Yakunin, a member of the Russian Supreme Soviet commission which investigated the role of the security organs in the 1991 putsch, said at a Washington news conference that he viewed KGB documents showing that Yakovlev was an informer against non-communist religious individuals. Gleb Yakunin, statement at news conference sponsored by the Jamestown Foundation, 340 Cannon House Office Building, Washington D.C., 20 March 1992. From author's notes.

9. Vladimir Kryuchkov, in *L'Unita* (Rome), 19 August 1989, pp. 6-7, trans. in FBIS-SOV-89-201, 19 October 1989, pp. 48-49.

10. Ivan Frolov, interview with *La Repubblica* (Rome), trans. in FBIS-SOV-89-074, 19 April 1989, p. 83, cited by Frederick Kagan, "The Secret History of Perestroika," *The National Interest*, Spring 1991, p. 33. Arbatov, head of the Institute on the USA and Canada, says he was "discovered" by Andropov's mentor Otto Kuusinen and cultivated by Andropov: "I am much indebted to these people as teachers." Georgiy Arbatov, interview in *Nedelya*, 23 March 1988, trans. in FBIS-SOV-88-073, 15 April 1988, p. 19.

11. Fyodor Burlatsky, cited by Stephen Cohen and Katrina vanden Heuvel, *Voices of Glasnost: Interviews with Gorbachev's Reformers* (New York: W. W. Norton and Company, 1989), p. 176, cited by Kagan, p. 38.

12. Burlatsky, p. 34. Burlatsky strains his credibility in the same interview series by alleging that Suslov wanted to ruin Andropov's political career by "forcing" him to become KGB chairman thereby making it "impossible for Andropov ever to return to leadership politics."

13. See Roy Godson, "'AIDS: Made in the USA': Moscow's Contagious Campaign," in Ladislav Bittman, ed., *The New Image-Makers: Soviet Propaganda and Disinformation Today* (Washington: Pergamon-Brassey's, 1988), pp. 221-226.

14. William R. Corson and Robert W. Crowley, *The New KGB: Engine of Soviet Power* (New York: Morrow, 1985), p. 381. This report was confirmed by a former KGB general in an interview with the author.

15. Amy W. Knight, *The KGB: Police and Politics in the Soviet Union* (Boston: Unwin, Hyman, 1988; rev. ed., 1990), pp. 95-97.

16. *Ibid.*, p. 98.

17. *Ibid.*, p. 110n.

18. Hedrick Smith noted what an unusual accomplishment it was for someone of Gorbachev's social standing and background to enter Moscow State University: "The odds against a farm boy from southern Russia making it into the nation's top university were tougher in 1950 than they would be for an American black from an urban ghetto getting into Harvard University in 1990." Hedrick Smith, *The New Russians* (New York: Random House, 1990), p. 44. There are

conflicting reports about the type of medal Gorbachev sported. Smith, as well as Vladimir Solovyov and Elena Klepikova, says it was the Order of the Red Banner of Labor, which seems improbable because this medal was reserved for high-level officials. Dmitry Mikheyev says it was merely a "silver medal."

19. Dmitry Mikheyev cites a number of such émigré observers including Abdurakhman Avtorkhanov, "Andropov's Coup d'Etat," *Posev*, No. 1, 1983; *idem*, "Round Table: Your Opinion About the New Secretary General," *Posev*, No. 4, 1985; Fridrikh Heznansky, "Politico-managerial Structures of the USSR," *Posev*, No. 11, 1985; *idem*, "The KGB and Glasnost," *Posev*, No. 9, 1989; and Aleksandr Vasiliev, "The Real Ideology of the Ruling Class," *Posev*, No. 9, 1985. Also, Peter Deriabin and T. H. Bagley, *KGB: Masters of the Soviet Union* (New York: Hippocrene Books, 1990), p. 111; Oleg Gordievsky, *Time*, 5 March 1990; and Leonid Gozman, "The Man of the Decade: Psychological Portrait of Mikhail Gorbachev," *Ogonek*, No. 49, 1991, p. 47.

20. Zhores Medvedev, *Gorbachev* (New York: Norton, 1987), p. 37. Said the late Peter Deriabin, who served in the Stalinist state security organs before defecting to the United States, "The roommates [were] invariably selected and assigned [by state security] with the specific task of watching foreigners." Deriabin and Bagley, p. 326. Hedrick Smith, making no reference to possible state security ties, called Gorbachev's friendship with Mlynar a "considerable risk at a time of Stalinist Cold War paranoia about spies and outside influences of any kind." Smith, p. 46.

21. Vladimir Solovyov and Elena Klepikova, *Behind the High Kremlin Walls* (New York: Dodd, Mead/Berkeley Books, 1986; rev. ed. 1987), pp. 173-176. The authors, journalists who interviewed some of Gorbachev's former classmates, record, "Judging from the accounts of former students at the law school, Gorbachev at first took part in [drinking] bouts, but he usually drank only a little. This set him rather apart from his comrades. One of his roommates recalls that many of them even wondered if he wasn't an informer. That suspicion was based on the fact that, the day after each of several drunken conversations on political subjects, many of the young men were called into the dean's office for interrogation. One of his classmates recalls, 'We all got drunk as lords and didn't remember a single thing the next day. He alone remained sober as a judge through the whole evening and remembered everything. Our suspicions grew stronger when we were sent out to serve internships. Some went here, some went there: to courtrooms, to the prosecutor's office, to prisons for regular criminals. But Misha chose the Lubyanka. That was in those very years when it was full of political prisoners, and the devil only knows what was done there! At that point, we stopped having doubts and tried to make sure he wasn't around when we had our parties. . . . And he himself, after he had joined the Party and made his connections at the Lubyanka, began to avoid us and stopped studying: he was beginning another career'" (pp. 174-175).

22. Gail Sheehy, *The Man Who Changed the World: The Lives of Mikhail S. Gorbachev* (New York: Harper Collins, 1990), p. 62.

23. Medvedev, p. 41. Without offering evidence, Medvedev writes that Gorbachev "almost certainly chose to do his apprenticeship in a procurator's office."

24. Sheehy, p. 63.

25. Lev Yudovich, *Wall Street Journal*, 12 March 1985, cited by Solovyov and Klepikova, p. 179.

26. Robert Kaiser, *Why Gorbachev Happened* (New York: Harper Collins, 1991), p. 30.

27. Dusko Doder and Louise Branson, *Gorbachev: Heretic in the Kremlin* (New York: Penguin, 1991), pp. 9-11; Sheehy, pp. 64-65, 82-84. Medvedev does not address the issue.

28. John-Thor Dahlburg, "The Rise and Fall of Gorbachev," *Los Angeles Times*, 26 December 1991.

29. This incident was recalled by one of the accused, Vladimir Lieberman. *Ibid.*, and Sheehy, p. 75.

30. From their own investigative work, Solovyov and Klepikova conclude, "Gorbachev also looked into the personnel files of other students and professors of non-Jewish origin and exposed as 'enemies of the people' those who, from his point of view, were lacking in Stalinist orthodoxy. In that urban, university milieu, the young man from the country . . . represented the common people and always managed to profit from his social [peasant] and ethnic [Russian] background, exposing the people's enemies in its name." Solovyov and Klepikova, pp. 179-180.

31. Sheehy, p. 76.

32. Mikheyev, p. 27.

33. Doder and Branson, Chapter 1; Medvedev, pp. 36-38; Smith, pp. 44-51.

34. Zdenek Mlynar, "Il mio compagno di studi Mikhail Gorbaciov," *L'Unita* (Rome), 9 April 1985. The article was published within weeks of Gorbachev's ascent as general secretary of the CPSU.

35. The Italian government reached an agreement with the Russian government in early 1992 stipulating that Moscow would supply documentation to Rome concerning its financial and material support to the Italian Communist Party. Documents given to the Italian government indicate the CPSU made cash transfers via the KGB to the ICP as late as 1987. See Aleksei Golyayev, ITAR-TASS/*Rossiyskaya gazeta*, 9 June 1992, first edition, p. 7, trans. in FBIS-SOV-92-116, 16 June 1992, pp. 5-6. As seen in chapter 8, the KGB used *L'Unita* to surface some of its most important international propaganda themes during the glasnost period.

36. Mlynar capitalized during the Gorbachev years by speaking about his friendship with the CPSU leader and bragging about his influence on him. Mlynar was a reform Communist who fled to exile in Austria in 1968. He acknowledged that Gorbachev, "like everyone else at the time was a Stalinist. In order to be a true reforming communist, you have to have been a true Stalinist." Doder and Branson, p. 11, citing Mlynar, "Il mio compagno di studi Mikhail Gorbaciov."

37. Solovyov and Klepikova, p. 180.

38. *San Francisco Chronicle*, 14 January 1990, cited in *ibid.*

39. Recalled by former classmate Fridrikh Nezansky, in Dahlburg; also Kaiser, pp. 29-30. Other former classmates cited above recall Gorbachev reporting to the authorities against fellow students who had committed indiscretions while drinking (see note 21).

40. Peter Deriabin and Frank Gibney, *The Secret World* (New York: Time, 1959; Ballantine, 1982), p. 229.

41. Robert Conquest, *Power and Policy in the USSR* (London: Macmillan, 1962), p. 45, cited by Mikheyev, *Op. cit.*, p. 28.

42. Sheehy, *Op. cit.*, p. 86. On pp. 84 and 85 she observes that somehow, Gorbachev still managed to avoid military conscription, and she speculates that it was because of sponsorship by state security.

43. *Stavropolskaya pravda*, 6 February 1979, cited by Solovyov and Klepikova, *Op. cit.*, p. 184. Mikheyev said that Komsomol work was a way of avoiding service in the Procuracy but agrees that it was humbling. Gorbachev's Komsomol post, the unsophisticated nature of which Mikheyev describes, would not have been a nomenklatura post. Mikheyev, pp. 46-48.

44. Deriabin and Gibney, p. 106

45. Amy Knight writes, "Judging from their activities as reported in the press, second secretaries, who have traditionally performed a watchdog role for the central party apparatus, have some responsibility for administrative organs. They attend all important functions concerning the internal affairs apparatus, the judiciary, and the Procuracy, as well as the KGB and the military. It is not uncommon for the second secretary to open meetings and address conferences of these institutions." Knight, p. 139. This assessment was confirmed by a former ranking KGB counterintelligence officer in an interview with the author.

46. Mikheyev, p. 28, citing personal interview with one of Gorbachev's neighbors in Stavropol, June 1989.

47. Kulakov hosted plotters Mikhail Suslov, Leonid Brezhnev, KGB Chairman Aleksandr Shelepin, and Marshal Roman Malinovsky at the Teberda Preserve in Stavropol where the conspiracy was hatched. Solovyov and Klepikova, pp. 189-190. Gorbachev biographer Christian Schmidt-Häuer writes that Gorbachev's promotion to Moscow "would hardly have been possible if the Stavropol Region had been controlled by a narrowminded bureaucrat. It wasn't. The Party chief from 1960 onward was Fedor Davidovich Kulakov, who, like Gorbachev, was the son of peasants and a supporter of cautious efforts to modernize agriculture. In spite of his youth—he was in his mid-forties—Kulakov was already one of Khrushchev's leading agricultural experts. . . . Kulakov's appointment showed Gorbachev that the important grain-growing region of Stavropol could be a vital springboard." Christian Schmidt-Häuer, *Gorbachev: The Path to Power* (London: I. B. Tauris, 1986), pp. 58-59.

48. *Pravda*, 10 December 1990, cited by Mikheyev, p. 28. In his biography of Gorbachev, Medvedev discounts suggestions that Andropov or Suslov might have recommended Gorbachev for the *kraykom* first secretary post.

49. Solovyov and Klepikova, pp. 196-199.

50. Schmidt-Häuer, p. 64.

51. Sheehy, pp. 116-118.

52. Solovyov and Klepikova, p. 28.

53. *Ibid.*, p. 209, citing *Pravda*, 21 September 1978.

54. Knight, pp. 140-141.

55. Oleg Gordievsky, in Christopher Andrew and Oleg Gordievsky, *KGB: The Inside Story* (New York: Harper Collins, 1990), p. 608. Canadian Members of

Parliament were impressed by Gorbachev's knowledge during his low-profile visit to Ottawa in May 1983. Medvedev, pp. 124-125.

56. Medvedev, p. 126.

57. *Ibid.*, pp. 119-136. Andropov promoted Chebrikov to become both chairman of the KGB and a candidate member of the Politburo in late 1982.

58. Andrew and Gordievsky, p. 624.

59. "Commentary by Alex Alexiev," appendix to Alexander Rahr, "Gorbachev and the Post-Chebrikov KGB," Radio Free Europe/Radio Liberty (RFE/RL) *Report on the USSR*, 22 December 1989, p. 21n, citing Aleksandr Pumpyansky, "Kak delnetsya istoria," *Novoye vremya*, No. 44, 1989. Another observer notes that at the 19th Party Congress of June and July 1988, Gorbachev's deputy, Yegor Ligachev, gave a speech "in which he listed Chebrikov *first* among a handful of promoters and patrons of Gorbachev who, he said, assured Gorbachev's appointment as general secretary." This seemingly innocuous order actually was an indication to the Party which enabled cadres to gauge who was closest to the center of power. Albert L. Weeks, "Gorbachev and the KGB," *Global Affairs*, Winter 1990, p. 75, citing *Pravda*, 2 July, 1988.

60. Medvedev writes that Chebrikov probably kept Grishin from becoming a candidate for general secretary by spreading rumors that Grishin's daughter-in-law was the illegitimate child of Beria. Gorbachev was chosen in a Politburo meeting on 10 March 1985. Medvedev, pp. 172-173.

61. *Ibid.*, p. 171.

62. Doder and Branson, p. 100.

63. "Commentary by Amy Knight," appendix to Alexander Rahr, "Gorbachev and the Post-Chebrikov KGB," RFE/RL *Report on the USSR*, 22 December 1989, p. 24.

64. Mikheyev, p. 156.

65. For a survey of this evidence, see J. Michael Waller, *The KGB and Its Successors Under Gorbachev and Yeltsin: Russian State Security and Elusive Civil Controls*, Ph.D. dissertation (Minneapolis: University Microfilms Inc., 1993), pp. 217-353.

66. See Françoise Thom, *The Gorbachev Phenomenon: A History of Perestroika*, trans. by Jenny Marshall (London and New York: Pinter, 1989), pp. 89-111.

67. See Knight, pp. 100-104.

68. *Pravda*, 12 September 1987, cited by Doder and Branson, p. 267; and in *ibid.*, pp. 103-104.

69. A. I. Lukyanov, *Promoting Democracy* (Moscow: APN Publishers, 1987), p. 21, cited by Doder and Branson, p. 272.

70. Richard Popplewell, "Themes in the Rhetoric of KGB Chairmen from Andropov to Kryuchkov," *Intelligence and National Security*, Vol. 6, No. 3, July 1991, p. 521.

71. *Pravda*, 13 April 1988, cited in *ibid.*, p. 520.

72. Rahr, "Gorbachev and the Post-Chebrikov KGB."

73. Doder and Branson, pp. 347-348.

74. Rahr, p. 17.

75. Chebrikov originally entered the KGB in 1967 as a Party official. He remained to become a career officer.

76. Weeks, p. 75. Weeks added that the former KGB chairman's growing authority "was particularly evident in a number of Chebrikov's speeches in 1988-89, including his lengthy front-page interviews with *Pravda*, 2 September 1988, and 19 August 1989. Chebrikov's broad discussion of legal matters in the latter interview bespoke not only the wide range of his authority but the harshness with which he appeared to be greeting the latest 'disarray' in the Soviet Union, including strikes and ethnic unrest, and protests by 'nationalist' groups and 'informal' non-official organizations. This was noted also by keen-eyed Russian émigrés writing in the West German, Frankfurt-based monthly *Posev* (issues of September and October 1989)."

77. Rahr, pp. 17, 18.

78. *Ibid.*

79. Cf., e.g., *Moskovskiye novosti*, 21 May 1989, and *Argumenty i fakty*, cited by Weeks, pp. 75-76.

80. Weeks, p. 76.

81. Alex Alexiev notes that in the wake of the Chebrikov-inspired brutalities in Tblisi, Georgia, Shevardnadze was dispatched to his native city to investigate and reported directly to Gorbachev: "Shevardnadze, a native Georgian, must have quickly found out exactly what had happened and to what degree Moscow had been involved. While maintaining the official line about 'extremists' at the time, he also used his clout to make it possible for the independent Georgian journalist Irakli Gotsiridze to interview the principals and establish the truth. It was Gotsiridze's investigation that first established Dmitrii Yazov's and ultimately Chebrikov's involvement in the tragic events (see *Molodezh gruzii*, May 27, 1989). Gorbachev, realizing how explosive the political impact of Moscow's and Chebrikov's involvement in the massacre would be, may have decided at that point that his KGB chief had become a liability. Subsequent events, such as the findings of the investigating commission of the Georgian Supreme Soviet (see *Zarya vostoka*, October 5, 1989) would seem to confirm this assessment." "Commentary by Alex Alexiev," appendix to Rahr, p. 21n.

82. Weeks, p. 59. Rahr observed prophetically, "Gorbachev should not be surprised if, in future, more KGB officials turn against him." Rahr, p. 19.

83. Theodore Karasik, "Post-USSR: The Apparatchiki," *Perspective* (Boston University Institute for the Study of Conflict, Ideology & Policy), Vol. 2, No. 4, March 1992, p. 1, citing *Nezavisimaya gazeta*, 30 October 1991.

84. Vadim Bakatin, interview with author, 25 September 1992.

85. Gordievsky, in Andrew and Gordievsky, p. 620. Gordievsky's point was later verified by the head of the KGB First Chief Directorate, who described the CPSU International Department as the main consumer of KGB foreign intelligence during the Gorbachev period. *Izvestiya*, 25 September 1991, union edition, p. 2, trans. in FBIS-SOV-91-191, 2 October 1991, p. 34.

86. Solovyov and Klepikova, p. 212.

87. Bakatin, to author.

Chapter 3

1. *Rossiyskaya gazeta*, citing Vadim Bakatin in *Der Spiegel*, 26 November 1991, first edition, p. 3, trans. in FBIS-SOV-91-231, 2 December 1991, p. 21.

2. For a description of the debate on the KGB in the USSR Supreme Soviet from late May to August 1989 and the issues of Soviet parliamentary oversight from 1989 to 1991, see J. Michael Waller, *The KGB and Its Successors Under Gorbachev and Yeltsin: Russian State Security and Elusive Civil Controls*, doctoral dissertation (Minneapolis: University Microfilms, Inc., 1993), pp. 149-216.

3. Alexander Rahr, "KGB Attack on Gorbachev and His Reforms," *Radio Liberty Report on the USSR*, 13 April 1990, p. 6.

4. Victor Yasmann, "Boris Yeltsin Says Russian 'KGB' Possible," *RFE/RL Daily Report*, No. 180, 20 September 1990, p. 1.

5. *Moskovskiye novosti*, No. 20, 19 May 1991, p. 10, trans. in FBIS-SOV-91-109, 6 June 1991, p. 43.

6. *Ibid.* This issue was not resolved until after the August putsch, when the Moscow KGB was made subordinate to the Moscow City Council. The Supreme Soviet member cited was Boris Bolshakov, a KGB colonel from Ivanovo who served at the time as deputy chairman of the Committee on Defense and Security of the Russian Federation Supreme Soviet.

7. Alexander Rahr, "Old KGB Remains Alive and Well in Post-Soviet Russia," *Post-Soviet/East European Report*, RFE/RL Research Institute, Vol. 9, No. 17, 10 March 1992.

8. Viktor Ivanenko, interview with Mark Urban, BBC Television Network in English (London), 2130 GMT, 6 September 1991, in FBIS-SOV-91-174, 9 September 1991, p. 77.

9. Viktor Ivanenko, cited by TASS international service in English, 0844 GMT, 28 August 1991, in FBIS-SOV-91-167, 28 August 1991, p. 81; Boris Yeltsin in Interfax, 1230 GMT, 23 August 1991, in FBIS-SOV-91-164, 23 August 1991, p. 76; and Leonid Shebarshin in TASS international service in English, 1233 GMT, 23 August 1991, in FBIS-SOV-91-164, 23 August 1991, p. 38.

10. These divisions were reported both prior to and subsequent to the putsch. Breakdowns in discipline were sporadically reported in various areas of the USSR in 1990 and 1991. Following the putsch, forty officers of the Maritime Kray KGB Directorate sent a telegram to President Yeltsin demanding the resignation of the kray KGB leaders for having compromised themselves. A "special commission" flew from Moscow to verify the assertions in the telegram. It was later reported that kray KGB Chairman K. Grigoryev was "suspended from his official duties" during the duration of the commission's investigation. His formal dismissal is not known to have been reported. *Komsomolskaya pravda*, 10 September 1991, p. 1, trans. in FBIS-SOV-91-177, 12 September 1991, pp. 79-80. Also see Waller, pp. 388-412.

11. Mark Galeotti, "The Role of the Security Forces," *Radio Liberty Report on the USSR*, Vol. 3, No. 36, 6 September 1991, p. 7.

12. Commission document cited by TASS in *Pravda*, 25 September 1991, p. 6, trans. in FBIS-SOV-91-191, 2 October 1991, p. 35. Stepashin was an instructor at a police training school in St. Petersburg.

13. Andrei Oligov, chief of the Public Relations Center of the Russian Federal Security Agency (AFB), to Yevgeniya Albats, "KGB-MSB-MBVD: Substantive Changes?" *Moscow News*, No. 12, 13 January 1992, p. 5.

14. TASS international service in English, 1614 GMT, 22 August 1991, in FBIS-SOV-91-164, 23 August 1991, p. 34.

15. TASS international service in English, 1419 GMT, 22 August 1991, in FBIS-SOV-91-164, 23 August 1991, p. 35. The English TASS announcement of Shebarshin's appointment was filed before the announcement that Kryuchkov had been removed. Also see FBIS Editorial Report of Moscow Central Television First Program Network (*Vzglyad*), 1845 GMT, 27 September 1991, in FBIS-SOV-91-191, 2 October 1991, p. 28.

16. Vadim Bakatin, interview with author, Washington, D.C., 18 September 1992. Bakatin explained in a televised interview a week after his appointment in August 1991, "I was constantly being hurried. The president's office rang; the president asks you to come in. . . . I kept saying that I would go, and for about an hour I did not go. They rang about five times and I thought that it probably concerned this. I did not go because I was to meet with several leaders of this [Alfa] group and prepare an appropriate document. After I had held this meeting, after I had prepared the document on resubordinating this group out of the KGB directly to the president, I then went with this file so he could sign it, and I thought that was about this. But completely unexpectedly I was told that I was expected in the Walnut Room. I went in and there were all the republican presidents—Boris Nikolayevich Yeltsin, [Kazakh President Nursultan] Nazarbayev, [Kyrgyz President Askar] Akayev, [Uzbek President Islam] Karimov—and they told me to sit down. The gathering said that 'we have decided to offer you the post of chairman of the KGB.'" Russian Television Network, 1731 GMT, 29 August 1991, trans. in FBIS-SOV-91-170, 3 September 1991, p. 45. He told the presidents, "You are sending me to the department which I have said on more than one occasion should be eliminated. So it turns out that I have come to destroy the Committee for State Security." Russian Television Network, 2000 GMT, 28 August 1991, trans. in FBIS-SOV-91-168, 29 August 1991, pp. 42-43. Bakatin also describes the episode in his KGB memoir, *Izbavlenie ot KGB* (Moscow: Novosti, 1992).

17. Bakatin, interview with author, 22 September 1992. A copy of the *ukase* is reproduced on the inside front cover of Bakatin, *Izbavleniye ot KGB* .

18. Mikhail Gorbachev, Russian Television Network (Moscow), 1308 GMT, 23 August 1991, trans. in FBIS-SOV-91-165, 26 August 1991, pp. 59-60. Boris Yeltsin, Radio Rossii (Moscow), 1230 GMT, 23 August 1991, trans. in FBIS-SOV-91-165, 23 August 1991, p. 76.

19. Bakatin, interview with author, 22 September 1992.

20. *Ibid.* In this interview, Bakatin showed me copies of the decree. This accunt is consistent with a report in *Izvestiya* the year before, which said that Bakatin made the actual dismissals and appointments in the KGB leadership and that his decisions were confirmed in decrees signed by USSR President Gorbachev. *Izvestiya*, 14 September 1991, union edition, p. 2, trans. in FBIS-SOV-91-182, 19 September 1991, pp. 23-24.

21. Bakatin, Russian Television Network, 1731 GMT, 29 August 1991, trans. in FBIS-SOV-91-170, 3 September 1991, p. 46. Temporary First Deputy Chairman Gennadiy Titov said in radio interview on 29 August that "the overwhelming majority" of collegium members had been removed. All-Union Radio Mayak Network, 1900 GMT, 29 August 1991, trans. in FBIS-SOV-91-170, 3 September 1991, p. 53.

22. Viktor Ivanenko, BBC Television Network (London) in English, 2130 GMT, 28 August 1991, in FBIS-SOV-91-168, 29 August 1991, p. 96.

23. Viktor Ivanenko, interview on All-Union Radio Mayak Network, 1900 GMT, 29 August 1991, trans. in FBIS-SOV-91-170, 3 September 1991, p. 51.

24. Bakatin, *Izbavleniye ot KGB*, pp. 66-68.

25. *Ibid.*, p. 67.

26. TASS international service in Russian, 1845 GMT, 25 August 1991, trans. in FBIS-SOV-91-165, 26 August 1991, p. 29; Russian Television Network, 1731 GMT, 29 August 1991, trans. in FBIS-SOV-91-170, 3 September 1991, p. 46; and TASS international service in English, 1618 GMT, 28 August 1991, in FBIS-SOV-91-168, 29 August 1991, p. 39.

27. Grushko is described as a specialist in Scandinavia and East Germany. As chief of Foreign Counterintelligence (Department KR of the First Chief Directorate) in the 1980s, he was tasked with infiltrating foreign intelligence services and Russian emigre organizations. His last foreign assignment was as chief adviser to the Stasi in East Germany. There is speculation that he may have been involved with attempts to control the direction of the revolutions of 1989. Grushko was observed in Prague just prior to the ouster of the Husak regime in 1989. Viktor Yasmann, "KGB Reshuffling May Signify New Approach to Opposition Groups," RFE/RL *Report on the USSR*, Vol. 8, No. 21, 22 February 1991.

28. Titov was expelled from Great Britain in 1971 and from Austria in 1984. Christopher Andrew and Oleg Gordievsky write, "Nicknamed 'the Crocodile,' Titov was deeply unpopular among his KGB colleagues (though not his superiors), and—save for a small group of proteges, feared by his subordinates. Gordievsky remembers Titov as the most unpleasant and unprincipled KGB officer he had ever met." Christopher Andrew and Oleg Gordievsky, *KGB: The Inside Story* (New York: Harper Collins, 1990), pp. 568-571.

29. TASS international service in Russian, citing a USSR presidential ukase, 1625 GMT, 29 August 1991, trans. in FBIS-SOV-91-169, 30 August 1991, p. 46.

30. Bakatin, interview with author, 22 September 1992. In his memoirs, Bakatin calls Oleynikov "An exceptionally able-bodied, ambitionless, experienced, benevolent person." Bakatin, *Izbavleniye ot KGB*, p. 68.

31. TASS international service in English, 0939 GMT, 29 August 1991, in FBIS-SOV-91-168, 29 August 1991, p. 39.

32. Ageyev was arrested following a 27 September authorization passed by the RSFSR Supreme Soviet. Russian Procurator General Valentin Stepankov said, "Acting on orders from Vladimir Kryuchkov, Ageyev organized measures to isolate the president of the USSR and deprive him of means of communication." The prosecutor added that on 19 August Ageyev had directed all KGB organs "to preclude the possibility of the transfer of information aimed at consolidating

forces opposing decisions of the State Committee for the State of Emergency." He added, "Later, Ageyev worked out concrete measures aimed at the seizure of the Russian parliament building and the removal from power of leaders of the republic. He ordered the internment of a large group of most active opponents to the State Committee for the State of Emergency, among them Russia's and USSR people's deputies." TASS international service in English, 1549 GMT, 27 September 1991, in FBIS-SOV-91-189, 30 September 1991, pp. 24-25.

33. *Izvestiya*, 14 September 1991, union edition, p. 2, trans. in FBIS-SOV-91-182, 19 September 1991, pp. 23-24.

34. Yevgeniya Albats, "KGB-MSB-MBVD: Substantive Changes?" *Moscow News*, 13 January 1992, p. 5.

35. TASS international service in English, 1219 GMT, 12 September 1991, in FBIS-SOV-91-179, 13 September 1991, p. 25.

36. *Moskovskiye novosti*, No. 38, 22 September 1991, p. 11, trans. in FBIS-SOV-91-197, 10 October 1991, p. 28; *Izvestiya*, 14 September 1991, union edition, p. 2, trans. in FBIS-SOV-91-182, 19 September 1991, p. 24.

37. Shebarshin has received mixed reviews as an intelligence professional. When Kryuchkov became USSR KGB chairman in September 1988, Shebarshin replaced him as head of foreign intelligence. An expert on Afghanistan, Pakistan, Iran, and India, he began his career in the Foreign Ministry and was transferred to the KGB after his second diplomatic tour of Pakistan which ended in 1968. He was trained at what became known as the Andropov Institute and then worked at First Chief Directorate headquarters. In 1971 he was sent to India as head of Line PR (political intelligence) and, from 1975 to 1977, served as main *rezident*. Following the 1979 Islamic revolution in Iran, he was rezident in Teheran until expelled in 1983. Subsequently he was deputy chief of Directorate RI at Yasenevo, where foreign intelligence reports were prepared for the Soviet leadership. Gordievsky credits Shebarshin's apparently pleasing reports to the Politburo for his rapid rise over superiors to become head of the First Chief Directorate in 1988 when Kryuchkov became KGB chairman. Andrew and Gordievsky, p. 620.

A more personal and negative description of Shebarshin can be found in the memoirs of Vladimir Kuzichkin, a defector who worked with Shebarshin in Teheran. Kuzichkin does credit Shebarshin in some areas, however. Vladimir Kuzichkin, *Inside the KGB: My Life in Soviet Espionage* (New York: Ballantine, 1992), chapters 14, 17, and 18.

38. Bakatin, interview with author, 23 September 1992.

39. Radio Rossii, cited by TASS international service in Russian, 0950 GMT, 20 September 1991, in FBIS-SOV-91-183, 20 September 1991, p. 15; and *Komsomolskaya pravda*, 2 October 1991, pp. 2-3, trans. in FBIS-SOV-91-193, 4 October 1991, pp. 20-22.

40. TASS international service in English, 1958 GMT, 21 September 1991, in FBIS-SOV-91-184, 23 September 1991, p. 24.

41. *Komsomolskaya pravda*, 2 October 1991, pp. 2-3, trans. in FBIS-SOV-91-193, 4 October 1991, pp. 20-22.

42. In a three-hour interview with American journalist David Wise, the acting intelligence chief used his real name and patronymic, Vyacheslav Ivanovich, with

the alias Artyomov. Wise says that he found "from other sources" that Artyomov's real name is Gurgenev. See Wise, "House of Cards," *The Times* (London), 30 November 1991.

43. Bakatin, interview with author, 25 September 1992. Primakov recalled that just before he was to travel to the Middle East as a special envoy in the aftermath of the Iraqi invasion of Kuwait, "I received a telephone call from Bakatin, and he made this offer. At first, I was unable to take this in at all. Then, I thought about it. 'You know,' I said to Bakatin, 'I am departing on a trip, let us not decide anything for the time being.' But when I returned, Bakatin (as I understood it) had already brought this up with Mikhail Sergeyevich Gorbachev and Boris Nikolayevich Yeltsin. The president of the country at first offered me the post of adviser on foreign policy and foreign economic questions, but he said that there was also another offer—intelligence." *Nezavisimaya gazeta*, 21 December 1991, pp. 1, 5, trans. in FBIS-SOV-92-002, 3 January 1992, p. 6.

44. Bakatin, *Izbavleniye ot KGB*, p. 89.

45. Avigdor Haselkorn and Christopher Coker, "The Spies Who Stayed in the Cold," *European Security Analyst* No. 20 (London: Institute for European Defence and Strategic Studies), August 1992, p. 2. Also see Yevgeniy Primakov, "Studio Nine" program, Moscow Television discussion on situation in Asia, 1540 GMT, 27 December 1980, trans. in BBC Summary of World Broadcasts (hereafter referenced as BBCSWB), 21 January 1981, p. SU/6628/C/1.

46. Primakov, "Studio Nine" program, Moscow Television discussion of Middle East issues for the Soviet Far East, 0815 GMT, 25 July 1981, trans. in BBCSWB, 31 July 1981, p. SU/6789/C/1.

47. Radio Moscow in Arabic, 1600 GMT, 5 July 1985, trans. in BBCSWB, 12 July 1985, p. SU/8001/A4/1.

48. Gary Lee, "Afghanistan Pullout Predicted; Soviet Official Assesses Peace Talks," *Washington Post*, 26 December 1986, p. A25.

49. Czechoslovak Press Agency in English, 1845 GMT, 9 April 1987, trans. in BBCSWB, 11 April 1987, p. EE/8540/C/1.

50. Reuter Library Report, 3 October 1990.

51. Oleg Kalugin, cited by Albats, "KGB-MSB-MBVD."

52. Uri Ra'anan, "Soviet Global Policy," *Naval War College Review*, Vol. 24, No. 1, p. 30.

53. Transcript of USSR Supreme Soviet proceedings, in "The New Supreme Soviet Meets—IV," *Izvestiya*, 12 June 1989, pp. 2-3, trans. in *Current Digest of the Soviet Press*, Vol. 41, No. 33, 13 September 1989, p. 20.

54. *Moskovskiye novosti*, No. 38, 22 September 1991, p. 11, trans. in FBIS-SOV-91-197, 10 October 1991, p. 27.

55. TASS international service in Russian, 1921 GMT, 13 September 1991, trans. in FBIS-SOV-91-179, 16 September 1991, p. 23.

56. Bakatin, *Izbavleniye ot KGB*, p. 69.

57. *Ibid.*, p. 90.

58. *Ibid.*, p. 73.

59. *Ibid.*

60. *Ibid.*

61. *Komsomolskaya pravda*, 2 October 1991, pp. 2-3, trans. in FBIS-SOV-91-193, 4 October 1991, p. 22.

62. Bakatin, on Russian Television Network, 1731 GMT, 29 August 1991, trans. in FBIS-SOV-91-170, 3 September 1991, p. 46; Albats, "KGB-MSB-MBVD: Substantive Changes?"

63. Bakatin, Russian Television, 1731 GMT, 29 August 1991, trans. in FBIS-SOV-91-170, 3 September 1991, p. 42.

64. *Izvestiya*, 30 August 1991, union edition, p. 1, trans. in FBIS-SOV-91-169, 30 August 1991, p. 46.

65. All-Union Radio Mayak Network, 1900 GMT, 29 August 1991, trans. in FBIS-SOV-91-170, 3 September 1991, p. 53.

66. Bakatin, *Izbavleniye ot KGB*, p. 82.

67. *Izvestiya*, 14 September 1991, union edition, p. 2, trans. in FBIS-SOV-91-182, 19 September 1991, pp. 23-24.

68. Bakatin, *Izbavleniye ot KGB*, p. 71.

69. Wise, "House of Cards."

70. *Komsomolskaya pravda*, 27 August 1991, p. 1, trans. in FBIS-SOV-91-169, 30 August 1991, p. 47.

71. Bakatin, *Izbavleniye ot KGB*, pp. 54-55.

72. In February 1993 in Moscow I viewed an official photograph of Leonov at a 1963 USSR-Cuba signing ceremony. Leonov, then a young officer, stood immediately to the right of Khrushchev during the ceremony. To Khrushchev's left stood Castro; to the Cuban leader's left stood Politburo member Mikhail Suslov. The photograph is in Leonov's collection.

73. Eighteen months after the fact, Leonov was unrepentant and reaffirmed what he saw as the righteousness of having worked with Soyuz. Nikolay Leonov, unpublished interview with Leonid Velhekov, February 1993.

74. *Moskovskiye novosti*, No. 38, 22 September 1991, p. 11, trans. in FBIS-SOV-91-197, 10 October 1991, pp. 26-27.

75. *Izvestiya*, 18 September 1991, union edition, p. 4, trans. in FBIS-SOV-91-183, 20 September 1991, pp. 15-16; and *Moskovskiye novosti*, No. 38, 22 September 1991, p. 11, trans. in FBIS-SOV-91-197, 10 October 1991, pp. 26-27.

76. Albats, "KGB-MSB-MBVD," and Bakatin, interview with author, 25 September 1992.

77. TASS international service in English, 1636 GMT, 28 August 1991, in FBIS-SOV-91-168, 29 August 1991, p. 39.

78. Savostyanov was a reserve lieutenant, but his service was not publicly identified. Victor Yasmann of Radio Liberty states that Savostyanov was a junior officer in the KGB Academic Reserve. He was the city official responsible for the sealing of the CPSU Central Committee building on Staraya Square to stem the hemorrhaging of documents following the putsch. He announced over the building intercom that all employees had one hour to leave the premises and later told a reporter, "I was so happy to get to make that announcement. Those were the 15 happiest minutes of my life." *Moskovskiye novosti*, No. 38, 22 September 1991, p. 11, trans. in FBIS-SOV-91-197, 10 October 1991, pp. 26-27; and Elizabeth Shogren, "Angry Muscovites Clamor for Justice," *Los Angeles Times*, 24 August

1991, p. 1. Also, author's interview with Savostyanov at Lubyanka, Moscow, 7 December 1991.

79. Savostyanov kept a photograph in his office of himself with Murashev leading a January 1989 anti-Communist demonstration in Moscow. Author's observation during meeting with Savostyanov at Lubyanka, 7 December 1991. For an in-depth profile of Murashev, see Jonas Bernstein, "Offbeat Russian Heat," *Insight*, 14 June 1992, pp. 6-11, 26-27.

80. Bakatin, *Izbavleniye ot KGB*, p. 73.

81. Savostyanov, interview with author.

82. Bakatin, interview with author, 23 September 1992.

83. TASS international service in English, 0939 GMT, 29 August 1991, in FBIS-SOV-91-168, 29 August 1991, p. 39. Stolyarov, a colonel, was a lecturer of Marxism-Leninism at the Gagarin Air Force Academy from 1980 to the time of his appointment to the KGB in 1991. Elected to the Party Control Committee of the Russian Federation in 1990, he was identified with the "akademocrat" faction. He joined Rutskoi as a founder of Communists for Democracy (subsequently renamed the Democratic Party of Russia) which called itself an alternative and legal structure of the Russian Communist Party. Victor Yasmann, "The KGB and Internal Security," *RFE/RL Research Report*, 3 January 1992, p. 21.

84. Bakatin, interview with author, 22 September 1992.

85. *Ibid.*

86. Bakatin, in *Izvestiya*, 2 January 1992, morning edition, p. 6, trans. in FBIS-SOV-92-002, 3 January 1992, pp. 4-5.

87. Bakatin, *Izbavleniye ot KGB*, p. 72.

88. *Ibid.*

89. Russian Television Network, 2108 GMT, 19 September 1991, trans. in FBIS-SOV-91-184, 23 September 1991, pp. 25-26.

90. Those generals, Bakatin said, were Plekhanov, Generalov, Beda, Gluzchenko, Rasshchepov, Karpukhin, Grushko, and Ageyev. *Moskovskiye novosti*, No. 36, 8 September 1991, p. 6, trans. in FBIS-SOV-91-182, 19 September 1991, pp. 22-23.

91. Col. Alexander Kichikhin, "Fortress Against Reform: The KGB Has Changed Its Name, but Not Much Else," *Crossroads*, was a KGB officer from 1977 to 1991, worked in the Fifth Chief Directorate. He was fired by KGB Chairman Kryuchkov for refusing to carry out orders during the putsch and became a harsh critic of the chekists. He served from October 1991 to April 1992 as an adviser to the Russian Supreme Soviet Commission to Investigate the Causes and Circumstances of the August Putsch, chaired by Lev Ponomarev.

92. Lev Ponomarev, chairman of the Russian parliamentary Committee to Investigate the Causes and Circumstances of the August Putsch (also known as the Ponomarev Commission), on All-Union Radio Mayak Network, Moscow, 1540 GMT, 25 December 1991, trans. in FBIS-SOV-91-248, 26 December 1991, p. 42. Aleksey Surkov, a member of the commission, told Radio Mayak that the commission found that militsiya leaders who supported the putsch were subsequently appointed to "major leading posts" in the USSR MVD. Another commission member, Deputy Lyushenkov, said that army commanders supportive of the putsch "are still occupying high-level posts and are being promoted." In

1993, a state security spokesman confirmed the approximate number of chekists removed. Lt. Col. Aleksey Petrovich Kandaurov, deputy chief of public affairs of the Ministry of Security, said that thirty officers were removed because of their involvement in the putsch. Aleksey Petrovich Kandaurov, presentation at "KGB: Yesterday, Today and Tomorrow," conference sponsored by the Glasnost Foundation, Moscow, 19 February 1993.

93. TASS international service in Russian, 1930 GMT, 11 September 1991, trans. in FBIS-SOV-91-178, 13 September 1991, pp. 35-36.

94. Russian Television Network, 1731 GMT, 29 August 1991, trans. in FBIS-SOV-91-170, 3 September 1991, p. 46.

95. Alexander Rahr, "Reform of Russia's State Security Apparatus." *RFE/RL Research Report*, Vol. 3, No. 8, 25 February 1994, pp. 19-30.

96. For his part, Bakatin said that Savostyanov, who ran day-to-day affairs in the Moscow City Council, impressed him as a capable administrator. Bakatin, *Izbavleniye ot KGB*, pp. 84-85.

97. Yevgeniy Savostyanov, *Nezavisimaya gazeta*, 6 September 1991, p. 2, trans. in *Soviet Press Digest*, 26 September 1991.

98. Russian Television Network, 2108 GMT, 19 September 1991, trans. in FBIS-SOV-91-184, 23 September 1991, pp. 25-26.

99. *Moscow News* in English, No. 41.

100. Oleg Zadkirov, statement at "KGB: Yesterday, Today and Tomorrow," conference sponsored by the Glasnost Foundation, Moscow, 20 February 1993. Zadkirov said that as a "non-conformist" he was expelled from the Communist Party and declared unfit for professional duties, after 15 years' service. Curiously, he added that the pressure for him to leave Smolensk included offers of a "promotion, transfer to another city, and higher rank." See Zadkirov, "System of Repressing KGB Personnel Members' Personality," *KGB: Yesterday, Today, Tomorrow (Collected Reports)* ed. and trans. E. Oznobkina and L. Isakova (Moscow: Glasnost Foundation/Znak -S.P. Gandalf, 1993), pp. 62-64.

101. Author's confidential interviews with Russian journalists and former KGB officers, Moscow, April 1994; and Victor Yasmann, "Domestic Aspects of the New Russian Military Doctrine," paper delivered to a conference organized by the Hanns Seidel Stiftung, Wildbad Kreuth, Germany, 21-23 March 1994, pp. 10-11.

102. Ibid., and author's confidential interview with a western businessman involved in minerals extraction.

103. RSFSR People's Deputy Nikolay Ryabov, deputy chairman of the State Commission to Investigate the Activity of State Security Organs, in *Rossiyskaya gazeta*, 18 September 1991, p. 1, trans. in FBIS-SOV-91-181, 18 September 1991, p. 25.

104. *Moscow News*, No. 41.

105. *Rossiyskaya gazeta*, citing Vadim Bakatin in *Der Spiegel*, 26 November 1991, first edition, p. 3, trans. in FBIS-SOV-91-231, 2 December 1991, p. 21.

106. *Literaturnaya gazeta*, No. 50, 18 December 1991, pp. 2, 3, trans. in FBIS-SOV-91-249, 27 December 1991, p. 14. Although he is by his own admission a product of the apparat, Bakatin's analysis is remarkably similar to the one Václav Havel expressed in his "corrupted moral environment" speech of 30

January 1990. Václav Havel, "New Year's Address," *Open Letters: Selected Writings, 1965-1990* (New York: Knopf, 1991), p. 390. For a greater discussion of the "contaminated moral environment" and what reformers under communism did to try to redeem their societies in Central and Eastern Europe, see George Weigel, *The Final Revolution: The Resistance Church and the Collapse of Communism* (New York and Oxford: Oxford University Press, 1992).

107. *Literaturnaya gazeta*, No. 50, p. 14.

108. Bakatin, in *Izvestiya*, 2 January 1992, morning edition, p. 6, trans. in FBIS-SOV-92-002, 3 January 1992, pp. 4-5.

109. Sergey Stepashin, on All-Union Radio Mayak Network, 1900 GMT, 29 August 1991, trans. in FBIS-SOV-91-170, 3 September 1991, p. 50.

110. All-Union Radio First Program Radio-1 Network, 1900 GMT, 29 August 1991, trans. in FBIS-SOV-91-169, 30 August 1991, pp. 47-48; All-Union Radio Mayak Network, 1900 GMT, 29 August 1991, trans. in FBIS-SOV-91-170, 3 September 1991, p. 50.

111. *Izvestiya*, 14 September 1991, union edition, p. 2, trans. in FBIS-SOV-91-182, 19 September 1991, p. 24.

112. Yevgeniya Albats, interview with author. She says that her ouster from the commission was engineered by Nikolay Kuznetsov after she would not yield in her insistence that the KGB be completely abolished.

113. Bakatin, interview with author, 25 September 1992.

114. TASS report in *Pravda*, 25 September 1991, single edition, p. 6, trans. in FBIS-SOV-91-191, 2 October 1991, p. 35.

115. *Ibid.*

116. *Ibid.*

117. Radio Rossii Network, 1000 GMT, 26 September 1991, trans. in FBIS-SOV-91-188, 27 September 1991, p. 16.

118. Bakatin, interview with author, 25 September 1992.

119. Kichikhin, p. 8.

120. *Izvestiya*, 30 August 1991, union edition, p. 1, trans. in FBIS-SOV-91-169, 30 August 1991, p. 46.

121. Yasmann, "The KGB and Internal Security," p. 21.

122. *Izvestiya*, 18 September 1991, union edition, p. 4, trans. in FBIS-SOV-91-183, 20 September 1991, pp. 15-17.

123. George Lardner, Jr., and Gary Lee, "Russian Security Group Meets with U.S. Intelligence to Seek Cooperation," *Washington Post*, 14 October 1991, p. A4.

124. All-Union Radio Mayak Network, 1900 GMT, 27 November 1991, trans. in FBIS-SOV-91-230, 29 November 1991, pp. 13-15.

125. Alexander Rahr, "Old KGB Remains Alive and Well in Post-Soviet Russia," *RFE/RL Post-Soviet/East European Report*, Vol. 9, No. 17, 10 March 1992.

126. *Komsomolskaya pravda*, 2 October 1991, pp. 2-3, trans. in FBIS-SOV-91-193, 4 October 1991, p. 22.

127. Bakatin, *Izbavleniye ot KGB*, p. 87.

128. *Ibid.*, p. 88.

129. TASS, 6 November 1991, cited by RFE/RL *Daily Report*, No. 213, 8 November 1991, p. 1.

130. Bakatin, *Izbavleniye ot KGB*, pp. 88-89.

131. Primakov, in *Nezavisimaya gazeta*, 21 December 1991, pp. 1, 5, trans. in FBIS-SOV-92-002, 3 January 1992, p. 8.

132. Bakatin, cited by David Wise, "House of Cards."

133. Bakatin, *Izbavleniye ot KGB*, pp. 84-85.

134. Yasmann, "The KGB and Internal Security," pp. 19-20. Vladimir Rubanov called it the General Communications Directorate while Yasmann termed the unit the Government Communications Committee. James Sherr called it the USSR President's Committee for Government Communications, in "Change and Continuity in the Former KGB," *Jane's Intelligence Review*, March 1993, p. 111.

135. Bakatin, *Izbavleniye ot KGB*, p. 82.

136. TASS, 6 November 1991, cited by *RFE/RL Daily Report*, No. 213, 8 November 1991, p. 1.

137. Mark Galeotti, "Police and Paramilitaries: Public Order Forces and Resources," *RL Report on the USSR*, 8 June 1990, pp. 8-9; Gabriel Schoenfeld, "Outer Limits: A Special Survey of the Former USSR's Multiple (and Multiplying) Border Problems," *Post-Soviet Prospects*, Center for Strategic and International Studies, No. 17, January 1993; and Wise, "House of Cards."

138. Natalya Gevorkyan, "The KGB: 'They Still Need Us,'" *The Bulletin of the Atomic Scientists*, January/February 1993, p. 37, citing Bakatin.

139. Deputy Chief of Staff Maj. Gen. Viktor Zemtsov, *Krasnaya zvezda*, 7 December 1991, first edition, p. 1, trans. in FBIS-SOV-91-240, 13 December 1991, p. 22.

140. TASS international service in Russian, 1400 GMT, 4 December 1991, trans. in FBIS-SOV-91-233, 4 December 1991, pp. 23-24. KGB Border Troops had been trained and deployed to operate internally against civil unrest. Mark Galeotti wrote in 1990, "Although the 175,000 border troops lack the training or equipment for maintenance of public order, one of the lessons learned in Azerbaijan was the importance of sealing off crisis areas. Border Troops Commander Lieutenant General (KGB) Ilya Kalinichenko took personal charge of this phase of the operation, and the leadership's view that this was a necessary precondition to 'pacification' was reflected in the emphasis given to similar operations in Lithuania. Baltic Border District Commandant Lieutenant General (KGB) Valentin Gaponenko confirmed that additional units were deployed to secure the republic's frontiers, both international and internal, while KGB *Okhrana osobykh* ('Special Installations Guards') were used alongside paratroopers to secure Party buildings in Vilnius." Galeotti, "Police and Paramilitaries."

141. Zemtsov.

142. TASS international service in Russian, 1400 GMT, 4 December 1991, trans. in FBIS-SOV-91-233, 4 December 1991, pp. 23-24.

143. Teleradiokompaniya Ostankino Television First Program Network (Moscow), 1800 GMT, 28 February 1992, trans. in FBIS-SOV-92-041, 2 March 1992, p. 9.

144. Author's interview with an American businessman who traveled through Georgia in May 1993, and sighted the Russian Border Troops units.

145. *Komsomolskaya pravda*, 20 September 1991, p. 2, trans. in FBIS-SOV-91-187, 26 September 1992, p. 22.

146. TASS in English, 1703 GMT, 4 September 1991, in FBIS-SOV-91-172, 5 September 1991, pp. 53-54.

147. Vadim Bakatin, in interview with author, 25 September 1992.

148. TASS, 6 November 1991, cited in *RFE/RL Daily Report*, No. 213, 8 November 1991, p. 1.

149. Bakatin, interview with author, 18 September 1992.

150. A week after becoming KGB chairman, Bakatin said, "As for military counterintelligence, let it be in the Army. I'm not saying that we shouldn't have any operational positions in the army from the point of view of intelligence. That's another matter. I'm talking about military counterintelligence which . . . performs the functions vested in it. Let the minister of defense answer for it. It should be part of the Army." Russian Television Network, 1731 GMT, 29 August 1991, trans. in FBIS-SOV-91-170, 3 September 1991, p. 46.

151. Bakatin, interview with author, 25 September 1992. The USSR KGB announced that an order had been issued to dissolve military counterintelligence as manifested by the Third Directorate. *Izvestiya*, 14 September 1991, union edition, p. 1, trans. in FBIS-SOV-91-183, 20 September 1991, p. 15.

152. Bakatin, p. 90.

153. *Ibid.*

154. *Ibid.*, p. 93.

155. *RFE/RL Daily Report*, No. 238, 17 December 1991, p. 2.

156. *Moskovskiye novosti*, No. 38, 22 September 1991, p. 11, trans. in FBIS-SOV-91-197, 10 October 1991, p. 27.

157. *Izvestiya*, 15 October 1991, union edition, p. 2, trans. in FBIS-SOV-91-202, 18 October 1991, p. 22.

158. Yevgeniy Savostyanov, interview with author at Lubyanka, Moscow, 7 December 1991. Savostyanov was RSFSR KGB deputy chairman, and chief of the KGB for Moscow and Moscow oblast until the RSFSR KGB was renamed the Federal Security Agency (Agentsvo federalnoy bezopasnosti, AFB) in November 1991. He retained the same ranks in the AFB. A journalist with unusually reliable sources reported, "This department was scrapped in the . . . central apparat: part of its personnel went over to counterintelligence, another part—to the Department for Combatting Organized Crime, and quite a few to the corridors of Russia's White House." Albats, "KGB-MSB-MBVD," p. 5.

159. Graham H. Turbiville and Harold S. Orenstein, "Observations from Rubanov Visit," Fort Leavenworth Soviet Army Studies, unpublished document, n.d., January 1992, based on interviews with MSB Analytical Directorate Chief Vladimir Rubanov, pp. 3-4.

160. Rubanov joined the KGB in 1971 in Voronezh and in 1982 was transferred to the Second Chief Directorate. Subsequently he served in the KGB Research Institute for Problems of Information. He helped initiate a program to lift secrecy in 1986, prior to the first wave of glasnost which began after the 26th CPSU Congress. In 1988 he published an article on secrecy in *International Affairs* for which Kryuchkov dismissed him from the KGB. Bakatin, then USSR MVD Minister, then hired him as a personal assistant. See Yasmann, "The KGB and

Internal Security," p. 21. Rubanov remains a vocal reform advocate and identifies with the Democratic Russia political movement.

161. Turbiville and Orenstein, pp. 5, 6. They note, "Part of the reason for this two-tiered process is evidently to make assessments or agreements palatable to their target audience, a factor much more important for a coordinating agency seeking consensus among republics than one that simply issued directives or unchallenged assessments. This group also plays a key role in concluding security treaties between the MSB and their republican analogs. Rubanov said, in illustration, that the higher analytical group would decide if a proposal to a republic government should be taken to the individuals themselves, if a delegation should go along, if the recipients should be invited to Moscow, or whatever seemed best designed to get a positive response. Rubanov allowed as how his own directorate could perform this second function as well, if required to do so."

162. *Ibid.*, p. 4.

163. *Ibid.*, p. 6; and Bakatin in *Izvestiya*, 2 January 1992, morning edition, p. 6, trans. in FBIS-SOV-92-002, 3 January 1992, p. 4.

164. Bakatin, speech to USSR Supreme Soviet, All-Union Radio Mayak Network, 1900 GMT, 27 November 1991, trans. in FBIS-SOV-91-230, 29 November 1991, pp. 13-15.

165. Bakatin, interview with author, 22 September 1992.

166. Bakatin, speech to USSR Supreme Soviet.

167. Bakatin, interview with author, 22 September 1992.

168. TASS world service in Russian, 1856 GMT, 16 December 1991, trans. in BBCSWB, 18 December 1991, p. SU/1258/A1/1; Radio Moscow world service in English, 2010 GMT, 18 December 1991, in BBCSWB, 20 December 1991, p. SU/1260/A1/1; and TASS world service in Russian, 1647 GMT, 23 December 1991, trans. in BBCSWB, 28 December 1991, p. SU/1264/B/1.

169. Postfactum (Moscow) in English, 1220 GMT, 20 December 1991, in FBIS-SOV-91-248, 26 December 1991, p. 60.

170. The Germany conference was sponsored in Potsdam by the International Freedom Foundation. The U.S. event was hosted by the Soviet Army Studies Center at Fort Leavenworth, Kansas.

171. *Izvestiya*, 14 September 1991, union edition, p. 1, trans. in FBIS-SOV-91-183, 20 September 1991, p. 15.

172. All-Union Radio First Program Radio-1 Network, 1540 GMT, 26 September 1991, trans. in FBIS-SOV-91-188, 27 September 1991, p. 15; and "Vesti," Russian Television Network, 2000 GMT, 26 September 1991, trans. in *ibid.*, p. 45.

173. *Moskovskiye novosti*, No. 38, 22 September 1991, p. 11, trans. in FBIS-SOV-91-197, 10 October 1991, p. 27.

174. All-Union Radio Mayak Network (Moscow), 1500 GMT, 27 September 1991, trans. in FBIS-SOV-91-189, 30 September 1991, p. 64.

175. RSFSR KGB Chairman Viktor Ivanenko, in Central Television First Program Network (Moscow), 1800 GMT, 25 September 1991, trans. in FBIS-SOV-91-187, 26 September 1991, p. 53.

176. Alexander Rahr, "Old KGB Remains Alive and Well."

177. Radio Rossii Network (Moscow), 1300 GMT, 5 October 1991, trans. in FBIS-SOV-91-194, 7 October 1991, p. 54.

178. Bakatin, interview with author, 25 September 1992. Bakatin said that if the Russian Federation had been permitted to absorb completely the KGB apparatus on Russian territory, the result would have been "every republic grabbing what it could from the Union."

179. Sources A and W, interviews with author.

180. Oleg Kalugin, statement at "KGB: Yesterday, Today and Tomorrow," conference sponsored by the Glasnost Foundation, Moscow, 19 February 1993.

181. Bakatin, interview with author, 25 September 1992.

182. Alexander Rahr, "Reform of Russia's State Security Apparatus," *RFE/RL Research Report*, Vol. 3, No. 8, 25 February 1994, p. 26.

183. *Rossiyskaya gazeta*, 28 November 1991, first edition, p. 1; and Moscow TASS international service in Russian, 1256 GMT, 29 November 1991, in FBIS-SOV-91-231, 2 December 1991, p. 43.

184. Lev Ponomarev, chairman of the Russian parliamentary Committee to Investigate the Causes and Circumstances of the August Putsch, on All-Union Radio Mayak Network, Moscow, 1540 GMT, 25 December 1991, trans. in FBIS-SOV-91-248, 26 December 1991, p. 42.

185. Igor Gvritishvili and Andrei Palaria, TASS world service in Russian, 1256 GMT, 29 November 1991, trans. in BBCSWB, 3 December 1991, p. SU/1245/B/1.

186. Savostyanov to author.

Chapter 4

1. For a discussion of the generational gap in the KGB, see Alexander Rahr, "Reform of Russia's State Security Apparatus," *RFE/RL Research Report*, Vol. 3, No. 8, 25 February 1994, pp. 19-30.

2. Yuriy Shchekochikhin, Russian Television Network, 1800 GMT, 20 December 1991, trans. in FBIS-SOV-91-246, 23 December 1991, p. 46.

3. *Ibid.*, pp. 46-47.

4. Yevgeniya Albats, "KGB-MSB-MBVD: Substantive Changes?" *Moscow News*, No. 12, 13 January 1992, p. 5.

5. *Ibid.*

6. *Izvestiya*, 2 January 1992, morning edition, p. 6, trans. in FBIS-SOV-92-002, 3 January 1992, pp. 4-5.

7. The decree instructed that the MBVD be created "on the basis of the disbanded USSR Ministry of Internal Affairs, the RSFSR Ministry of Internal Affairs, the Inter-Republican Security Service and the RSFSR Federal Security Agency. To establish that, under the legislation in force, all the buildings and constructions, as well as the material-technical means, data bases and systems, official documents and other property of the disbanded ministries and agencies will become the state property of the RSFSR." Text of decree, in *Postfactum* in English, 1630 GMT, 19 December 1991, trans. in BBCSWB, 21 December 1991, p. SU/1261/B/1.

8. Vadim Bakatin, interview with author, 22 September 1992; and Yuri Shchekochikhin, *Literaturnaya gazeta* investigative journalist and former USSR people's peputy interview with author, 31 March 1992.

9. Bakatin, interviews with author, 22 and 25 September 1992.

10. Barannikov later told the Russian Supreme Soviet, "Development of the new combined ministry has been in progress since 1990. In November, 1991, there was a state soviet meeting where the decision was made whereby the two leaders of the authorities--the Union MVD and the Union Ministry of Security [*sic;* Barannikov means the Inter-republic Security Service]--were instructed to develop this structure. Then, you know, the union structure was done away with. And the President then decided to create these structures." Viktor Barannikov, testimony before the Russian Federation Supreme Soviet Hearings Concerning the Events Associated with the Attempted Coup d'Etat of August 19-21, 1991, Moscow, 4 February 1992. A translation in English is housed in the Special Collections at Mugar Library, Boston University.

11. *Izvestiya,* 21 December 1991, union edition, p. 1, trans. in FBIS-SOV-91-247, 24 December 1991, pp. 23-24.

12. Sergei Shakhrai, interview with Oleg Ivanov on "Facing Russia," Russian television 1645 GMT, 6 January 1992, trans. in BBCSWB, 8 January 1992, p. SU/1272/B/1.

13. MVD Major General Vladislav Nasinovsky, in Interfax in English, 1633 GMT, 28 January 1992, in FBIS-SOV-92-019, 29 January 1992, pp. 31-32.

14. I. Kadulin, *Komsomolskaya pravda,* 26 December 1991, p. 1, trans. in *Soviet Press Digest,* 26 December 1991.

15. TASS world service in English, 2303 GMT, 26 December 1991, trans. in BBCSWB, 30 December 1991, p. SU/1265/B/1.

16. Bakatin, interview with author, 25 September 1992.

17. *Moskovsky komsomolets,* 20 December 1991, p. 1, trans. in *Soviet Press Digest,* 20 December 1991; *Izvestiya,* 21 December 1991, union edition, p. 1, trans. in FBIS-SOV-91-247, 24 December 1991, p. 23. RSFSR Supreme Soviet First Deputy Chairman Sergey Filatov said that he "had a telephone conversation with First Deputy Chairman of the RSFSR Government Gennadiy Burbulis in which the latter was puzzled by the signing of the decree." *Postfactum* in English, 1638 GMT, 20 December 1991, in FBIS-SOV-91-246, 23 December 1991, p. 47.

18. *Postfactum,* 1630 GMT, 19 December 1991, trans. in BBCSWB, 21 December 1991, p. SU/1261/B/1.

19. TASS in English, 1536 GMT, 24 December 1991, in FBIS-SOV-91-248, 26 December 1991, pp. 41-42.

20. Yuriy Rostov, Russian television, 1800 GMT, 20 December 1991, trans. in BBCSWB, 23 December 1991, p. SU/1262/B/1. Rostov commented, "I don't think the failure to explain all these things is intentional. Anybody who knows anything about present Russian structures would agree with this. This is simply the result of a failure to ensure that the decisive actions now being taken are always thought out and, most important of all, prepared properly. Not all members of the government service are sufficiently competent."

21. *Izvestiya,* 21 December 1991, union edition, p. 1, trans. in FBIS-SOV-91-247, 24 December 1991, p. 23.

22. FBIS editorial report citing *Postfactum* in English, 1638 GMT, 20 December 1991, in FBIS-SOV-91-246, 23 December 1991, p. 47.

23. A. A. Aslakhanov, in FBIS editorial report of Russian Television Network, 1653 GMT, 28 December 1991, FBIS-SOV-92-251, 31 December 1991, p. 35.

24. Nikolai N. Kuznetsov, chairman of the Subcommittee on Security of the Committee on Defense and Security of the Russian Supreme Soviet and a career KGB officer, on *Postfactum*, 1630 GMT, 19 December 1991, trans. in BBCSWB, 21 December 1991, p. SU/1261/B/1.

25. *Nezavisimaya gazeta*, 24 January 1992, p. 2, trans. in *Soviet Press Digest*, 24 January 1992. Kuznetsov pointed to Barannikov as the author. Interfax in English, 2046 GMT, 24 December 1991, in FBIS-SOV-91-247, 24 December 1991, p. 48.

26. Bakatin, interview with author, 22 September 1992.

27. Shchekochikhin, Russian Television Network, 1800 GMT, 20 December 1991, trans. in FBIS-SOV-91-246, 23 December 1991, p. 47.

28. Russian television, 1800 GMT, 20 December 1991, trans. in BBCSWB, 23 December 1991, SU/1262/B/1.

29. V. Shuykov, secretary of the Russian Supreme Soviet Committee on Defense and Security, Central Television First Program Network, 1000 GMT, 26 December 1991, trans. in FBIS-SOV-91-248, 26 December 1991, p. 48.

30. Yuriy Rostov and Yuriy Shchekochikhin, Russian television, 1800 GMT, 20 December 1991, trans. in BBCSWB, 23 December 1991, p. SU/1262/B/1.

31. Valeriy Rudnev, *Izvestiya*, union edition, 31 December 1991, trans. in BBCSWB, SU/1267/B/1, 1 January 1992.

32. TASS international service in English, 0034 GMT, 21 December 1991, in FBIS-SOV-91-246, 23 December 1991, p. 45.

33. Yuriy Shchekochikhin, Russian Television Network, 1800 GMT, 20 December 1991, trans. in FBIS-SOV-91-246, 23 December 1991, p. 46.

34. Albats, "KGB-MSB-MBVD: Substantive Changes?" p. 5.

35. Interfax in English, 2022 GMT, 30 January 1992, in FBIS-SOV-92-023, 4 February 1992, pp. 54-55.

36. TASS world service in English, 1514 GMT, 25 December 1991, in BBCSWB, 28 December 1991, p. SU/1264/B/1.

37. Radio Rossii, 0300 GMT, 2 January 1992, citing *Nezavisimaya gazeta*, trans. in BBCSWB, 3 January 1992, SU/1268/B/1.

38. The chief of the Federal Security Agency (AFB) in Buryat called the decree a "mistake" and said, "Boris Yeltsin is now creating a still more mighty monster, which is analogous to the NKVD." The Commander of the Novosibirsk Higher Courses of Military Counterintelligence conceded that Yeltsin might not have had an alternative to creating the MBVD to protect the structures from claims by non-Russian republics but expressed hope that the transition period would be short and that state security and MVD organs "should exist separately." FBIS editorial report from *Postfactum* in English, 1639 GMT, 20 December 1991, in FBIS-SOV-91-246, 23 December 1991, pp. 47-48.

39. *Rossiyskaya gazeta*, 28 December 1991, first edition, p. 1, trans. in FBIS-SOV-91-251, 31 December 1991, p. 34.

40. *Komsomolskaya pravda*, 26 December 1991, p. 1, trans. in FBIS-SOV-92-001, 2 January 1992, p. 53.

41. It was noted, "The MVD gains access to the special equipment, the scientific and analytical potential, and the information base of the former KGB." *Rossiyskaya gazeta*, 28 December 1991, first edition, p. 1, trans. in FBIS-SOV-91-251, 31 December 1991, p. 34.

42. Petrov and Ilyushin "accompany the President during his tours around the country to arrange meetings with local *nomenklatura* bureaucrats who influence the President's decisions in a most negative way." *Nezavisimaya gazeta*, 24 January 1992, p. 2, trans. in *Soviet Press Digest*, 24 January 1992.

43. *Ibid.*

44. Sergei Shakhrai, interview with Oleg Ivanov on "Facing Russia," Russian television 1645 GMT, 6 January 1992, trans. in BBCSWB, 8 January 1992, p. SU/1272/B/1.

45. News conference coverage, Central Television First Program Network, 1900 GMT, 24 December 1991, trans. in FBIS-SOV-91-251, 31 December 1991, p. 33.

46. Barannikov interviews, All-Union Radio Mayak, 1100 GMT, 28 December 1991, trans. in BBCSWB, 30 December 1991, p. SU/1265/C3/1; and *Izvestiya*, union edition, 31 December 1991, trans. in BBCSWB, 1 January 1992, p. SU/1267/B/1.

47. Barannikov, on All-Union Radio Mayak Network, 1100 GMT, 28 December 1991, trans. in FBIS-SOV-92-001, 2 January 1992, pp. 56-57.

48. Barannikov interview, in *Izvestiya*, union edition, 31 December 1991, trans. in BBCSWB, 1 January 1992, p. SU/1267/B/1.

49. See Chapter 6.

50. *Moskovsky komsomolets*, 17 January 1992, p. 1, trans. in *Soviet Press Digest*, 17 January 1992.

51. Presidential decree No. 42, "On the formation of the Russian Federation Ministry of Security," 24 January 1992, published in *Rossiyskaya gazeta*, first edition, 30 January 1992, trans. in BBCSWB, 1 February 1992, SU/1293/B/1.

52. Aleksandr Gurov, deputy chief of public relations, Ministry of Security, interview with RFE/RL Russian Service, 25 August 1992, cited by Victor Yasmann, "Where Has the KGB Gone?" *RFE/RL Research Report*, Vol. 2, No. 2, 8 January 1993.

53. Lev Ponomarev, Chairman, Supreme Soviet Commission to Investigate the Causes and Circumstances of the August Putsch, in news conference sponsored by the Jamestown Foundation and the Ethics and Public Policy Center, Cannon House Office Building, Washington DC, 20 March 1992.

54. A clause in the decree that created the MB allowed Barannikov to "move his people from the internal affairs system to the federal security bodies which actually means a merger of these agencies," according to Aleksandr Tsopov, chairman of the Moscow City Council Anti-Criminality Subcommission, in Interfax in English, 2022 GMT, 30 January 1992, in FBIS-SOV-92-023, 4 February 1992, pp. 54-55.

55. Sergey Beloborodov, questioning Barannikov, testimony before the Russian Federation Supreme Soviet Hearings Concerning the Events Associated with the

Attempted Coup d'Etat of August 19-21, 1991, Moscow, 4 February 1992, pp. 103-104.

56. Oleynikov said, "At the moment I sit in my office and am formally considered unemployed. I have not yet received any offers from Barannikov. And I do not know whether I will be needed in this work." *Izvestiya*, 22 January 1992, morning edition, p. 2, trans. in FBIS-SOV-92-018, 28 January 1992, p. 40.

57. Beloborodov, p. 104.

58. People's Deputy Surkov, questioning Barannikov, testimony before the Russian Federation Supreme Soviet Hearings Concerning the Events Associated with the Attempted Coup d'Etat of August 19-21, 1991, Moscow, 4 February 1992, p. 106. Barannikov did not take issue with Surkov's assertion that Trubin had supported the coup attempt.

59. Decree No. 42 of the RSFSR President "On the Formation of the RSFSR Ministry of Security and Internal Affairs," 24 January 1992, *Rossiyskaya gazeta*, 30 January 1992, first edition, p. 3, trans. FBIS-SOV-92-021, 31 January 1992, pp. 30-31.

60. *Moskovskaya pravda*, 4 September 1992, cited by Yasmann, "Where Has the KGB Gone?"

61. Vadim Bakatin, *Izbavleniye ot KGB* (Moscow: Novosti, 1992), p. 46.

62. *Krasnaya zvezda*, 14 March 1992, p. 2, trans. in FBIS-SOV-92-042, 3 March 1992, pp. 45-46.

63. Natasha Gevorkyan, "The KGB: They Still Need Us," *The Bulletin of the Atomic Scientists*, January-February 1993, p. 38; and Gevorkyan, "Revanchism in the Security Forces," *Crossroads*, 15 March 1993, citing Bakatin.

64. The KGB was described as a "bloated" bureaucracy as early as 1974. See John Barron, *KGB: The Secret Work of Soviet Secret Agents* (New York: Reader's Digest Press/Bantam, 1974), p. 10.

65. Bakatin, *Izbavleniye ot KGB*, p. 40.

66. *Ibid.*, p. 46.

67. *Ibid.*, pp. 46-47.

68. Vyacheslav Trubnikov, first deputy head of the First Chief Directorate, *Nezavisimaya gazeta*, 16 September 1992.

69. *Izvestiya*, 22 January 1992, morning edition, p. 2, trans. in FBIS-SOV-92-018, 28 January 1992, p. 40.

70. Rahr, "Reform of Russia's State Security Apparatus," p. 28.

71. *Moskovskaya pravda*, 4 September 1992, and *Komsomolskaya pravda*, 14 November 1992, cited by Rahr, "Reform of Russia's State Security Apparatus," p. 28.

72. See Victor Yasmann, "Domestic Aspects of the New Russian Military Doctrine," paper delivered at the Hanns Seidel Stiftung, Wildbad Kreuth, Germany, 21-23 March 1994, pp. 11-12.

73. At a February 1993 conference on the KGB in Moscow, a Ministry of Security spokesman refused to divulge even a general number of officers on payroll. Instead, Col. Aleksey Kandaurov, deputy director of the MB public relations office, tried an old method—quoting foreign press reports—but was rebuffed by the audience. From author's notes at "KGB: Yesterday, Today and

Tomorrow," conference sponsored by the Glasnost Foundation, Moscow, 19-21 February 1993. Also see Gevorkyan, "Revanchism in the Security Forces," p. 4.

74. U.S. security and intelligence services total approximately 85,000 employees, not including military intelligence personnel. The Central Intelligence Agency consists of approximately 20,000 personnel, and the National Security Agency of approximately 20,000 to 24,000, according to Jeffrey Richelson, *The U.S. Intelligence Community*, 2nd ed. (New York: Harper Business Publishers, 1989), pp. 13, 23. The Federal Bureau of Investigation contains approximately 24,000 agents and staff members, and the Drug Enforcement Administration and Secret Service consist of 7,200 and 4,600 personnel respectively, according to the public affairs officers of each agency (various interviews with author). The U.S. Border Patrol is staffed below its authorized limit of 4,700 uniformed personnel, according to Jerry Seper, "A Thin Line Guards U.S. Boundaries," *Washington Times*, 5 July 1993.

75. *Kuranty*, 15 June 1992, p. 2.

76. Bakatin, *Izbavleniye ot KGB*, p. 81.

77. Amy Knight notes that there is no reliable estimate of guard troops. She cites a 1986 International Institute for Strategic Studies figure of 40,000 KGB special troops, which include the Kremlin Guard, Special Guards and Signal Guards. Amy Knight, *KGB: Police and Politics in the Soviet Union* (Boston: Unwin, Hyman, 1988, 1990), p. 226.

78. Bakatin, *Izbavleniye ot KGB*, p. 46.

79. Gordievsky writes that the First Chief Directorate had 12,000 staffers in the mid-1980s. Christopher Andrew and Oleg Gordievsky, *KGB: The Inside Story* (New York: Harper-Collins, 1990), p. 611. Source E, in an interview with the author, reported that the number increased markedly—to 16,000—by the time of the putsch in 1991. Knight puts the number in late 1991 at 15,000. Amy Knight, "Russian Security Services Under Yel'tsin," *Post-Soviet Affairs*, Vol. 9, No. 1, January-March 1993, p. 44, citing *Izvestiya*, 26 October 1991 and Interfax, 1700 GMT, 24 October 1991.

80. Knight, *ibid.*

81. Victor Yasmann, "The KGB and Internal Security," *The USSR and Successor States, RFE/RL Research Report*, 3 January 1992, pp. 19-20. In 1990 Lt. Gen. Nikolay Nikolayevich Andreyev, head of the KGB Eighth Chief Directorate responsible for electronic intelligence said that the unit employed substantially fewer persons than the 70,000 he attributed to his counterpart in the United States, the National Security Agency (NSA). However, there is no means of verifying Andreyev's statement. *Pravda*, 16 September 1990, second edition, p. 2, trans. in FBIS-SOV-90-185, 24 September 1990, p. 65. Andreyev says, "According to the foreign press there are about 25,000 specialists in NSA alone and approximately another 45,000 workers employed in the interests of NSA at radio intercept stations. . . . The amount of personnel and finances that we allocate in our country to counteract Western electronic intelligence is several times less than what is spent by NSA alone. . . ." Andreyev appeared to speak only of Soviet electronic counterintelligence, and did not address the size of the Eighth Chief Directorate.

82. Bakatin, interview with author, 17 September 1992. He told Amy Knight that "only a hundred or so" were fired. Knight, "Russian Security Services Under Yel'tsin," p. 44.

83. Member of the Supreme Soviet Commission on the Budget and Taxation and three other people's deputies, private conversation with author, July 1993.

84. Knight, "Russian Security Services Under Yel'tsin," pp. 48-49.

85. Observed Alexander Rahr: "The former KGB apparatus may still function to such a degree that it could be exploited by an authoritarian regime. Yeltsin seems to be repeating Gorbachev's mistake in trying to secure his personal power base by relying extensively on the structures of the Ministry of Security. . . . After he took control over the entire state security machine from Mikhail Gorbachev, Yeltsin stopped purges inside the state security organization and seemed to become more reluctant to open KGB archives to the public." Alexander Rahr, "Old KGB Remains Alive and Well in Post-Soviet Russia." *Post-Soviet/East European Report,* RFE/RL Research Institute, Vol. 9, No. 17, 10 March 1992.

86. *Ibid.*

87. Bakatin, interview with author, 20 September 1992.

88. *RFE/RL Daily Report,* No. 81, 28 April 1992, pp. 1-2.

89. The announcement was not officially made until 17 June, while President Yeltsin was abroad in the United States. However, *Komsomolskaya pravda* reported the personnel shakeup on 12 June. See FBIS-SOV-92-117, 17 June 1992, p. 28.

90. Gevorkyan, "The KGB: 'They Still Need Us,'" p. 37.

91. Interfax in English, 1607 GMT, 17 June 1992, in FBIS-SOV-92-118, 18 June 1992, p. 22. Radio Liberty transliterates the name from the Ukrainian as Mykola Holushko. Golushko started in the KGB in 1963. He served in the Keremovo KGB administration until 1974, and then to the central apparatus until 1987. From 1987 to 1991 he headed the Ukrainian KGB. Alexander Rahr, "Former Ukrainian KGB Chief Gets Top Security Post in Russia," *RFE/RL Daily Report,* No. 117, 23 June 1992, pp. 2-3. Knight reports that he was politically connected with hard-line former Politburo member Yegor Ligachev. Earlier, Golushko had served as KGB chief in Tomsk, where Ligachev was Party chief. Knight, "Russian Security Services Under Yel'tsin," pp. 47-48.

92. *Krasnaya zvezda,* 25 December 1992, p. 1, trans. in FBIS-SOV-92-249, 28 December 1992, p. 19.

93. *Komsomolskaya pravda,* 16 June 1992, p. 1, trans. in FBIS-SOV-92.

94. Sergei Mostovshchikov, "Border Guards Return to Chekists' Ranks," *Izvestiya,* 17 June 1992, morning edition, p. 2, trans. in FBIS-SOV-92-119, 19 June 1992, p. 40. Shlyakhtin was previously chief of the Central Asian District Border Troops, according to Michael Parrish, *Soviet Security and Intelligence Organizations, 1917-1990* (Westport, Connecticut: Greenwood Press, 1992), p. 394.

95. The text of the order, Presidential Decree 620, was published while Yeltsin was abroad, in *Rossiyskaya gazeta,* 16 June 1992, first edition, p. 5, trans. in FBIS-SOV-92-117, 17 June 1992, p. 24.

96. Source K, a former internal security officer, interview with author, Moscow, October 1992; and statements of former KGB Col. Vladimir Rubanov

and former KGB Maj. Gen. Oleg Kalugin, at "KGB: Yesterday, Today and Tomorrow," conference sponsored by the Glasnost Foundation, Moscow, 20 February 1993.

97. *Krasnaya zvezda*, 28 July 1992, p. 1, trans. in FBIS-SOV-92-145, 28 July 1992, p. 42.

98. John Dziak, *Chekisty: A History of the KGB* (Lexington, Massachusetts: Lexington Books, 1988), p. 112.

99. Lt. Col. Aleksandr Kichikhin, former officer of KGB Fifth Chief Directorate, *Komsomolskaya pravda*, 19 August 1992, cited by Yasmann, "Where Has the KGB Gone?"

100. Law on Federal Organs of State Security, *Rossiyskaya gazeta*, 12 August 1992, trans. FBIS-USR-92-121, 24 September 1992, pp. 21-28.

101. Anatoliy Oleynikov, in *Trud*, cited by TASS in English, 1155 GMT, 27 February 1992, in FBIS-SOV-92-042, 3 March 1992, pp. 45-46.

102. Interfax in English, 1736 GMT, 22 October 1992, in FBIS-SOV-92-206, 23 October 1992 p. 33.

103. Former KGB Col. Petr Nikulin, statement at a seminar sponsored by the Glasnost Foundation, Moscow, 9 April 1994. From author's notes.

104. Gurov.

105. Bakatin, *Izbavleniye ot KGB*, p. 41.

106. Viktor Barannikov, interview with *Izvestiya*, union edition, 31 December 1991, trans. in BBCSWB, 1 January 1992, p. SU/1267/B/1.

107. See J. Michael Waller, "The KGB Is Back in Business," *Wall Street Journal Europe*, 30 October 1992; and Knight, "Russian Security Services Under Yel'tsin," *Op. cit.*, p. 48. Also see Boris Pustintsev, "Die Arbeit der 'Bürgerkontrolle' in St. Petersburg," *Die Stasi und der KGB--Möglichkeiten der Kontrolle der Geheimdienste, Dokumentation des Wochenendseminars* (Berlin: Bildungswerk für Demokratie und Umweltschutz e.V, 3-4 April 1993), pp. 19-22.

108. *Komsomolskaya pravda*, 23 December 1993, p. 1, trans. in FBIS-SOV-93-245, 23 December 1993, p. 28.

109. Boris Yeltsin, interview with Ostankino television, 16 November 1993, cited by Alexander Rahr, "Reform of Russia's State Security Apparatus," *RFE/RL Research Report*, Vol. 3, No. 8, 25 February 1994, p. 26.

110. Zhirinovskiy's KGB connections had long been presumed, but St. Petersburg Mayor Anatoliy Sobchak claims personal knowledge of how the KGB backed his rise as a political figure. Sobchak was a member of Gorbachev's presidential council in 1989 when the Soviet government repealed Article 6 of the Constitution which had given the CPSU a monopoly on power. According to Sobchak, Gorbachev stated that the Soviet leadership should set up the first alternative political party, which it would effectively control, leaving the details to the KGB. The KGB then employed Zhirinovskiy to lead the new Liberal Democratic Party, named deliberately to mislead; the LDP then was the first party to register officially, even before the CPSU. ITAR-TASS World Service in Russian, 0724 GMT, 12 January 1994, trans. in FBIS-SOV-94-008, 12 January 1994, p. 34. Also see Rahr, "Reform of Russia's State Security Apparatus," p. 26.

111. Ostankino television, 15 December 1993; and *Moskovskiye vedomosti*, No. 22, 1993, cited by Victor Yasmann, "Security Services Reorganized: All Power to

the Russian President?" *RFE/RL Research Report*, Vol. 3, No. 6, 11 February 1994, p. 8.

112. ITAR-TASS world service in Russian, 1704 GMT, 21 December 1993, trans. in FBIS-SOV-93-244, 22 December 1993, p. 35.

113. First Deputy Minister of Security Sergey Stepashin claimed he "knew nothing" about the decree in advance. See his interview in *Rossiyskaya gazeta*, 12 January 1994, first edition, p. 2, trans. in FBIS-SOV-94-008, 12 January 1994, p. 33. Also see Aleksandr Kudakayev, *Segodnya*, 23 December 1993, p. 1, trans. in FBIS-SOV-93-245, 23 December 1993, pp. 28-29; and Yasmann, "Security Services Reorganized," p. 9.

114. Yasmann, "Security Services Reorganized," p. 9; and ITAR-TASS World Service in Russian, 1555 GMT, 21 December 1993; ITAR-TASS World Service in Russian, 1520 GMT, 21 December 1993; and ITAR-TASS in English 0922 GMT, 22 December 1993; and *Kommersant-Daily*, 21 December 1993, p. 3; trans. in FBIS-SOV-93-244, 22 December 1993, pp. 36-38.

115. Oleg Lobov, interview in *Nezavisimaya gazeta*, 2 February 1994, p. 1, trans. in FBIS-SOV-94-023, 3 February 1994, p. 22.

116. Edict No. 19 of the President of the Russian Federation "On Ratifying the Statute of the Federal Counterintelligence Service of the Russian Federation," *Rossiyskaya gazeta*, 11 January 1994, first edition, p. 5, trans. in FBIS-SOV-94-007, 11 January 1994, p. 28.

117. KGB Col. Petr Nikulin, remarks at seminar sponsored by the Glasnost Foundation, Moscow, 9 April 1994, from author's notes.

118. FKS Director Nikolay Golushko, interview with Valeriy Yakov, *Izvestiya*, first edition, 3 February 1994, pp. 1, 6, trans. in FBIS-SOV-94-024, 4 February 1994, p. 18.

119. Stepashin, *Rossiyskaya gazeta*, p. 33.

120. Yasmann, "Security Services Reorganized," p. 9.

121. Edict No. 19 of the President of the Russian Federation, pp. 27-28.

122. Olga Semenova, ITAR-TASS dispatch in English, 25 March 1994, citing Sergey Stepashin.

123. Stepashin, *Rossiyskaya gazeta*, p. 33.

124. *Ibid.*; and *Komsomolskaya pravda*, 11 January 1994, p. 1, trans. in FBIS-SOV-94-008, 12 January 1994, pp. 31-32; and *Krasnaya zvezda*, 11 January 1994, p. 1, trans. in FBIS-SOV-94-007, 11 January 1994, p. 27.

125. Sergey Stepashin, news conference statement, 25 March 1994, trans. by Federal Information Systems Corporation.

126. Nikolay Golushko, *Izvestiya*, p. 19. The translation is also "operational reserve," from ofitsery deystvuyushchego rezerva.

127. Stepashin, *Rossiyskaya gazeta*, p. 33.

128. Sergey Stepashin, interview on "Itogi," St. Petersburg Fifth Channel Television, 1800 GMT, 30 January 1994, trans. in FBIS-SOV-94-025, 7 February 1994, p. 20.

129. Oleg Lobov, Secretary of the Russian Security Council, interview in *Nezavisimaya gazeta*, 2 February 1994, p. 1, trans. in FBIS-SOV-94-023, 3 February 1994, p. 22.

130. Oleg Lobov, interview on "Itogi," St. Petersburg Fifth Channel Television, 1800 GMT, 30 January 1994, trans. in FBIS-SOV-94-025, 7 February 1994, p. 20. Other members of the commission were Lobov, his deputy Vladimir Rubanov, presidential national security adviser Yuriy Baturin, Security Minister Nikolay Golushko, and First Deputy Security Minister Stepashin.

131. Author's interviews with former fellow members of the Supreme Soviet Committee on Human Rights, which Kovalev chaired, April 1994.

132. *Segodnya*, 26 March 1994, cited in *Crossroads*, 15 April 1994, p. 1.

133. Stepashin, news conference, 25 March 1994.

134. Stepashin, "Itogi," p. 21.

135. Oleg Lobov, *Krasnaya zvezda*, 26 March 1994, p. 1, trans. in FBIS-SOV-94-059, 28 March 1994, p. 22; and Stepashin, 25 March 1994 news conference.

136. *Komsomolskaya pravda*, 11 January 1994, p. 1, trans. in FBIS-SOV-94-008, 12 January 1994, p. 31; and Stepashin, *Rossiyskaya gazeta*, p. 32.

137. Stepashin, 25 March 1994 news conference.

138. Yasmann, "Security Services Reorganized," p. 13; and *Komsomolskaya pravda*, 11 January 1994, p. 1, trans. in FBIS-SOV-94-008, 12 January 1994, pp. 31-32.

139. Sergey Stepashin, interview with "Novosti" newscast, Ostankino First Channel Television Network, 1800 GMT, 5 March 1994, trans. in FBIS-SOV-94-044, 17 March 1994, p. 22.

140. *Ibid.*

141. Radio Rossii, 1000 GMT, 1 March 1994, citing Interfax, trans. in FBIS-SOV-94-040, 1 March 1994, p. 17; and Aleksandr Kudakayev, *Segodnya*, 1 March 1994, p. 1, trans. in FBIS-SOV-94-040, 1 March 1994, p. 17.

142. Natalya Gevorkyan, "Appointments," *Moscow News*, No. 13, April 1994, electronic mail version. The article did not appear in the printed English-language edition. Stepashin provided Gevorkyan with the information on the new officials, but notably gave no details about Strelkov and Timofeyev. He did say that Vladimir Tsekhanov, his new deputy for economic counterintelligence, had supported dissident human rights activist Andrey Mironov when he was imprisoned for "anti-Soviet" activity in early 1986.

143. Stepashin, "Novosti" newscast, 5 March 1994.

144. Stepashin, "Itogi," p. 21-22.

145. Aleksandr Krolakyev, *Segodnya*, 23 December 1993, p. 1, trans. in FBIS-SOV-93-245, 23 December 1993, p. 28. This article was a rare exception to the newspaper's hands-off attitude toward the chekists.

146. Human rights leader Sergey Grigoryants and former KGB Maj. Gen. Oleg Kalugin verified Stepashin's "enemies" and "terrorists" statement to the author in interviews in Moscow, April 1994.

147. Rahr, p. 25.

148. *Rossiyskaya gazeta*, 28 December 1991, first edition, p. 2. FBIS-SOV-92-001, 2 January 1992, p. 57. For more on the Communications Troops, see *Krasnaya zvezda*, 18 February 1993, p. 2, trans. in FBIS-SOV-93-032, 19 February 1993, pp. 21-22.

149. Vera Selivanova, "All Information to Have One Color: KGB Will Determine Which One," *Segodnya*, No. 38, 30 July 1993, p. 2, trans. in FBIS-SOV-93-147, 3 August 1993, pp. 10-11.

150. *Ibid.*

151. *Izvestiya*, 5 November 1992, morning edition, p. 5, trans. in FBIS-SOV-92-215, 5 November 1992, p. 16; Pascal Fletcher, "Moscow, Havana Ink Pact," Reuters, 4 November 1992.

152. Yasmann, "The KGB and Internal Security," *Op. cit.*, p. 20. Also, James Sherr, "Change and Continuity in the Former KGB," *Jane's Intelligence Review*, March 1993, p. 112.

153. Selivanova.

154. *Ibid.*

155. *Kommersant-Daily*, 23 February 1994, p. 2, trans. in FBIS-SOV-94-037, 24 February 1994, pp. 29-30.

156. ITAR-TASS, 21 March 1993, and *Selskaya zhizn*, 31 August 1993, cited by Yasmann, "Security Services Reorganized," p. 11.

157. TASS international service in Russian, 1925 GMT, 26 August 1991, trans. in FBIS-SOV-91-167, 28 August 1991, p. 35.

158. Interfax in English, 2000 GMT, 22 August 1991, in FBIS-SOV-91-164, 23 August 1991, p. 91; *Komsomolskaya pravda*, 24 August 1991, p. 1, trans. in FBIS-SOV-91-166, 27 August 1991, pp. 14-15; and TASS international service in Russian, 1925 GMT, 26 August 1991, trans. in FBIS-SOV-91-167, 28 August 1991, p. 36.

159. Mikhail Barsukov, interview with Sergey Mostovshchikov, *Izvestiya*, 8 October 1993, first edition, p. 2, trans. in FBIS-SOV-93-194, 8 October 1993, p. 16; and J. Michael Waller, "Yeltsin's Debt to the Old KGB," *Wall Street Journal Europe*, 21 October 1993.

160. TASS international service in English, 1714 GMT, 26 September 1991, trans. in FBIS-SOV-91-188, 27 September 1991, pp. 16-17. The murder of President Amin and his children is reported by Edward Girardet, *Afghanistan: The Soviet War* (New York: St. Martin's Press, 1986), p. 14.

161. Interfax in English, 1215 GMT, 22 February 1994, in FBIS-SOV-94-035, 22 February 1994, p. 32.

162. *Ibid.*

163. FBIS editorial report summarizing "Vesti," Russian Television Network, 1700 GMT, 2 February 1994, in FBIS-SOV-94-023, 3 February 1994, p. 31.

164. Valeriy Yakov, *Izvestiya*, 16 April 1994, p. 2, trans. in FBIS-SOV-94-075, 19 April 1994, pp. 26-27; and Interfax, 22 February 1994.

165. Interfax in English, 1328 GMT, 19 April 1994, citing Russian Interior Troops Commander Col. Gen. Anatoliy Kulikov, trans. in FBIS-SOV-94-076, 20 April 1994, pp. 41-42.

166. Yan Ulanskiy, *Kuranty*, 24 March 1994, p. 1, trans. in FBIS-SOV-94-057, 24 March 1994, p. 8.

167. Igor Nikulin, chairman of a subcommittee of the Russian Federation Supreme Soviet Committee on Defense and Security, *Komsomolskaya pravda*, 20 October 1992, pp. 1-2, trans. in FBIS-SOV-92-204, 21 October 1992, pp. 21-23.

168. *Ibid.*

169. Interfax in English, 1153 GMT, 24 November 1992, in FBIS-SOV-92-228, 25 November 1992, pp. 41-42.

170. Igor Nikulin, p. 23.

171. Yasmann, "Security Services Reorganized," p. 12.

172. Sherr, pp. 110-111.

173. *Komsomolskaya pravda*, 17 January 1992, p. 3, trans. in FBIS-SOV-92-014, 22 January 1992.

174. For commentary on the challenge of guarding post-Soviet borders, see Gabriel Schoenfeld, "Outer Limits," *Post-Soviet Prospects* No. 17, Center for Strategic and International Studies, January 1993.

175. Text of edict on federal restructuring, ITAR-TASS World Service in Russian, 1406 GMT, 10 January 1994, trans. in FBIS-SOV-94-007, 11 January 1994, pp. 23-26; Yuriy Baturin, interview, *Izvestiya*, 11 January 1994, first edition, p. 3, trans. in FBIS-SOV-94-007, 11 January 1994, pp. 28-29.

176. Yasmann, "Where Has the KGB Gone?"

177. Col. Petr Nikulin, Glasnost Foundation, 9 April 1994.

178. Yasmann, "Security Services Reorganized," p. 11.

179. *Ibid.*, p. 12.

180. The GRU, however, increased its foreign intelligence activities markedly in 1992, according to the FBI and the CIA. For a detailed and generally reliable description of the GRU, purportedly an insider's account but apparently containing substantial information from British intelligence, see Viktor Suvorov (pseud.), *Inside Soviet Military Intelligence* (New York: Macmillan, 1984).

181. *RFE/RL Daily Report*, No. 82, 30 April 1992, p. 1.

182. Carey Schofield, "Interview with the Head of Russian GRU," *Jane's Intelligence Review*, March 1993, p. 113.

183. Interfax, 1440 GMT, 20 December 1991, in FBIS-SOV-91-246, 23 December 1991, p. 45.

184. TASS international service in Russian, 1650 GMT, 26 December 1991, trans. in FBIS-SOV-91-249, 27 December 1991, p. 33.

185. TASS world service in Russian, 1650 GMT, 26 December 1991, trans. in BBCSWB, 31 December 1991, p. SU/1266/B/1.

186. Bakatin, interview with author, Washington, D.C., 17 September 1992.

187. SVR Directorate press secretary Tatyana Samolis, in *Nezavisimaya gazeta*, 20 February 1992, p. 1, trans. in FBIS-SOV-92-035, 21 February 1992, p. 45.

188. Tatyana Samolis, ITAR-TASS, 25 March 1992, trans. in *RFE/RL Weekly Review*, 10 April 1992, p. 56.

189. Vadim Kirpichenko, statement at Kennan Institute Washington, D.C., 11 January 1993. He said that the SVR operates only abroad, and that it considers the three Baltic states "foreign countries," as opposed to the other former Soviet republics, which are not "foreign" but considered part of the "near abroad." He did not say whether the SVR considered Georgia, which was not part of the CIS at the time, a "foreign" state.

190. Presidential Decree No. 1147, "On the System of Central Organs of Federal Executive Power," 30 September 1992, trans. in FBIS-SOV-92-195, 7 October 1992, pp. 11-12.

191. *Rossiyskaya gazeta*, 3 February 1993, first edition, p. 7, trans. in FBIS-SOV-93-025, 9 February 1993, p. 17.

192. Primakov was a top adviser to Gorbachev and chairman of the Council of the Union of the USSR Supreme Soviet. Although Security Minister Barannikov served as USSR minister of internal affairs, he did so only after the putsch and at Yeltsin's direction. Prior to that Barannikov was RSFSR MVD minister. Many other Russian Federation leaders served in the Soviet regime, but not at the highest echelons.

193. Radio Rossii, 0900 GMT, 13 June 1992, trans. in FBIS-SOV-92-117, 17 June 1992, p. 30.

194. Victor Yasmann, *RFE/RL Daily Report*, No. 12, 20 January 1992, p. 3; and Stephen Foye, citing "Vesti," 22 July 1992, in *RFE/RL Daily Report*, No. 139, 23 July 1992, p. 3.

195. Bakatin, interview with author, 11 September 1992.

196. "Gorelovsky Joins Foreign Intelligence," *RFE/RL Research Report*, 31 January 1992, pp. 67-68.

197. "Russian Foreign Intelligence Service Delegation Biographies," Center for Democracy, Washington, D.C., January 1993.

198. Kirpichenko to author, 11 January 1993; and interview with *Patriot* (Moscow), No. 34, in *RFE/RL Daily Report*, No. 169, 3 September 1992, p. 2.

199. Dziak writes that Directorate S absorbed Department V for "wet affairs" after the 1971 defection of Oleg Lyalin from that department to Great Britain. Kirpichenko, an Arabist who as *rezident* in Egypt had warned of Sadat's imminent expulsion of the Soviets, became Directorate S chief in 1974. According to Vladimir Kuzichkin, who served in Directorate S before defecting to the United States, the unit was responsible for training foreign terrorists. Dziak, pp. 162-163.

200. See Jillian Becker, *The PLO: The Rise and Fall of the Palestine Liberation Organization* (New York: St. Martin's Press, 1984); Christopher Dobson and Ronald Payne, *The Never-Ending War: Terrorism in the '80s* (New York and Oxford: Facts On File, 1987), pp. 101-112; Roberta Goren, *The Soviet Union and Terrorism* (London: George Allen & Unwin, 1984), pp. 106-141; Michael Ledeen, "Intelligence, Training, and Support Components," in Uri Ra'anan, Robert Pfalzgraff, Richard H. Shultz, Jr., Ernst Halperin, and Igor Lukes, eds., *Hydra of Carnage: The International Linkages of Terrorism--The Witnesses Speak* (Lexington, Massachusetts: Lexington Books, 1986), pp. 155-168; Ra'anan et. al., "Surrogate Actors in the Middle East," in *ibid.*, pp. 519-527, 544-547; and Richard H. Shultz, Jr., *The Soviet Union and Revolutionary Warfare: Principles, Practices, and Regional Comparisons* (Stanford: Hoover Institution, 1988), pp. 76-114.

201. Even the most reformist of former KGB professionals have a difficult time reconciling with their colleagues who defected from the Soviet Union to the West. In writing the preface to the Russian edition of a book by former KGB Col. Oleg Gordievsky who defected to the West, retired KGB Maj. Gen. Oleg Kalugin said the book raised many valid points about the Soviet intelligence service, but began by stating flatly that Gordievsky is a "traitor."

202. Nikolay Semenenko, *Rossiyskiye vesti*, 4 August 1993, p. 7, trans. in FBIS-SOV-93-148, 4 August 1993, pp. 25-26.

203. SVR Public Relations Director Col. Yuriy Kobaladze and Lt. Gen. Vadim Kirpichenko, remarks at Kennan Institute, 11 January 1993.

204. "Bulgaria to Sack Diplomats Who Spied for Communists," Reuter Library Report, 4 March 1992. President Zhelyu Zhelev ordered the fundamental reform of Bulgaria's intelligence services and had new intelligence officers trained by the United States. Bulgarian Telegraph Agency (BTA) in English, 1501 GMT, 17 December 1991, in BBCSWB, 19 December 1991, p. EE/1259/B/1; and BTA in English, 1415 GMT, 18 December 1991, in BBCSWB, 23 December 1991, p. EE/1262/B/1.

205. Bill Gertz, "Russia, China Sign Pact Restoring Intelligence Ties," *Washington Times,* 21 October 1992, p. A7.

206. Interfax in English, 1440 GMT, 20 December 1991, in FBIS-SOV-91-246, 23 December 1991, p. 45.

207. Source L, interview with author, late 1992. For a pro-SVR statement about its "new" structure and purpose, see Semenenko, pp. 24-26.

208. The author questioned Kirpichenko after his Kennan Institute speech in Washington on 11 January 1993: "Do you still maintain your networks of illegals, and if so, why?" Kirpichenko responded, "Of course, we are maintaining our illegals. We need them. Our country is in very bad shape, and we need our illegals." Then he caught himself and said, "What am I talking to you about illegals for?" and walked away. He later told the *Washington Post,* "We think that 'illegal intelligence' is one of the legitimate forms of intelligence gathering. But we no longer have goals of a subversive character." Michael Dobbs and R. Jeffrey Smith, "From Inside the KGB: A Tale of Incompetence," *Washington Post,* 21 February 1993, p. A26.

209. Kirpichenko, *ibid.*

210. Bakatin, *Izbavleniye ot KGB* , p. 86.

211. Kirpichenko publicly stated at the Kennan lecture and in other January 1993 gatherings in Washington that the SVR no longer practiced "active measures." These remarks were covered by Bill Gertz, "Russians Discard Tactics of KGB," *Washington Times,* 12 January 1993. In response to a question at the Kennan lecture about whether Service A had been abolished, Kirpichenko said that it had.

212. Evgueni Novikov, *RFE/RL Daily Report,* No. 211, 6 November 1991, p. 2.

213. Col. Yuriy Kobaladze, during exchange at the third international conference on "KGB: Yesterday, Today and Tomorrow," sponsored by the Glasnost Foundation, Moscow, 3 October 1993. From author's notes. The remarks were also recorded on videotape by the Cultural Initiative Foundation of philanthropist George Soros.

214. First Deputy Prime Minister Gennadiy Burbulis, in TASS world service in English, 2303 GMT, 9 January 1992, in FBIS-SOV-92-007, 10 January 1992, p. 22; SVR Public Relations Center Chief Yuriy Kobaladze, in TASS world service in English, 2100 GMT, 6 March 1992, in FBIS-SOV-92-047, 10 March 1992, p. 25.

215. Bakatin, interview with author, 22 September 1992. The same percentages were given more than two years later in unofficial SVR propaganda. For examples, see Semenenko; and Matt Campbell, "Ex-KGB Colonels Find Eager Audiences," *Kansas City Star* dispatch, *Washington Times,* 5 November 1993.

216. Bakatin, *Izbavleniye ot KGB*, p. 39.

217. *Ibid.*

218. Vadim Kirpichenko and Yuriy Kobaladze, statements at the Kennan Institute, 11 January 1993.

219. Dobbs and Smith, p. A26.

220. Vyacheslav Trubnikov, interview in *Nezavisimaya gazeta*, 16 September 1992.

221. A KGB First Chief Directorate training and operations manual published at the height of glasnost makes this exact point. The secret 108-page manual, *Political Intelligence from the Territory of the USSR* (Moscow: Red Banner Yu. V. Andropov Institute of the KGB, 1989), describes at great length the easier recruitment and agent servicing processes.

222. Igor Nikulin, member, Supreme Soviet Committee on Questions of Legality, Law, Order, and Combatting Crime, on Radio Rossii, 1300 GMT, 24 January 1992, trans. in FBIS-SOV-92-019, 29 January 1992, p. 48.

223. First Chief Directorate First Deputy Director Vyacheslav Trubnikov, on Teleradiokompaniya Ostankino Television First Program Network, 1100 GMT, 9 September 1992, trans. in FBIS-SOV-92-176, 10 September 1992, p. 21.

224. See, for example, the story of Captain Yuriy Shvets, who served at the Soviet Embassy in Washington from 1985 to 1987. He told the *Washington Post* that most officers stationed in the U.S. capital when he was there were more committed to earning hard currency and enjoying life in the United States than they were to working. Shvets said the decline in the Washington *rezidentura* began in 1982. Corruption allowed the FBI to recruit one officer, and then a second, to spy on the rezidentura for the United States. Said the *Post*, "By the time Shvets reported for duty in Washington, a general atmosphere of paranoia reigned at the KGB residency on the fourth floor of the Soviet Embassy. To discourage anyone from clandestinely photographing secret documents, officers were required to work in their shirtsleeves." Dobbs and Smith, pp. 1, 26.

225. Yevgeniy Primakov, interview in *Nezavisimaya gazeta*, 21 December 1991, pp. 1, 5, trans. in FBIS-SOV-92-002, 3 January 1992, p. 8.

226. Vyacheslav Trubnikov, on Teleradiokompaniya Ostankino Television First Program Network, 1100 GMT, 9 September 1992, trans. in FBIS-SOV-92-176, 10 September 1992, p. 21.

227. Mark Almond, "Introducing KGB PLC," *The Spectator* (London), 10 July 1993. Almond is author of *Still Serving Silently: Soviet Bloc Spies Under New Masters* (London: Institute for European Defence and Strategic Studies, 1993).

228. Mark Deich, *Golos*, No. 42/43, October 1992, cited by Rahr, "Reform of Russia's State Security Apparatus," p. 28.

229. Daniel Southerland, "Former Foes In Espionage Form Alliance: Ex-Officers at NSA, KGB To Offer Services in Russia," *Washington Post*, 5 February 1993.

230. Olga Krishtanovskaya, "'I'm Tired of Politics: Let's Get Down to Business,'" *Nezavisimaya gazeta* international edition in English, Vol. 4, Nos. 4-5, August 1993, p. 8.

231. Tatyana Samolis, in *Kuranty*, 20 February 1992, p. 3, trans. in FBIS-SOV-92-035, 21 February 1992, p. 45.

232. Yuriy Kobaladze, remark at Glasnost Foundation seminar, Moscow, 10 April 1994, from author's notes.

233. Krishtanovskaya.

234. Erich Inciyan, "Russian Spies at the Heart of Nuclear Secrets," *Le Monde*, 3 November 1992, p. 14, trans. FBIS-WEU-92-216, 6 November 1992, p. 25.

235. Krishtanovskaya.

236. Maj. Gen. Oleg Kalugin, interview with *Nepszabadsag*, Budapest, 10 March 1994, p. 7, trans. in FBIS-SOV-94-048, 11 March 1994, pp. 14-15.

237. William E. Conner, "National Classification System Update," *National Security Law Report*, Vol. 16, No. 3-4, March-April 1994, pp. 1, 4. The proposal was in a draft of PRD-29 issued by President Clinton on 26 April 1993.

238. Kobaladze, Kennan Institute, from author's notes.

239. Józef Darski, "Police Agents in the Transition Period," *Uncaptive Minds*, Vol. 4, No. 4, Winter 1991-1992, p. 16.

240. Petr Toman, spokesman of the Parliamentary Investigative Commission for the Clarification of the Events of 17 November 1989, to Czechoslovak Federal Assembly, 22 March 1991, trans. as "Collaborators Revealed: The Parliamentary Commission's Report," *Uncaptive Minds*, Vol. 4, No. 2, Summer 1991, p. 9.

241. Darski, pp. 15-16.

242. *Izvestiya*, 29 November 1991, union edition, pp. 1, 6, trans. in FBIS-SOV-91-232, 3 December 1991, pp. 36-37.

243. Avigdor Haselkorn and Christopher Coker, "The Spies Who Stayed in the Cold," *European Security Analyst* (London: Institute for European Defence and Strategic Studies), No. 20, August 1992, p. 1.

244. Anna Tomforde, "Moscow 'Widens Spy Network,'" *Guardian* (Manchester and London, U.K.), 30 June 1992.

245. Haselkorn and Coker.

246. *Der Spiegel*, Hamburg, 31 August 1992, pp. 16-17, trans. in FBIS-WEU-92-170, 1 September 1992, p. 4.

247. Henning Thiesen, deputy commissioner of Danish Police Intelligence Services (PET), in Agence France Presse, 26 May 1992.

248. *Semanario*, Lisbon, 28 November 1992, p. 6, trans. in FBIS-WEU-92-244, 18 December 1992, p. 39.

249. *ABC*, Madrid, 1 May 1993, p. 25, trans. in FBIS-WEU-93-090, 12 May 1993, p. 42.

250. Darski, p. 24.

251. Stephen B. Cohen, "Today's Czech Politics, with Swears and Laughter," *Washington Post*, 3 June 1990; and Czechoslovak Vice Minister of Interior Jiri Ruml, interview, *Le Monde*, 21 September 1990, p. 10, trans. in FBIS-EER-90-148, 26 October 1990, p. 5.

252. Says James Sherr, "Intelligence gathering against NATO countries has not diminished; indeed, the FBI and German BfV report a 12 percent increase in combined GRU/SVR activity in their respective countries since the collapse of the August 1991 coup. Sherr, p. 112.

253. Andrew and Gordievsky, pp. 621-623; Philip Hanson, "Soviet Industrial Espionage," *Bulletin of the Atomic Scientists*, April 1987, pp. 25-29. For a journalistic investigation of Soviet technological espionage in the early 1980s, see Linda Melvern, David Hebditch, and Nick Anning, *Techno-Bandits: How the*

Soviets Are Stealing America's High-Tech Future (Boston: Houghton Mifflin, 1984).

254. Michael Smith, "A New Order for the Spies," *Daily Telegraph*, 24 January 1992, p. 17; Inciyan, p. 25.

255. "KGB Defector Helping CIA, Report Says," Reuter Library Report, 5 March 1992; Bill Gertz, "CIA Learning from KGB Defector," *Washington Times*, 5 March 1992, p. A3.

256. Vyacheslav Trubnikov, cited by Natalya Gorodetskaya and Yelena Tregubova, *Nezavisimaya gazeta*, 10 September 1992, pp. 1-2, trans. in FBIS-SOV-92-180, 16 September 1992, pp. 19-20.

257. J. Michael Waller, "Former KGB Still Targets Western Business and Industry," *Perspectives on Post-Soviet Business*, Vol. 2, No. 4, 27 May 1992, p. 1.

258. William S. Sessions, transcript of Hearing of the Judiciary Committee, Subcommittee on Economic and Commercial Law, U.S. House of Representatives, 29 April 1992, in Federal News Service.

259. *Nezavisimaya gazeta*, 21 December 1991, pp. 1, 5, trans. in FBIS-SOV-92-002, 3 January 1992, p. 8.

260. Russian official with firsthand knowledge of the operation, conversation with author, 1993.

261. "Ex-Soviet States Building Up Spy Network, Says German Official," Reuter Library Report, 8 February 1992.

262. *Handelsblatt* in German (Düsseldorf), 14-15 August 1992, p. 5, trans. in FBIS-WEU-92-160, 18 August 1992, p. 11.

263. *Der Spiegel*, Hamburg, 31 August 1992, pp. 16-17, trans. in FBIS-WEU-92-170, 1 September 1992, p. 4; *Bild*, Hamburg, 23 September 1992, p. 2, trans. in FBIS-WEU-92-186, 24 September 1992, p. 11; and *Die Welt*, 2 October 1992, p. 1, trans. in FBIS-WEU-92-194, 6 October 1992, p. 5. Also see interview with Bernd Schmidbauer in *Focus*, Munich, 22 February 1993, p. 12, trans. in FBIS-WEU-93-034, 23 February 1993, p. 14.

264. DPA, Hamburg, 0953 GMT, 20 October 1992, trans. in FBIS-WEU-92-203, 20 October 1992, p. 7.

265. Waller, "Former KGB Still Targets Western Business and Industry."

266. Roger Faligot, "Russian Spy Ring Smashed," *The European*, 29 October 1992; "Paris Expelling 4 as Russian Spies," *International Herald Tribune*, 24-25 October 1992, p. 5; Thierry Oberle, "The French Spies Who Were Still Working for Moscow," *Le Figaro*, Paris, 23 April 1992, p. 10, trans. in FBIS-WEU-92-088, 6 May 1992, pp. 23-24; France Inter-Radio Network, 1300 GMT, 23 October 1992, trans. in FBIS-WEU-92-207, 26 October 1992, p. 15; and Inciyan, p. 24.

267. *RFE/RL Daily Report*, No. 80, 27 April 1992, p. 3.

268. Arkady Prisyazhny, "Russian Citizens Traveling on Forged Documents Detained," ITAR-TASS, 21 May 1992; Reuter Library Report, 22 May 1992.

269. Sveriges Radio Network, Stockholm, 1445 GMT, 15 July 1992, trans. in FBIS-WEU-92-137, 16 July 1992, p. 30.

270. Reuter Library Report, citing *Svenska Dagbladet*, 2 March 1992.

271. Sveriges Radio Network, Stockholm, 1600 GMT, 9 September 1992, trans. in FBIS-WEU-92-177, 11 September 1992, p. 34.

272. Mikael Holmstrom, "Secret Organization Behind It," *Svenska Dagbladet*, 21 June 1992, p. 6, trans. in FBIS-WEU-92-145, 28 July 1992, pp. 33-34.

273. Yuriy Kobaladze, Radio Rossii, 0800 GMT, 4 May 1992, trans. in BBCSWB, 6 May 1992, p. SU/1373/A1/1; author's interview with a former First Chief Directorate officer, 20 May 1992.

Chapter 5

1. The unit of the CPSU directly responsible for the KGB was the Administrative Organs Department. As part of Gorbachev's 1989 reforms to transfer Party power to the state (but with Party members holding those state positions), the Administrative Organs Department was renamed the Legal Affairs (or Policy) Commission and headed by Viktor Chebrikov, who was transferred to the commission from his post as KGB chairman.

2. The earliest officers to go public with their criticisms were Col. Vladimir Rubanov, who was fired from the KGB in 1988 for writing an article in the Party journal *Kommunist* alleging that the KGB made up many foreign threats to the USSR, and Maj. Gen. Oleg Kalugin, who left the KGB and went public in 1989.

3. Vadim Bakatin, testimony to the Russian Constitutional Court, trans. by Interfax in English, 1932 GMT, 12 October 1992, in FBIS-SOV-92-206-S, 23 October 1992, pp. 7-8.

4. The definitive CPSU account of the structure and functions of the Congress of People's Deputies, authored by Yevgeniy Primakov, a Party toady whom Gorbachev named chief of the Soviet of the Union chamber of the USSR Supreme Soviet, was issued in Russian, English, French, and other languages and distributed in airport lounges for foreigners. See Yevgeniy Primakov, *Perestroika Has Given the People an Opportunity to Know Themselves Better* (Moscow: Novosti, 1990).

5. Dawn Mann and Julia Wishnevsky, "Composition of Congress of People's Deputies," *RL Report on the USSR*, Vol. 1, No. 18, 5 May 1989, pp. 1-5. Also, Kenneth C. Farmer, *The Soviet Administrative Elite* (New York: Praeger, 1992), p. 271. Farmer, citing Mann and Wishnevsky, writes, "Overall, one of every five Party officials was defeated. Even though 88 percent of the deputies elected were Party members, these tended not to be Party officials, workers, or prominent conservatives [*sic*]. . . Of 121 military candidates, 79 were elected, as were 9 republican KGB chairmen."

6. Alexander Rahr, "Kryuchkov, the KGB, and the 1991 Putsch," *RFE/RL Research Report*, Vol. 2, No. 31, 30 July 1993, pp. 21, 22.

7. There had been debates within the Party, none of which ever took center stage, over the fate of the KGB. One idea in 1988 was to establish local commissions to govern KGB and MVD activities. Another was to take the KGB out of "law enforcement" completely. *Komsomolskaya pravda*, 7 June 1988, cited by Dusko Doder and Louise Branson, *Gorbachev: Heretic in the Kremlin* (New York: Penguin, 1991), p. 315.

8. Hélène Carrére d'Encausse, trans. Franklin Philip, *The End of the Soviet Empire: The Triumph of the Nations* (New York: New Republic/Basic Books,

1993), pp. 73-95; and John P. Dunlop, "Crackdown," *The National Interest*, Spring 1991, p. 25. Also see Eduard Gudava, "The Tragedy of Georgia," *Glasnost*, English international edition, May-July 1989, pp. 4-10.

9. Soviet state television, monitored and trans. in FBIS-SOV-89-104S, 31 May 1989 and FBIS-SOV-89-111-S, 12 June 1989.

10. Congress of USSR People's Deputies, "Verbatim Report," *Izvestiya*, 2 June 1989, pp. 1-10, trans. in *The Current Digest of the Soviet Press*, 26 July 1989. An alternative translation appears in FBIS-SOV-89-111-S, 12 June 1989.

11. Esther B. Fein, "Pointed Questions for Chief of KGB," *New York Times*, 15 July 1989, p. 1. Fein recalls the opening of the Congress six weeks before, although her coverage of the opening was not published. Bill Keller, who covered Vlasov's speech, reported, "When Mr. Vlasov finished, hundreds of deputies rose in a standing ovation, while others—including members of the Communist Party's ruling Politburo and head of the KGB, Vladimir A. Kryuchkov—sat with stares frozen on their faces. President Mikhail S. Gorbachev applauded briefly." Bill Keller, "Olympic Star, in Passionate Talk, Attacks KGB in Soviet Congress," *New York Times*, 1 June 1989, p. 1.

12. Congress of USSR People's Deputies, "Verbatim Report."

13. Vladimir Kryuchkov, introductory remarks to USSR Supreme Soviet, "Excerpts from 199-minute Recording of Morning Sitting Continued from SU/0511 C/7," transcript of USSR Supreme Soviet proceedings from Soviet television, 1400 GMT, 14 July 1989, trans. in BBCSWB, 20 July 1989, p. SU/0513/C/1. Hereafter referenced as "Excerpts."

14. David Remnick, "KGB Chief Wins Reappointment from Legislature," *Washington Post*, 15 July 1989, p. A17. Committee Chairman Vladimir Lapygin declared that the Soviet government held no political prisoners.

15. Quentin Peel, "Soviet Deputies Grill KGB Chief," *Financial Times*, 15 July 1989, p. 3.

16. "Excerpts."

17. *Ibid.*

18. *Ibid.*

19. *Ibid.*

20. Michael Parks, "Supreme Soviet Approves Security Chief; Reforms for KGB Promised," *Los Angeles Times*, 15 July 1989, p. 4.

21. Kryuchkov, "Excerpts."

22. *Ibid.*

23. Peel.

24. Kryuchkov was making reference to the Fifth Chief Directorate which was renamed but not abolished until after the Soviet Union collapsed. The Fifth was created under Andropov as the main "political police" subunit within the KGB to monitor and carry out operations against individual dissidents and organizations.

25. John Kampfner, "Soviet MPs Back KGB Chief After Glasnost Pledge," *Daily Telegraph*, 15 July 1989, p. 9.

26. "Excerpts."

27. *Ibid.*

28. *Ibid.*

29. *Ibid.*

30. *Ibid.*

31. Parliamentary Correspondent, "KGB Chief Kryuchkov—Confirmation Hearing Details," TASS, 14 July 1989. This English-language dispatch was unquestioning in its support for Kryuchkov, reporting how the KGB chairman "answered all manner of questions—serious, naive and bitter, born of recollections of the Stalin times when the secret service kept tabs on the entire society. Kryuchkov formally assured the deputies that the KGB today does not maintain a network of informants, does not keep any files on people who have not committed state crimes, and does not tap telephone calls. . . . One idea repeatedly stressed during the debate was that the distorted image of the KGB was due to people's generally poor knowledge about it."

32. BBC editorial commentary, BBCSWB, 20 July 1989, p. SU/0513/C/1; Parks, p. 4. The Supreme Soviet did not rubber stamp all Kremlin appointments. The summer 1989 session of the USSR Supreme Soviet rejected eleven ministers proposed by Prime Minister Nikolay Ryzhkov. Kampfner, p. 9.

33. "Commentary by Amy Knight," appendix to Alexander Rahr, "Gorbachev and the Post-Chebrikov KGB," *RL Report on the USSR*, 22 December 1989, p. 23.

34. Charles M. Madigan *et al.*, "Ideology Failing Test of Reality," *Chicago Tribune*, 23 July 1989.

35. Sources D and N, two USSR people's deputies, interviews with author, Moscow, December 1991.

36. Primakov, known to have had strong ties to the KGB throughout his career as a journalist and Middle East expert, was reportedly recruited as an active informant with the cryptonym "Maxim" as early as 1957. A KGB First Chief Directorate officer operating under journalistic cover, Oleg Kalugin, first made contact with Primakov, then a broadcast journalist, in 1960, and he relayed this story in 1991. Yevgeniya Albats, "KGB-MSB-MBVD: Substantive Changes?" *Moscow News*, No. 2, 13 January 1992, p. 5.

37. See, for example, the confusion and questions from the floor directed at Supreme Soviet Council of the Union Chairman Primakov during the election of chairmen of the joint committees of the USSR Supreme Soviet, in *Izvestiya*, 12 June 1989, pp. 2-3, trans. in *Current Digest of the Soviet Press*, Vol. 41, No. 33, 13 September 1989, p. 20.

38. Jennifer Scheck Lee, *The Supreme Soviet Defense and Security Committee: Limited Oversight Capabilities* (Palo Alto: Global Outlook, 1991), pp. 4-5.

39. The body's original name was the Committee on Defense and State Security. Its original membership numbered thirty-eight people, none of them from the Baltic states. Five more members, including Balts, were added by the time the full membership list was published on 14 July 1989.

40. Robert G. Kaiser, *Why Gorbachev Happened* (New York: Touchstone, 1992), p. 291.

41. Amy Knight, *The KGB: Police and Politics in the Soviet Union* (Boston: Unwin, Hyman, 1988, 1990), p. 142. She writes, "He served at one time for the Council of Ministers' Legal Commission, which may have involved him with the KGB, and his first deputy was P. P. Laptev, a former KGB official and Andropov aide." Lukyanov was one of the main plotters of the August 1991 putsch.

42. "A Little Light on the KGB," *The Economist Foreign Report*, 5 April 1990, pp. 4-5.

43. Lee, pp. 20-21. Lee cites committee member Sergey Tsypliayev, who diplomatically said, "The majority of our members are big leaders of our industry and of science. They are very busy outside the committee. It is a disadvantage of the system that they are working [on the committee] as a part-time job. They have no time to think about things, to work on these problems, and then to work actively to achieve some goals."

44. "The New Supreme Soviet Meets—IV," *Izvestiya*, 12 June 1989, No. 164, pp. 2-3, trans. in *Current Digest of the Soviet Press*, Vol. 41, No. 33, 13 September 1989, p. 20.

45. "A Little Light on the KGB."

46. "Commentary by Mikhail Tsypkin," appendix to Rahr, "Gorbachev and the Post-Chebrikov KGB," p. 30; citing "Komitety Verkhovnogo Soveta SSSR i postoyannye komissii Sovets Soyuza i Soveta Natsional'nostei," *Izvestiya*, 13 July 1989, and "Kommyunike zasedaniya Baltiiskogo Soveta," *Atmoda*, 23 October 1989. Observer Georgii Sturua claimed that 90 percent of the committee members held simultaneous positions in the Ministry of Defense or the military-industrial complex. Georgii Sturua, "Komitet po voprosam oborony i gostudarstvennoy bezopasnosti: pervyye mesyatsy raboti (The Defense and State Security Committee: The First Months of Work)" MEIMO No. 1, January 1990, p. 83, cited by Lee, p. 21.

47. Lee, *ibid.*, p. 2.

48. Akhromeyev was identified as a Lukyanov adviser by TASS in Russian for abroad, 1307 GMT, 8 August 1989, trans. in BBCSWB, 25 August 1989, p. SU/0544/A1/1.

49. Source E, interview with author. Apparently Lapygin was too ineffective; he resigned for "health reasons" after only a year as chairman.

50. The KGB had penetrated virtually every movement in the Soviet Union. For example, in Lithuania, after lengthy investigations, the Supreme Court found that Virgilijus Cepaitis, a leader of Sajudis and close ally of President Vytautas Landsbergis, and former Prime Minister Kazimiera Prunskeine, were KGB agents. Both were disgraced and suspended from the Lithuanian parliament. See *RFE/RL Daily Report*, No. 69, 8 April 1992, p. 6; *RFE/RL Daily Report*, No. 107, 5 June 1992, p. 6.

51. "The New Supreme Soviet Meets—IV," pp. 2-3

52. Source L, interview with author.

53. Said Primakov, "After a great deal of thought, after debates and so forth, we settled on the candidacy of Comrade Lapygin. Vladimir Lavrentyevich Lapygin, born in 1925, a Russian. . . . What guided us? Comrade Lapygin is a prominent designer. Very prominent. He works in a field that is connected with both military and civilian production, and he understands very well that, naturally, we must strengthen the defense of our country, and no one should get away from that. At the same time, he realizes that part of our military industry has to be converted, and that practical experience in this conversion has to be created." "The New Supreme Soviet Meets—IV," pp. 2-3.

54. *Ibid.* The deputy was not introduced by name.

55. *Ibid.*

56. *Ibid.*

57. *Ibid.*

58. Yevgeniy P. Velhikov, vice president of the USSR Academy of Sciences and an adviser to Gorbachev, was nominated from the floor as "a person who is known the world over" to be committee chairman, but he declined, saying, "I don't think we should exaggerate the role of chairman at this time," and added that he would work with Lapygin. *Ibid.*

59. *Ibid.*

60. Michael R. Gordon, "Soviets Are Trying Out Legislative Oversight of Military," *New York Times*, 14 August 1989, p. 7.

61. Françoise Thom, "The Red Army: A New Role?" *Perspective* (Boston University Institute for the Study of Conflict, Ideology & Policy), Vol. 1, No. 3, February 1991, p. 6.

62. *Ibid.*

63. *The Economist Foreign Report*, 5 April 1990, pp. 4-5.

64. Tsypkin, citing Vladimir Lapygin, "Rassmatrivaetsa oboronnyi byudzhet," *Krasnaya zvezda*, 5 October 1989; V. Kosarev, "Poiski optimal'nogo resheniya," *Krasnaya zvezda*, 13 October 1989; and Andrei Romanov, "Ot imeni naroda," *Moskovskiye novosti*, 29 October 1989.

65. TASS international service in English, "Soviet Parliament on Defence and State Security," 5 April 1990. KGB Deputy Chairman Viktor Glushko gave the briefing, delivered the report, answered questions, and hosted an exhibit "featuring means used by foreign secret services in their intelligence activities against the Soviet Union." TASS reported, "The committee adopted a resolution on the matter."

66. BBCSWB, abstract of reports SU/0531/i, TASS dispatches in Russian and English between 7 and 17 August 1989, trans. in BBCSWB, 25 August 1989, p. SU/0544/A1/1.

67. Peter Almond, "Soviet Lawmakers' Visit Fails to Answer Aspin's Questions," *Washington Times*, 19 February 1990, p. A7. Aspin did state, however, "It seems they are trying to be more than just a rubber stamp for Gorbachev."

68. TASS, "End of Third Session," in English, 1828 GMT, 14 June 1990, in BBCSWB, 16 June 1990, p. SU/0792/C1/1.

69. Oleg Kalugin, interview with author, 23 September 1992. Kalugin was told that he had been invited to join the committee, but he never actually became a member. Victor Yasmann, citing TASS, 16 October 1990, in *RFE/RL Daily Report*, No. 198, 17 October 1990.

70. Lee, pp. 11-12.

71. Lukyanov interview, Moscow Central Television, 27 April 1991, trans. in FBIS-SOV-91, 15 May 1991, p. 37. Cited in *ibid.*

72. Lee, pp. 1, 8-10. In contrast, a former U.S. diplomat in Moscow responsible for following the Committee on Defense and Security claimed that the Committee had a "big effect on defense policy" due to its work on charters for the KGB and the Ministry of Defense. *Ibid.*, p. 13.

73. Sources D, N, O, and S, interviews with author at the Kremlin, Moscow, 4 December 1991. The four were members of the USSR Supreme Soviet Committee on Defense and Security.

74. Lee, p. 23.

75. Sergey Tsypliayev, member of the Committee on Defense and Security, interview with author, Moscow, December 1991.

76. Sources D, N, O and S.

77. Lee, p. 23.

78. "A Little Light on the KGB," p. 4.

79. KGB Lt. Col. Valentin Korolev, cited in Victor Yasmann, "Law on the KGB Published," *RL Report on the USSR*, 2 August 1991, p. 12.

80. KGB Deputy Chairman Valeriy Lebedev, in TASS in English, 1016 GMT, 2 March 1991, in FBIS-SOV-91-042, 4 March 1991, pp. 26-27.

81. Korolev.

82. KGB Colonel of Justice Semen Martirosov, *Rabochaya tribuna*, 5 March 1991, p. 2, trans. in FBIS-SOV-91-049, 13 March 1991, p. 36. Martirosov was asked by an interviewer, "Is it not a paradox that the law is being prepared by employees of the Committee [on State Security (KGB)] itself, and not by a group, for example, of indepndent experts. Could this not influence the objectivity of the draft?" He replied, "Independent experts? But where do you get them 'from the outside?' We cannot invite specialists from the CIA or the FBI to prepare the document. And, indeed, where does one find competent specialists on Soviet intelligence and counterintelligence, if not in the 'competent organs' themselves?"

83. *Ibid.*; V. I. Ilyukhin, chief of the administration of the USSR Procuracy, the organ responsible for checking on the implementation of laws on the KGB, and member of the board of the USSR Procuracy, *Literaturnaya gazeta*, 17 October 1990, cited in *Literaturnaya gazeta* No. 46, 14 November 1990. Also see Kryuchkov's address to the Supreme Soviet joint session, 5 March 1991 carried by TASS international service in Russian, 1427 GMT, 5 March 1991, trans. in FBIS-SOV-91-044, 6 March 1991, pp. 23-27.

84. V. M. Savitskiy, Institute of State and Law of the USSR Academy of Sciences, in *Literaturnaya gazeta*, No. 46, 14 November 1990, p. 11, trans. in FBIS-SOV-90-227, 26 November 1990, p. 67. Savitskiy was also a member of the scientific consultative councils of the USSR Supreme Soviet, Procuracy, and Ministry of Justice.

85. *Ibid.*, p. 68.

86. *Ibid.*, pp. 68-69.

87. Natalya Gevorkyan, "Deputy Proposes, the KGB Disposes," *Moscow News*, No. 11, 17-24 March 1991, p. 6. KGB Colonel of Justice Semen Yenokovich Martirosov of the USSR KGB Inspection Directorate said that the law "was presented to the Supreme Soviet at the end of last year [1990] by the USSR Council of Ministers. Unfortunately, the draft was not reviewed then, as I understand it, because of an unusually heavy agenda." *Rabochaya tribuna*, 5 March 1991, p. 2, trans. in FBIS-SOV-91-049, 13 March 1991, p. 35.

88. TASS in English, 1016 GMT, 2 March 1991, in FBIS-SOV-91-042, 4 March 1991, pp. 27-28.

89. Vladimir Kryuchkov, address to the USSR Supreme Soviet, transcript in TASS international service in Russian, 1427 GMT, 5 March 1991, trans. in FBIS-SOV-91-044, 6 March 1991, pp. 23-25, esp. p. 23.

90. Gevorkyan.

91. *Ibid.*

92. FBIS editorial report summarizing Moscow Domestic Service, 1200 GMT, 5 March 1991, in FBIS-SOV-91-045, 7 March 1991, p. 26. The group of deputies was composed mostly of young members of the Committee for Youth Affairs, which they used as a platform to attack the Supreme Soviet leadership, the armed forces, and the KGB. Most of the members belonged to the Interregional Group. Sources D, N, O and S.

93. Leonid Sharin, interviewed in IAN Press Release in English, Moscow, 3 April 1991, in FBIS-SOV-91-069, 10 April 1991, pp. 36-37.

94. James Rosen, "Law Gives KGB New Powers," United Press International, 16 May 1991.

95. The law's provisions are comprehensively discussed by Yasmann, "Law on the KGB Published."

96. "USSR Law on State Security Bodies in the USSR" [*sic*] Articles 2, 9, and 10, *Izvestiya*, 25 May 1991, union edition, pp. 3-4, trans. in FBIS-SOV-91-102, 28 May 1991.

97. Sharin.

98. "USSR Law on State Security Bodies in the USSR," Article 11; and Yasmann, "Law on the KGB Published," p. 13, citing *Izvestiya TsK KPSS*, No. 3, 1991, pp. 56-59.

99. The most prolific examples are Rubanov, who was fired, and Kalugin, who after his resignation was stripped of his rank, decorations, and pension.

100. "USSR Law on State Security Bodies in the USSR," Article 13, Part 1, Paragraph 16.

101. *Ibid.*, Article 9, which kept the KGB in charge of military and MVD counterintelligence.

102. *Ibid.*, Article 14, Paragraph 2.

103. *Ibid.*, Article 4.

104. *Ibid.*, Article 14, Paragraph 3.

105. *Ibid.*, Article 13, Part I, Paragraph 17.

106. *Ibid.*, Article 4.

107. *Ibid.*, Article 5.

108. *Ibid.*, Article 14, Paragraph 16.

109. Ernst Orlovskiy, *Novoye vremya*, No. 23, June 1991, pp. 34-35, trans. in FBIS-SOV-91-115, 14 June 1991, pp. 25-27.

110. "USSR Law on State Security Bodies in the USSR," Article 13, Part 3, Paragraph 5; Article 14, Paragraph 13; Article 3, Paragraph 14, cited by Yasmann, "Law on the KGB Published," p. 17. Yasmann notes that the existence of other Soviet bureaucracies administering satellites—the USSR Ministry of Space Defense Troops and the Administration of Far Space Communications of the Ministry of Communications—were secrets at that time despite glasnost.

111. Gevorkyan.

112. "USSR Law on State Security Bodies in the USSR," Article 15, Part III, Paragraphs 3 and 5.

113 *Ibid.*, Article 14, Paragraph 9.

114. Orlovskiy.

115. "USSR Law on State Security Bodies in the USSR," Article 15, Part II, Paragraph 5.

116. *Ibid.*, Article 16.

117. *Ibid.*, Articles 19 and 20.

118. Orlovskiy.

119. *Ibid.*

120. *Ibid.*

121. Kalugin, in *Komsomolskoye Znamya* (Kiev), 16 September 1990, pp. 8-9, trans. in FBIS-SOV-90-193, 4 October 1990, p. 55. Kalugin's assertion that the nomenklatura were protected was confirmed in June 1991 by former KGB counterintelligence officer Valentin Yuryevich Korolev on a Soviet television broadcast 1445 GMT, 30 June 1991, trans. in BBCSWB, 2 July 1991.

122. Dr. Boris Pugachev, investigator, Russian Supreme Soviet Commission to Investigate the Causes and Circumstances of the August Putsch, Mayak Radio Network (Moscow), 1420 GMT, 4 February 1992, trans. in FBIS-SOV-92-024, 5 May 1992, pp. 61-62.

Chapter 6

1. Aleksandr Kichikhin, "Fortress Against Reform: The KGB Has Changed Its Name, But Not Much Else," *Crossroads*, Jamestown Foundation, 15 August 1993, p. 10.

2. Tim Zimmerman, "Storm Warnings on the Russian Front," *U.S. News and World Report*, 1 November 1993, p. 54.

3. *Informatsionnyi byulleten KGB USSR*, No. 2, 1990, cited by Alexander Rahr, "Kryuchkov, the KGB, and the 1991 Putsch," *RFE/RL Research Report*, Vol. 2, No. 31, 30 July 1993, p. 19.

4. In the course of private conversations in 1992 and 1993 with at least ten Russian lawmakers of different political persuasions (including some with jurisdiction over the organs) I could find none who understood the mechanisms of control over the Ministry of Security, the External Intelligence Service, or other services.

5. Alexander Rahr, "The Revival of a Strong KGB," *RFE/RL Research Report*, Vol. 2, No. 20, 14 May 1993, p. 76.

6. Law No. 2646-1 of the Russian Federation, "On Security," signed by Russian President Boris Yeltsin at the Russian House of the Soviets, Moscow, 5 March 1992, *Rossiyskaya gazeta*, 6 May 1992, first edition, p. 5, trans. in FBIS-SOV-92-088, 6 May 1992, p. 34. Note: FBIS erroneously cites the date of passage and signature as 5 May 1992.

7. Alexander Rahr, "El'tsin Sets Up New System for Governing Russia," *RL Report on the USSR*, Vol. 3, No. 34, 23 August 1991.

8. There were three State Councillors in the Yeltsin government following the putsch: State Councillor for Legal Affairs Sergey Shakhray, State Councillor for Social Affairs Boris Stankevich, and State Councillor for Regional Affairs Yuriy Skokov. Only Shakhray would attempt to remain true to democratic reform. In late 1992 Stankevich associated himself with the military-industrialist Civic Union, led by Arkadiy Volsky. Skokov's political base was within the same sector.

9. Miroslav Buzhkevich, *Pravda*, 12 February 1992, p. 2, trans. in FBIS-SOV-92-030, 13 February 1992, pp. 48-50.

10. Official Kremlin News Broadcast, text of decree, trans. in Federal News Service, 27 February 1992.

11. *RFE/RL Daily Report*, 1 June 1992.

12. Andrey Illesh and Valeriy Rudnev, *Izvestiya*, 29 July 1993, first edition, pp. 1, 2, trans. in FBIS-SOV-93-144, 29 July 1993, p. 17.

13. Vadim Bakatin, interview with author, 18 September 1992. Said Bakatin, "Ilyushin opens the door for Yeltsin, not vice-versa." As USSR KGB chairman and chief of the Inter-Republic Security Service from August to December 1991, and as a personal friend of Barannikov and other Russian officials who kept his pulse on inside political developments, Bakatin was well positioned to make such an assessment.

14. Law No. 2646-1 of the Russian Federation, "On Security," Section III.

15. Rahr, "El'tsin Sets Up New System for Governing Russia."

16. Law No. 2646-1 of the Russian Federation, "On Security," Article 13.

17. Vasiliy Kononenko, *Izvestiya*, 21 May 1992, morning edition, p. 1, trans. in FBIS-SOV-92-099, 21 May 1992, pp. 49-50.

18. Aleksei Kirpichnikov, "Yuriy Skokov: New Top Man," *Kommersant*, No. 28, 6-13 July 1992, p. 2, trans. in FBIS-SOV-92-137, 16 July 1992, p. 37.

19. Vladimir Orlov, "Chief of Russia's Diplomacy: Yuri Skokov," *Moscow News*, No. 7, 11 February 1993, p. 9.

20. "Statement by Boris Yeltsin at the First Session of the RF Security Council," Official Kremlin International News Broadcast, Federal News Service, 21 May 1992; Gennadiy Talalayev, "Yeltsin Warns Security Council Against Becoming New KGB," ITAR-TASS in English, 20 May 1992.

21. Vice Premier Sergey Shakhray lost his duties as State Councillor on June 15. Yeltsin signed Security Minister Barannikov's decree for the Ministry of Security to absorb the independent Border Guard forces on 16 June. The decree was approved in violation of a January agreement with the Supreme Soviet that no major structural changes in the security services would take place until after 1 July. On 17 June he approved Security Minister Barannikov's decision to fire First Deputy Security Minister Anatoliy Oleynikov, who had carried out Bakatin's reforms of the KGB, and to install in his place former Ukrainian KGB Chairman Nikolay Golushko in his place. On the same date he supported Barannikov's purge of about eighty other officers. The Russian president appointed extremist Col. Gen. Boris Gromov (a charismatic leader with a fanatical following) as deputy minister of defense on 29 June. During the same

period Yeltsin named a number of figures from the "industrialist lobby" to prominent government posts.

22. ITAR-TASS World Service in Russian, 0915 GMT, 15 June 1992, trans. in FBIS-SOV-92-115, 15 June 1992, p. 15.

23. Alexander Rahr, "Yeltsin Courts Industrial Lobby in Order to Reduce Threat from the Right," *RFE/RL Post-Soviet/East European Report*, Vol. 9, No. 28, 1 July 1992, p. 1.

24. Sergey Chugayev, "Yuriy Skokov Receives Power at Premier Level," *Izvestiya*, 11 July 1992, morning edition, p. 2, trans. in FBIS-SOV-92-134, 13 July 1992, pp. 32-33.

25. *Ibid.*, p. 33; Kirpichnikov.

26. *RFE/RL Daily Report*, No. 135, 17 July 1992, p. 1, citing ITAR-TASS, 16 July 1992.

27. "Reform Lawyer Brands Yeltsin Unit a Politburo," *Washington Times*, 9 August 1992, p. A10, citing *Komsomolskaya pravda*.

28. Security Council Secretary (and former CIS Marshal) Yevgeniy Shaposhnikov, interview, *Megapolis-Ekspress*, 28 July 1993, cited in *RFE/RL Daily Report*, No. 144, 30 July 1993, p. 1.

29. *RFE/RL Daily Report*, No. 148, 5 August 1992, p. 1, citing *Nezavisimaya gazeta*, 4 August 1992. If this account of events is true, it could indicate a move by Vice President Rutskoi against the president's authority. Lebed's new assignment followed the surprising appointment of another hard-line officer, Gen. Boris Gromov, who commanded Soviet forces in Afghanistan, as deputy minister of defense. Rutskoi, Lebed, and Russian Minister of Defense Pavel Grachev had served under Gromov in Afghanistan.

30. Edict No. 1571 of the Russian Federation President, "On the Formation of the Interdepartmental Foreign Policy Commission of the Russian Federation Security Council," 16 December 1992, *Rossiyskaya gazeta*, 18 December 1992, first edition, p. 1, trans. in FBIS-SOV-92-247, 23 December 1992, pp. 19-20. For a discussion of the Foreign Policy Commission of the Security Council, see Suzanne Crow, "Processes and Policies," *RFE/RL Research Report*, Vol. 2, No. 20, 14 May 1993, pp. 47-52.

31. Peter Conradi, "Silent Rise of the Invisible Man," *The European*, 28 January 1993.

32. Radio Rossii Network, 0900 GMT, 13 November 1992, trans. in FBIS-SOV-92-220, 13 November 1992, p. 56.

33. Bakatin to author, 18 September 1992.

34. Shaposhnikov.

35. *Kommersant-Daily*, 26 October 1993, p. 3, trans. in FBIS-SOV-93-206, 27 October 1993, p. 22.

36. Vladimir Rubanov to author at a seminar on civil control sponsored by the Glasnost Foundation, Moscow, 9 April 1994.

37. *Komsomolskaya pravda*, 15 January 1992, cited by Julia Wishnevsky, "Russian Constitutional Court: A Third Branch of Government?" *RFE/RL Research Report*, Vol. 2, No. 7, 12 February 1993, p. 1.

38. TASS world service in Russian, 2025 GMT, 28 December 1991, trans. in BBCSWB, SU/1265/B/1, 30 December 1991; Russian Central Television, First All-Union Programme, 1900 GMT, 29 December 1991, trans. in BBCSWB, 31 December 1991, p. SU/1266/B/1.

39. *Izvestiya*, 16 January 1992, morning edition, p. 1, trans. in FBIS-SOV-92-015, 23 January 1992, pp. 42-44.

40. *Ibid*.

41. Interfax in English, 2100 GMT, 15 January 1992, in FBIS-SOV-92-012, 17 January 1992, p. 37.

42. *Izvestiya*, 16 January 1992, morning edition, p. 1, trans. in FBIS-SOV-92-015, 23 January 1992, pp. 42-44.

43. *Ibid*.

44. For a discussion of this question see Wishnevsky, pp. 1-8.

45. Herman Schwartz, "The New East European Constitutional Courts," *Michigan Journal of International Law*, Vol. 13, Summer 1992, p. 137.

46. Law No. 2646-1 of the Russian Federation, "On Security," Article 22; Law No. 3245-1 of the Russian Federation, "On Foreign Intelligence," Section 25, signed by President Boris Yeltsin at the Russian Soviet Center, 8 July 1992, *Rossiyskaya gazeta*, 11 August 1992, p. 4, trans. in FBIS-USR-92-110, 1 September 1992, p. 26.

47. "Russia's Congress of People's Deputies," *Washington Post*, 2 December 1992, p. A34.

48. Kichikhin, "Fortress Against Reform," p. 9.

49. *Megapolis-Express*, No. 11, 1993, cited by Victor Yasmann, "Legislation on Screening and State Security in Russia," *RFE/RL Research Report*, Vol. 2, No. 32, 13 August 1993, p. 16.

50. Rahr, "Kryuchkov, the KGB, and the 1991 Putsch," p. 19.

51. Yevgenia Albats, "Subjects of the KGB," *Moscow News*, No. 14, 1 April 1992.

52. *Ibid*.

53. Author's private discussions with several Russian Supreme Soviet members in 1993.

54. *Izvestiya*, 5 February 1992, morning edition, p. 3, trans. in FBIS-SOV-92-024, 5 February 1992, pp. 60-61.

55. Source W, a member of the Russian Supreme Soviet, interview with author, 1993.

56. *Izvestiya*, 8 February 1992, morning edition, p. 2, trans. in FBIS-SOV-92-031, 14 February 1992, p. 55.

57. Yasmann, "Legislation on Screening and State Security in Russia." The draft law was presented by Democratic Russia leader Galina Starovoitova at the second "KGB: Yesterday, Today and Tomorrow" conference sponsored by the Glasnost Foundation, Moscow, 29-31 May 1993.

58. Rolandas Barysas, "Court Rules Lithuanian Nationalist Worked for KGB," Reuter Library Report, 26 March 1992.

59. Kazis Uscila, ITAR-TASS, 26 March 1992.

60. The woman was Rita Dapkus of Chicago. Michael Kates, "Chicago Woman: I Led Two Lives for Lithuania," *Chicago Tribune*, 27 March 1992; Baltfax in English, 1902 GMT, 2 April 1992, in FBIS-SOV-92-065, 3 April 1992; and Barysas.

61. Vladas Burbulis, ITAR-TASS world service in Russian, 1254 GMT, 14 September 1992, trans. in FBIS-SOV-92-179, 15 September 1992, p. 57.

62. *Izvestiya*, 8 February 1992, morning edition, p. 2, trans. in FBIS-SOV-92-031, 14 February 1992, pp. 54-55.

63. *Komsomolskaya pravda*, 4 February 1992, p. 1, trans. in FBIS-SOV-92-025, 6 February 1992, p. 35. The FBIS translation refers to the SVR as "FIS" (Foreign Intelligence Service).

64. Lev Ponomarev, Russian Television, 2000 GMT, 6 March 1992, trans. in BBCSWB, 9 March 1992, p. SU/1324/B/1; and Radio Moscow World Service in English, 1810 GMT, 6 March 1992, in BBCSWB, 9 March 1992, p. SU/1324/B/1.

65. Ponomarev, Russian Television, 6 March 1992.

66. Lev Ponomarev and Rev. Gleb Yakunin, a commission member, news conference at Cannon House Office Building, Washington, D.C., 20 March 1992; and Ponomarev, interview with author, Jamestown Foundation, Washington, D.C., 27 March 1992. Ponomarev and Yakunin said that Orthodox Patriarch of Moscow Aleksi and External Intelligence Service Director Yevgeniy Primakov asked Khasbulatov to stop the commission, which Khasbulatov then did.

67. Ponomarev to author, 27 March 1992.

68. The hearings circulated around Moscow in photocopy form. An English translation, *Hearings, Russian Federation Supreme Soviet Hearings Concerning the Events Associated with the Attempted Coup d'Etat of August 19-21, 1991*, is housed in the Special Collection at Boston University's Mugar Library.

69. Law No. 3246/1-1 of the Russian Federation, "On the Federal Organs of State Security," Article 21, *Rossiyskaya gazeta*, 12 August 1992, pp. 1, 4, trans. in FBIS-USR-92-121, 24 September 1992, p. 27; Law No. 3245-1 of the Russian Federation "On Foreign Intelligence," Section 25.

70. Law No. 2646-1 of the Russian Federation "On Security," Article 21.

71. Decree No. 3246-1 of the Russian Federation Supreme Soviet "On Execution of Law of Russian Federation 'On Foreign Intelligence,'" 8 July 1992, *Rossiyskaya gazeta*, 11 August 1992, p. 4, trans. in FBIS-USR-92-110, 1 September 1992, p. 26.

72. Members of the Commission on the Budget, Plans, taxes and Prices, the Committee on Defense and Security, and the Committee on Human Rights, confidential interviews with the author, 1993.

73. Sergey Ivanov, member, Committee on Defense and Security, interviewed by Amy Knight, "Russian Security Services Under Yel'tsin," *Post-Soviet Affairs*, Vol. 9, No. 1, January-March 1993, p. 62.

74. Alexander Rahr of Radio Liberty reports that the Committee on Defense and Security "largely consists of former KGB officers." Rahr, "Old KGB Remains Alive and Well in Post-Soviet Russia," *Post-Soviet/East European Report*, RFE/RL Research Institute, Vol. 9, No. 17, 10 March 1992.

75. Martin McCauley, ed., *Directory of Russian MPs* (Harlow, Essex: Longman Current Affairs, 1992), p. The directory, compiled by a team of Russian academic experts, journalists, and political observers and translated into English, contains biographies and political profiles of most members of the Russian Supreme Soviet as of July 1992.

76. Interfax in English, 1801 GMT, 6 October 1992, in FBIS-SOV-92-195, 7 October 1992, p. 10.

77. McCauley, pp. 45-46.

78. Nikolay Kuznetsov, remarks at "KGB: Yesterday, Today and Tomorrow" conference sponsored by the Glasnost Foundation, Moscow, 19 February 1993. From author's notes and verified in transcript.

79. Nikolay Kuznetsov, interview with author, 19 February 1993.

80. Source C, interview with author.

81. Nanette van der Laan, "Parliament Committee Monitors Former KGB," *Moscow Times*, 15 July 1993. Also see A. Peslyak, *Vesti*, Russian Television Network, 1600 GMT, 14 July 1993, trans. in FBIS-SOV-93-134, 15 July 1993, p. 23; and Vladimir Suprun, ITAR-TASS in English, 1322 GMT, 14 July 1993, in FBIS-SOV-93-154, 15 July 1993, pp. 23-24.

82. George Lardner, Jr., and Gary Lee, "Russian Security Group Meets with U.S. Intelligence to Seek Cooperation," *Washington Post*, 14 October 1991, p. A4.

83. Sergey Stepashin, chairman, Committee on Defense and Security, Supreme Soviet of the RSFSR, letter to author, 22 January 1992.

84. Committee Staff Director Sergei Kondrakhin spent a month in Washington and worked briefly out of the office of a House Armed Services Commitee member in 1992. Also see, for example, "Trip Report from a Congressional Delegation's Visit to Moscow, Russian Federation, February 20-24, 1992," prepared by the office of Rep. Jon Kyl (R-Arizona).

85. One of the main organizers was Committee on Defense and Security Secretary Nikolay Kuznetsov, who invited the author to attend.

86. Committee on Defense and Security members were have to visited Washington to study the U.S. oversight system in an exchange I developed at the International Freedom Foundation with a grant from the United States Information Agency. The Supreme Soviet was dissolved before the trip took place.

87. Igor Nikulin, *Komsomolskaya pravda*, 20 October 1992, pp. 1-2, trans. in FBIS-SOV-92-204, 21 October 1992, pp. 22, 23.

88. *Ibid.*

89. *Ibid.*

90. Minister of Security Viktor Barannikov, testimony before the Russian Federation Supreme Soviet Hearings Concerning the Events Associated with the Attempted Coup d'Etat of August 19-21, 1991, Moscow, 4 February 1992, p. 102.

91. Russian Federation People's Deputy Beloborodov, member, Committee on Defense and Security, testimony before the Russian Federation Supreme Soviet, *Ibid.*, pp. 103-104.

92. Sergei Boskholov, Deputy Chairman, State Duma Committee on Security, interview with the author, 9 April 1994.

93. See Ariel Cohen, "Russia's Draft Constitutions: How Democratic Are They?" Heritage Foundation *Backgrounder*, No. 949, 30 June 1993, analyzing Constitutional Commission Draft Constitution, trans. in FBIS-SOV-93-091-S, 13 May 1993.

94. Barannikov, testimony before the Russian Federation Supreme Soviet, p. 107.

95. For discussions of Russian law and society, see three chapters in Uri Ra'anan, Keith Armes, and Kate Martin, eds., *Russian Pluralism: Now Irreversible?* (New York: St. Martin's Press, 1992): Nina Belyaeva, "Toward a Law-Abiding State?" pp. 71-92; Yelena Bonner, "Individual and Group Rights," pp. 93-102; Richard Schifter, "Human Rights: Established or Precarious?" pp. 103-123. Also see Carla Thorson, "Russia: Toward the Rule of Law," *RFE/RL Research Report*, Vol. 1, No. 27, 3 July 1992, pp. 41-49.

96. Barannikov, testimony, p. 106.

97. Law No. 2646-1 of the Russian Federation "On Security," Article 10.

98. *Ibid.*

99. *Ibid.*, Article 11.

100. *Ibid.*, Article 10.

101. *Ibid.*, Article 5.

102. *Ibid.*, Article 3.

103. *Ibid.*, Article 1.

104. *Ibid.*, Article 8.

105. *Ibid.*, Article 12.

106. *Ibid.*, Article 2.

107. *Ibid.*, Article 20.

108. Source P, a high-ranking Russian state security officer, interview with author. Also see Mark Almond, "Introducing KGB PLC," *The Spectator*, London, 10 July 1993, p. 9.

109. *RFE/RL Daily Report*, No. 213, 8 November 1991, p. 1, citing *Moskovskaya pravda*, 6 November 1991.

110. Source P. Many of the advertisers in the newspapers were companies affiliated with the chekists who bought space specifically to support the papers.

111. Law No. 2646-1 of the Russian Federation "On Security," Article 7.

112. Law No. 3246/1 of the Russian Federation "On Federal Organs of State Security," *Rossiyskaya gazeta*, 12 August 1992, pp. 1, 4, trans. in FBIS-USR-92-121, 24 September 1992, pp. 21-28.

113. *Ibid.*, Article 1.

114. *Ibid.*, Article 2.

115. See Chapter 7.

116. Barannikov interview, *Izvestiya*, Union edition, 31 December 1991, trans. in BBCSWB, 1 January 1992, p. SU/1267/B/1.

117. Law 3246-1/1 of the Russian Federation, "On Federal Organs of State Security," Article 4.

118. *Ibid.*, Article 5.

119. *Ibid.*, Article 6, clause 2.

120. *Ibid.*, Article 11.

121. *Ibid.*, Article 12, clause g [sic].
122. *Ibid.*
123. Lev Fedorov and Vil Mirzayanov, "Poisoned Politics," *Moscow News* No. 38, 20 September 1992, p. 16. The authors are chemists. Also see Andrei Illesh and Sergei Mostovshchikov, "Any Journalist Can Be a 'Traitor to the Motherland' Nowadays," *Izvestiya*, 24 October 1992, morning edition, p. 1, trans. in FBIS-SOV-92-207, 26 October 1992, pp. 30-31.
124. Vladimir Petrenko, interview with author, Moscow, May and October 1993.
125. Commonwealth of Independent States customs declaration forms, obtained by author on incoming flights to Moscow and St. Petersburg, and at the Sheremetyevo and Pulkovo airports between 1991 and 1994.
126. Law 3246-1/1 "On Federal Organs of State Security," Article 15.
127. *Ibid.*, Article 13.
128. Sergei Grigoryants, interview with author, 8 April 1994.
129. ***Ibid.***, Article 13, clause f [sic].
130. *Ibid.*, Article 15, section 4.
131. *Ibid.*, Article 12, clause l [sic].
132. Alexander Rahr, "Reform of Russia's State Security Apparatus," p. 29.
133. Sergei Zamoshkin, "Special Services Get More Powers Than Is Good for Citizens," Moscow News, 27 May 1992, p. 22.
134. *Ibid.*
135. *Ibid.*
136. *Ibid.*
137. Law No. 2646-1 "On Security," Articles 2 and 7; and Zamoshkin.
138. Thorson, p. 44.
139. Zamoshkin.
140. Law No. 3245-1 "On Foreign Intelligence," signed by President Boris Yeltsin and dated the Russian Soviet Center, 8 July 1992; and Decree No. 3246-1 of the Russian Federation Supreme Soviet "On Execution of Law of Russian Federation 'On Foreign Intelligence,'" signed by Supreme Soviet Chairman R. I. Khasbulatov, Russian Soviet Center, 8 July 1992, *Rossiyskaya gazeta*, 11 August 1992, p. 4, trans. in FBIS-USR-92-110, 1 September 1992, pp. 21-26, and 26-27.
141. *Ibid.*, Section 4.
142. *Ibid.*, Sections 10 and 12.
143. *Ibid.*, Section 12.
144. *Ibid.*, Section 13.
145. *Ibid.*, Section 19.
146. *Ibid.*, Section 20.
147. *Ibid.*, Section 13.
148. Vadim Kirpichenko to author, Washington, D.C., 11 January 1993.
149. Col. Yuriy Kobaladze, in public exchange with author at the third international conference "KGB: Yesterday,Today and Tomorrow," sponsored by the Glasnost Foundation, Moscow, 3 October 1993. Kobaladze's remarks were videotaped.
150. Law No. 3245-1, "On Foreign Intelligence," Section 7.

151. *Ibid.*
152. *Ibid.*, Section 5.
153. *Ibid.*, Section 11.
154. *Ibid.*, Section 6.
155. See the law "On State Secrets," below. Vil Mirzayanov, who served for 26 years in a top secret chemical weapons laboratory before emerging as a dissident to expose continued covert chemical weapons production, told the author that he was unable to acquire a passport for foreign travel as of May 1994.
156. Certain scientists and engineers involved with military and intelligence programs are forbidden to leave the country. Several cities where military and intelligence programs are designed and produced remained closed by late 1993. Among them are Chelyabinsk-65 and Chelyabinsk-70, which were renamed Ozersk and Snezhinsk. ITAR-TASS, *Izvestiya*, 10 July 1993, first edition, p. 2, trans. in FBIS-SOV-93-133, 14 July 1993, p. 40.
157. Law No. 3245-1, "On Foreign Intelligence," Section 7.
158. *Ibid.*, Section 18.
159. Zamoshkin.
160. Law No. 3245-1, "On Foreign Intelligence," Section 9.
161. Col. Yuriy Kobaladze, SVR Public Relations Bureau chief, statement at Kennan Institute, Woodrow Wilson Center, Smithsonian Institution, Washington, D.C., 11 January 1993.
162. Oleg Glushakov, *Krasnaya zvezda*, 23 July 1993, p. 1, trans. in FBIS-SOV-93-142, 27 July 1993, pp. 42-43.
163. Yuriy Filippov, ITAR-TASS in English, 0744 GMT, 23 July 1993, in FBIS-SOV-93-140, 23 July 1993, p. 36.
164. See Nicholas Daniloff, "Yeltsin, the Press and the New Constitution," *Demokratizatsiya: The Journal of Post-Soviet Democratization*, Vol. 2, No. 1, Winter 1993-1994, pp. 52-64.

Chapter 7

1. Jean Davidson, "UCI Scientists Told Moscow's Aim Is to Deprive U.S. of Foe," *Los Angeles Times*, 12 December 1988, metro section, p. 1.
2. "KGB Adopting a Revised, Friendlier Image," *Washington Post*, 8 September 1985, cited by John Lenczowski, "Military Glasnost' and Strategic Deception," *International Freedom Review*, Winter 1990, p. 38.
3. George Popoff, *The Tcheka: The Red Inquisition* (London: A. M. Philpot, Ltd., 1925), pp. 238-239.
4. *Ibid.*, p. 240.
5. See, for example, Jeremy Murray-Brown, "Sakharov, the KGB, and the Mass Media," in Ladislav Bittman, ed., *The New Image-Makers: Soviet Propaganda and Disinformation Today* (Washington: Pergamon-Brassey's, 1988), pp. 159-200.
6. Transcript of session of the CPSU TsK Politburo, 29 August 1985, published in *Rossiiskie vesti*, 3 October 1992, p. 3, trans. in *Perspective* (Boston: Institute for

the Study of Conflict, Ideology & Policy at Boston University), Vol. 3, No. 2, November 1992, pp. 5, 7.

7. Dusko Doder and Louise Branson, *Gorbachev: Heretic in the Kremlin* (New York: Penguin, 1991), p. 172.

8. "New thinking" was a nebulous term used to characterize the new Party worldview enunciated by Gorbachev. Most practitioners were really Party revisionists instead of real new thinkers, and the "newness" of their thought remained, by and large, within the narrow confines of the Party. Some truly saw the need for democratic and free-market reforms and jettisoned (successfully or otherwise) their ideological baggage. On the foreign policy front, new thinkers were often cynical maneuverers aiming to preserve Soviet power abroad, as Françoise Thom discusses in *Moscow's 'New Thinking' as an Instrument of Foreign Policy* (Toronto: Mackenzie Institute, 1987).

9. Richard Popplewell, "Themes in the Rhetoric of KGB Chairmen from Andropov to Kryuchkov," *Intelligence and National Security*, Vol. 6, No. 3, July 1991.

10. Mihajlo Mihajlov, "The KGB Goes Public," *Disinformation: Soviet Active Measures and Disinformation Forecast*, No. 10, Fall 1988, pp. 13, 14.

11. Popplewell, pp. 520-521; Chebrikov quote cited from *Pravda*, 11 September 1987.

12. *Ibid.*

13. International front organizations directed by the CPSU International Department and funded via the KGB found it difficult to adopt the new line. Insatiable consumers of hard currency and long discredited, they lost their utility, although they continued to be maintained by the Russian state after the dissolution of the USSR. Fund transfers were personally approved by Gorbachev. For a study of these instruments, see Richard H. Shultz and Roy Godson, *Dezinformatsiya: Active Measures in Soviet Strategy* (Washington, D.C.: Pergamon-Brassey's, 1984).

14. The January 1920 Cheka decree to abolish the death penalty is a case in point. It did not change the Cheka's conduct but was purely for foreign consumption, according to Simon Wolin and Robert M. Slusser, eds., *The Soviet Secret Police* (New York: Praeger, 1957), p. 8.

15. Stanislav Levchenko, "Soviet Active Measures in 1989," in Ladislav Bittman, ed., *The Messages from Moscow 1989: Propaganda, Disinformation, Persuasion*, Boston University College of Communication Program for the Study of Disinformation Papers, Vol. 3, No. 1, Summer 1990, pp. 15-16.

16. *Ibid.*, p. 16.

17. *Ibid.*, p. 18.

18. Popplewell, p. 531.

19. Francis X. Clines, "Protesters March to KGB Headquarters," *New York Times*, 31 October 1989.

20. Levchenko, p. 27.

21. *Ibid.*, pp. 26-27.

22. Vladimir Kryuchkov, on Soviet television, 24 June 1989, trans. in BBCSWB, 30 June 1989, p. SU/0496/B/1; and "KGB Adopting a Revised, Friendlier Image."

23. Maj. Gen. Oleg Kalugin, former director of KGB foreign counterintelligence, interview with author, May 1993.

24. Vadim Bakatin, interview with author, 19 September 1992.

25. Christopher Andrew and Oleg Gordievsky, *KGB: The Inside Story* (New York: Harper Collins, 1990), pp. 534-535.

26. Vladimir Kryuchkov, interview on "Around Midnight" television program, Moscow, 30 June 1989, trans. in BBCSWB, 30 June 1989, p. SU/0496 B/1.

27. Alexander Rahr, "Gorbachev and the Post-Chebrikov KGB," Radio Free Europe/Radio Liberty *Report on the USSR*, 22 December 1989, citing Karpovich in *Ogonek* No. 29, 1989.

28. *New Times* in English, 8-14 August 1989, cited by Popplewell, pp. 533-534.

29. *Moskovskaya pravda*, 14 September 1989, p. 4, trans. in FBIS-SOV-89-187, 28 September 1989, pp. 75-76.

30. R. Ignatyev, "Perestroika in the KGB," *Izvestiya*, 27 October 1989, p. 3, trans. in FBIS-SOV-89-207, 27 October 1989, pp. 65-66.

31. *Ibid.*, p. 67.

32. Moscow in English to North America, 0100 GMT, 18 October 1989, in FBIS-SOV-89-201, 19 October 1989, pp. 43-44.

33. "KGB Adopting a Revised, Friendlier Image."

34. *Ibid.*

35. "And Now, the Selling of the KGB," *Washington Post*, 14 September 1989, and "KGB Goes Wimp with Video Showing Its 'Just Folks' Side," *Washington Times*, 14 September 1989, cited by Lenczowski, p. 39.

36. Vadim Bakatin, *Izbavleniye ot KGB* (Moscow: Novosti, 1992), pp. 40-41. Bakatin says that KGB officers "were not at all delighted with the fact that many had to train for a new profession as trade inspectors."

37. Sociology Institute of the Russian Academy of Sciences and Circon poll of 1,530 individuals in nine Commonwealth of Independent States republics, December 1991-January 1992, cited by Olga Krishtanovskaya, "Advocates and Antagonists of the KGB," *Nezavisimaya gazeta* international edition in English, Issue 4-5, August 1993, p. 3. Only 13 percent surveyed were opposed to KGB foreign intelligence.

38. Vladimir Kryuchkov, in *L'Unita* (Rome) in Italian, 19 August 1989, pp. 6-7, trans. in FBIS-SOV-89-201, 19 October 1989, p. 50.

39. *Argumenty i fakty*, no. 48, December 1990, pp. 6-7, trans. in FBIS-SOV-90-235, 6 December 1990, pp. 46-48.

40. Aleksandr Karbainov, KGB public relations chief, interview in *Milliyet* (Istanbul) in Turkish, 28 November 1990, p. 14, trans. in FBIS-SOV-91-008-S, 11 January 1991, pp. 21-22.

41. *Pravda Ukrainy* (Kiev), 3 September 1989, p. 2, trans. in FBIS-SOV-89-180, 19 September 1989, p. 55.

42. KGB Maj. Gen. Anatoli Petrovich Bondarev, BBCSWB, 6 November 1989, p. SU/0606/C2/9, cited by Andrew and Gordievsky, p. 616.

43. A photograph appears in *Soviet Intelligence and Active Measures* (formerly *Disinformation: Soviet Active Measures and Disinformation Forecast*), Nos. 15/16, Summer/Fall 1990, p. 24.

44. KGB Major General Igor Ivanovich Ustinov, in V. Galenkin, "Law, Truth, and Glasnost: KGB Staffers Answer Workers' Questions," *Trud*, 19 August 1989, p. 3, trans. in FBIS-SOV-89-166, 27 August 1989, pp. 71-72.

45. Vladimir Abarinov, *The Murderers of Katyn* (New York: Hippocrene, 1991).

46. Col. Peter S. Nikulin, in E. Oznobkina and L. Isakov, eds., *KGB: Yesterday, Today, Tomorrow* (Moscow: Znak-SP/Gandalf, 1993), p. 155.

47. Moscow International Service in Slovak, 1600 GMT, 16 October 1989, trans. in FBIS-SOV-89-199, 17 October 1989, p. 71. Kryuchkov's foreign intelligence chief, Leonid Shebarshin, later said he still thought defectors like Oleg Gordievsky should be assassinated. See John Kampfner, "Fury of the Defiant Diehard," *The Daily Telegraph*, n.d., December 1990.

48. Stanislav Levchenko, interview with author, June 1993.

49. "The KGB from the Horse's Mouth," *New Times* in English, 8-14 August 1989, cited by Popplewell, p. 524.

50. United States Information Agency, *Soviet Active Measures in the 'Post-Cold War' Era, 1988-1991* (Washington, D.C.: USIA, June 1992), pp. 77-79, citing the *New York Times*, 1 April 1987; John Marks and Brian Jenkins, "Talking Terrorism with Moscow," *Washington Post*, 5 March 1989; *Izvestiya*, 11 February 1989.

51. John Marks and Igor Beliaev, eds., *Common Ground on Terrorism* (New York: W. W. Norton, 1991).

52. Patrick Clawson, review, *Orbis*, Fall 1991, p. 607.

53. Michael Dobbs, "Yeltsin Aides Seek to Link Gorbachev to Terrorism," *Washington Post*, 6 June 1992, p. A19. The *Los Angeles Times* quotes Poltaranin: "These groups, for example, were ready to demolish pipelines or kill American businessmen or British or others . . . and [the Communist Party leaders] supplied them with rifles, guns, hand grenades, submachine guns, etc." Elizabeth Shogren, "Soviets Accused of Funding Terrorism Until '91," *Los Angeles Times*, 6 June 1992; Vladimir Isachenkov, "Archives: KGB Gave Millions to Terrorists for Stolen Art," Associated Press, 10 June 1992. For documentation on Soviet support for terrorism under Brezhnev and Andropov, see Jillian Becker, *The Soviet Connection: State Sponsorship of Terrorism* (London: Institute for European Defence & Strategic Studies, 1985); Ray S. Cline and Yonah Alexander, *Terrorism: The Soviet Connection* (New York: Crane Russak, 1984); Roberta Goren, *The Soviet Union and Terrorism* (London: George Allen & Unwin, 1984); Uri Ra'anan, Robert L. Pfaltzgraff, Jr., Richard H. Shultz, Ernst Halperin, and Igor Lukes, eds., *Hydra of Carnage: International Linkages of Terrorism: The Witnesses Speak* (Lexington, Massachusetts: Lexington Books, 1986); Herbert Romerstein, *The Soviet Union and International Terrorism* (Washington, D.C.: Foundation for Democratic Education, 1981); Richard H. Shultz, Jr., *The Soviet Union and*

Revolutionary Warfare (Stanford: Hoover Institution Press, 1988); Claire Sterling, *The Terror Network* (New York: Holt, Rinehart Winston/Reader's Digest Press, 1981); U.S. Senate, Committee on the Judiciary, Subcommittee on Security and Terrorism, *Soviet, East German and Cuban Involvement in Fomenting Terrorism in Southern Africa* (Washington, D.C.: U.S. Government Printing Office, November 1982); and U.S. Senate, Committee on the Judiciary, Subcommittee on Security and Terrorism, *State-Sponsored Terrorism* (Washington, D.C.: U.S. Government Printing Office, June 1985). For a survey of Soviet military and other support for the African National Congress (ANC) of South Africa while it was engaged in terrorist activity, based on official Soviet records, see Vladimir Abarinov, "ANC Keeps Significant Soviet Arms Stockpiles," *Nezavisimaya gazeta,* international edition in English, August 1992, pp. 8-9; and Abarinov, "The Generous Hand of Moscow: The African National Congress Received from the Soviet Union Not Only Socks, but Also Saxophones," *Nezavisimaya gazeta,* 2 September 1992, p. 4.

54. Radio Moscow in English to North America, 2300 GMT, 28 October 1989, in FBIS-SOV-89-201, 29 October 1989, pp. 44-45.

55. Brochure cited and described in United States Information Agency, *Soviet Disinformation in the 'Post-Cold War Era,' 1989-1991,* USIA Report to Congress (Washington, D.C.: USIA, June 1992).

56. Vladimir Kryuchkov, in *Soyuz,* No. 47, November 1990, pp. 3, 10-11, trans. in FBIS-SOV-90-240, 13 December 1990, p. 49.

57. Moscow in English to North America, 0100 GMT, 18 October 1989.

58. TASS in English, 2353 GMT, 30 October 1989, in FBIS-SOV-89-209, 31 October 1989.

59. *Moskovskaya pravda,* 14 September 1989, p. 4, trans. in FBIS-SOV-89-187, 28 September 1989, pp. 75-76. The column was edited by Yu. Shabanov, chief of the newspaper's Communist Education Department, who "previously served in all the subdivisions of the USSR KGB Administration for Moscow and Moscow oblast."

60. Yu. Savin, "KGB Officials Respond to Questions," *Argumenty i fakty,* No. 32, 12-18 August 1989, p. 7, trans. in FBIS-SOV-89-161, 22 August 1989, pp. 63-64; and text of Ustinov.

61. *Pravda,* 15 June 1990, cited by Popplewell, p. 533.

62. *Pravda,* 21 June 1990, cited in *ibid.,* p. 538.

63. *Ibid.,* p. 536.

64. After the putsch investigators found that plans were already being made within the top levels of the KGB in 1990. According to former USSR People's Deputy Sergey Belozertsev, USSR Supreme Soviet Chairman Anatoliy Lukyanov held a meeting in March 1990, where participants decided that if they could not "curb Russia" in six months with Gorbachev, that is, by September, they would have to impose a state of emergency. Assault troops under KGB jurisdiction were stationed around Moscow in September 1990. *Kuranty,* 1 February 1992, p. 1, trans. in FBIS-SOV-92-023, 4 February 1992, pp. 38-39.

Decrypted KGB documents leaked to *Komsomolskaya pravda* showed that "the idea of imposing a state of emergency in the country occurred to Chairman Kryuchkov apparently as early as December of last year [1990], when he first instructed Zhizhin, former deputy chief of PGU [First Chief Directorate] (Intelligence), and Yegorov, an aide to former USSR KGB First Deputy Grushko, to 'effect a study of possible primary measures of imposition of a state of emergency.' Kryuchkov's instructions were carried out, and the KGB chairman made use of the materials prepared as late as early August." *Komsomolskaya pravda*, 21 December 1991, p. 3, trans. in FBIS-SOV-91-251, 31 December 1991, p. 12.

65. Diane Sawyer, *Prime Time Live*, ABC News, 20 September 1990. Also see Richard Popplewell, "KGB Chairman Seeks New Image," *Soviet Intelligence & Active Measures* (formerly *Disinformation: Soviet Active Measures and Disinformation Forecast*), Nos. 15-16, p. 15.

66. Including Eighth Chief Directorate head Lt. Gen. Nikolay Nikolayevich Andreyev, *Pravda*, 16 September 1990, second edition, p. 2, trans. in FBIS-SOV-90-185, 24 September 1990, pp. 64-68.

67. *RFE/RL Daily Report*, No. 184, 26 September 1990, p. 7, citing *Sobesednik*, No. 38.

68. TASS, in *Komsomolskaya pravda*, 4 April 1991, p. 3., trans. in FBIS-SOV-91-067, 8 April 1991, p. 39.

69. Source H, interview with author. This account coincides with an earlier report that shortly prior to his appointment as Public Relations Center chief, Karbainov worked in the "dissident" directorate of the KGB. *Rabochaya tribuna*, 31 August 1991, p. 2, trans. in FBIS-SOV-91-177, 12 September 1991, pp. 31-32.

70. *La Repubblica*, Rome, in Italian, 24 August 1991, p. 7, trans. in FBIS-SOV-91-167, 28 August 1991, p. 36.

71. *Ibid*.

72. *Bild am Sonntag*, Hamburg, in German, 1 December 1991, p. 19, trans. in FBIS-SOV-91-234, 5 December 1991, p. 29.

73. Source H, to author.

74. *Rabochaya tribuna*, 9 May 1990, cited in *Soviet Intelligence and Active Measures*, Nos. 15-16, p. 13.

75. *Izvestiya*, 18 July 1991, union edition, p. 3, trans. in FBIS-SOV-91-140, 22 July 1991.

76. Lenczowski, p. 39.

77. Lt. Gen. Nikolay N. Andreyev, in *Pravda*, 16 September 1990, second edition, p. 2, trans. in FBIS-SOV-90-185, 24 September 1990, pp. 64-68.

78. *Rabochaya tribuna*, 5 March 1991, p. 2, trans. in FBIS-SOV-91-049, 13 March 1991, pp. 35-36.

79. *Pravda*, 16 September 1990, second edition, p. 2, trans. in FBIS-SOV-90-185, 24 September 1990, pp. 64-68.

80. *Soyuz*, No. 47, November 1990, pp. 3, 10, 11, trans. in FBIS-SOV-90-240, 13 December 1990, pp. 48-52.

81. *Argumenty i fakty*, no. 48, December 1990, pp. 6-7, trans. in FBIS-SOV-90-235, 6 December 1990, pp. 46-48.

82. TASS international service in Russian, 1040 GMT, 16 December 1990, trans. in FBIS-SOV-90-242, 17 December 1990, p. 42. Shebarshin's name and position were made public earlier in 1990 by defector Vladimir Kuzichkin, *Inside*

the KGB: My Life in Soviet Espionage (New York: Ballantine/Ivy, 1990, 1992), p. 383.

83. *Pravda,* 20 December 1990, second edition, p. 6, trans. in FBIS-SOV-90-245, 20 December 1990, p. 51. The Bolshevik Council of People's Commissars (Sovnarkom) issued the order to establish the All-Russian Extraordinary Commission to Combat Counterrevolution and Sabotage (known as the Cheka) on 20 December 1917. On the third anniversary of the Cheka, Dzerzhinskiy ordered that the Foreign Department (*Inostranyy otdel,* INO) be created. John J. Dziak, *Chekisty: A History of the KGB* (Lexington: Lexington Books, 1988), pp. 13, 14. The Russian Ministry of Security and External Intelligence Service (SVR) were founded on 20 December 1991.

84. *Washington Post,* 12 December 1990, p. A18.

85. *Pravda,* 13 December 1990, second edition, pp. 1, 2, trans. in FBIS-SOV-90-240, 13 December 1990, p. 47.

86. *Izvestiya,* 15 December 1990, union edition, p. 4, trans. in FBIS-SOV-90-242, 17 December 1990, pp. 39-42.

87. Transcript in BBCSWB, 21 January 1991.

88. Moscow Domestic Service, 1900 GMT, 17 January 1991, trans. in FBIS-SOV-91-013, 18 January 1991, pp. 26-27.

89. Central Television First Program Network, Moscow, 1800 GMT, 18 January 1991, trans. in FBIS-SOV-91-014, 22 January 1991, pp. 44-45.

Chapter 8

1. *Izvestiya,* 31 December 1991, union edition, trans. in BBCSWB, 1 January 1992, p. SU/1267/B/1.

2. Col. Aleksey Kandaurov, remarks for the record, in E. Oznobkina, ed., *KGB: Yesterday, Today and Tomorrow: Proceedings of the 1st International Conference Plenary Session,* trans. A. Shkarubo (Moscow: Glasnost Foundation, 1993), p. 30.

3. Sociology Institute of the Russian Academy of Sciences/Circon poll of 1,530 individuals in nine CIS republics, commissioned by the Inter-republican Security Service, December 1991-January 1992, reported by Olga Kryshtanovskaya, "Advocates and Antagonists of the KGB: Neither Have a Decided Advantage," *Nezavisimaya gazeta,* English international edition, Vol. 4, Issue 4-5, August 1993, p. 3.

4. *Ibid.*

5. Observations of author inside Moscow KGB headquarters and around the perimeter of the Lubyanka complex on various occasions from 1991 to 1994.

6. Vil Mirzayanov, interview with author, April 1994. Mirzayanov, a disident former chemical weapons scientist, was imprisoned in Lefortovo in October 1992 and brought back to the facility for processing in late 1993.

7. For example, I asked Lt. Gen. Vadim Kirpichenko, chairman of the SVR Advisory Council, why the SVR was not dispensing with Dzerzhinskiy iconolatry given the state terror he perpetrated. Kirpichenko grew somewhat agitated and began an emotional defense of the Cheka founder, saying that people

do not remember him for all the good things he did. The exchange occurred in Washington, D.C., on 13 January 1993. At a 20 October 1993 news conference, I asked the same question of Col. Yuriy Totrov, who retired in 1992 but in Washington to begin a five-week unofficial SVR propaganda tour of the United States sponsored by the Association of National Security Alumni. When pressed, Totrov strongly defended Dzerzhinskiy and said that the Russian intelligence services would never shed their chekist legacy because "you can't take our history away from us." From author's notes.

8. Kirpichenko, exchange with author, 13 January 1993.

9. The selections below are representative of a larger collection of quotations and statements issued by the Ministry of Security or by MB officials in 1992.

10. Viktor Barannikov, Russian Television, 1500 GMT, 27 April 1992, trans. in BBCSWB, 29 April 1992, p. SU/1367/B/1.

11. *Ibid.*

12. Anatoliy Oleynikov, in *Trud,* cited by TASS in English, 1155 GMT, 27 February 1992, in FBIS-SOV-92-042, 3 March 1992, pp. 45-46.

13. Viktor Barannikov, interview in *Krasnaya zvezda,* 14 May 1992, p. 2, trans. in FBIS-SOV-92-099, 21 May 1992, p. 70. Dzerzhinskiy spoke thusly in 1922: "The Vecheka . . . with honor has fulfilled the difficult task it was entrusted with. At the very height of the civil war, when we were caught in the fiery grip of the blockade, when we suffered from hunger, cold and devastation, when the white guards at home and the imperialists abroad approached the heart of the republic, the Vecheka and its local organs carried out self-sacrificing, heroic work. . . .The Vecheka is proud of its heroes and martyrs, who perished in the struggle." G. A. Belov, et al., eds., *Iz istorii vserossiiskoi chrezvychainoi kommissii, 1917-21 gg. Sbornik dokumentov* (Moscow: Politizdat, 1958), pp. 474-475, cited by Amy W. Knight, *The KGB: Police and Politics in the Soviet Union* (Boston: Unwin Hyman, 1988, 1990), p. 13.

14. Barannikov, *Krasnaya zvezda,* pp. 69-70.

15. *Rossiyskiye vesti,* 25 July 1992, p. 1, trans. in FBIS-SOV-92-145, 28 July 1992, p. 42.

16. Grigoriy Yavlinsky, interview in *Nezavisimaya gazeta,* 25 December 1993, pp. 1, 3, trans. in FBIS-SOV-93-246, 27 December 1993, pp. 46-47.

17. Anatoliy Oleynikov, transcript of news conference, Official Kremlin International News Broadcast, 27 February 1992, trans. in Federal News Service, 28 February 1992.

18. Barannikov, *Krasnaya zvezda,* 14 May 1992, p. 69.

19. Knight, p. 14.

20. Barannikov, *Krasnaya zvezda,* 14 May 1992, p. 69.

21. Natalya Gevorkyan, "Revanchism in the Security Forces," *Crossroads,* Jamestown Foundation, 15 March 1993, p. 4.

22. Oleynikov, in *Trud,* TASS world service in Russian, 1145 GMT, 25 February 1992, trans. in FBIS-SOV-92-038, 26 February 1992, p. 35; Barannikov, Russian Television, 27 April 1992. The MB announced the creation of a new counterterrorism unit in July 1992; see ITAR-TASS world service in Russian, 1355 GMT, 24 July 1992, trans. in FBIS-SOV-92-146, 29 July 1992, pp. 17-18.

23. *Izvestiya,* 22 January 1992, morning edition, p. 2, trans. in FBIS-SOV-92-018, 28 January 1992, p. 40.
24. United Press International, 27 February 1992; TASS world service in Russian, 1220 GMT, 27 February 1992, trans. in FBIS-SOV-92-042, 3 March 1992, p. 44.
25. *Izvestiya,* 31 December 1991, union edition, trans. in BBCSWB, 1 January 1992, p. SU/1267/B/1.
26. A. Drubnov, "Vesti," Russian Television Network, 1100 GMT, 10 January 1994, trans. in FBIS-SOV-94-006, 10 January 1994, p. 22.
27. Aleksey Kandaurov, interview in *Panorama* (Italy), 4 February 1994, p. 72, trans. in FBIS-SOV-94-026, 8 February 1994, p. 11.
28. TASS in English, 1927 GMT, 4 February 1992, in FBIS-SOV-92-024, 5 February 1992, p. 63.
29. Barannikov, Russian Television, 27 April 1992.
30. *Ibid.* Many Russians who comment on reform of the security organs refer to the industrialized democracies in the West as "civilized countries," thereby implying that their own country is not civilized. In discussiong civil controls with Russian political, juridical and chekist figures, I found that use of the term is used by people of widely differing backgrounds, professions and political persuasions.
31. Oleynikov, Official Kremlin International News Broadcast, 27 February 1992.
32. Oleynikov, in *Trud.*
33. Gen. Andrei Chernenko, chief of public relations, Ministry of Security, in *Pravda,* 30 September 1992, p. 2, trans. in FBIS-SOV-92-195, 7 October 1992, pp. 32-33.
34. Oleynikov, in *Trud.*
35. *Ibid.*
36. Viktor Barannikov, testimony before the Russian Federation Supreme Soviet Hearings Concerning the Events Associated with the Attempted Coup d'etat of August 19-21, 1991, Moscow, 4 February 1992, Boston University transcript, Mugar Library, Special Collections, p. 100.
37. Gevorkyan, p. 5.
38. Russian Federation Council of Ministers, Government Decree No. 685, 20 July 1993, "On Additional Measures to Ensure the Procedure for Russian Federation Citizens to Leave the Russian Federation," *Rossiyskiye vesti,* 3 August 1993, p. 5, trans. in FBIS-SOV-93-148, 4 August 1993, p. 22.
39. Interfax in English, 1437 GMT, 27 October 1992, p. 27, in FBIS-SOV-92-208, 27 October 1992, p. 27.
40. TASS in English, 1927 GMT, 4 February 1992, in FBIS-SOV-92-024, 5 February 1992, p. 63.
41. Gen. Andrei Chernenko, in *Literaturnaya gazeta,* No. 51, cited in *RFE/RL Daily Report,* No. 242, 17 December 1992, p. 2.
42. Yevgeniya Albats, former *Moscow News* reporter and analyst, presentation at the School of Advanced International Studies, Johns Hopkins University, 20 November 1992, cited by Amy Knight, "Russian Security Services Under Yel'tsin," *Post Soviet Affairs,* Vol. 9, No. 1, January-March 1993, p. 51. Reporters and

editors from three Moscow newspapers confirmed Albats's allegations in individual and confidential discussions with the author in 1993.

43. Mary Dejevsky, "Moscow Sheds Light on Mystery of Missing U.S. Spy Planes," *The Times* (London), 28 February 1992.

44. Anatoliy Oleynikov, cited in *The Proper Role of an Intelligence Service in a Democracy* (Washington, D.C.: Center for Democracy, 1992), p. 50.

45. Andrei Gurov, deputy director, Ministry of Security Public Relations Center, cited by Interfax in English, 1355 GMT, 27 February 1992, in BBCSWB, 3 March 1992, p. SU/1319/A1/1.

46. ITAR-TASS world service in Russian, 1355 GMT, 24 July 1992, trans. in FBIS-SOV-92-146, 29 July 1992, pp. 17-18.

47. *RFE/RL Daily Report*, No. 31, 16 February 1993, p. 2. Also see commentary on Barannikov's speech to the Congress of People's Deputies in *RFE/RL Daily Report*, No. 240, 15 December 1992.

48. *Izvestiya*, 8 February 1992, morning edition, p. 8, trans. in FBIS-SOV-92-030, 13 February 1992, pp. 50-51.

49. *Ibid.*

50. *Ibid.*

51. Igor Andreyev and Valeriy Yakov, *Izvestiya*, 24 December 1993, first edition, pp. 1-2, trans. in FBIS-SOV-93-246, 27 December 1993, p. 45.

52. *Izvestiya*, 28 February 1992, morning edition, p. 2, trans. in FBIS-SOV-92-044, 5 March 1992, p. 44.

53. At the February 1993 Glasnost Foundation conference, I spoke about the shallowness of the Ministry of Security's anticorruption campaign, and cited several breaches and abuses which the chekists either permitted or ignored. I alleged that Minister Barannikov "deliberately" ignored the activity of certain organized criminal elements, and argued that because of that, the U.S. should refrain from rendering assistance to fight organized crime. At that, MB spokesman Col. Aleksei Kandaurov jumped up from his seat and shouted me down, saying that I should not be allowed to make such statements. Five months later, Barannikov was fired—in part because of his own alleged involvement in criminal activity. For a transcript of my remarks, see J. Michael Waller, "K probleme obobshcheniya nekotorykh zzakonodatelnykh aspektov," E. Oznobkina and L. Isakova, eds., *KGB: Vchera, segodnya, zavtra* (Moscow: Znak-SP/Galdalf, 1993), pp. 108-114.

54. Anatoliy Oleynikov represented the Ministry of Security at a conference sponsored by U.S. Center for Democracy President Allen Weinstein and Bulgarian President Zhelyu Zhelev, Sofia, Bulgaria, 8-10 April 1992. For proceedings, see *The Proper Role of an Intelligence Service in a Democracy* (Washington, D.C.: Center for Democracy, 1992). MB officials also participated in open conferences and roundtables in Moscow sponsored by the Supreme Soviet Committee on Defense and Security and by the Academy of Sciences, as well as in the February, May, and October 1993 conferences on the "KGB: Yesterday, Today and Tomorrow," sponsored in Moscow by human rights activist Sergey Grigoryants.

55. Official Kremlin International News Broadcast, "Press Conference with the RF Secret Services," 7 April 1994, trans. by Federal Information Systems Corporation, on Nexis.

56. Sergey Grigoryants, interview with author, 10 April 1994.

57. Olga Kryshtanovskaya, Institute of Applied Sciences, presentation at the second conference on the "KGB: Yesterday, Today, and Tomorrow," in E. Oznobkina and L. Isakova, eds., *KGB: Yesterday, Today, Tomorrow (Collected Papers)*, Moscow: Znak-SP, Gandalf, 1993), pp. 139-140.

58. Teleradiokompaniya Ostankino Television First Program Network, 1425 GMT, 10 July 1992, trans. in FBIS Editorial Report, FBIS-SOV-92-136, 15 July 1992, p. 28.

59. Rodion Morozov, *Obshchaya gazeta*, No. 22/24, 17-23 December 1993, trans. in FBIS-SOV-93-242, 20 December 1993, p. 66.

60. *RFE/RL Daily Report*, No. 168, 2 September 1992, pp. 2-3.

61. Warren Christopher, U.S. secretary of state, response to question by the Minority of the Senate Committee on Foreign Relations, 4 November 1993.

62. *RFE/RL Daily Report*, No. 168, p. 2.

63. Barannikov, *Krasnaya zvezda*, p. 69.

64. Chernenko, *Pravda*, 30 September 1992.

65. The main organizer was *Demokratizatsiya* founder Fredo Arias-King. Participants included former KGB Foreign Counterintelligence chief Maj. Gen. Oleg Kalugin and former KGB Col. Vladimir Rubanov (who subsequently became deputy secretary of President Yeltsin's security council). For a report on the work that led to the Moscow State University conference, see Fredo Arias-King, "On the Path to Reforming the KGB: Proposals and Projects," *Demokratizatsiya: The Journal of Post-Soviet Democratization*, Vol. 1, No. 1, Summer 1992, pp. 98-110. Also see J. Michael Waller, "When Will Democrats Control the Former KGB?" *ibid.*, pp. 27-40.

66. Interfax in English, 1745 GMT, 29 October 1992, in FBIS-SOV-92-211, 30 October 1992, p. 9.

67. Andrew Higgins, "New KGB Lashes Out At 'Foreign Meddling,'" *The Independent* (London), 28 January 1993.

68. In the case of the International Freedom Foundation (IFF), Chernenko was referring to the program that I developed at Boston University's Institute for the Study of Conflict, Ideology, and Policy (as a byproduct of my research for a Ph.D. dissertation) to assist government officials, Supreme Soviet members, journalists, and others by providing them with information and expertise on the principles and mechanics of civil control of security and intelligence services in Western societies. IFF had worked for a year with some of the organizers of the conference. The Heritage Foundation, which recently had opened an office in Moscow, publicized the upcoming event in the United States and urged American experts to attend.

69. Higgins.

70. Aleksandr Miroshnikov, "Special Services: Monitoring of State Security with Soros's Money," *Rossiyskaya gazeta*, 4 August 1993, first edition, p. 5.

71. Stepashin was referring specifically to Sergey Grigoryants, former KGB Maj. Gen. Oleg Kalugin, and investigative journalist Yevgeniya Albats, according to Grigoryants and Kalugin in interviews with the author, Moscow, April 1994.

72. Bill Gertz, "Russia, China Sign Pact Restoring Intelligence Ties," *Washington Times*, 21 October 1992, p. A7.

73. Pascal Fletcher, "Russia Keeps Ear Tuned in Cuba: Listening Post Stays Under New Accords," Reuters dispatch, *Washington Post*, 4 November 1992. The listening post is not operated by the SVR but by the Federal Agency for Government Communications.

74. *Nezavisimaya gazeta*, 21 December 1991, pp. 1, 5, trans. in FBIS-SOV-92-002, 3 January 1992, p. 7.

75. Among the most responsive to this theme was David Wise, "Closing Down the KGB," *The New York Times Magazine*, 24 November 1991; and Wise, "House of Cards," *The Times*, London, 30 November 1991. The headlines and leads did not reflect more critical analysis in the text. Wise was one of the few Western journalists to visit foreign intelligence headquarters at Yasenevo.

76. Kirpichenko, presentation at the Kennan Institute, Washington, D.C., 11 January 1993. From author's notes.

77. The Russian Federal Agency for Government Communications, responsible for cryptography, also compares itself favorably to its American counterpart. Created by decree on 28 December 1991 from the Soviet Government Communications Committee—the former USSR KGB Eighth Chief Directorate, 16th Directorate, and Communications Troops—the new unit's existence was announced immediately in the official *Rossiyskaya gazeta*. Said the official announcement: "The agency has been created by analogy with the U.S. National Security Agency. In addition to supplying the top leaders of the republic with all types of scrambled communications, its functions include the development of encoding and decoding apparatus, which are used in the interests of Russian ministries and departments. So far the department's services are also used by the sovereign states belonging to the former USSR. The agency also engages in the interception and decoding of information. This function is extremely important, because it provides a source of information for the state's top leaders that is independent of the special services." See *Rossiyskaya gazeta*, 28 December 1991, first edition, p. 2, trans. in FBIS-SOV-92-001, 2 January 1992, p. 57.

78. Radio Rossii, 1300 GMT, 24 January 1992, trans. in FBIS-SOV-92-019, 29 January 1992, p. 48; and *RFE/RL Daily Report*, No. 84, 4 May 1992, p. 1.

79. SVR Director General Yevgeniy Primakov, to *The Sunday Times* (London), 27 September 1992, in *RFE/RL Daily Report*, No. 186, 28 September 1992, p. 3; Kirpichenko, Kennan Institute, 11 January 1993. From author's notes.

80. SVR Press Bureau Chief Yuriy Kobaladze, Radio Rossii Network, 1100 GMT, 2 November 1992, trans. in FBIS-SOV-92-213, 3 November 1992, p. 47.

81. Yuriy Kobaladze, presentation at the Kennan Institute, Washington, D.C., 11 January 1993. From author's notes. Kobaladze's figures were disputed at the conference by Amy Knight.

82. Yuriy Kobaladze, statement at the third international conference on "KGB: Yesterday, Today, and Tomorrow," Glasnost Foundation, Moscow, 3 October 1993. From author's notes. Also, statement of Cols. Yuri Totrov, Vladimir Barkovsky, Vsevelod Gapon, and Yuri Modin, sponsored by the Association of National Security Alumni, National Press Building, Washington, D.C., 20 October

1993. From author's notes. Barkovsky and Modin were espionage officers for Stalin; Modin served as a case officer for atom bomb spy Klaus Fuchs. Also see Matt Campbell, "Ex-KGB Colonels Find Eager Audiences," *Kansas City Star/Washington Times*, 5 November 1993.

83. Yuriy Kobaladze, cited by Victoria Clark, *London Observer* dispatch, "Russian Spy Service Called Dying Body," *Washington Times*, 8 March 1994.

84. Stanislav Levchenko, interview with author, 22 October 1993.

85. Aleksandr Chernyak, *Pravda*, 28 February 1992, pp. 1, 3, trans. in FBIS-SOV-92-044, 5 March 1992, pp. 12-13.

86. Kirpichenko, presentation at the Kennan Institute.

87. Yuriy Kobaladze, *Izvestiya*, 4 May 1992, cited in *RFE/RL Daily Report*, No. 85, 5 May 1992, p. 2. The reports were extremely well documented. A Soviet/Russian industrial espionage ring based in Belgium was destroyed when KGB First Chief Directorate officer Igor Cherpinsky, stationed in Brussels, defected in 1990. Late the following year Soviet Embassy First Secretary Vladimir Konopolev, who defected in place to the CIA, fled to the United States in April 1992, shortly before Kobaladze made his remark. The Konopolev defection compromised a vast Russian military technology theft ring in Belgium and France. Avigdor Haselkorn and Christopher Coker, "The Spies Who Stayed in the Cold," *European Security Analyst* (London: Institute for European Defence and Strategic Studies), No. 20, August 1992, p. 2.

88. "I Have the Honor—Intelligence Service," Teleradiokompaniya Ostankino Television First Program Network, 1850 GMT, 13 August 1992, trans. in FBIS-SOV-92-160, 18 August 1992, pp. 33-34.

89. In lengthy conversations with reform figures, I found that even Russians who are most strongly against the state security services, including former dissidents, human rights activists, and members of the Democratic Russia Party, view the former First Chief Directorate in a rather positive light. Much of the elation felt in the aftermath of the Ames affair seemed not to be hostility toward the U.S. as much as it was a sense of national victory at having accomplished something great, as in an Olympic competition.

The Inter-republic Security Service poll taken in December 1991 and January 1992 found that only 13 percent of the population opposed the foreign intelligence service outright, with an unspecified majority saying that KGB foreign intelligence was necessary. Kryshtanovskaya, "Advocates and Antagonists of the KGB."

90. Tatyana Samolis, press secretary to SVR Director Primakov, Mayak Radio Network, 1520 GMT, 19 February 1992, trans. in FBIS-SOV-92-034, 20 February 1992, pp. 59-60.

91. ITAR-TASS in English, 1316 GMT, 18 December 1992, in FBIS-SOV-92-245, 21 December 1992, pp. 45-46.

92. Radiostantsiya Ekho Moskovy, 1605 GMT, 21 March 1994, trans. in FBIS-SOV-94-055, 22 March 1994, p. 19.

93. The exchange took place at a Moscow seminar sponsored by the Glasnost Foundation, 9 April 1994.

94. "I Have the Honor—Intelligence Service."

95. V. Kantorov, head of the SVR Legal Department, and Vyacheslav Trubnikov, SVR first deputy director, "Novosti" newscast, Teleradiokompaniya Ostankino Television First Program Network, 1100 GMT, 9 September 1992, trans. in FBIS-SOV-92-176, 10 September 1992, p. 21.

96. Kobaladze, in exchange with author at "KGB: Yesterday, Today, and Tomorrow," Glasnost Foundation, Moscow, 3 October 1993. From author's notes.

97. Kirpichenko, presentation at the Kennan Institute, Washington, D.C., 11 January 1993. From author's notes.

98. Tatyana Samolis, press secretary to SVR Director Primakov, Interfax in English, 1549 GMT, 29 September 1992, in FBIS-SOV-92-192, 2 October 1992, pp. 16-17.

99. Kobaladze, in exchange with author at "KGB: Yesterday, Today, and Tomorrow," Glasnost Foundation, Moscow, 3 October 1993. From author's notes.

100. Kirpichenko, presentation at the Kennan Institute, Washington, D.C., 11 January 1993. From author's notes.

101. *Komsomolskaya pravda,* 18 March 1992, p. 1, trans. FBIS-SOV-92-054, 19 March 1992, p. 50.

102. TASS world service in English, 1727 GMT, 2 October 1991, trans. in FBIS-SOV-91-192, 3 October 1991, pp. 17-18.

103. *RFE/RL Daily Report*, No. 80, 27 April 1992, p. 3.

104. Pavel Koltsov, *Nezavisimaya gazeta,* 26 February 1994, p. 2, trans. in FBIS-SOV-94-039, 28 February 1994, p. 34.

105. "I Have the Honor—Intelligence Service."

106. Radio Rossii Network, 1300 GMT, 26 February 1992, trans. in FBIS-SOV-92-039, 27 February 1992, p. 35.

107. Walter Pincus, "Ames Met Two Russians in the '70s, and Therein Lies a Tale of Deceit," *Washington Post,* 27 April 1994, p. A15.

108. Kirpichenko, Kennan Institute, 11 January 1993.

109. The tour was sponsored by the U.S. Association of National Security Alumni (ANSECA), whose officials refer to Philip Agee as a "charter member" and who was an early leader of the organiation. I attended ANSECA's 20 October 1993 news conference at the National Press Club at which Totrov and the others spoke, and observed longtime Agee partner Louis Wolf, a member of the ANSECA board of directors, organizing the event and destributing literature.

110. Author's observations from ANSECA news conference, 20 October 1993. The KGB veterans present were Col. Vladimir B. Barkovsky, who began his chekist career in Stalin's secret service and retired in 1984; Col. Yuriy I. Modin, who also began work in the chekist organs under Stalin and who retired in 1988; Col. Vsevelod I. Gapon, who worked for the KGB from 1962 to 1991; and Col. Yuriy H. Totrov, who was with the KGB from 1960 to 1992. The ANSECA press kit contained the names of seven of its own participants at the news conference, but notably failed to include Louis Wolf.

111. Yuriy Kobaladze, in TASS in English, 2100 GMT, 6 March 1992, in FBIS-SOV-92-047, 10 March 1992, p. 25.

112. Interfax in English, 1549 GMT, 29 September 1992, in FBIS-SOV-92-192, 2 October 1992, pp. 16-17.

113. *RFE/RL Daily Report*, 28 September 1991.

114. Also see Primakov's speech at a 16 December 1992 roundtable sponsored by the Supreme Soviet Committee on Defense and Security, reported by ITAR-TASS in English, 1316 GMT, 18 December 1992, in FBIS-SOV-92-245, 21 December 1992, pp. 45-46.

115. Yuriy Kobaladze, Central Television First Program Network, 1540 GMT, 15 December 1991, trans. in FBIS-SOV-91-247, 24 December 1991, p. 23.

116. TASS in English, 2110 GMT, 30 September 1991, in FBIS-SOV-92-184, 30 September 1991, pp. 23-24; Yevgeniy Primakov, text of news conference, Official Kremlin International News Broadcast, trans. in Federal News Service, 2 October 1991.

117. *Ibid.*

118. Source I, interview with author.

119. Yuriy Kobaladze, exchange with author, third "KGB: Yesterday, Today and Tomorrow" conference, Moscow, 3 October 1993. The exchange was videotaped by staff members of the Moscow office of the Cultural Initiative Foundation.

120. SVR Public Relations Bureau telephone: (095) 923-62-13; fax: (095) 923-81-91.

121. Yuriy Kobaladze, *Izvestiya*, 18 February 1992, morning edition, p. 4, trans. in FBIS-SOV-92-040, 28 February 1992, pp. 21-22; Vadim Kirpichenko, *Krasnaya zvezda*, 21 December 1993, p. 3, trans. in FBIS-SOV-93-245, 23 December 1993, pp. 31-33.

122. Radio Rossii Network, 2000 GMT, 18 December 1991, trans. in FBIS-SOV-91-244, 19 December 1991, pp. 13-14.

123. *Komsomolskaya pravda*, 18 March 1992, p. 1, trans. in FBIS-SOV-92-054, 19 March 1992, p. 50.

124. Kirpichenko was the SVR representative at the Bulgaria conference. For his remarks, see *The Proper Role of an Intelligence Agency in a Democracy*.

125. FBIS Editorial Report of Teleradiokompaniya Ostankino Television First Program Network, 1850 GMT, 13 August 1992, trans. in FBIS-SOV-92-160, 18 August 1992, pp. 33-34.

126. Radio Slavyanka to Tajikistan, 1700 GMT, 10 March 1994, trans. in FBIS-SOV-94-048, 11 March 1994, p. 24.

127. ITAR-TASS world service in Russian, 24 June 1992, trans. in FBIS-SOV-92-124, 26 June 1992, pp. 16-17.

128. The officer was Vadim Kirpichenko, former chief of Administration C of Directorate S of the KGB First Chief Directorate, later chief of Directorate S, and then director of the SVR Advisory Council, in *Patriot*, No. 34, cited by Victor Yasmann, *RFE/RL Daily Report*, No. 169, 3 September 1992, p. 2. Kirpichenko denied he was trying to reassure illegals but confirmed emphatically that Russia would continue to use them. Kirpichenko, interview with author, Kennan Institute, 11 January 1993.

129. Yuriy Kobaladze, third "KGB: Yesterday, Today and Tomorrow" conference, Moscow, 3 October 1993.

130. Wise, "Closing Down the KGB"; and "House of Cards."

131. Bill Gertz, "Russians Discard Tactics of KGB," *Washington Times*, 12 January 1993.

132. Yevgeniy Primakov, text of news conference, Official Kremlin International News Broadcast, trans. in Federal News service, 2 October 1991.

133. Yevgeniy Primakov, testimony before the Russian Federation Supreme Soviet Hearings Concerning the Events Associated with the Attempted Coup d'Etat of August 19-21, 1991, Moscow, 4 February 1992, Boston University transcript, Mugar Library, Special Collections, p. 109; TASS international service in Russian, 1550 GMT, 4 February 1992, trans. in FBIS-SOV-92-024, 5 February 1992, pp. 62-63.

134. *Izvestiya*, 19 March 1992, morning edition, p. 3, trans. in FBIS-SOV-92-059, 26 March 1992, pp. 39-40. Also, "Russian Spy Chief Admits KGB Cooked Up AIDS-CIA Link," Reuter Library Report, 18 March 1992.

135. *Ibid.*

136. See Thomas P. Melady and John F. Kikoski, "The Attempted Assassination of the Pope," *Orbis*, Winter 1985, pp. 775-801.

137. Claire Sterling, *The Time of the Assassins: Anatomy of an Investigation* (New York: Holt, Rinehart and Winston, 1983); Paul B. Henze, *The Plot to Kill the Pope* (New York: Charles Scribner's, Inc., 1983).

138. Sterling, citing *Paese-Sera* reprint of a *Pravda* article, 6 January 1983, p. 168. The Italian Communist Party, which spread the allegations, as Soviet documents later proved, was at the time funded by the CPSU International Department via the KGB. The Italian and Russian governments agreed in 1992 that Moscow would provide documentation of Soviet funding and support for the Italian Communist Party and other groups in Italy. See "Yeltsin Wants Proposals for Inquiry into CPSU Financial Activities in Italy," Interfax (Moscow) in English, 1858 GMT, 23 April 1992, in BBCSWB, 25 April 1992, p. SU/1364/A1/1; Aleksey Golyayev, "The CPSU Money: Secrets of 'Clandestine Funds,'" ITAR-TASS in *Rossiyskaya gazeta*, 9 June 1992, first edition, p. 7, trans. in FBIS-SOV-92-116, 16 June 1992, pp. 5-6

139. Roy Godson, "AIDS—Made in the USA: Moscow's Contagious Campaign," in Ladislav Bittman, ed., *The New Image-Makers: Soviet Propaganda and Disinformation Today* (Washington, D.C.: Pergamon-Brassey's, 1988), p. 222, citing Valentin Zapevalov, "Panic in the West, or What Is Hidden Behind the Sensation Around AIDS," *Literaturnaya gazeta*, 30 October 1985, p. 14. Zapevalov later became a deputy chairman of the Russian Supreme Soviet Committee on Foreign Affairs.

140. Kalugin first made the revelation to Radio Liberty in early 1991, and spoke about the Markov assassination in interviews with the author in January and September 1992.

141. TASS world service in English, 1933 GMT, 20 February 1992, in FBIS-SOV-92-035, 21 February 1992, p. 30.

Conclusion

1. Galina Starovoitova, transcript of remarks at the plenary session of the first international conference on "KGB: Yesterday, Today, Tomorrow," Moscow, Glasnost Foundation, February 1993; E. Oznobkina, ed., *KGB: Yesterday, Today, Tomorrow, Report of the First International Conference,* trans. A. Shkarubo. (Moscow: Glasnost Foundation, 1993), p. 19.

2. John Lenczowski, "How to Measure Changes in the USSR," unpublished study, n.d., 1990. Also see Lenczowski, "What Ever Happened to the Evil Empire? Moral Distinctions in the Age of Glasnost," *Crisis,* October 1988, pp. 18-24.

Bibliography

Abarinov, Vladimir. "More Troubled Waters in KGB Archives." *Demokratizatsiya: The Journal of Post-Soviet Democratization,* Vol. 1, No. 2, Winter 1992-1993, pp. 41-48.

Adams, Jefferson. "Destasification: A Midcourse Appraisal." *Demokratizatsiya: The Journal of Post-Soviet Democratization,* Vol. 1, No. 3, Summer 1993.

_____. "Destasification: Perils and Prospects." Presented as part of the panel "Assisting Democratic Control of Intelligence Agencies in Former Warsaw Pact Nations," at conference "Intelligence in a Post Cold War World," American Bar Association Standing Committee on Law and National Security, 30 April-1 May 1992.

Albats, Yevgeniya. "A Time Bomb, or a Political Portrait of the KGB." *Moscow News,* No. 16, 16 April 1991, pp. 8-9.

_____. "KGB-MSB-MBVD: Substantive Changes?" *Moscow News,* No. 2, 13 January 1992.

_____. "The Next Putsch Will Be Unannounced." *Moscow News,* No. 41, 1991, p. 6.

_____. *A State Within A State.* New York: Farrar, Strauss & Giroux, 1994.

_____. "Subjects of the KGB." *Moscow News,* No. 14, 1 April 1992.

Albats, Yevgeniya. and Natalya Gevorkyan. "What's to Become of the KGB?" *Moscow News,* 2 September 1991.

Alexiev, Alex. Commentary on "Gorbachev and the Post-Chebrikov KGB," Radio Free Europe/Radio Liberty (RFE/RL) *Report on the USSR,* December 22, 1989, pp. 20-22.

Almond, Mark. "Introducing KGB PLC." *The Spectator,* London, 10 July 1993, pp. 9-11.

_____. *Still Serving Secretly: Soviet Bloc Spies Under New Masters.* London: Institute for European Defence and Strategic Studies, 1992.

Arias King, Fredo. "On the Path to Reforming the KGB: Proposals and Projects." *Demokratizatsiya: The Journal of Post-Soviet Democratization,* Vol. 1, No. 1, Summer 1992, pp. 98-110.

Armes, Keith. "Chekists in Cassocks: The Orthodox Church and the KGB." *Demokratizatsiya: The Journal of Post-Soviet Democratization,* Vol. 1, No. 4, Autumn 1994, pp. 72-83.

Azrael, Jeremy, and Alexander Rahr. *The Formation and Development of the Russian KGB, 1991-1994.* Santa Monica: RAND, 1993.

Bakatin, Vadim. *Izbavleniye ot KGB.* Moscow: Novosti, 1992.

Basta, Jaroslav. "Dismantling the Czechoslovak Police State." *Demokratizatsiya: The Journal of Post-Soviet Democratization*, Vol. 1, No. 3, Summer 1993, pp. 108-109.

_____. "How Czechoslovakia Confronted the Security Police: Successes and Pitfalls in Dismantling the StB." Paper delivered at the International Studies Association national conference, Washington, D.C., 31 March 1994.

Belyaeva, Nina. "Toward a Law-Abiding State?" Uri Ra'anan, Keith Armes, and Kate Martin, eds., *Russian Pluralism: Now Irreversible?* New York: St. Martin's Press, 1992, pp. 71-92.

Beschel, Robert P., Jr. "Jaroslav Basta and the Difficult Case of Jan Kavan." Unpublished study for Project Liberty, John F. Kennedy School of Government, 1993.

Bittman, Ladislav. *The KGB and Soviet Disinformation: An Insider's View.* Washington, D.C.: Pergamon-Brassey's, 1985.

Blank, Stephen. "Contending with Russia's Military Machine." *Demokratizatsiya: The Journal of Post-Soviet Democratization*, Vol. 2, No. 1, Winter 1994, pp. 120-137.

Bonner, Yelena. "Individual and Group Rights." Uri Ra'anan, Keith Armes, and Kate Martin, eds., *Russian Pluralism: Now Irreversible?* New York: St. Martin's Press, 1992, pp. 93-102.

Bren, Paulina. "Lustration in the Czech and Slovak Republics." *RFE/RL Research Report*, Vol. 2, No. 29, 16 July 1993, pp. 16-22.

Bukovsky, Vladimir. "Boris Yeltsin's Hollow Victory." *Commentary*, Vol. 95, No. 6, June 1993, pp. 31-36.

Center for Democracy. *The Proper Role of an Intelligence Agency in a Democracy.* Sofia, Bulgaria, and Washington, D.C.: Center for Democracy, 8-10 April 1992.

Colby, Gale, and Irene Goldman. "When Will Russia Abandon Its Secret Chemical Weapons Program?" *Demokratizatsiya: The Journal of Post-Soviet Democratization*, Vol. 2, No. 1, Winter 1994, pp. 148-154.

Crozier, Brian. *Free Agent: The Unseen War, 1941-1991.* New York: Harper Collins, 1993.

_____. "Intelligence Requirements in the Post-Cold War Era." *Laissez-faire*, London, Vol. 1, No. 3, Winter 1992, pp. 23-26.

Daniloff, Nicholas. "Yeltsin, the Press, and the New Constitution." *Demokratizatsiya: The Journal of Post-Soviet Democratization*, Vol. 2, No. 1, Winter 1994, pp. 52-64.

Darski, Józef. "Police Agents in the Transition Period." *Uncaptive Minds*, Vol. 4, No. 4, Winter 1991-1992, pp. 15-28.

d'Encausse, Hélène Carrère. *The End of the Soviet Empire: The Triumph of Nations.* New York: New Republic/Basic Books, 1993.

de Weydenthal, Jan B. "Building a National Security System [In Poland]." RFE *Report on Eastern Europe*, 14 June 1991.

Dimitrov, Philip. "Freeing the Soul from Communism." *Wall Street Journal*, 23 March 1992.

Douglas-Home, Jessica. "East Europe's Unfinished Revolution." *Laissez-faire*, London, Vol. 1, No. 3, Winter 1992, pp. 31-35.

Dunlop, John B. "KGB Subversion of Russian Orthodox Church." *RFE/RL Research Report*, Vol. 1, No. 12, 20 March 1992, pp. 51-53.

Dziak, John J. *Chekisty: A History of the KGB*. Lexington: Lexington Books, 1988.

Ebon, Martin. *KGB: Death and Rebirth*. Westport: Praeger, 1994.

Efron, Sonni. "'New' KGB: On Top or on Skids?" *Los Angeles Times*, 3 March 1994, pp. 1, 8.

Engelbrekt, Kjell. "Bulgaria's State Security Archives: Toward a Compromise?" *RFE/RL Research Report*, Vol. 3, No. 5, 4 February 1994, pp. 21-27.

_____. "The Lasting Influence of the Secret Services." RFE *Report on Eastern Europe*, 19 July 1991.

_____. "Probing Into the Secret Services' Past Activities Abroad." RFE *Report on Eastern Europe*, 12 July 1991.

_____. "Redefining National Security in the New Political Environment." RFE *Report on Eastern Europe*, 26 July 1991.

_____. "The *Stasi* Revisited." *RFE/RL Research Report*, Vol. 2, No. 46, 19 November 1993, pp. 19-24.

Fairbanks, Charles H., Jr. "The Nature of the Beast." *The National Interest*, Spring 1993, pp. 46-56.

Foster, Richard B. "Affirmative Strategy and Moral Vision." *Global Affairs*, Vol. 3, No. 3, Summer 1988, pp. 105-109.

Foye, Stephen, and Alexander Rahr. "Gorbachev Appoints Temporary Heads of Army, KGB, and MVD." RL *Report on the USSR*, 30 August 1991.

Galeotti, Mark. "The Role of the Security Forces." RL *Report on the USSR*, 6 September 1991.

_____. "Russia's Police Moves Towards Independence." RL *Report on the USSR*, 26 October 1990.

Gamayunov, Igor, "Monitoring the KGB?" *Literaturnaya Gazeta International*, Vol. 1, No. 18, December 1990, pp. 16-17.

Gates, Robert M. "CIA and the Collapse of the Soviet Union: Hit or Miss?" Speech to the Foreign Policy Association, New York, 20 May 1992.

Gauck, Joachim. "Disposing of the Stasi Legacy: Germany's Experience with the Preservation and Disposal of the GDR Secret Police Files." *Demokratizatsiya: The Journal of Post-Soviet Democratization*, Vol. 1, No. 3, Summer 1993, pp. 104-107.

Gertz, Bill. "FBI Watching KGB's Future after Putsch," *Washington Times*, 23 August 1991.

_____. "The KGB and Soviet Reform." *The World & I*, May 1988, pp. 115-121.

_____. "New Life for Old Warriors of KGB." *Washington Times*, 15 November 1992, pp. 1, 6.

_____. "Russian Spies Remain in U.S. Despite KGB's Fall." *Washington Times*, 15 November 1992, p. 6.

Gevorkyan, Natasha. "A 'Case' Which Is None of Our Business," *Moscow News*, No. 31, 1990.

_____. "Deputy Proposes, KGB Disposes," *Moscow News*, No. 11, 17-24 March 1991, p. 6.

_____. [Natalija Geworkjan]. *Der KGB lebt* [The KGB Lives]. Berlin: edition q Verlags-GmbH, 1992.

_____. "The KGB: They Still Need Us." *The Bulletin of the Atomic Scientists*, January-February 1993, pp. 36-38.

_____. "Revanchism in the Security Forces," *Crossroads*, Jamestown Foundation, Vol. 2, No. 5, 15 March 1993, pp. 4-5.

Grigoryants, Sergey, ed. *State Security and Democracy*. Moscow: Glasnost Foundation, February, March, and April 1993.

Hammel, Claus. *Reflections on Feliks D.* East Berlin: Herausgeber: Solidaritätskomitee der DDR, 1979.

Hartwig, Hanna. "The Shock of the Past." *Uncaptive Minds*, Vol. 5, No. 1, Spring 1992, pp. 99-104.

Havel, Václav. *Open Letters: Selected Writings, 1965-1990*. Trans. and ed. Paul Wilson. New York: Vintage, 1991.

Hershberg, James G. "Soviet Archives: The Opening Door." *Cold War International History Project Bulletin*, Woodrow Wilson International Center for Scholars, Issue 1, Spring 1992, pp. 1, 12-15, 23-27.

Hollander, Paul. "Soviet Terror, American Amnesia." *National Review*, 2 May 1994, pp. 28-39.

Holloway, David. "State, Society, and the Military Under Gorbachev." Alexander Dallin and Gail W. Lapidus, eds., *The Soviet System in Crisis*. Boulder: Westview, 1991, pp. 616-632.

Holmes, James L., III. "Behind the Scenes, Communists Cling to Power: Internal Security in the Soviet Bloc." *West Watch*, May 1990, pp. 1, 4-6.

Jameson, Donald. "Covert Activities and New Priorities." *Laissez-faire*, London, Vol. 1, No. 3, Winter 1992, pp. 27-30.

Kalugin, Oleg. "Restructuring the KGB." In Carl Runde and Greg Voss, eds., *Intelligence and the New World Order: Former Cold War Adversaries Look Toward the 21st Century*. Hamburg: International Freedom Foundation, 1992, pp. 157-164.

Karpinski, Jakub. "Files into Ashes." *Uncaptive Minds*, Vol. 4, No. 2, Summer 1991, pp. 5-7.

Kichikhin, Aleksandr. "Fortress Against Reform: The KGB Has Changed Its Name, But Not Much Else," *Crossroads*, Jamestown Foundation, 15 August 1993, pp. 8-10, 15.

Klyamkin, Igor. "The Emergence of Democracy and Russia's New Role." RL *Report on the USSR*, 11 October 1991.

Knight, Amy W. Commentary on "Gorbachev and the Post-Chebrikov KGB," RFE/RL *Report on the USSR*, 22 December 1989, pp. 22-24.

_____. *The KGB: Police and Politics in the Soviet Union*. Boston: Unwin, Hyman, 1988, 1990.

_____. "Russian Security Services Under Yel'tsin." *Post-Soviet Affairs*, Vol. 9, No. 1, January-March 1993, pp. 40-65.

Kuzio, Taras. "The Security Service of Ukraine: A Transformed Ukrainian KGB?" *Jane's Intelligence Review*, March 1993, pp. 115-117.

Lally, Kathy. "The KGB 's Power: In Some Ways, Little Has Changed." *Baltimore Sun*, 6 March 1994.

Lee, Jennifer Scheck. *The Supreme Soviet Defense and Security Committee: Limited Oversight Capabilities*. Palo Alto: Global Outlook, July 1991.

Lenczowski, John. "How to Measure Changes in the USSR." Unpublished paper, 1989.

_____. "Military *Glasnost'* and Strategic Deception." *International Freedom Review*, Vol. 3, No. 2, Winter 1990, pp. 3-44.

_____. *The Sources of Soviet Perestroika*. Ashland, Ohio: Ashland University, John M. Ashbrook Center for Public Affairs, 1990.

_____. "What Ever Happened to the Evil Empire? Moral Distinctions in the Age of Glasnost." *Crisis*, October 1988, pp. 11-24.

Lepingwell, John W. R. "Towards a Post-Soviet Army." *Orbis*, Vol. 36, No. 1, Winter 1992, pp. 87-104.

Levchenko, Stanislav. "Kto vy, Doktor Totrov?" *Vestnik*, Vol. 5, No. 24 (74), 30 November 1993, pp. 13-15.

Levchenko, Stanislav, and Herbert Romerstain. *The KGB Against the 'Main Enemy.'* Lexington: Lexington Books, 1989.

Lovás, Zoltán. "After Danubegate." *Uncaptive Minds*, Vol. 4, No. 2, Summer 1991, pp. 15-18.

Lukashuk, Alexander. "Belarus's KGB: In Search of an Identity." *RFE/RL Research Report*, Vol. 1, No. 47, 27 November 1992, pp. 17-21.

Mihalisko, Kathleen. "Defense and Security Planning in Ukraine." RL *Report on the USSR*, 6 December 1991.

Mikheyev, Dmitry. *The Rise and Fall of Gorbachev*. Indianapolis: The Hudson Institute, 1992.

Miklaszewska, Marta. "An Exceptionally Delicate Matter." *Uncaptive Minds*, Vol. 4, No. 2, Summer 1991, pp. 13-15.

Miller, Stephen. "The Soviet Coup and the Benefits of Breakdown." *Orbis*, Vol. 36, No. 1, Winter 1992, pp. 69-86.

Moore, John Norton. "An Overview Democratic Strategy of Strength and Principle." *Global Affairs*, Vol. 3, No. 3, Summer 1988, pp. 76-78.

Müller, Pawel. "The Gauck Commission." *Uncaptive Minds*, Vol. 5, No. 1, Spring 1992, pp. 95-98.

Novikov, Evgueni. "Ideology Still Central to Soviet Propaganda." *Soviet Intelligence and Active Measures*, Nos. 15/16, Summer/Fall 1990.

Obrman, Jan. "The New Intelligence Services [in Czechoslovakia]." RFE *Report on Eastern Europe*, June 28, 1991.

_____. "The New Police Forces [in Czechoslovakia]." RFE *Report on Eastern Europe*, September 13, 1991.

Orlov, Vladimir. "Yeltsin Unfettered: It May Not Be a Classic Dictatorship, But Russia Might Be in for an Extended Period of One-Man Rule." *Crossroads*, October 1993, pp. 8-9.

Oznobkina, E., ed. *KGB: Yesterday, Today and Tomorrow: Proceedings of the First International Conference Plenary Session.* Trans. A. Shkarubo. Moscow: Glasnost Foundation, 1993.
Parrott, Bruce. "Soviet National Security Under Gorbachev." Alexander Dallin and Gail W. Lapidus, eds., *The Soviet System in Crisis.* Boulder: Westview, 1991, pp. 573-615.
Pehe, Jiri. "International Front Organizations Survive in Prague." RFE *Report on Eastern Europe,* 21 June 1991.
Pipes, Richard. "Proposal for a U.S. Affirmative Strategy on Soviet Nationalities." *Global Affairs,* Vol. 3, No. 3, Summer 1988, pp. 74-75.
Plater-Zyberk, Henry. "The Future of the Russian Security Services." *Jane's Intelligence Review,* September 1992, pp. 396-398.
Popplewell, Richard. "KGB Chairman Seeks New Image." *Soviet Intelligence and Active Measures,* Nos. 15/16, Summer/Fall 1990.
_____. "Themes in the Rhetoric of KGB Chairmen from Andropov to Kryuchkov." *Intelligence and National Security,* Vol. 6, No. 3, July 1991, pp. 513-547.
Pustintsev, Boris. "Die Arbeit der 'Bürgerkontrolle' in St. Petersburg." In *Die Stasi und der KGB: Möglichkeiten der Kontrolle der Geheimdienste: Dokumentation des Wochenendseminars.* Berlin: Bildungswerk für Demokratie und Umweltschutz, 1993, pp. 19-22.
_____. "Die Entwicklung des KGB nach dem Putsch." In *Die Stasi und der KGB: Möglichkeiten der Kontrolle der Geheimdienste: Dokumentation des Wochenendseminars.* Berlin: Bildungswerk für Demokratie und Umweltschutz, 1993, pp. 3-9.
Ra'anan, Uri, Keith Armes, and Kate Martin, eds. *Russian Pluralism: Now Irreversible?* New York: St. Martin's Press, 1992.
Radosh, Ronald, and Eric Breindel. "Bombshell: The KGB Fesses Up." *The New Republic,* 10 June 1991, pp. 10-12.
Rahr, Alexander. "El'tsin Sets Up New System for Governing Russia," RL *Report on the USSR,* 23 August 1991.
_____. "The Future of Russian Reforms," *RFE/RL Research Report,* Vol. 3, No. 5, 4 February 1994, pp. 7-11.
_____. "Gorbachev and the Post-Chebrikov KGB," RFE/RL *Report on the USSR,* 22 December 1989, pp. 16-20.
_____. "KGB Attack on Gorbachev and His Reforms." RL *Report on the USSR,* 13 April 1990, pp. 4-6.
_____. "The KGB's Foreign Branch Goes Public." RL *Report on the USSR,* 23 November 1990.
_____. "The KGB Survives Under Yeltsin's Wing." *RFE/RL Research Report,* Vol. 1, No. 13, 27 March 1992, pp. 1-4.
_____. "Kryuchkov, the KGB, and the 1991 Putsch." *RFE/RL Research Report,* Vol. 2, No. 31, 30 July 1993, pp. 16-23.
_____. "The October Revolt: Mass Unrest or Putsch?" *RFE/RL Research Report,* Vol. 2, No. 44, 5 November 1993, pp. 1-4.
_____. "'Power Ministries' Support Yeltsin." *RFE/RL Research Report,* Vol. 2, No. 40, 8 October 1993, pp. 8-11.

_____. "Power Struggle in the White House." RL *Report on the USSR,* 25 October 1991.
_____. "Reform of Russia's State Security Apparatus." *RFE/RL Research Report,* Vol. 3, No. 8, 25 February 1994, pp. 19-30.
_____. "The Revival of a Strong KGB." *RFE/RL Research Report,* 14 May 1993, pp. 74-79.
_____. "Russia: The Struggle for Power Continues." *RFE/RL Research Report,* Vol. 2, No. 6, 5 February 1993, pp. 1-9.
Ramet, Sabrina Petra. "The New Poland: Democratic and Authoritarian Tendencies." *Global Affairs,* Vol. 7, No. 2, Spring 1992.
Reddaway, Peter. Commentary on "Gorbachev and the Post-Chebrikov KGB," RFE/RL *Report on the USSR,* 22 December 1989, pp. 24-27.
_____. "The Quality of Gorbachev's Leadership." Alexander Dallin and Gail W. Lapidus, eds., *The Soviet System in Crisis.* Boulder: Westview, 1991, pp. 210-223.
Robbins, James S. "New Sources on Soviet Military Counterintelligence in the Great Patriotic War (SMERSH)." Unpublished paper delivered at the New England Slavic Association annual conference, Providence College, Providence, Rhode Island, 3 April 1993.
Romerstein, Herbert. "In Crisis: The Rulers of the Soviet Union." *International Freedom Review,* Vol. 3, No. 2, Winter 1990, pp. 65-80.
Rostow, Eugene V. "The Double Crisis in Europe: A Strategic Opportunity for the West." *Global Affairs,* Vol. 3, No. 3, Summer 1988, pp. 65-73.
Rubanov, Vladimir. "Defence Gets the Best, Economy the Rest." *International Affairs,* No. 1, 1991, pp. 3-12.
_____. "The New KGB." In Carl Runde and Greg Voss, eds., *Intelligence and the New World Order: Former Cold War Adversaries Look Toward the 21st Century.* Hamburg: International Freedom Foundation, 1992, pp. 165-170.
Rurarz, Zdzislaw. "Nothing Has Ended Yet." *Uncaptive Minds,* Vol. 4, No. 4, Winter 1991-1992, pp. 29-34.
Russian Federation. Supreme Soviet. *Hearings Concerning the Events Associated with the Attempted Coup d'Etat of August 19-21, 1991.* Moscow: 22 October 1991, 4 February 1992, and 10 February 1992. English translation of transcripts, Special Collections, Mugar Library, Boston University.
Schifter, Richard. "Human Rights: Established or Precarious?" In Uri'Ra'anan, Keith Armes, and Kate Martin, eds. *Russian Pluralism: Now Irreversible?* New York: St. Martin's Press, 1992.
Schwartz, Herman. "The New East European Constitutional Courts." *Michigan Journal of International Law,* Vol. 13, Summer 1992, pp. 101-145.
Serio, Joseph. "Organized Crime in the Soviet Union and Beyond." *Low Intensity Conflict and Law Enforcement,* Vol. 1, No. 2, Autumn 1992, pp. 127-151.
Sellars, Duncan, ed. *Where Do We Go from Here? A Blueprint for U.S. Aid to Emerging Democracies.* Washington, D.C.: International Freedom Foundation, 1990.
Sharlet, Robert. "The Russian Constitutional Court: The First Term." *Post-Soviet Affairs,* Vol. 9, No. 1, January-March 1993, pp. 1-39.

Sherr, James. "Change and Continuity in the Former KGB." *Jane's Intelligence Review*, March 1993, pp. 110-112.

Sheymov, Victor. *Tower of Secrets*. Annapolis: Naval Institute Press, 1993.

Sturzda, Mihai. "The Files of the [Romanian] State Security Police." RFE *Report on Eastern Europe*, 13 September 1991.

Sustrova, Petruska. "The Lustration Controversy." *Uncaptive Minds*, Vol. 5, No. 2, Summer 1992, pp. 129-134.

Thom, Françoise. "The Second Echelon." *Uncaptive Minds*, Vol. 4, No. 4, Winter 1991-1992, pp. 5-10.

Tismaneanu, Vladimir, and Patrick Clawson, eds. *Uprooting Leninism, Cultivating Liberty*. Philadelphia and Lanham, Maryland: Foreign Policy Research Institute/University Press of America, 1992.

Todres, Vladimir. "The Center and the Regions: Before and After." *Crossroads*, October 1993, pp. 6-7, 12.

Tolz, Vera. "New Situation for CPSU and KGB Archives." RL *Report on the USSR*, 20 September 1991.

Tolz, Vera, and Julia Wishnevsky. "The Russian Government Declassifies CPSU Documents." *RFE/RL Research Report*, Vol. 1, No. 26, 26 June 1992, pp. 8-11.

Toman, Petr. "Collaborators Revealed: The Parliamentary Commission's Report." *Uncaptive Minds*, Vol. 4, No. 2, Summer 1991, pp. 8-12.

Trimble, Jeff. "New Act, Old Tricks." *U.S. News and World Report*, 8 February 1993, pp. 42-44.

Tsypkin, Mikhail. "Commentary on 'Gorbachev and the Post-Chebrikov KGB,'" RFE/RL *Report on the USSR*, 22 December 1989, pp. 27-30.

_____. "The Committee for Defense and State Security of the USSR Supreme Soviet." RL *Report on the USSR*, 11 May 1990.

_____. "A Split in the KGB?" RL *Report on the USSR*, 28 September 1990.

Uzzell, Lawrence. "The Russian Press: Delusions of Freedom." *Crossroads*, 15 April 1994, pp. 4-5.

_____. "Upheaval: The Black House Perspective." *Crossroads*, October 1993, pp. 4-5, 11.

Vinton, Louisa. "Walesa and the Collaboration Issue." *RFE/RL Research Report*, Vol. 2, No. 6, 5 February 1993, pp. 10-17.

Voslensky, Mikhail. *Nomenklatura: The Soviet Ruling Class*. New York: Doubleday, 1984.

Waller, J. Michael. "Civil Authority and the Security Organs." In Uri Ra'anan, Keith Armes, and Kate Martin, eds. *Russian Pluralism: Now Irreversible?* New York: St. Martin's Press, 1992.

_____. "Commonwealth of Chekists." John Blaney, ed. *The Successor States*. Washington: Foreign Service Institute/Congressional Quarterly, 1994.

_____. "Delay Expansion of NATO—For the Right Reason." *Wall Street Journal Europe*, 10 January 1994.

_____. "The KGB and Its 'Successors': State Within a State," *Perspective*, Institute for the Study of Conflict, Ideology, and Policy, Boston University, Vol. 4, No. 4, April-May 1994, pp. 5--9.

_____. "The KGB Is Back In Business." *Wall Street Journal Europe,* 30 October 1992.

_____. "The KGB Isn't Dead Yet." *Wall Street Journal Europe,* 28 January 1992.

_____. "The KGB Lingers Unreformed." *Wall Street Journal Europe,* 2 August 1993.

_____. "KGB: The Perils of Arbitrary Power." *Perspective,* Institute for the Study of Conflict, Ideology, and Policy, Boston University, Vol. 2, No. 1, September 1991, pp. 1, 4-5, 7.

_____. "New KGB Spymaster, Same Nasty Tricks," *Wall Street Journal Europe,* 10 October 1991.

_____. "Old Guard Is Entrenched in New Russian Security Services," *National Security Analysis,* American Security Council Foundation, 27 January 1992.

_____. "Phoenix Rising: The KGB and the World Today." *terra nova,* Vol. 1, No. 4, Autumn 1992, pp. 21-30.

_____. "Post-Soviet Sakharovs: Renewed Persecution of Dissident Scientists and the American Response." *Demokratizatsiya: The Journal of Post-Soviet Democratization,* Vol. 2, No. 1, Winter 1994, pp. 138-147.

_____. "Russia's Biggest 'Mafia' Is the KGB," *Wall Street Journal Europe,* 22 June 1994.

_____. "Russia's Legal Foundations for Civil Repression: Are Soviet Practices Being Reformed or Legalized?" *Demokratizatsiya: The Journal of Post-Soviet Democratization,* Vol. 1, No. 3, Summer 1993, pp. 110-115.

_____. "Russia's Security and Intelligence Services Today." *National Security Law Report,* American Bar Association Standing Committee on Law and National Security, June 1993.

_____. "Trial of a New Russian Dissident." *Wall Street Journal,* 4 February 1994.

_____. "When Will Democrats Control the Former KGB? Opportunities for Russian-U.S. Cooperation." *Demokratizatsiya: The Journal of Post-Soviet Democratization,* Vol. 1, No. 1, Summer 1992, pp. 27-39.

_____. "Yeltsin's Debt to the Old KGB." *Wall Street Journal Europe,* 21 October 1993.

Weeks, Albert. "Gorbachev and the KGB," *Global Affairs,* Vol. 5, No. 1, Winter 1990, pp. 58-77.

Weigel, George. *The Final Revolution: The Resistance Church and the Collapse of Communism.* New York: Oxford University Press, 1992.

White, Jennifer. "Dualities in Foreign Aid Policies." In Duncan Sellars, ed. *Where Do We Go from Here? A Blueprint for U.S. Aid to Emerging Democracies.* Washington, D.C.: International Freedom Foundation, 1990.

_____. "Perestroika and Western Dollars: The Continuity of Ends." *International Freedom Review,* Vol. 3, No. 3, Spring 1990, pp. 39-64.

Wishnevsky, Julia. "Russian Constitutional Court: A Third Branch of Government?" *RFE/RL Research Report,* Vol. 2, No. 17, 12 February 1993, pp. 1-8.

_____. "The Russian Media After the State of Emergency." *RFE/RL Research Report,* Vol. 3, No. 6, 11 February 1994, pp. 1-6.

Sherr, James. "Change and Continuity in the Former KGB." *Jane's Intelligence Review*, March 1993, pp. 110-112.

Sheymov, Victor. *Tower of Secrets*. Annapolis: Naval Institute Press, 1993.

Sturzda, Mihai. "The Files of the [Romanian] State Security Police." RFE *Report on Eastern Europe*, 13 September 1991.

Sustrova, Petruska. "The Lustration Controversy." *Uncaptive Minds*, Vol. 5, No. 2, Summer 1992, pp. 129-134.

Thom, Françoise. "The Second Echelon." *Uncaptive Minds*, Vol. 4, No. 4, Winter 1991-1992, pp. 5-10.

Tismaneanu, Vladimir, and Patrick Clawson, eds. *Uprooting Leninism, Cultivating Liberty*. Philadelphia and Lanham, Maryland: Foreign Policy Research Institute/University Press of America, 1992.

Todres, Vladimir. "The Center and the Regions: Before and After." *Crossroads*, October 1993, pp. 6-7, 12.

Tolz, Vera. "New Situation for CPSU and KGB Archives." RL *Report on the USSR*, 20 September 1991.

Tolz, Vera, and Julia Wishnevsky. "The Russian Government Declassifies CPSU Documents." *RFE/RL Research Report*, Vol. 1, No. 26, 26 June 1992, pp. 8-11.

Toman, Petr. "Collaborators Revealed: The Parliamentary Commission's Report." *Uncaptive Minds*, Vol. 4, No. 2, Summer 1991, pp. 8-12.

Trimble, Jeff. "New Act, Old Tricks." *U.S. News and World Report*, 8 February 1993, pp. 42-44.

Tsypkin, Mikhail. "Commentary on 'Gorbachev and the Post-Chebrikov KGB,'" RFE/RL *Report on the USSR*, 22 December 1989, pp. 27-30.

_____. "The Committee for Defense and State Security of the USSR Supreme Soviet." RL *Report on the USSR*, 11 May 1990.

_____. "A Split in the KGB?" RL *Report on the USSR*, 28 September 1990.

Uzzell, Lawrence. "The Russian Press: Delusions of Freedom." *Crossroads*, 15 April 1994, pp. 4-5.

_____. "Upheaval: The Black House Perspective." *Crossroads*, October 1993, pp. 4-5, 11.

Vinton, Louisa. "Walesa and the Collaboration Issue." *RFE/RL Research Report*, Vol. 2, No. 6, 5 February 1993, pp. 10-17.

Voslensky, Mikhail. *Nomenklatura: The Soviet Ruling Class*. New York: Doubleday, 1984.

Waller, J. Michael. "Civil Authority and the Security Organs." In Uri Ra'anan, Keith Armes, and Kate Martin, eds. *Russian Pluralism: Now Irreversible?* New York: St. Martin's Press, 1992.

_____. "Commonwealth of Chekists." John Blaney, ed. *The Successor States*. Washington: Foreign Service Institute/Congressional Quarterly, 1994.

_____. "Delay Expansion of NATO—For the Right Reason." *Wall Street Journal Europe*, 10 January 1994.

_____. "The KGB Is Back In Business." *Wall Street Journal Europe*, 30 October 1992.

_____. "The KGB Isn't Dead Yet." *Wall Street Journal Europe*, 28 January 1992.

_____. "The KGB Lingers Unreformed." *Wall Street Journal Europe,* 2 August 1993.

_____. "KGB: The Perils of Arbitrary Power." *Perspective,* Institute for the Study of Conflict, Ideology, and Policy, Boston University, Vol. 2, No. 1, September 1991, pp. 1, 4-5, 7.

_____. "New KGB Spymaster, Same Nasty Tricks," *Wall Street Journal Europe,* 10 October 1991.

_____. "Old Guard Is Entrenched in New Russian Security Services," *National Security Analysis,* American Security Council Foundation, 27 January 1992.

_____. "Phoenix Rising: The KGB and the World Today." *terra nova,* Vol. 1, No. 4, Autumn 1992, pp. 21-30.

_____. "Post-Soviet Sakharovs: Renewed Persecution of Dissident Scientists and the American Response." *Demokratizatsiya: The Journal of Post-Soviet Democratization,* Vol. 2, No. 1, Winter 1994, pp. 138-147.

_____. "Russia's Legal Foundations for Civil Repression: Are Soviet Practices Being Reformed or Legalized?" *Demokratizatsiya: The Journal of Post-Soviet Democratization,* Vol. 1, No. 3, Summer 1993, pp. 110-115.

_____. "Russia's Security and Intelligence Services Today." *National Security Law Report,* American Bar Association Standing Committee on Law and National Security, June 1993.

_____. "Trial of a New Russian Dissident." *Wall Street Journal,* 4 February 1994.

_____. "When Will Democrats Control the Former KGB? Opportunities for Russian-U.S. Cooperation." *Demokratizatsiya: The Journal of Post-Soviet Democratization,* Vol. 1, No. 1, Summer 1992, pp. 27-39.

_____. "Yeltsin's Debt to the Old KGB." *Wall Street Journal Europe,* 21 October 1993.

Weeks, Albert. "Gorbachev and the KGB," *Global Affairs,* Vol. 5, No. 1, Winter 1990, pp. 58-77.

Weigel, George. *The Final Revolution: The Resistance Church and the Collapse of Communism.* New York: Oxford University Press, 1992.

White, Jennifer. "Dualities in Foreign Aid Policies." In Duncan Sellars, ed. *Where Do We Go from Here? A Blueprint for U.S. Aid to Emerging Democracies.* Washington, D.C.: International Freedom Foundation, 1990.

_____. "Perestroika and Western Dollars: The Continuity of Ends." *International Freedom Review,* Vol. 3, No. 3, Spring 1990, pp. 39-64.

Wishnevsky, Julia. "Russian Constitutional Court: A Third Branch of Government?" *RFE/RL Research Report,* Vol. 2, No. 17, 12 February 1993, pp. 1-8.

_____. "The Russian Media After the State of Emergency." *RFE/RL Research Report,* Vol. 3, No. 6, 11 February 1994, pp. 1-6.

Woodard, Joseph K. "Perestroika and Grand Strategy." *Global Affairs,* Vol. 5, No. 1, Winter 1990, pp. 19-37.

Yasmann, Victor. "Corruption In Russia: A Threat to Democracy?" *RFE/RL Research Report,* 15 March 1993, pp. 15-18.

_____. "Domestic Aspects of the New Russian Military Doctrine," paper delevered at conference of the Hanns Seidel Stiftung, Wildbad Kreuth, 21-23 March, 1994.

_____. "The KGB [1989 Year in Review]." RL *Report on the USSR*, 29 December 1989, pp. 8-10.

_____. "The KGB and Internal Security." *RFE/RL Research Report*, 3 January 1992, pp. 19-21.

_____. "The KGB and the Party Congress." RL *Report on the USSR*, 3 August 1990, pp. 12-14.

_____. "Law on the KGB Published." RL *Report on the USSR*, 2 August 1991, pp. 12-18.

_____. "Legislation on Screening and State Security in Russia." *RFE/RL Research Report*, Vol. 2, No. 32, 13 August 1993, pp. 11-16.

_____. "The Power of the Soviet Internal Security Forces." RL *Report on the USSR*, 26 October 1990.

_____. "Reshuffle at the Top of the KGB." RL *Report on the USSR*, 1 March 1991, pp. 6-12.

_____. "Security Services Reorganized: All Power to the Russian President?" *RFE/RL Research Report*, Vol. 3, No. 6, 11 February 1994, pp. 7-14.

_____. "Where Has the KGB Gone?" *RFE/RL Research Report*, Vol. 2, No. 2, 8 January 1993.

About the Book and Author

As the world watches a new generation of Russian leaders struggle to establish democratic institutions after the fall of the Soviet Union, a persistent question arises: What has happened to the former KGB? The official line following the attempted coup of August 1991 was that the KGB was abolished and dispersed. In this provocative book, J. Michael Waller demonstrates that in reality the leaders and officers of the KGB have been able to maintain their power and privilege through "new" security and intelligence services, the emerging democratic political process, and the developing market economic system.

Waller makes use of new revelations in Russia and draws on interviews with former and current KGB officers to trace the history and evaluate the present state of the KGB's institutions of internal repression and external aggression. He offers a new perspective on Mikhail Gorbachev's meteoric rise to power by examining Gorbachev's relations with the KGB and his insulation of the KGB from the reforms of perestroika.

A central theme of this book is the problem of civilian control and oversight of the security forces—a perennial dilemma for all democracies but especially vexing in the shifting sands of contemporary Russian politics. Waller argues that following the August 1991 putsch, there were no serious attempts to make the security agencies more accountable to the public. Consequently, Boris Yeltsin enjoyed the benefits and the perils of a strong but independent internal security agency as a part of his newly enhanced presidential powers.

Maintaining a set of deeply inculcated professional traditions developed and refined since the Bolsheviks founded the Cheka, today's Russian security and intelligence officers continue to refer to themselves as *chekisti*. In so doing they consciously carry forward the legacy of a security organ designed to deprive citizens of their civil, political, economic, and human rights. This book reveals that fearful lineage and assesses the threat posed to Russia's fledgling democracy by its own security forces.

J. Michael Waller is a Senior Fellow at the American Foreign Policy Council in Washington, D.C. He pioneered a program to work with Russian lawmakers, government officials, journalists, legal experts, and human rights workers in developing theories and mechanisms of civil control and oversight of the Russian state security services. He is executive editor of *Demokratizatsiya: The Journal of Post-Soviet Democratization*, published in association with the American University and Moscow State University. He holds a Ph.D. in International Security Studies from Boston University, where he was an Earhart Fellow at the Institute for the Study of Conflict, Ideology, and Policy.

Index